Hearts Turned to the Fathers

Exterior portals of the Granite Mountain Records Vault, ca. 1963. The vault assures the long-term perservation of the original microfilm copies of genealogical records from around the world.

Hearts Turned to the Fathers:
A History of the Genealogical Society of Utah, 1894–1994

by

James B. Allen

Jessie L. Embry

Kahlile B. Mehr

BYU Studies

Brigham Young University

Provo, Utah

BYU Studies Monographs

B. H. Roberts, *The Truth, The Way, The Life*

The Journals of William E. McLellin, 1831–1836

Hearts Turned to the Fathers

Mormon Americana: A Guide to Collections

 For information about subscribing to *BYU Studies*, a quarterly multidisciplinary LDS journal, write to 403 CB, Brigham Young University, Provo, Utah 84602.

Library of Congress Catalog Card Number: 95-5504

ISBN 0-8425-2327-8

Printed in the United States of America
10 9 8 7 6 5 4 3 2 1

Table of Contents

Illustrations

Preface

The year 1994 marks the one hundredth anniversary of the founding of the Genealogical Society of Utah, the predecessor of the present Family History Department of The Church of Jesus Christ of Latter-day Saints. Since the inception of the Genealogical Society in 1894, the Church has developed the most extensive genealogical research facility and record-gathering program in the world. We hope this volume of history is a fitting contribution to the centennial celebration.

This work was originally prepared at the request of the Genealogical Society. It was to be a reference work for the Society, but it was written also for the benefit of anyone interested in the story of how the genealogical and family history program of the Church developed. Many readers will be Latter-day Saints, but we believe there will also be interest on the part of others. We have therefore provided some details relating to Mormon history and doctrine in order to help place the development of genealogical interest in its broader historical and religious contexts.

Work on this book began in the mid-1970s, when the History Division of the Historical Department of the Church was asked by Elder Theodore M. Burton, vice president and general manager of the Genealogical Society, to prepare a complete history of the Society. Leonard J. Arrington, Church historian, happily accepted the challenge on behalf of the Historical Department. He gave the assignment to Bruce D. Blumell, then a research associate in the History

Division. It was not long, however, before Blumell resigned his position in order to go to law school. James B. Allen, assistant Church historian, was then asked to take the assignment. Because of other pressing assignments, Allen obtained the assistance of Jessie L. Embry, an employee of the Historical Department, 1976–77. Allen and Embry cooperated on the research, conducted oral histories, and consulted on chapter content and outlines. Embry then prepared the initial chapter outlines, after which Allen drafted the chapters.

In 1979 Allen, who had been dividing his time between Brigham Young University and the Historical Department, returned to BYU full time. Embry also accepted a position at BYU. Their university responsibilities absorbed their attention and the history of the Genealogical Society was placed on the "back burner." In the mid-1980s, after considerable friendly prodding by George D. Durrant and other members of the Genealogical Department of the Church, a draft of the history was finally completed. It was then deposited with the Genealogical Department.

Neither Allen nor Embry was satisfied with the manuscript, however. They asked for and received suggestions from a number of people whom they had asked to read various sections. In 1993 they finished revising the manuscript, still complete only to 1975. With the approach of the centennial year, the Genealogical Department, now the Family History Department, decided to publish a centennial history. When it became clear that Allen and Embry would be unable to accomplish this, Kahlile Mehr, a full-time staff member of the Family History Department was assigned to the project and given time to work on it. Because of his expertise, he was able to add some important new material to the original chapter on microfilming, as well as write two completely new chapters and bring the history up-to-date. In addition, he did the initial work of condensing the entire work to make it of publishable size.

The three of us wish to thank the various people who have worked with us on this project, and those who have both prodded and supported us. We are particularly appreciative of the painstaking work of Nancy Lund of *BYU Studies,* who edited the finished manuscript. We also appreciate the work and suggestions of John W. Welch, editor of *BYU Studies,* as well as Doris Dant and their staff of student interns. We are also grateful to Jennifer Hurlbut for her work on the index and to Daniel B. McKinlay, who provided the extensive bibliography. The photographs were gathered by Kahlile Mehr. Unless otherwise indicated, they are provided courtesy of the Family History Library of The Church of Jesus Christ of Latter-day Saints. As always, we take sole responsibility for accuracy and the views expressed in this volume. We have enjoyed working on the project, and we hope the readers will find it of interest and value.

JAMES B. ALLEN
JESSIE L. EMBRY
KAHLILE MEHR
November 1994

Prologue

The Spirit of Elijah

In 1894, The Church of Jesus Christ of Latter-day Saints (commonly called the Mormon Church) founded the Genealogical Society of Utah. Genealogical research had been undertaken by many people for various reasons since ancient times, but it holds a unique spiritual meaning for Latter-day Saints. Impelled by what they refer to as the Spirit of Elijah, Church members seek to identify their ancestors and then perform sacred ordinances in their behalf in the temples. The Society was founded to help the Saints achieve that purpose. Since its modest beginnings, the Society, now officially known as the Family History Department of the Church, has extended its influence to all quarters of the globe, quietly amassing a treasure house of the world's ancestry and providing the information contained therein not only to Church members, but to all those interested in becoming acquainted with their heritage.

To understand the significance of the Society's history, one should know something of the historical setting in which the Society arose. This prologue will briefly review that setting as well as the essential doctrines that make genealogical work so vital to Latter-day Saints.

Ancient Genealogies

The word *genealogy,* derived from Greek, refers to the study of family or race and to the identification of lines of descent.

Mormons believe that the family of Adam and Eve were the first genealogists, for LDS scripture says that Adam and Eve's family kept a "book of remembrance" and that "a genealogy was kept of the children of God" (Moses 6:5, 8). These records were kept for religious purposes, particularly to support claims to priesthood authority. The Hebrew patriarch Abraham, for example, possessed records dating from himself back "to the beginning of the creation;" these "records of the fathers" concerned the right of priesthood (Abr. 1:28, 31).

The Bible contains some of the earliest known genealogies. As was the case with the earlier records, one purpose was to ensure proper tracing of priesthood lineage. In ancient Israel, a priest had to prove himself a descendant of Aaron before he could claim his priestly office (Ezra 2:61-62; Neh. 7:63-64).[1] Another purpose for these records was to provide all Israelites with the means to see themselves as literal descendants of Jacob (Israel) and partakers of the special blessings of Abraham and Sarah.

Ancient peoples in various parts of the world were committed to keeping track of lineage. Ancient genealogies, including some of those in the Bible, were handed down by oral tradition and later recorded, sometimes by unusual methods. The Incas of Peru, for example, used a system of ropes and knots, while the New Zealand Maoris invented a complex system of beads. Most oral genealogies eventually were written down, but for several reasons they are often unreliable. European royal families, for example, sometimes corrupted an oral tradition in order to force it into biblical lines. Some genealogies in the Islamic world may have been altered to portray individuals as descendants of Mohammed. Similarly, the genealogies of the kings of Rome may have been distorted to satisfy national pride. The Roman emperor Vespasian (A.D. 69-79), for example, usually made fun of the magnificent pedigrees that his courtiers prepared for him, reminding them that he descended from humble farmers.[2]

Most early genealogical records were kept for the benefit of royal families. Their interest was natural and pragmatic: the records were essential in confirming one's right to the throne or other royal inheritance. One exception was in China, where the tradition of ancestor worship resulted in very long pedigrees among nonroyal families. Indeed, some Chinese claim they can trace their lineage as far back as Confucius.

In Europe, records tracing the lineage of common folk were not created until the sixteenth century. English parish records, for example, which include baptismal, marriage, and burial dates, were begun in 1538. The creation of such records was partly related to the rise of national states, where monarchs needed accurate information about their subjects for purposes such as taxation and conscription.

The Mission of Elijah

The Latter-day Saint commitment to genealogy has its roots in the Bible. The Old Testament concludes with two enigmatic verses in which God said to the prophet Malachi:

> Behold, I will send you Elijah the prophet before the coming of the great and dreadful day of the Lord: And he shall turn the heart of the fathers to the children, and the heart of the children to the fathers, lest I come and smite the earth with a curse. (Mal. 4:5–6)

In the centuries that followed, the expectation that this prophecy would be fulfilled became so strong that when Jesus began his ministry he was sometimes mistaken for Elijah (Matt. 16:14; Mark 6:15; 8:28; John 1:21).[3] Even today, Jews leave a vacant seat at their tables at Passover in symbolic anticipation of Elijah's return. The exact nature of Elijah's mission was not clear in the Bible, but in the nineteenth century, the Latter-day Saints received enlightenment on the reason for his return. This can best be understood in the context of the Mormon concept of the restoration of the gospel.

According to LDS belief, Jesus established his Church during his ministry and left it in the hands of ordained apostles and prophets. Eventually, however, the Church fell into apostasy, altering certain essential truths and losing the priesthood, or the authority to act in the name of God. But New Testament prophets foresaw a day of restoration. Peter, for example, referred to the "times of restitution of all things" (Acts 3:21), while Paul told the Ephesians about the "dispensation of the fulness of times," in which the Lord would "gather together in one all things in

Christ, both which are in heaven, and which are on earth; even in him" (Eph. 1:10).

Latter-day Saints believe the fulness of the gospel to have been restored through the Prophet Joseph Smith, as is explained in a revelation dated 1 November 1831:

> Wherefore, I the Lord, knowing the calamity which should come upon the inhabitants of the earth, called upon my servant Joseph Smith, Jun., and spake unto him from heaven, and gave him commandments; . . . to lay the foundation of this church, and to bring it forth out of obscurity and out of darkness, the only true and living church upon the whole earth. (D&C 1:17, 30)[4]

Included in this restoration was the doctrine of salvation for the dead. As Joseph Smith explained, when Malachi foretold the return of Elijah, he "had his eye fixed on the restoration of the priesthood, the glories to be revealed in the last days, and in an especial manner this most glorious of all subjects belonging to the everlasting gospel, namely, the baptism [salvation] for the dead" (D&C 128:17).

The Restoration began during the spring of 1820 in western New York state. In the midst of a series of religious revivals that swirled around him, Joseph Smith, then only fourteen years old, became dismayed at the confusion and bad feelings he saw among the various religious denominations. As he recalled in 1835, "I knew not who was right or who was wrong, but considered it of the first importance to me that I should be right."[5] Under these circumstances, young Joseph was deeply impressed when he read a biblical passage, James 1:5, that promised wisdom to those who would ask of God. "Never did any passage of scripture come with more power to the heart of man than this did at this time to mine," he wrote. "At length I came to the conclusion that I must either remain in darkness and confusion, or else I must do as James directs, that is, ask of God" (JS-H 1:12–13).

This determination led Joseph to a grove of trees, where he knelt in fervent prayer. After a considerable spiritual struggle with forces that seemed to almost overwhelm him, he suddenly saw a pillar of light that shone "above the brightness of the sun at noon day." Within the light stood two persons. One called Joseph by name and, pointing to the other, announced, "This is My Beloved Son. Hear Him!" As the vision continued, Joseph was informed, among other things, that he should join none of the existing churches, for God did not recognize the authority or teachings of those who led them.

Three years later, on the night of 21 September 1823, Joseph Smith received a second vision. A heavenly being named Moroni appeared and told him of the ancient records from which he would translate the Book of Mormon. Moroni also quoted Malachi's prophecy of Elijah, though with some significant modifications. Instead of saying, "I will send you Elijah," Moroni quoted Malachi 4:5 as: "I will reveal unto you the Priesthood, by the hand of Elijah the prophet." The next verse was also modified: "And he shall plant in the hearts of the children the promises made to the fathers, and the hearts of the children shall turn to their fathers. If it were not so, the whole earth would be utterly wasted at his coming" (D&C 2).

Joseph Smith received more visions and revelations that eventually led to the organization of the Church. The visions included visits from other heavenly beings, who restored the priesthood. In 1829, John the Baptist appeared to Joseph Smith and Oliver Cowdery and restored the priesthood of Aaron, which included the authority to baptize. Later, the Apostles Peter, James, and John restored the Melchizedek, or higher, Priesthood.

The Church was organized on 6 April 1830. Immediately, the handful of believers set out to gather new converts. Within a month, any question that might have lingered concerning the Church's exclusive authority to administer ordinances was settled by revelation. When converts who had been previously baptized in other churches wanted to join the restored Church without re-baptism, the Lord revealed the following through Joseph Smith:

> Behold, I say unto you that all old covenants have I caused to be done away in this thing; and this is a new and an everlasting covenant, even that which was from the beginning. Wherefore, although a man should be baptized an hundred times it availeth him nothing, for you cannot enter in at the strait gate by the law of Moses, neither by your dead works. For it is because of your dead works that I have caused this last covenant and this church to be built up unto me, even as in days of old. (D&C 22:1–3)

Because of religious harassment and the expectation of better acceptance in the West, Joseph Smith and his followers soon moved to Kirtland, Ohio. There the Church grew dramatically, although Church members suffered economic troubles and continued to face persecution.

In December 1832, the Prophet received a revelation commanding the Saints to erect a sacred building that would become "a house of prayer, a house of fasting, a house of faith, a house of learning, a house of glory, a house of order, a house of God" (D&C 88:119). This was the Kirtland Temple, forerunner of many temples to be constructed by the Church.

The dedication of the Kirtland Temple on 27 March 1836, was accompanied by dramatic spiritual outpourings—the sounds of rushing winds, a shaft of light over the temple, speaking in

The Kirtland Temple. On the day of Passover, 3 April 1836, the prophet Elijah and other resurrected beings appeared to Joseph Smith and Oliver Cowdery in this temple and committed to them the priesthood keys for directing ordinance work for the dead. Photograph by LaMar C. Berrett. Courtesy College of Religious Education, Brigham Young University.

tongues, and the visitation of angels.[6] Then, on 3 April, the day of the Passover that year,[7] Joseph Smith and Oliver Cowdery concluded a general meeting by retiring to the pulpit at the west end of the temple. After drawing a curtain to assure privacy and bowing themselves in solemn and silent prayer, they experienced a vision: "The veil was taken from our minds, and the eyes of our understanding were opened. We saw the Lord standing upon the breastwork of the pulpit, before us" (D&C 110:1–2). The Lord spoke to them, accepted the temple, and foretold its influence among the Saints and throughout the world. Other visions were opened to their minds, and then, at last, the following was manifested:

> After this vision had closed, another great and glorious vision burst upon us; for Elijah the prophet, who was taken to heaven without tasting death, stood before us, and said: Behold, the time has fully come, which was spoken of by the mouth of Malachi—testifying that he [Elijah] should be sent, before the great and dreadful day of the Lord come—To turn the hearts of the fathers to the children, and the children to the fathers, lest the whole earth be smitten with a curse—Therefore, the keys of this dispensation are committed into your hands; and by this ye may know that the great and dreadful day of the Lord is near, even at the doors. (D&C 110:13–16)[8]

Elijah had come, thus fulfilling the prophecy of Malachi. The full meaning of his appearance would become clear a few years later, after Joseph Smith instituted the practice of performing proxy baptisms in behalf of deceased ancestors.

Proxy Ordinances

The Saints believed that baptism, together with the laying on of hands for the gift of the Holy Ghost, was essential to salvation, but that these ordinances were invalid unless performed by priesthood authority. Many, therefore, wondered about the salvation of family members and friends who had died with no chance to accept the restored gospel or be baptized by someone holding the priesthood. The question may have arisen in Joseph Smith's mind in January 1836, when, in a remarkable vision, he saw his deceased brother Alvin inhabiting the celestial kingdom of God. As the Prophet wondered how this could be, since Alvin had not been baptized, the voice of the Lord came to him with these words:

> All who have died without a knowledge of the Gospel, who would have received it if they had been permitted to tarry, shall be heirs of the celestial kingdom of God; also all that shall die henceforth without a knowledge of it, who would have received it with all their hearts, shall be heirs of that kingdom for I, the Lord, will judge all men according to their works, according to the desire of their hearts.[9]

Joseph Smith first preached the doctrine of baptism for the dead in August 1840. Two months later, he officially notified the Quorum of the Twelve Apostles, who were in England, of the new doctrine:

> I presume the doctrine of "baptism for the dead" has ere this reached your ears, and may have raised some inquiries in your minds respecting the same. I cannot in this letter give you all the information you may desire on the subject; but aside from knowledge independent of the Bible, I would say that it was certainly practiced by the ancient churches; and St. Paul endeavors to prove the doctrine of the resurrection from the same, and says, "Else what shall they do which are baptized for the dead, if the dead rise not at all: Why are they then baptized for the dead?" I first mentioned the doctrine in public when preaching the funeral sermon of Brother Seymour Brunson; and have since then given general instructions in the Church on the subject. The Saints have the privilege of being baptized for those of their relatives who are dead, whom they believe would have embraced the Gospel, if they had been privileged with hearing it, and who have received the Gospel in spirit, through the instrumentality of those who have been commissioned to preach to them while in prison.[10]

Brigham Young later recalled that he had thought about this concept even before it was taught in the Church. Therefore, he said:

> It made me glad when I heard it was revealed through his servant Joseph, and that I could go forth and officiate for my fathers, for my mothers, and for my ancestors, of the earliest generation, who have not had the privilege of helping themselves; that they can yet arise to the state of glory and exaltation as we that live have a privilege of rising to ourselves.[11]

As Joseph Smith continued to preach on the subject, he emphasized the same theme:

> This doctrine presents in a clear light the wisdom and mercy of God, in preparing an ordinance for the salvation of the dead, being baptized by proxy, their names recorded in heaven and they judged according to the deeds done in the body. This doctrine was the burden of the scriptures. Those Saints who neglect it in behalf of their deceased relatives, do it at the peril of their own salvation.[12]

In the fall of 1840, Church members began to perform proxy baptisms in the Mississippi River. That did not continue, however, for in January 1841, Joseph Smith received a revelation commanding the Saints to build a temple in Nauvoo where sacred ordinances, known as the endowment, would be administered. In addition, the revelation declared, this would be the proper place to perform vicarious baptisms:

> For a baptismal font there is not upon the earth, that they, my saints, may be baptized for those who are dead—For this ordinance belongeth to my house, and cannot be acceptable to me, only in the days of your poverty, wherein ye are not able to build a house unto me. But I command you, all ye my saints, to build a house unto me; and I grant unto you a sufficient time to build a house unto me; and during this time your baptisms shall be acceptable unto me. (D&C 124:29–31)

In October 1841, Joseph Smith announced that no more baptisms for the dead should be conducted until they could be performed in the temple.[13] Only thirty-six days later, a temporary font was dedicated in the unfinished basement of the newly begun edifice. Constructed of tongued and grooved pine timber, it was oval shaped, measured sixteen feet long by twelve feet wide, had a basin four feet deep, and was trimmed with a molding of "beautiful carved work in antique style."[14] The sides were paneled and a flight of stairs led into each end of the font. Reminiscent of the brazen sea in the temple of Solomon, it rested on the backs of twelve oxen (1 Kgs. 7:25). Carved by Elijah Fordham from pine planks glued together, these oxen were patterned after "the most beautiful five-year-old steer that could be found in the country."[15] On 21 November, members began to perform baptisms for the dead in this remarkable font.

Church members eagerly performed baptisms in behalf of deceased relatives and friends. At first it mattered little to them whether men were being baptized for women or vice versa. The important thing was to do the work: "I went and was baptized for all my friends, grandmothers, and aunts, as those of the male sex," recalled Wilford Woodruff. Then, commenting on the instructions later given to the Church, he added, "Why, by-and-by, it was revealed, through the servants of the Lord, that females should be baptized for females, and males for males; but the full particulars of this order was not revealed till after the days of Joseph; therefore this shows an advance in the building up of the kingdom."[16]

On 6 September 1842, Joseph Smith clarified further the significance of Elijah's mission. Explaining Malachi's assertion that without the coming of Elijah the earth would be smitten with a curse, the Prophet said:

> It is sufficient to know, in this case, that the earth will be smitten with a curse unless there is a welding link of some kind or other between the fathers and the children, upon some subject or other—and behold what is that subject? It is the baptism for the dead. For we without them cannot be made perfect; neither can they without us be made perfect. . . . Let us, therefore, as a church and a people, and as Latter-day Saints, offer unto the Lord an offering in righteousness; and let us present in his holy temple, when it is finished, a book containing the records of our dead, which shall be worthy of all acceptation. (D&C 128:18, 24)

Baptism was not the only temple ordinance instituted for the deceased. During the construction of the Nauvoo Temple, Joseph Smith began to prepare the Saints to receive the endowment: a series of symbolic representations, special instructions, and sacred covenants that would give them greater insight into their eternal origins and destinies as well as their earthly responsibilities.[17] Reserved only for worthy Church members, the endowment was to be administered exclusively in the temple and was necessary for the exaltation of the individual. In May 1842, Joseph Smith introduced the endowment ceremony to a small group of specially selected Saints, including members of the Quorum of the Twelve, in an upper room of his store in Nauvoo. Members of this group, which was gradually enlarged to include both men and women, were thus prepared to administer the endowment to other Church members once the temple was ready.[18]

The Prophet also taught the Saints the principle of eternal marriage. Family relationships were at the heart of the gospel

The Nauvoo Temple. Beginning 21 November 1841, proxy baptisms for deceased individuals were performed in a wooden font in a dedicated basement room of this temple while it was under construction. Courtesy College of Religious Education, Brigham Young University.

message, and it was the plan of the Lord that marriage bonds should be eternal (D&C 132:18, 19). A marriage performed by priesthood authority, therefore, would last through eternity, and the children produced from that marriage would be part of an eternal family union. The temple ordinances creating these eternal family bonds became known as sealings.

The Saints believed, however, that the endowment and sealing ceremonies were essential not only to their own salvation, but also to the salvation of their dead family members. Church members were taught that these ordinances were necessary in order to form connecting links within their families all the way back to Adam and Eve. For this reason, Joseph continued to preach about the urgency of concern for the dead. Less than three months before his death, he explained again the very close connection between this world and eternity: "We are looked upon by God as though we were in eternity." Then, referring to the eternal responsibility of the Saints toward their ancestors, he proclaimed, "The greatest responsibility in this world that God has laid upon us is to seek after our dead."[19]

After the death of Joseph Smith in June 1844, the Saints continued to work toward completion of the temple in Nauvoo, even though it became apparent that they must eventually leave that city. By the end of November 1845, the temple was far enough along that Brigham Young and other members of the Council of the Twelve Apostles could dedicate several finished rooms for the purpose of giving the endowment to Church members. The first endowments in the temple were administered on 10 December 1845. The Saints were so eager to receive their endowments that the ordinance work often went on around the clock. At the same time, many couples were married for eternity by the power of the priesthood. By the time they were forced to leave Nauvoo, over five thousand Church members had received the promised blessings.

The exodus from Nauvoo began in February 1846. The next year, Brigham Young led the vanguard pioneer company from Winter Quarters, Iowa, to the Great Basin, where the Church established a new gathering place for the Saints. One of Brigham Young's first acts after arriving in the Salt Lake Valley was to designate a spot for building another temple, and work commenced in 1853. Although the Salt Lake Temple was not dedicated until 1893, three other temples were completed in Utah prior to that date so the sacred temple ordinances could again be enjoyed by the Saints. In the meantime, some proxy baptisms and sealings, along with endowments of the living, were administered in places approved temporarily, including the Endowment House (1855–89) erected on Temple Square in Salt Lake City.

Proxy endowments, however, were delayed until the completion of the temple in St. George. Even though that temple was not officially dedicated until April 1877, baptisms in behalf of the dead were performed after a preliminary dedication on 9 January. The first to be baptized was Susa Young Gates, a daughter of Brigham Young. Two days later, the first endowments in behalf of the dead were administered. That day Brigham Young, so afflicted with rheumatism that he had to be carried from place to place, stood proxy for his father.[20] President Young also addressed the group on the significance of what they were doing. With special reference to the dead, he remarked:

> What do you suppose the fathers would say if they could speak from the dead? Would they not say: 'We have lain here thousands of years in this prison house, bound and fettered in the association of the filthy and corrupt.' If they had the power the very thunders of heaven would resound in our ears. All the angels in heaven are looking to this little handful of people. When I think upon this subject I want the tongue of seven thunders to awaken the people to action. When we closed the Endowment House many people of the north came to us crying. They begged the privilege to be baptized for their dead. They can now come here, do the work and bid the prisoners go free.[21]

This, then, was the Spirit of Elijah at work among the Saints. They were concerned with baptisms, endowments, and sealings not just for themselves, but also in behalf of the dead. They knew that the ultimate validity of their proxy work would depend on the righteousness of the deceased beneficiaries and their personal acceptance of the work. Nevertheless, it was the obligation of the living to do all they could for the dead by searching them out and then performing the necessary ordinances in their behalf.

Meanwhile, general interest in genealogical research was growing. The Saints were delighted, for they saw it all as further evidence of the hand of God in history and of the outpouring of the Spirit of Elijah. In 1885 the editor of the Church-owned *Deseret News* wrote:

> The same motive does not prompt the members of the various genealogical societies of New England and other places as urges the Saints to make similar researches; in fact, it might be difficult for many persons who have during recent years become so wonderfully exercised over genealogical matters that it amounts to a mania with them, to tell just why they are so affected. . . . And so the work of forming these societies and collecting and publishing genealogical data goes on in this and other countries; and thousands of men are laboring assiduously to prepare the way, though unconsciously, for the salvation of the dead.
>
> In all this the Saints recognize the hand of the Lord, shaping the destiny of his work, and preparing the way for its accomplishment.

> They have no difficulty in assigning a reason for the unusual interest in the subject referred to which now prevails in the world. It is a result of that power which will in time come to be made manifest in revealing to the Saints in sacred places those links in their ancestry which cannot be traced by human means, so that the saving work might be done for all who are worthy, and the chain of redemption through the power of the Gospel rendered complete all the way back to Father Adam.[22]

The American Setting

Before 1844 there were no organized societies in the United States devoted primarily to genealogical research, but many Americans were nevertheless engaged in the quest for ancestral roots. Among them were prominent families who had long taken an interest in their lineage. Benjamin Franklin and George Washington were among the numerous illustrious Americans who collected and recorded their ancestral lines. In addition, genealogy was among the interests of the eleven state historical societies that existed prior to 1844, as well of as the American Antiquarian Society, founded in 1812.

Most people did not publish their findings, although the first published genealogy in America appeared in 1771. By 1915 only about 3,000 family histories had been published. After that, a flood tide seemed to hit; in less than thirty years, another sixteen thousand titles were added to the list.[23] The family histories and genealogies in print today probably number into the hundreds of thousands.

In the eighteenth and early nineteenth centuries, genealogy still carried the aura of an aristocratic pastime. More common Americans, who deplored aristocratic tendencies, often ridiculed genealogical records and considered it bad taste even to speak of their ancestors. However, the organization of societies specifically dedicated to general genealogical research, not solely to compilations for the benefit of the rich and the wellborn, helped counter such disdain. The founders of the New England Historic Genealogical Society were convinced that all people should become acquainted with their progenitors. "They who care nothing for their ancestors," someone later said, "are wanting in respect for themselves and deserve only contempt by their posterity."[24]

A barely averted genealogical tragedy in 1844 ignited the spark that led to the organization of the first American genealogical society. A Boston merchant, William H. Montague, was horrified one cold day when he discovered a janitor about to stoke the fires of the Boston Custom House with the 1798 U.S. District Tax rolls for Massachusetts and Maine. He quickly intervened and saved some twenty folio volumes. Other Boston citizens were also concerned with the destruction of public documents and family papers. In October 1844, a small group met in Montague's home to discuss forming an organization to prevent such historical catastrophes. In December the New England Historic Genealogical Society was founded. The following March, the Massachusetts legislature approved the society's incorporation and granted it a charter "for the purpose of collecting, preserving and occasionally publishing genealogical and historic matter relating to New England." By April 1846, the society had nearly 150 members, including former U.S. president John Quincy Adams and distinguished historian George Bancroft. A hundred years later, the society boasted a membership of over 2,350 people and a library of 168,000 bound volumes and over 50,000 pamphlets and manuscripts.

The next major American organization, the New York Genealogical and Biographical Society, was incorporated on 16 March 1869. By the time of its centennial in 1969, the society housed over 54,000 printed volumes and nearly 22,500 manuscripts at its New York City library.

Meanwhile, an emphasis by some Americans on their distinctive lineage led to the creation of various societies based on royal descent. Not concerned with proving a title, their members simply wanted the satisfaction derived from being part of a royal family. Royal societies formed in the United States included the Order of the Crown in America (1898), consisting of descendants of royalty; the Baronical Order of Magna Charta (1898); the National Society of Americans of Royal Descent (1908), in which membership is by invitation only; the Daughters of the Baron of Runnymede (1921); and the Descendants of Royal Bastards (1952). All these are exclusivist organizations in which at least one major motivation for keeping genealogical records is the prestige that comes from a hereditary attachment to royalty.

Other Americans became interested in genealogy because their ancestors belonged to distinctive groups other than royalty. This interest resulted in the organization of a number of hereditary and lineage societies. In general, these were also patriotic societies, devoted to promoting respect and reverence for the deeds of those who played a role in the great events of national history. The Society of the Cincinnati, for example, was founded in 1783 by officers of the American Continental Army, with George Washington as the first president. Membership remains strictly hereditary. In the latter part of the nineteenth century, such societies multiplied profusely. They included the Sons of the Revolution, the Sons of the American Revolution, the Union Veterans of the Civil War, the Society of Colonial Wars, the Daughters of the American Revolution, the National Society of Colonial Dames in America, the United Daughters of the Confederacy, and the Society of the Mayflower Descendants. Societies limited to descendants of other American wars and many more such groups continued to multiply in the twentieth century. Some of these hereditary societies have made important contributions to genealogical research by preserving wills, notices of births, marriages and deaths, church records, and various private records.

Samuel Eliot Morison has called the period from 1870 to 1900 the era of "the American joiner," in which a variety of needs and interests led growing numbers of Americans, especially among the rising urban middle class, to look for new social outlets and new sources of fellowship. Societies based on ancestry were among those they eagerly joined.[25] All this interest provided a tremendous boost to genealogical research in America. Genealogical and ancestral societies helped create wider interest in family history and promote more responsible record keeping and gathering on the part of churches as well as government.[26] Forty years after its founding, the president of the New England society reported that its library was being used widely by people from all over the United States. Members of the society, he said, had awakened the interest of many others "till at the present time a spirit of genealogical inquiry pervades the whole country." In addition, the society had been influential in bringing about the preservation and collection of many priceless manuscripts.[27]

As the twentieth century progressed, genealogical societies appeared in state after state. "A tidal wave of ancestry-searching has swept over the country," reported one genealogist in 1911. "Libraries and the custodians of public records bear record to this great movement. . . . So onerous has become the work of handing out historical and genealogical books that in some large libraries such works have been gathered into alcoves which are thrown open to the public, where the ancestry-hunter may help himself."[28]

The significance of this tidal wave was not lost upon the Latter-day Saints. Long before their own genealogical society was formed, many Church members were eagerly engaged in the ancestor search. They were quick to take advantage of the opportunities being created by others. In 1877, Benjamin F. Cummings, one of the earliest professional genealogists among the Mormons, visited the library of the New England society in Boston. He was surprised at the vastness of its program and was especially pleased with the skill and knowledge of John Ward Dean, the librarian. "It seemed that all I had to do was to tell him the name of the family concerning which I desired information and he could readily tell me whether its history and genealogy had ever been written or arranged, and if so, who by, and where I could get more information."[29] "How gratifying . . . it must be," the Church newspaper editorialized, for the Saints "to learn that others as well as themselves are aroused to the necessity of searching the misty records of the past and tracing the history of families as to remote a period as possible."[30] "Surely," wrote Benjamin Cummings, "it must be the Spirit of God at work among the people that causes them to thus seek out a knowledge of their ancestry and arrange the same with such care and precision."[31]

As the organization of genealogical societies and the publications of journals, genealogies, and family histories accelerated, many genealogists began to feel the need for better coordination on a national scale. Most local and state organizations seemingly could provide little help outside their own areas or libraries. Providing such aid was one of the purposes of the National Genealogical Society, organized in 1903. It welcomed genealogical inquiries, kept a record of the families on which its members were working, and willingly sent to inquirers the names and addresses of others working on the same families. In 1912 it began publishing *The National Genealogical Society Quarterly*. The society did not do genealogical research itself, but was devoted to assisting its members in research and to collecting and preserving genealogical data. The National Genealogical Society now has the largest membership of any such society in the United States.

In recent years, the interest in genealogical research has gone far beyond the search for pedigrees and other traditional family information. Historians who were once disdainful of genealogy as a discipline are now using it for a variety of professional purposes. As social history, demography, and family studies have become more prominent within the profession, historians have turned to genealogical and family records to help create a better understanding of the past. "In fact," wrote one prominent scholar, "the frequently expressed disdain by historians concerning the usefulness of these records, often allowed to decay by neglect, borders on archival irresponsibility."[32] The same historian made an eloquent plea for greater cooperation:

> When the social historian begins to work with family history and to focus on a broader network of kinship relationships over time, and the genealogist begins to spend time and effort in indexing the same manuscript census returns that historians use, it is time for the two groups to examine their common ground.[33]

In that spirit, some history professors have even begun to have their students write their own family histories, placed and interpreted in historic context, for three or four generations back.

New Revelation and the Continuing LDS Challenge

For Church members, the growing interest in genealogy and family history, the formation of so many genealogical and historical societies, and the expanding availability of family history sources were all evidence of the outpouring of the Spirit of Elijah.[34] That feeling was enhanced in 1918 when a revelation to President Joseph F. Smith provided the Saints with a significant new insight into the spirit world and how the dead could receive the gospel.

Church members already understood that preaching the gospel to the dead was begun by the Savior himself during the three days his body lay in the tomb. During that time, the Apostle Peter taught, "he went and preached unto the spirits in prison; which sometime were disobedient, when once the longsuffering of God waited in the days of Noah, while the ark was a preparing" (1 Pet. 3:19–20). Peter also reminded the New Testament Saints that "for this cause was the gospel preached also to them that are dead, that they might be judged according to men in the flesh, but live according to God in the spirit"(1 Pet. 4:6). But Church president Joseph F. Smith wondered how the Savior could have preached to all the dead in so short a time. While he was pondering the question on 3 October 1918, a vision was opened to his mind. He beheld the Savior in the spirit world and saw him organize missionary work among the spirits of the dead:

> I perceived that the Lord went not in person among the wicked and the disobedient who had rejected the truth, to teach them; But behold, from among the righteous, he organized his forces and appointed messengers, clothed with power and authority, and commissioned them to go forth and carry the light of the gospel to them that were in darkness . . . and thus was the gospel preached to the dead. (D&C 138:29–30)

Since then, the Saints have understood that missionary work continues in the spirit world. The responsibility for genealogical research and the opportunity for temple worship connected with it are both virtually unlimited—at least for the time being. Recently temple building has expanded into many nations, spurring genealogical research worldwide. In 1977, President Spencer W. Kimball explained the responsibility of the Saints:

> We do not know how many millions of spirits are involved. We know that many have passed away in wars, pestilence, and various accidents. We know that the spirit world is filled with the spirits of men who are waiting for you and me to get busy. . . . We wonder about our progenitors—grandparents, great-grandparents, great-great-grandparents, etc. What do they think of you and me? We are their offspring. We have the responsibility to do their temple work. . . . We have a grave responsibility that we cannot avoid, and may stand in jeopardy if we fail to do this important work.[35]

The coming of Elijah on 3 April 1836 ushered in the distinctive efforts of Latter-day Saints to seek out their ancestors and perform saving ordinances in their behalf. What follows is the story of their organized efforts to achieve that goal. The Genealogical

Society of Utah, succeeded by the Family History Department of the Church, has contributed in a most fundamental way to turning the hearts of the children to the fathers.

NOTES

[1]Today, a literal descendant of Aaron, if otherwise worthy, can claim the office of bishop in the LDS Church (D&C 68:15–20; 107:16, 69–70).

[2]Much of this and the following paragraph is based on L. G. Price, "Genealogy," in *Collier's Encyclopedia* (New York: Crowell, Collier, and Macmillan, 1967), 1613–16.

[3]These verses use the name Elias, which is the New Testament form of Elijah.

[4]For further insight into the LDS concept of the apostasy and restoration of the gospel, see Joseph Fielding Smith, *The Restoration of All Things* (Salt Lake City: Deseret News, 1945). In particular, see chapter 1, "The Dispensation of the Fulness of Times"; chapter 8, "The Church Restored"; and chapters 18 and 19, both of which deal with the coming of Elijah. See also James E. Talmage, *The Great Apostasy* (Salt Lake City: Deseret News, 1909); B. H. Roberts, *A Comprehensive History of The Church of Jesus Christ of Latter-day Saints, Century One,* 6 vols. (Salt Lake City: Deseret News, 1930), 1:introduction.

[5]For Joseph Smith's full statement on his early visions and revelations and the origin of the Church, see Joseph Smith—History, in the Pearl of Great Price. See Dean C. Jessee, "The Early Accounts of Joseph Smith's First Vision," *BYU Studies* 9 (Spring 1969): 275–94, for photographic reproductions of other statements by Joseph Smith concerning his first vision. The quotation above is from the 1835 account. The best recent history of the years before the Church was organized is Richard L. Bushman, *Joseph Smith and the Beginnings of Mormonism* (Urbana: University of Illinois Press, 1984). For an overview of the history of the Church, see James B. Allen and Glen M. Leonard, *The Story of the Latter-day Saints,* 2d ed., rev. and enl. (Salt Lake City: Deseret Book, 1992).

[6]Joseph Smith Jr., *The History of The Church of Jesus Christ of Latter-day Saints,* ed. B. H. Roberts, 2d ed. rev., 7 vols. (Salt Lake City: Deseret Book, 1971), 2:428 (hereafter cited as *History of the Church*).

[7]Stephen D. Ricks, "The Appearance of Elijah and Moses in the Kirtland Temple and the Jewish Passover," *BYU Studies* 23 (Fall 1983): 483–86.

[8]For an authoritative statement by an LDS Church leader on the mission of Elijah, see Joseph Fielding Smith, *Elijah the Prophet and His Mission* (Salt Lake City: Deseret Book, 1957).

[9]*History of the Church* 2:380. See also D&C 138, which is an account of Joseph F. Smith's vision of the celestial kingdom.

[10]Joseph Smith, to the Traveling High Council and Elders of The Church of Jesus Christ of Latter-day Saints in Great Britain, 19 October 1840, *History of the Church* 4:231. See also D&C 138, which is an account of Joseph F. Smith's vision of the celestial kingdom.

[11]Speech delivered by Brigham Young in Nauvoo, 6 April 1845, as reported in *Millennial Star* 6 (1 October 1845): 119–22.

[12]*History of the Church* 4:426.

[13]*History of the Church* 4:426.

[14]*History of the Church* 4:426.

[15]*History of the Church* 4:446.

[16]Brigham Young and others, *Journal of Discourses,* 26 vols. (Liverpool: F. D. Richards, 1855–86), 5:85 (9 April 1857).

[17]For authoritative statements on the nature of temples and temple work, see James E. Talmage, *The House of the Lord* (Salt Lake City: Deseret News, 1912); Boyd K. Packer, *The Holy Temple* (Salt Lake City: Bookcraft, 1980).

[18]See D. Michael Quinn, "Latter-day Saint Prayer Circles," *BYU Studies* 19 (Fall 1978): 79–105.

[19]*History of the Church* 6:313.

[20]Relief Society lesson on "Testimony and Genealogy," *Relief Society Magazine* 7 (October 1920): 600. See also Matthias F. Cowley, *Wilford Woodruff: History of His Life and Labors as Recorded in His Daily Journals* (Salt Lake City: Deseret News, 1909), 491–95.

[21]Cowley, *Wilford Woodruff,* 494–95.

[22]"Genealogical Matters," *Deseret News Weekly,* 1 April 1885, 174.

[23]Frederick Adams Virkus, *The Handbook of American Genealogy* 4 (Chicago: Institute of American Genealogy, 1943): preface.

[24]As quoted by Kenneth Scott, "Genealogical Societies: Introduction, General Description and Brief History," in the Report on the World Conference on Records and Genealogical Seminar, vol. 2, Salt Lake City, 1969.

[25]Samuel Eliot Morison, *The Oxford History of the American People* (New York: Oxford University Press, 1965), 787.

[26]*Deseret Evening News,* 5 November 1875.

[27]Address reported in *Deseret News Weekly,* 1 April 1885.

[28]Frank Allaben, "Concerning Genealogies," *The Utah Genealogical and Historical Magazine* 2 (April 1911): 96 (hereafter cited as *UGHM*).

[29]B. F. Cummings Jr., to the *Deseret News,* 7 May 1877, in *Deseret News,* 6 June 1877.

[30]*Deseret News Weekly*, 1 April 1885.

[31]Cummings to *Deseret News,* 7 May 1877.

[32]Samuel P. Hays, "History and Genealogy: Patterns of Change and Prospects for Cooperation," *Prologue: The Journal of the National Archives* 7 (Spring 1975): 40.

[33]Hays, "History and Genealogy," 39.

[34]When the *Utah Genealogical and Historical Society Magazine* published a 1913 article on eugenics and genealogy, the Mormon editor added the following comment: "To the many reasons for the study of genealogy which the author of the following article so interestingly sets forth, the Latter-day Saints will add another, more far-reaching and fraught with vastly more good to the human race than any other—that of salvation for the dead. 'The Spirit of Elijah' actuates the 'New Genealogy,' though the world, as yet, may not recognize the fact." Editor's note at head of Charles K. Bolton, "The New Genealogy," *UGHM* 4 (July 1913): 126–29, reprinted from the *Boston Transcript,* 23 October 1909.

[35]Spencer W. Kimball, "The Things of Eternity—Stand We in Jeopardy?" *Ensign* 7 (January 1977): 5.

President Wilford Woodruff received a revelation in 1894 on the importance of tracing ancestry for the purpose of temple work. The revelation led to the establishment of the Society. Courtesy LDS Church Archives.

Chapter 1

Small Beginnings

Long before the Latter-day Saints founded a genealogical society, a number of Church members made extraordinary efforts to gather family information. While these attempts to locate genealogical records were largely individual, the Church offered encouragement and assistance when possible. The major impediment to genealogical research in nineteenth-century Utah was the inaccessibility of sources. The ancestral records of the typical Utah resident were scattered far outside the territory and usually outside the country in homes, institutions, archives, offices, churches, and cemeteries. The Saints' continuing personal and cooperative search for these records together with an important doctrinal revelation to President Wilford Woodruff helped set the stage for the founding of the Genealogical Society of Utah in 1894.

Personal Genealogical Activities

Among the Saints in Utah, Church leaders often set the example in the search for family records. The brothers Orson and Parley P. Pratt, both Apostles, were among the first to begin an organized search for family records. In 1853, while serving a mission in Washington, D.C., Orson Pratt responded to a newspaper advertisement placed by the Reverend Frederick W. Chapman requesting information concerning the descendants of William Pratt of Massachusetts. Chapman provided Elder Pratt the connecting links between him and his earliest New England forebear.

Elder Pratt later published a Pratt family genealogy, thereby becoming the first Latter-day Saint to systematically research and publish his family history. In 1873 he reported that his ancestry had been traced back eleven generations and that the families of the Pratt brothers had been baptized for about three thousand of their ancestors.[1]

Likewise, Wilford Woodruff, who became President of the Church in 1889, was an exemplary part-time genealogist. While doing missionary work in London in 1840 and again in 1846, he spent part of his time gathering Woodruff genealogy. Eventually he gathered hundreds of Woodruff names, obtained a family coat of arms, and traced his direct ancestry in America to some of the earliest New England settlers.

Apostle Franklin D. Richards was one of the most well known of the nineteenth-century genealogists in the Church. He served as assistant Church historian for many years and from 1889 until his death in 1899 as Church historian and general Church recorder. In a patriarchal blessing, Elder Richards was told that he should be involved in work relating to the dead.[2] He gathered genealogical records in England and the United States through letters and personal research. On 23 November 1885, he wrote in his journal, "I find that I have 2,801 names of Richards and those who had married in connection with the Richards race baptized for and recorded in my family record book."[3] He spent the next three days working on his books and by 26 November had recorded 3,434 names of persons for whom vicarious baptism had been done.[4]

In 1884 Elder Richards's personal library became the basis for the first Church genealogical library when he agreed to sell it at cost to the Church Historian's Office.[5] An avid collector of books, he continued to add to the collection, and by 1889 the library contained over two hundred publications of the New England Historic Genealogical Society as well as many other valuable genealogical publications.[6] Known for his extensive work even outside Utah, that same year Elder Richards accepted an invitation to join the New England society.

Elder Richards did much to help other Saints. He frequently ordered books for other people and for the temples. Church members

Elder Franklin D. Richards, first president of the Genealogical Society, 1894–99.

often turned to him for advice on building their own genealogical libraries.[7]

On 23 May 1890, Elder Richards and his son Charles started out on a genealogical excursion—a twenty-three-day trip that took them to several eastern states where they sought out relatives, visited graveyards, searched town records, and gathered all the family names they could. It was an effort later emulated by other Church members both in that century and this. In Pittsfield, Massachusetts, they found a cousin and spent an enjoyable evening with her family. They found the graves of several family members, including that of Elder Richards's great-grandmother. They ended their eastern tour in Philadelphia, where they copied many names from the city directory. Upon returning to Utah, Elder Richards wrote in his journal, "Thanks and praise to God for the information that I was enabled to obtain . . . of men whom I never saw before concerning our Dead that I may prepare a proper Record of my work such as will be acceptable when the dead shall be judged out of the Books that shall have been written."[8]

Church members in the Territory of Utah used various other means of gathering information. They corresponded with members elsewhere on genealogical matters. Those who left on proselyting missions were often pressed into research service by relatives and friends. Presumably the missionaries helped when they could, although too much time spent on genealogical work could drastically interfere with missionary labors. In one case, Elder Franklin D. Richards received a letter from a woman who wanted a list of all missionaries going to Europe so she could ask them to help with her genealogies. This, of course, was inappropriate, but Elder Richards suggested that she write the president of the British Mission in Liverpool, providing the names of her parents and the parish and shire where they and their ancestors had lived. The mission president would then ask the Elder in that area to visit the parish clerk to see if the appropriate records were there and to find out how much it would cost to have them copied. Elder Richards astutely commented that they should not tell the parish clerk that the information was for temple work. The religious purpose might antagonize him, but since other people were doing genealogy simply for family interest, this approach would be more likely to persuade him to furnish the material at a reasonable cost.[9]

One missionary, Benjamin F. Cummings, provided an unusual amount of help. He went on two missions within the United States, one from 1876 to 1877 and another in 1878. During his first mission, he interspersed his missionary work with genealogical work for other people. Before his second, he was specifically assigned by Orson Pratt and others to search records and gather genealogies.[10] Charles C. Rich of the Council of the Twelve publicly recognized the work of Cummings in 1878, when he told a Paris, Idaho, audience that "an opportunity is now offered by Brother Cummings, by which some of us may obtain our genealogies, and we should improve it as much as possible. I feel happy in being able to send to the States where many of my ancestors have lived and died, so as to get the names."[11]

Cummings devoted the rest of his life to genealogical and temple work. In 1892 he went on an extended tour of the eastern United States to learn about their record-keeping systems. His goal was to develop a kind of national clearinghouse for both genealogical and temple work. In an 1893 letter to the First Presidency of the Church, he proposed to invite all American families to send him their genealogies. He would index them, collect published works, and attempt to prevent duplications while facilitating research. He felt he could save work and expense for many researchers by putting related people in touch with each other. He also wanted to help arrange genealogical material for temple work and agreed that since this work was sacred, he would keep the cost low and not do it for "speculation."[12] Though given approval by the First Presidency, he was unable to pursue this project before his death in 1899.

For Church members, perhaps the most readily available source of help for genealogical research in the 1880s and 1890s was the Church Historian's Office, particularly through the dedicated work of Elder Franklin D. Richards. One of the duties of the Historian's Office was collecting genealogical information from missionaries as they came to Church headquarters on their way to their mission fields. In addition, Elder Richards provided personal research assistance to many people who wrote or came to the office. Sometimes he charged a nominal fee for the time spent.[13] On other occasions, he simply gave advice. With all his other responsibilities, however, he had less and less available time. By 1893 he was directing some inquiries to Benjamin F. Cummings Jr.[14]

During these early years, some Church members attempted to establish their own genealogical organizations. Scottish members pioneered this effort. In 1879 a notice appeared in the Church-owned *Deseret Evening News* calling for a meeting of all Saints of Scottish descent who were interested in a united effort to promote research. David McKenzie of Salt Lake City and Alexander F. McDonald of St. George attempted to collect the names of interested people. The meeting was to be held in Salt Lake City during the October 1879 general conference.[15] The results of that meeting remain unknown, but that same year Alexander McDonald was called to preside over the Saints in Salt River Valley in Arizona.

While not in a position to actively participate in a Utah-based organization, McDonald did not give up on the idea of a united effort. In 1888 he proposed the creation of a genealogical bureau, particularly for the benefit of Scottish members of the Church. His dream, which he soon realized was somewhat unrealistic, was ultimately to have all the Scottish records copied and the copies brought to Utah.[16]

On 20 June 1888, John Nicholson, one of McDonald's collaborators, wrote President Wilford Woodruff about the Scottish plan. President Woodruff was delighted, for he, too, was concerned that individual efforts were often costly. More cooperative efforts, he believed, could save money as well as provide more thorough research. Besides, he observed, "there is danger also of much work being done twice in the temple, for the want of system on the part of those who officiate."[17]

President Woodruff fully endorsed the plans being formulated by Nicholson, McDonald, and others.[18] The result was the founding of the Latter-day Saints' Genealogical Bureau, with John Nicholson as president and Douglas A. Swan as secretary. The Bureau's initial emphasis was to be on Scottish research. Nicholson and Swan, along with Alexander F. McDonald, William Budge, and Duncan McAllister, were also directors. The impetus was initially provided by Nicholson and Swan. The other three directors did not even reside in Salt Lake City at the time. Duncan McAllister, for example, was on a mission in England, acting as manager of business affairs in the Church office at Liverpool. He must have been surprised when he received a letter written on 24 September 1888 on Latter-day Saints' Genealogical Bureau letterhead, with his name listed as a director. "You will see by the enclosed circular," Nicholson and Swan explained to him, "that we have used your name in connection with an enterprise that you will doubtless deem laudable. . . . When you come home, all business will be open to your inspection. Please do not object to the use of your name in so good a cause; you were so far off that we could not reach you in time to consult you."[19]

Nicholson and Swan also wrote to George Teasdale, president of the European Mission, asking permission to use John Hays, a missionary in the Edinburgh district, to work for them. They wanted Hays to devote part of his time to obtaining genealogical information from the civil registry office in that city. They were willing to reimburse him for his time, thus making his missionary expenses less burdensome. They hastened to assure the mission president that theirs was no money-making scheme. They intended to charge their clients "barely sufficient to cover expenses."[20]

The founders had ambitious plans for the new bureau. They proposed to establish a permanent agent at the headquarters of the Church in Liverpool who would know the location of all missionaries. Family research requests would be sent to the missionary nearest the parish designated. This missionary "tracer" would send his report to the Liverpool agent. If more information might be obtained in another parish, the agent would forward the request to the appropriate missionary. The genealogists believed this plan would save considerable money by eliminating the need for one person to travel widely around the country.[21] The Latter-day Saints' Genealogical Bureau sent out circulars and advertised in the press.

Nicholson and Swan's ambitious plan was the natural result of the frustration of many dedicated Mormon genealogists who saw an important work floundering for want of organized cooperative efforts. How long the organization lasted is not clear, but by the time the Genealogical Society of Utah was founded in 1894, the Latter-day Saints' Genealogical Bureau was not functional.

Other Church members also provided professional help in genealogical research. Hiring a professional was usually much less expensive to individuals and families than an attempt to do the research on their own. In 1892 the services of James B. Walkley of London were publicized in the *Deseret Evening News:*

> Any of our friends who desire to obtain genealogical information in England can gain it on reasonable terms by engaging the services of Brother James B. Walkley of 19 Burton Street Euston Road London. He has been working at the business with good results for some time.
>
> He can collect all necessary data concerning persons who have died from 1837 to date, at the rate of $7.50 per hundred names or if preferred at twenty-five cents per name. It costs him about $6.00 per hundred names and the $1.50 is what he charges per day for his work. For dates previous to 1837, outside of London, he would require traveling expenses. We are informed that he is capable and reliable and those who avail themselves of his aid may confidently expect to receive satisfaction.[22]

Genealogical Missionaries

It was almost inevitable that the Mormon custom of calling missionaries for almost every important project should be adapted to genealogical work.[23] The genealogical missionaries seldom, if ever, received official calls to be missionaries. Theirs were self-appointed missions. Once they decided to go, however, they were invited to Salt Lake City to receive a blessing for their missions from a General Authority. Also, they were often given missionary cards, which allowed them travel discounts. The trip to Chicago in 1883, for example, would cost the missionary only $6.25.[24] Franklin D. Richards's journal is replete with entries concerning blessings he gave to people for genealogical missions.[25]

Armed with missionary zeal, missionary cards, letters of appointment, and a special blessing from a Church authority, the genealogical missionaries set out. They visited relatives, copied family Bibles and other records, and asked an unending stream of questions regarding their ancestors. They visited parish churches, where they spent long hours searching through old registers, and trekked to cemeteries seeking the gravestones of their relatives. Many missionaries reported spiritual experiences that gave them firm assurance that the Lord was with them and had miraculously directed them to their needed sources.

The surviving missionary records are incomplete, but it is clear that between 1885 and 1900 at least 178 Saints became genealogical missionaries.[26] Most were middle-aged or elderly men; however, some young men and women, as well as a few couples also went. A few came from Arizona and Idaho, but most were from Utah. The majority went to Great Britain. There was no set length of service, and the time spent varied from a few weeks to over three years.[27]

The story of one genealogical missionary illustrates the nature of their activities. John Adams Wakeham was converted to Mormonism in Boston in 1845 and returned to New England as a regular missionary in 1882. Nine years later, at age sixty-nine, he returned again, this time as a genealogical missionary. Wakeham spent about three and one-half years on his genealogical mission, most of the time in the vicinity of his ancestral home in New Hampshire. On one occasion, he walked four miles to the home of James H. Neals, seeking a relative he had never met. To Mrs. Neals, who answered the door, he explained in his customary fashion that he was a relative of the Copp family, some of whom had settled in that area, and that he was seeking to know more about his kindred. "I was directed to you as being the granddaughter of William H. Copp," he told the woman. "Therefore if you will give such information as you possess of the history of the family, I will be greatly obliged." For fifteen minutes, the suspicious woman interrogated the missionary about his ancestors but finally said that even though she was alone, she would let him in because he had an honest face. She had been attempting to gather genealogy herself, although with limited success.

Wakeham did not spend all his time doing genealogy. At times he stopped to see old friends, sometimes staying long enough to help them with their work. He spent parts of two summers on the farm of A. H. Wentworth helping with the harvest. All his friends and relatives were kind, but he was saddened at the end of his mission that he had been unable to convert any of them to the Church.

One of Wakeham's most helpful genealogical contacts was Doctor John R. Ham. While examining Ham's extensive genealogical library, Wakeham found the name of Edward Wakeham, his great-great-grandfather. He also learned that one of his great-grandfathers was a Native American. This information confirmed a family tradition, but it was also particularly significant to Wakeham. His patriarchal blessing had identified him as a literal descendant of the biblical Joseph who was sold into Egypt. Church teachings identified many Native Americans as descendants of Joseph, and for Wakeham, this genealogical discovery in Dr. Ham's library was a welcome confirmation of a sacred personal blessing.[28]

Most genealogical missions were of relatively short duration. The success of the missionaries varied, but in the end their efforts resulted in many additional family records being brought to Utah, as well as in the completion of considerable amounts of vicarious temple work.

A New Revelation

With the dedication of the Salt Lake Temple in April 1893, the Church began a new era of temple work. Because the temple was located in the major metropolitan center of the Church, the potential for temple attendance increased dramatically. Members in Salt Lake City no longer had to travel sixty miles north to Logan or hundreds of miles south to Manti or St. George to perform proxy ordinances.

The next year, President Wilford Woodruff made a pivotal doctrinal announcement that had an important effect on genealogical work and temple activity. At the time of the dedication of the Salt Lake Temple, sealing ordinances were limited to the first generation beyond the first family member to join the Church. Husbands and wives were sealed for eternity by the power of the priesthood, and men and women were sealed by proxy to their parents if their parents were deceased. But it was also a custom for a man and his family to be "adopted" into the family of a Church official or other prominent priesthood bearer.[29] The Saints apparently believed this action would secure the salvation of their families in a worthy priesthood lineage if their own progenitors did not accept the gospel in the next life. The request for this ordinance was usually initiated by those wishing to be adopted into a given line. As the requests came, Church leaders willingly responded, and the "adoption" ceremony was performed in the temple.[30] Some members chose to be adopted directly by a Church leader, while others were sealed to their natural parents and then had their parents adopted by a Church leader.

Thus many, and perhaps most, Church members were more concerned with simply collecting names of ancestors than with organizing those names into specific family units. While proxy baptisms and endowments were administered for deceased progenitors as a matter of course, it was not incumbent upon the living to also perform proxy sealings. The lack of emphasis on sealings reduced the importance of extending family lines beyond one generation.

The practice of adoption raised doctrinal questions about the organization of eternal families.[31] President Wilford Woodruff was so concerned that he made the issue a matter of special prayer. The result was a new revelation which the President discussed in depth with the First Presidency and the Council of the Twelve on 5 and 6 April 1894.[32] After obtaining their endorsement, he presented the revelation to the membership of the Church during a general conference address on 14 April.

Significantly, President Woodruff's announcement was based on the doctrine of continuing revelation, which held that the Lord would "give unto the faithful line upon line, precept upon precept," as they were prepared for new ideas or information (D&C 98:12).[33] Joseph Smith, President Woodruff said, "accomplished all that God required at his hands. But he did not receive all the revelations that belong to this work, neither did President Taylor, nor has Wilford Woodruff. There will be no end to this work until it is perfected." Then, after emphasizing how fervently he and his brethren in the leadership of the Church had prayed for a better understanding, President Woodruff announced the change in policy:

> Now, what are the feelings of Israel? They have felt that they wanted to be adopted to somebody. . . . When I went before the Lord to know who I should be adopted to (we were then being adopted to prophets and apostles,) the Spirit of God said to me, "Have you not a father, who begot you?" "Yes, I have," "Then, why not honor him? Why not be adopted to him?" "Yes," says I, "that is right." I was adopted to my father, and should have had my father sealed to his father, and so on back; and the duty that I want every man who presides over a Temple to see performed from this day henceforth and forever, unless the Lord Almighty commands otherwise, is, let every man be adopted to his father. When a man receives the endowment, adopt him to his father; not to Wilford Woodruff, not to any other man outside the lineage of his father. That is the will of God to this people. . . . We want the Latter-day Saints from this time to trace their genealogies as far as they can, and to be sealed to their fathers and mothers. Have children sealed to their parents, and run this chain through as far as you can get it. . . . This is the will of the Lord to his people, and I think when you come to reflect upon it you will find it to be true.[34]

At the conclusion of President Woodruff's sermon, his first counselor, George Q. Cannon, recognizing that the practice of adoption had resulted in some haphazard policies so far as family units were concerned, commented on the impact the new policy would have on genealogical work:

> There has been a disposition manifested among our people, to some extent, for some men and women to gather up all the names of families, whether they were related or not, and perform ordinances for them. I am a believer in this when it does not interfere with the rights of heirship. We should do all we can for those for whom we have friendship, or to whom we are attached in any way, and who have no living representatives that we know of in the Church. But you can see the advantage of pursuing now the course that is pointed out by the word of God to us. It will make everyone careful

> to obtain the connection, and to get the names properly of the sons and daughters of men, to have them sealed to their parents. It will draw the line fairly. It will define lineage clearly. "But," says one, "that may take a long time." Well, we have got a thousand years to do it in. We need not be in such a hurry as to create confusion.[35]

The question of validity naturally arose in regard to ordinances already performed which had adopted people to someone other than their natural parents. The First Presidency and the Twelve ruled that old records would be left standing, leaving it to the wisdom of God to deal with the problems of human error.[36]

A Society Is Organized

The change in the law of adoption was an important step toward the organization of a genealogical society. The new revelation required Latter-day Saints to commit themselves even more fully to collecting and organizing accurate family records.

Discussion of a Church-sponsored genealogical organization actually had begun at least as early as the administration of Church president John Taylor (1880–1887), but nothing was done at the time.[37] In 1893, Duncan McAllister, previously associated with the Latter-day Saints' Genealogical Bureau, importuned the Church on this issue. On 16 February, he wrote President Wilford Woodruff, decrying the unnecessary expense of individual research. He estimated that about fifty people each year went to Europe for genealogical purposes at a cost of about $500 each, which meant an average annual outlay of $25,000. This was in addition to the expenditures of regular missionaries, who often spent part of their time in genealogical research. McAllister was concerned that most of these people were unskilled in research techniques. He estimated that one person with ordinary accounting skills could, with occasional help, accomplish more than fifty unskilled persons working in the haphazard manner of many enthusiastic travelers and at one-tenth the cost. To prevent such inefficiency, he urged the formation of a Church genealogical bureau that would concentrate initially on the British Isles, where most research trips were being conducted, and then expand. The bureau should function under Church auspices, he suggested, so that the Saints would have confidence in it and so that duplication in temple work could be prevented.[38]

McAllister was only one of several genealogists pressing for a Church-sponsored organization that would make record gathering a more cooperative, productive effort and at the same time reduce the cost to individuals. In personal meetings with the First Presidency, a number of genealogists urged the need for an organized effort. At the same time, the external pressures on the Church were easing, leaving it with the ability to turn its attention to other, more vital pursuits. Wilford Woodruff, an avid genealogist, was President of the Church and had received an important revelation related to temple work. The time was ripe for the formation of a permanent, official genealogical association through which the Church could more effectively support the genealogical activity important to the work of the temple.

At least as early as 27 July 1894, Franklin D. Richards, John Jaques, and A. Milton Musser were examining versions of a proposed genealogical library corporation.[39] On 1 November 1894, at their regular Thursday meeting, the First Presidency and Council of the Twelve approved the articles of incorporation of the Genealogical Society of Utah. They instructed Elder Richards to begin organizing the Society, and they appointed him to become the first president.[40] The official organizational meeting was held in the Historian's Office on 13 November with Elder Richards acting as chair. Also in attendance were other prominent Church historians and genealogists: assistant Church historians John Jaques, A. Milton Musser, and Andrew Jenson; James H. Anderson, a member of the editorial staff of the *Deseret News;* James B. Walkley, who had spent years doing genealogical work in England and who is credited with writing the first letter to the leaders of the Church urging the organization of a society; and Duncan McAllister, assistant recorder in the Salt Lake Temple.

The Articles of Association of the Genealogical Society of Utah announced three types of purposes for the organization: benevolent, educational, and religious. The benevolent goal was to be met by establishing and maintaining a genealogical library for the benefit of Society members and others; the educational purpose was to disseminate information regarding genealogical matters; and the religious goal was to acquire records of the dead in order to enable the performance of Church ordinances on their behalf. Clearly the overriding concern was religious, and the articles provided that the association would "be conducted in harmony with the rules and order of the said Church." To house the new society, Elder Richards offered the free use of an upstairs room in the Historian's Office. The offer was accepted with gratitude.[41]

Elder Richards's first official act was to telegraph the presidents of the Logan, Manti, and St. George Temples, informing them of the new organization and inviting them to become members. The next day, he received telegrams from each of them, all agreeing to join.[42] On 19 November, Franklin D. Richards was officially elected president, with John Nicholson as vice president and James H. Anderson as secretary. A. Milton Musser was elected treasurer, John Jaques was made the librarian, and Andrew Jenson became a director. The following day George Reynolds was also elected a director. These seven men constituted the first board of directors of the Society.[43]

Old Historian's Office, 1908, at 58 East South Temple, Salt Lake City, was the location of the Genealogical Society, 1894–1917.

On 21 November, Franklin D. Richards, James H. Anderson, and A. Milton Musser appeared in the Salt Lake County Probate Court and filed the Society's articles of incorporation. The filing cost was $16.25, and the Certificate of Incorporation was issued the next day.[44] The Genealogical Society of Utah was a legal entity.

Significantly, the new society did not focus on helping only Church members. Membership in the Society was open to anyone "of good moral character."[45] This decision set the precedent for the work of the Genealogical Society in providing assistance to all interested persons, a policy the Society follows to this day.

The Library

In order to provide research materials for members, the Society began to build a library collection. Two days after the Society was organized, Bishop George Taylor of the Salt Lake Fourteenth Ward sent a carpenter to the Historian's Office to construct shelves on the allotted floor. On 22 November, President Wilford Woodruff ordered the existing library—Elder's Richards's personal collection of three hundred books previously purchased by the Church—to be delivered to the Society within a week.[46]

The collection grew slowly—most of the additions coming from continuing donations by Elder Richards and a few others. Elder Richards used a general conference priesthood meeting in 1896 to urge stake presidents and bishops to visit the library and donate to it.[47] In addition, he obtained funds from membership dues and other fees to purchase books as he became aware of them.

Elder Richards industriously examined book catalogs and solicited donations from Church members and other acquaintances. He also recruited missionaries as agents to collect books. In 1896, for example, George Shorter was sent to England. Elder Richards gave him a certificate identifying him as a member of the Genealogical Society of Utah, as an "honorable and trustworthy gentleman," and as one who could do business for the Society. Shorter was authorized to receive donations of money and books, and potential contributors were reminded that the library was the only one of its character between the Mississippi and the Pacific Ocean.[48] Shorter was able eventually to purchase a few books for the Society, as well as to perform other genealogical tasks for Elder Richards.[49]

Library books were hard to come by; the money to purchase them depended upon membership fees and donations. Nevertheless, within six years the library had increased its holdings by 50 percent—from 300 volumes to 450.[50] Seven years later it boasted 800 volumes.[51]

Initially, use of the library was restricted to members of the Society, but fees were low enough to encourage all serious ancestor seekers to join. The entrance fee was first set at $2.00, though it was later raised to $3.00, and the annual fee was $1.00. Life membership was set at $12.00.[52] Despite these modest rates, the membership grew slowly. In 1896 there were twenty annual and twenty-eight lifetime members. Three years later, there were forty lifetime members.[53] After another decade, the number had increased to 173—most of them lifetime memberships.

The Society soon provided a number of services to its patrons. Clerical help was available to copy genealogical material.

Genealogical Society Library reading room, ca. 1917, located on the upper floor of the old Historian's Office. Shown (left to right) are Genealogical Society staff members Nephi Anderson, Lillian Cameron, Joseph Christenson, Joseph Fielding Smith, and Bertha Emery.

Members were charged $3.00 or $3.50 per day at first, though by 1900 they were paying forty or fifty cents per hour. As a rule, those not having a Society membership paid 50 percent more.[54] Such clerical services apparently began in 1895, when a temple worker was assigned to spend part of his time doing research for library patrons,[55] but soon other clerks began to spend more time at this work. The Society also provided genealogical forms designed by a committee. By 1897 the Society had printed circulars about its program and distributed them to the various wards and stakes of the Church.[56] It also assisted families in organizing their records for temple work.

The clerks who performed this service were undoubtedly dedicated people, for they apparently received relatively small compensation for their labors. Neither the Society itself nor the Historian's Office had the funds to pay them. In one case, according to Elder Richards, one faithful assistant librarian was doing clerical work without pay until President George Q. Cannon of the First Presidency of the Church authorized him an allowance of $25.00 per month in "tithing orders."[57]

Foreign Agents

Among the initial aspirations of the founders of the Society was a network of paid genealogical agents outside Utah who would do research for others. The Society believed that genealogical research could be the most effective and the least expensive if done by experienced researchers. On 15 June 1897, three directors of the Society wrote a letter to their colleagues lamenting the fact that their operations would be limited until the Society could establish agents in different parts of the world. This could be done, they said, only by having the First Presidency designate various agents to fill the orders of the Society. George Carpenter, Henry H. Kinsman, and Julius Billeter were prime candidates. They would work in London, the eastern United States, and Germany, respectively.[58] The proposal was apparently approved, for the Society soon contacted a few people and asked them to work.

Henry H. Kinsman was a missionary in New England at the time. He had thirty-one years of business experience before going on his mission. When he received this new request, he replied that he was unable to do much at the moment, as he was responsible for a new area and several new missionaries. During cold weather, however, and after he finished his mission, he would be happy to cooperate.[59] Later he accepted the terms offered him by the Society—to meet the actual expenses involved in his research and to give him fair and reasonable compensation for his time and efforts. As a member of the Society, he agreed to charge only the lowest rates, but since this work would require him to remain in New England after his mission, he asked the Society to pay his transportation home.[60] By 16 November 1897, terms had been agreed upon with both Henry Kinsman and Julius Billeter, and the Society had its first official field agents.[61]

To generate work for the newly appointed agents, the Society undertook an advertising campaign. A notice was published in the *Deseret News* on 1 May 1898, informing the public that the Society was ready to receive orders for research through its agents in New England, Germany, Switzerland, and Scotland. The Society also urged that this notice be read by stake presidents and bishops in public meetings. It promised three services: (1) it would procure the names of ancestors as far back as records would permit, (2) it would ascertain the relationship of the clients to these ancestors, and (3) it would arrange the accumulated names in family groups "as far as practicable." The prospective client must make an initial deposit of $10.00 with the Society. The balance of the cost could be paid either in installments or when the names were furnished. The following month, another advertisement published the names of "competent search agents." Henry Kinsman was already in New England and would remain there. William Leggat would work in Edinburgh, Scotland. Julius Billeter Jr. would leave that fall for an assignment in Germany and Switzerland and in the meantime would do research in Utah for those who were interested.[62]

The response was not immediate. In September there were still not enough orders to justify the full-time employment of a European agent.[63] But at least the Society had agents available for those who were willing to pay. How many agents were employed in these early years is not clear, but the activity of Julius Billeter Jr. stands out and serves to illustrate their work.[64]

An immigrant from Switzerland, Billeter returned to his homeland as a missionary in 1892. This was a turning point in his career, for while in Europe, he took time to work in the genealogical records of both Switzerland and Germany. His appetite was whetted, and he soon developed a commitment to genealogical research that would last the rest of his life. After his return, he found himself in demand among the Swiss and German Church members who needed help in genealogical work. He determined he could be of best service if he went back to Switzerland and operated from there. This was the beginning of a career in professional genealogical work that would last until his death in 1957.

Billeter returned to Switzerland armed with numerous letters of recommendation intended to help him open doors to more research facilities. The Society gave him a letter certifying him as its agent and requesting any reasonable assistance that could be offered him. He also had a letter from the governor of the State of Utah, identifying him as "reputable and respected citizen of this State"; a letter of personal recommendation from Utah historian Orson F. Whitney; and a letter from Karl G. Maeser, a German convert who was serving as general superintendent of schools for the Church.

Billeter received his pay directly from the Society, based on the amount of work accomplished. The Society billed the client, adding 20 percent to the agent's fee in the case of Society members and 50 percent in the case of nonmembers. Even so, the Society believed that its fees were at least 50 percent less than those of other societies.[65] Billeter apparently accepted those conditions at first, but after a few years he became dissatisfied, partly because he was not receiving his money regularly. By 1903 he had begun to accept work independently of the Society, and soon he was working completely on his own.

It was probably inevitable that Billeter should have a few disagreements with the Society. The records suggest he likely had the same problems that often plagued other professional researchers. Some clients became dissatisfied when they did not receive all the information they thought their money should buy. They did not always understand why the agent could not do more in the time available to him. The agent could explain the situation, but long-distance misunderstanding sometimes led to criticism and harsh words from both sides. In addition, agents were sometimes frustrated when their clients did not make agreed-upon payments. The agents' work was not just a religious commitment; it was also their livelihood, and they could ill afford to do research without pay. Yet the Society could hardly afford to send additional money until the client had paid. Apparently, such collection problems were among those that caused Julius Billeter discomfort and led him at times to criticize the policies of the Society.[66]

Nevertheless, even after he resigned as a full-time agent, Julius Billeter's important contribution to genealogical work in the Church was well recognized and respected. He continued to work part-time for the Society, and he was recommended by the Society to people who wanted research done. His life's work, which he pursued doggedly over a period of sixty years, was to compile Church-oriented genealogies. He not only collected names for his clients, but also put them in appropriate order for temple work.[67]

The Society constantly advised inexperienced Saints that they could get their work done more cheaply and efficiently if they would work through professional agents rather than try to do the research themselves, but it also warned them against hiring researchers who were untrustworthy or irresponsible. Great care must be taken in recording vital data accurately, and the Saints were told that the Society's agents would be reliable. A typical warning was issued in 1905 in the *Deseret Evening News:*

> The Saints here should, therefore, not entrust that work to irresponsible persons. When they cannot attend to it themselves, they should apply to the Genealogical Society with headquarters at the Historians' Office . . . in order that they may know that their genealogy will be traced correctly and as perfectly as the Old Country records permit.[68]

Small Beginnings, Great Anticipations

The growth of the Genealogical Society of Utah during its early years was modest. The library collection grew steadily. Membership growth was equally gradual, standing at 173 in 1908. Sporadic research requests were sufficient to sustain only a handful of research agents in the eastern United States and Europe.

Yet this humble beginning did not limit the vision of the Society's founders, epitomized in 1912 in the words of Nephi Anderson:

> In conclusion, let me suggest the future of this work. I see the records of the dead and their histories gathered from every nation under heaven to one great central library in Zion—the largest and best equipped for its particular work in the world. Branch libraries may be established in the nations, but in Zion will be the records of last resort and final authority. Trained genealogists will find constant work in all nations having unpublished records, searching among the archives for families and family connections. Then, as temples multiply, and the work enlarges to its ultimate proportions, this Society, or some organization growing out of this Society, will have in its care some elaborate, but perfect system of exact registration and checking, so that the work in the temples may be conducted without confusion or duplication. And so throughout the years, reaching into the Millennium of peace, this work of salvation will go on, until every worthy soul that can be found from earthly records will have been searched out and officiated for; and then the unseen world will come to our aid, the broken links will be joined, the tangled threads will be placed in order, and the purposes of God in placing salvation within the reach of all will have been consummated.
>
> We live in a day of small beginnings, as far as this is concerned. We are still pioneers. We are but helping to lay the foundation of the "marvelous work and a wonder that is about to come forth among the children of men."[69]

NOTES

[1]Brigham Young and others, *Journal of Discourses,* 26 vols. (Liverpool: F. D. Richards, 1855–86), 16:300.

[2]Among the Latter-day Saints, a patriarchal blessing is a special blessing given by an ordained patriarch; it is intended to give direction in the lives of the faithful. It also indicates one's lineage. Receiving more than one such blessing officially is uncommon, though in the early days the practice was more loosely regulated. Franklin D. Richards's several blessings are recorded in his letterbooks. The blessing of 11 April 1859 told him, "You shall minister for many who shall be heirs of salvation, even many who have gone before you behind the veil." On 19 July 1875, he was told, "Much of your labor shall be devoted to the redemption of your dead. Your family also shall assist you and co-operate with you in your labors." The blessing of 7 October 1883 said, "Thou shalt do a great work in the earth both for the living and the dead." Franklin D. Richards letterbook, Richards Family collection, Archives Division, Historical Department, The Church of Jesus

Christ of Latter-day Saints, Salt Lake City (hereafter cited as LDS Church Archives). See also William J. Mortimer, "Patriarchal Blessings," *Encyclopedia of Mormonism,* ed. Daniel H. Ludlow, 5 vols. (New York: Macmillan, 1992), 3:1066–67 (hereafter cited as *EM*).

[3]Franklin D. Richards journal, 23 November 1885, Richards Family collection, LDS Church Archives.

[4]Richards journal, 26 November 1885.

[5]Richards journal, 16 April, and 4 June 1884, Richards Family collection, LDS Church Archives. At the time, Elder Richards calculated the value of his library to be $527.89.

[6]The New England Genealogical Society publications included the quarterly journal that had been published since 1846. Other valuable works included a file of the *New York Genealogical and Biographical Record*, published quarterly since 1850. Franklin D. Richards to W. Cabell Truman, 19 December 1889, Richards letterbook, Richards Family collection, LDS Church Archives.

[7]His journal included many entries suggesting this. For example, 4 June 1884 he ordered two books for the Logan Temple, one a pronouncing gazetteer and the other a world geography; 14 April 1885 he placed an order for forty-one volumes of genealogical works to send to the Logan Temple to aid the Saints in the area; 27 June 1888 he corresponded with the Manti Temple president about genealogical books and records for the Manti Temple Association; 22 August 1888 he sent 192 volumes of genealogical works to the Manti Temple Association (but on 29 August 1893, the First Presidency and Council of the Twelve decided to transfer the Manti Temple's genealogical library to the Salt Lake Temple, for there it would be accessible to more of the Saints generally). See also Franklin D. Richards to J. D. T. McAllister, 29 August 1893, Richards letterbook. The journal entry of 23 November 1893 indicates that he was supplying lists of available genealogical works to many Saints in the Territory of Utah.

[8]Richards journal, 15 June 1890.

[9]Franklin D. Richards to Mrs. Maria Newman, 19 May 1893, Richards letterbook, Richards Family collection, LDS Church Archives.

[10]Benjamin F. Cummings to the First Presidency, 8 March 1893, Genealogical Society correspondence, Family History Department of the Church of Jesus Christ of Latter-day Saints (hereafter cited as FHD).

[11]*Journal of Discourses* 19:255.

[12]Cummings to the First Presidency.

[13]For example, he noted on 25 October 1884 that he received $10.00 from George B. Spencer for "genealogy labor." Richards journal, Richards Family collection, LDS Church Archives. His journal contains many references to people coming in for help and advice in this period.

[14]Franklin D. Richards to the Cragin brothers, 13 December 1893, Richards letterbook, Richards Family collection, LDS Church Archives.

[15]*Deseret Evening News,* 2 July 1879.

[16]*Deseret Evening News,* 12 September 1888.

[17]Wilford Woodruff to John Nicholson, 22 June 1888, First Presidency letterbooks, LDS Church Archives.

[18]Woodruff to Nicholson.

[19]John Nicholson and Douglas A. Swan to Duncan McAllister, 24 September 1888, Duncan M. McAllister papers, LDS Church Archives.

[20]John Nicholson and Douglas A. Swan to George Teasdale, 24 September 1888, Duncan M. McAllister papers, LDS Church Archives.

[21]Douglas A. Swan to Duncan M. McAllister, 8 October 1888, Duncan M. McAllister papers, LDS Church Archives.

[22]*Deseret Evening News,* 5 January 1892.

[23]In pioneer days, Mormon settlers were called by the Church as missionaries not only to preach the gospel, but also to do a variety of tasks associated with building the kingdom. The establishment of many early settlements was the result of missionary calls. Missionaries were called to go to the gold fields, collect rags during paper shortages, open iron mines in southern Utah, and promote the Church's youth program and Sunday School. People were even "called," though not officially as missionaries, to study art in Europe and to become educated in other fields in the better schools of the United States. As would be expected, this practical application of the missionary tradition found its way into the genealogical impulses of the Mormons.

[24]Franklin D. Richards to C. M. Hubbard, 23 November 1883, Richards letterbook, Richards Family collection, LDS Church Archives.

[25]To cite only a few: 24 June 1885, "Sister Amelia Folsom Young desired that I would bless her for her journey East to assist her relatives in Ohio, Michigan, Mass and Conn to get genealogy. . . . I blessed her in the name of the Lord"; 25 September 1885, "Took genealogy and set apart Elders Wesley K. Walton and Aubury E. Easton both of Woodruff in Utah to go and visit their kindred to get genealogy of their ancestors in Maine. Gave them appointments"; 4 May 1886, "Blessed Elder Wm. Wallace White of the 11 ward SL City for a mission to visit, settle up the affairs of his father lately deceased and gather up his fathers family and their genealogy and bring them to Zion"; 6 July 1886, "Set apart Louie B. Felt and Charlotte E. Taylor to go to Wales to search for genealogy"; 18 May 1887, "Blessed Joseph Bull Jr. for a business visit of about 3 mos to England to get genealogies"; 9 March 1888, "I blessed Nils Bengtson of 8th ward and John Ludwig Berg a H P from Showlow of Apache Co AZ for missions to Scandinavia. Gave them regular certificates of appointment and each of them a letter of introduction to Priests Teasdale and Flygare stating their unusually great ages and their objects in going to do business, get genealogy and minister what they can."

[26]The following statistics were compiled by Jessie Embry from Missionary Record (1830–1906), Missionary Department, Church Library; and Richards journal. For further insight, see Jessie L. Embry, "Missionaries for the Dead: The Story of the Genealogical Missionaries of the Nineteenth Century," *BYU Studies* 17 (Spring 1977): 355–60.

[27]The profile of the 178 known missionaries, as compiled by Jessie Embry, follows. Note that some figures do not add up to 178, because the full information was not always available.

Age: under 20, 1; 20–30, 6; 30–40, 7; 40–50, 32; 60–70, 16; 70 and over, 6.
Sex: male, 135; female, 43.
Home residence: Utah, 128; Idaho, 7; Arizona, 2.
Mission to: Great Britain, 90; United States and Canada, 51; European continent, 2.

[28]John Adams Wakeham, autobiography, John A. Wakeham collection, LDS Church Archives.

[29]For a full discussion of this practice, see Gordon Irving, "The Law of Adoption: One Phase of the Development of the Mormon Concept of Salvation, 1830-1900," *BYU Studies* 14 (Spring 1974): 291-314; *EM* 2: 810.

[30]One example of a request for "adoption" is reflected in a letter from President Wilford Woodruff to Mrs. Mary Pixton:

> Dear Sister: In the matter of adoption of yourself and Brother Pixton to me, as referred to by letter from President Wm Paxman to-day—I will say that I am quite willing to have that ordinance attended to when it [is] convenient for me to be at the Temple. I will endeavor to keep this matter in mind so that when I am at the Temple and you being also present your wishes may be granted. Should you hear of my going to Manti in the near future you can then be present.

Wilford Woodruff to Mrs. Mary Pixton, 17 November 1890, Wilford Woodruff letterbooks, LDS Church Archives.

[31]See Irving, "The Law of Adoption," 310-11, for examples of certain modifications that were being made even before the announcement of President Woodruff's revelation.

[32]Wilford Woodruff journal, 5 and 6 April 1894, Wilford Woodruff collection, LDS Church Archives.

[33]See also *Journal of Discourses* 19:12; "Article of Faith," 9.

[34]President Woodruff's address may be found in several places, including *Deseret Evening News,* 14 April 1894; *Deseret Weekly,* 21 April 1894, 541-44; *The Utah Genealogical and Historical Magazine* 13 (October 1922): 145-52 (hereafter cited as *UGHM*); and James R. Clark, comp., *Messages of the First Presidency of The Church of Jesus Christ of Latter-day Saints, 1833-1964,* 6 vols. (Salt Lake City: Bookcraft, 1966), 3:252-60.

[35]The full text of President Cannon's sermon may be found in *UGHM* 13 (October 1922): 152-58; and the *Deseret News,* 14 April 1894.

[36]Irving, "The Law of Adoption," 313. See citations listed in his footnote.

[37]Wilford Woodruff to John Nicholson, 22 June 1888, First Presidency letterbooks, LDS Church Archives.

[38]Duncan M. McAllister to Wilford Woodruff, 16 February 1892 [1893], Duncan M. McAllister papers, LDS Church Archives.

[39]Richards journal, 27 July 1894, Richards Family collection, LDS Church Archives.

[40]See journals of Wilford Woodruff, Franklin D. Richards, and Abraham H. Cannon, LDS Church Archives for 1 November 1894.

[41]Genealogical Society Minutes, 13 November 1894, FHD; Richards journal, 13 November 1894, Richards Family collection, LDS Church Archives.

[42]Richards journal, 13 and 14 November 1894, Richards Family collection, LDS Church Archives.

[43]Richards journal, 19 and 20 November 1894; Genealogical Society Minutes, 20 November 1894.

[44]Richards journal, 21 and 22 November 1894, Richards Family collection, LDS Church Archives.

[45]Genealogical Society Minutes, 13 November 1894; *UGHM* 25 (October 1934): 164.

[46]Richards journal, 12 and 15 November 1894, Richards Family collection, LDS Church Archives.

[47]Richards journal, 7 April 1896, Richards Family collection, LDS Church Archives.

[48]Franklin D. Richards to George Shorter, 20 March 1896, Richards letterbook, Richards Family collection, LDS Church Archives.

[49]Franklin D. Richards to George Shorter, 31 August, and 4 November 1896, Richards letterbook.

[50]John Jaques to Newel Knight Palmer, 27 July 1900, Genealogical Society correspondence, FHD.

[51]Genealogical Society Minutes, 15 October 1907, proposed circular letter; *Deseret Evening News,* 2 November 1907.

[52]Genealogical Society Minutes, 19 January 1895; George W. Willis to Nellie Hawkes, 19 July 1900, Genealogical Society correspondence, FHD; *Deseret Evening News,* 2 November 1907.

[53]Genealogical Society Minutes, 18 April 1896; Richards journal, 28 April 1899, Richards Family collection, LDS Church Archives.

[54]Genealogical Society Minutes, 19 January 1895, 28 March 1896; Wm. H. Perkes to Mary A. Thomas, 8 February 1897; William Willis to George Mason, 21 November 1900, Genealogical Society correspondence, FHD.

[55]Genealogical Society Minutes, 18 June 1895.

[56]Genealogical Society Minutes, 19 November 1897, 2 May, 28 June, and 19 July 1898.

[57]*Deseret News,* 5 September 1896; William Perkes to Ebenezer Bryce, 28 December 1899; Franklin D. Richards to James Jack, 30 April 1897, Genealogical Society correspondence, FHD.

[58]John Nicholson, George Reynolds, and A. Milton Musser to the President and Board of Directors of the Genealogical Society of Utah, 15 June 1897, Genealogical Society correspondence.

[59]Henry H. Kinsman to John Nicholson, 7 October 1897, Genealogical Society correspondence.

[60]Henry H. Kinsman to John Nicholson, 10 November 1897, Genealogical Society correspondence.

[61]John Nicholson, George Reynolds, and A. Milton Musser to the President and Board of Directors of the Genealogical Society of Utah, 16 November 1897, Genealogical Society correspondence.

[62]*Deseret Evening News,* 18 June 1898.

[63]Genealogical Society Minutes, 20 September 1898.

[64]The following information is based on memoranda by Henry E. Christiansen, temple ordinance coordinator of the Genealogical Department of the Church, dated 21 September 1976 and 2 December 1976, located in his files in the Genealogical Society office, as well as miscellaneous entries in the Genealogical Society Minutes and the Richards journal. Christiansen obtained much of his information from Julius Billeter's son and from his own research in the minutes.

[65]John Jaques to Julius Billeter, 11 December 1900, Genealogical Society correspondence, FHD.

[66]All this is only implicit in the sketchy information available, but it fits the pattern of problems described by Henry Christiansen, who for many years served as supervisor of the research department of the Genealogical Society. The record is abundantly clear that Billeter and the Society had disagreements and that money was one of the major issues involved.

[67]In addition, Billiter built a magnificent personal file of genealogical material, which he willingly placed at the disposal of the Church mission office in Switzerland in 1946. In Salt Lake City, meantime, the board of directors of the Genealogical Society authorized the preparation of a typed transcript of his records, to be housed in Salt Lake City. The file was so voluminous that after two typists had worked for two years they still had covered only about 20 percent of the material. It was estimated that it would take a total of ten years to complete the project, so the Society decided in 1949 to have the records sent to Salt Lake City for microfilming. Julius Billeter's life-long commitment was exemplary, and through his career as a professional genealogist he made an invaluable contribution to the Church.

[68]*Deseret Evening News,* 27 April 1905.

[69]Nephi Anderson, "Genealogy's Place in the Plan of Salvation," *UGHM* 3 (January 1912): 21-22.

Chapter 2

Coming of Age, 1907–1920

Much of the credit for the early accomplishments of the Genealogical Society of Utah goes to two forceful advocates who shared a common vision of the Society's possibilities and doggedly pursued that vision: Susa Young Gates and Joseph Fielding Smith. Susa Young Gates constantly labored towards expanding the influence of the Society throughout the Church and represented it well before other genealogical organizations. She pursued her agenda not only through the Genealogical Society, but also under the auspices of the Relief Society, which for almost a decade carried the responsibility of getting the genealogical program into the homes of Church members. During the same period, Joseph Fielding Smith sought to make genealogy—which was often a low priority among the Saints—equal to the other programs occupying the time of Church members. The Society would absorb a great deal of his adult life.

Joseph Fielding Smith and Susa Young Gates contributed not only to expanding the services of the Society in Salt Lake City, but also to taking the genealogical program to stakes and wards throughout the Church. They exported classes and instructional materials, promoted the growth of local genealogical institutions, started classes at Brigham Young University, and instituted an annual "Genealogy Sunday" in the Church. Participation in the International Congress of Genealogy at the San Francisco World's Fair in 1915 was a high point in this welter of activity. Yet the difficulty of making genealogical research a high priority in the lives of

Church members who were fully occupied with family, job, and other Church activities limited what even the most tireless leaders could accomplish.

Susa Young Gates

Around 1918, Susa Young Gates was preparing a history of Latter-day Saint women. One chapter dealt with the women's contribution to the genealogical program and suggested an important reality: despite male leadership in the Genealogical Society of Utah, the women of the Church were doing the most genealogical research and temple work. In a witty commentary on the role she thought the women were playing, Gates observed, "The old-time motto of the women's auxiliary committee of the Genealogical Society of Utah ran thus: 'Let us provoke the brethren to good works, yet not provoke the brethren while we work.'"[1] Although respectful of priesthood authority, Gates and her colleagues were not reluctant to vigorously seek new directions, to strive for what they believed the Church needed most, and to goad their brethren when they thought them lax or derelict in their genealogical responsibilities.

Susa Young Gates won respect both nationally and internationally even beyond her work in genealogy. She was the mother of thirteen children and was prominent as a suffragist, a prolific writer and editor, a publisher, a public speaker, and an educator. She was a leader in the Relief Society and the Young Ladies' Mutual Improvement Association (YLMIA) and founder of *The Young Women's Journal.* Active in the National Council of Women, she represented the YLMIA seven times at its national meetings. For three years, she chaired the press committee of the national organization. In 1899 she was a speaker at the International Quinquennial held in London. Two years later, she was the sole delegate of the National Council of Women at a meeting of the International Council in Copenhagen, Denmark.

Gates's commitment to genealogy and temple work, however, was lifelong. She helped compile a thirteen-volume genealogical record of the Young family that contained twenty thousand names. Later, in order to avoid duplication of temple work, she

Susa Young Gates, daughter of Brigham Young. As a Society staff member, Gates assiduously promoted the Genealogical Society's work, 1905–20. Courtesy LDS Church Archives.

directed the preparation of an index to the Young family records and deposited a copy in each temple.[2]

Her dedication to genealogical work increased after a remarkable experience in 1901. Taken seriously ill while returning from the Copenhagen conference, she was confined for several weeks at a friend's home in Geneva. After receiving a blessing from the missionaries, she was finally able to travel to England, but her condition remained critical. "She was ready to die," recalled John A. Widtsoe, "or at least we thought so." Then came the miracle. Francis M. Lyman, an Apostle and president of the European Mission, gave her a blessing. Certain she would die, he began with an admonition not to fear death. Suddenly he stopped, and, as Gates recalled later, waited for nearly two minutes before he continued, "There has been a council held in heaven, and it has been decided you shall live to perform temple work, and you shall do a greater work than you have ever done before."[3]

Gates became well enough to travel home but did not completely recover at once. Horribly emaciated and weighing only eighty-five pounds, she continued to fight for life. When she next went to the temple, she had to be carried in a chair. Gradually she recovered, and from then until her death in 1933, she was constantly involved in temple and genealogical work. In addition to giving one-tenth of her income to the Church as tithing, she also donated another 10 percent for genealogical purposes.[4]

Joseph Christenson, secretary of the Society, was aware of Susa Young Gates's great interest in her ancestors and in temple work.

One day in 1904, shortly after Gates moved from Provo to Salt Lake City, he asked her, "Sister Gates, why don't you go over to the Genealogical Library and hunt out the names of the Young family?" Gates replied that she did not even know there was a library in Salt Lake City.[5]

After discovering the Genealogical Library, she was dismayed to find it so full of rich material not being used effectively. Patrons had no instruction in research methods, and an overworked librarian could not oversee all their efforts. As someone wrote later, "No one knew where to begin or how to continue, and, indeed, no one tried except the Library attendant who worked a little in the books for the benefit of a few clients."[6] Gates later recalled:

> I felt that I must do something more, something to help all the members of the Church with their genealogy and temple work. There was practically no book of lessons in genealogy in existence. Beginners were forced to blunder into record keeping without guide or compass; there were no classes in schools or printed instructions to enlighten them.[7]

Her lifetime efforts to correct this problem included editing a weekly newspaper article on genealogy; organizing and teaching classes under the auspices of the Daughters of Utah Pioneers, the Genealogical Society, and the Relief Society; writing genealogical manuals; arranging genealogical conventions; and developing programs to help Latter-day Saints gather the names of their ancestors and do their temple work.

Susa Young Gates's organizational leadership in genealogy began within the Daughters of Utah Pioneers (DUP), which she helped found in 1901. This hereditary organization, having a natural genealogical interest, urged its members to collect genealogies. In 1904, Gates was asked to become president, but she accepted only on condition that the organization inaugurate a program for more effectively training the women in genealogy and encouraging them in temple work. The DUP agreed, and Gates was installed in April 1905. She wasted no time in getting started; her first two activities through the DUP were a weekly newspaper column and the establishment of genealogical classes.

Publicizing and Teaching

In 1906, Joseph Christenson suggested that Sister Gates ask the *Deseret Evening News* to run a section on genealogy.[8] She approached the newspaper, and the *News* accepted her offer to write weekly genealogical articles. Her new section first appeared on 1 January 1907. A year later, the *Herald-Republican* added a similar weekly column, which Gates also produced.[9] Published each Saturday, it carried genealogical news, genealogical data on various Church leaders, and other items of interest.

After the first year and a half of publication, the board of the Society passed a resolution on 21 July 1908 "requesting that the articles on Genealogy now appearing in the *Deseret Evening News* under the auspices of the DUP be published hereafter under the direction of the Society and that a committee of sisters to assist in the work be appointed."[10] Joseph Fielding Smith, secretary of the board, wrote to Susa Young Gates explaining the contents of the resolution and asking the sisters to accept the "calling."[11]

Gates readily agreed to the Society's request for several reasons. First, she believed the column had become so significant that it should be part of the Church's official genealogical organization.[12] She was also in the midst of a serious disagreement within the DUP over how far its genealogical activities should range. Some, including Gates and her friend Elizabeth Claridge McCune, wanted to subdivide the large organization into groups with special hereditary interests in great LDS historical epochs, such as Daughters of the Founders of the Church, Daughters of Kirtland, Daughters of the Mormon Battalion, Daughters of the Pioneers from Great Britain, and so on. Seeing the increasing secularization of the DUP as a hindrance to their plans for temple work, they wanted the DUP to become a Church organization rather than a state society. When their suggestions for reorganization were rejected, they took the matter to Church leaders. In response, Anthon H. Lund, a member of the First Presidency and president of the Genealogical Society, invited them to bring their work over to the Society.[13] Almost immediately Gates resigned as DUP president and shifted all her genealogical programs to the Genealogical Society's newly organized Women's Committee, which she chaired. She also encouraged all the women she had been working with to join the Society.[14] Her committee represented the first active involvement by women in that organization.

Gates continued to edit the genealogical department in the *Deseret Evening News* for ten years. But in 1918, faced with the wartime scarcity of paper, the management of the *News* planned to reduce the size of the Saturday paper and eliminate genealogy. Gates was outraged. On 26 August with the approval of the Board of Directors of the Genealogical Society, she sent a thousand circulars to Relief Societies throughout the Church, calling upon the women to send letters of protest to the Church-owned newspaper. "Sometimes business men are more interested in finances, and city dwellers are more interested in society than in topics pertaining to our spiritual advancement," she wrote with righteous indignation. But, she urged, "the right of petition is always ours and the women in the Church may well take advantage of this right to convince our Deseret News Management that we are vitally interested in the work of genealogy and temple work generally."[15]

As Susa Young Gates hoped, a number of women soon wrote to the newspaper expressing their concern. At the end of September, however, the *News* countered by sending a form letter to all the Relief Societies that had responded, explaining that the department had not been discontinued; it had only been condensed and would appear less frequently because of the paper shortage. The letter added that the *News* would publish matters "of the greatest interest to its readers, and that it is the best judge of what should and should not appear in its columns in these days of stress and government regulations."[16] A stamped envelope was enclosed with the letter. The sisters were asked to deliver the message to whoever had told them the genealogical articles would no longer appear. They dutifully flooded Susa Young Gates with letters.[17]

Dismayed at the attitude of the *News,* Gates was unwilling to take what she considered undeserved criticism. She wrote to Joseph Fielding Smith on 17 October, explaining that she wanted the *News* to know she had obtained his approval before she mailed the letters to the Relief Societies. "I think I would like to clear my own skirts," she explained, "for the *Deseret News* letter would indicate that I was both untruthful and out of harmony with the powers [that] be." She added, "However, I do not care very much about it and am willing to do whatever you think best."[18]

As another possible way to lean on the newspaper, Gates wrote a strongly worded letter to the board of the Society on 29 August. She vehemently protested the loss of the column, reminding the brethren of its inestimable value in providing communication between genealogists and in making genealogy "a settled part of our daily life and communication." She also lamented that "if this department ceases, and if the Relief Society genealogical classes should be discontinued, as some people wish they were, it might so cripple our genealogical interests that the people's temple activities would suffer irreparable loss." She was convinced, however, that a male voice would carry more weight:

> For some time I have felt that the department should be turned over to your Society and the name of the Secretary, Joseph F. Smith, Jr., placed there in lieu of my own. . . . And although this seems to be a strange time in which to turn over the department to your Society, I now formally do so and beg of you to resurrect it in the columns of the News and thus serve the people who greatly need that help.[19]

Although no evidence indicates that Gates responded directly to the *Deseret Evening News,* whatever pressures were applied by others apparently had an effect. The genealogy column was absent for a few weeks in August, but it began again as a regular feature in September, even as the controversy continued to simmer. Nephi Anderson, prominent writer and genealogist, eventually replaced Gates as editor.[20]

Another of Susa Young Gates's enterprises was the development of genealogical classes. As president of the DUP, she obtained the use of a room in the historic Lion House, then being used by the Latter-day Saints University. Formal genealogical classwork began in the fall of 1906.[21] Gates directed the meetings and asked both men and women to give the lessons. Among the early lecturers was Duncan McAllister, who was the Salt Lake Temple recorder, an avid genealogist, and Gates's personal friend. Other genealogical stalwarts who participated included Joseph Christenson, Elizabeth McCune, and Joseph Fielding Smith. One of the lectures, Elder Smith's "Salvation Universal," was eventually printed in pamphlet form and circulated widely in the Church.[22]

The classes were so successful that the DUP continued them on a regular basis. Weekly classwork began in the fall of 1907. The women in charge were surprised when sixty people showed up for the first class, and they had to postpone instruction in order to move to larger accommodations. In addition, they conducted a special class on 7 October for those attending the Church's semi-annual general conference.[23]

The following year, the Society absorbed not only the newspaper column, but all the genealogical programs of the DUP. At the first meeting of the Women's Committee on 4 September 1908, Joseph Christenson asked the members to arouse greater interest in genealogical work and increase membership in the Society, "not slackening in their labors until a sufficiently large membership had been secured which would enable the Society to purchase every genealogical book now published or to be published."[24]

This was an ambitious charge, but the women pursued it avidly. They wrote stake presidents, asking permission to speak on genealogy and temple work in the various wards.[25] The committee continued the lessons and lectures that had been started under the auspices of the DUP and also held a series of balls and other social activities commemorating historical events and memorializing Church leaders.[26] In 1909 the Women's Committee began publication of a yearbook that contained information about meetings and classes. The result of the committee's activity was so impressive that the January 1910 issue of the *Utah Genealogical and Historical Magazine* reported a great awakening in the past two years and acknowledged that the Women's Committee was one of the chief factors.[27] Four years later, the First Presidency also complimented the women:

> The sisters in charge of that [classwork] have labored with zeal and efficiency and have accomplished wonders, not only in the direction mentioned, but in arousing interest in it through the Church and greatly increasing the membership of the Society.[28]

In 1910 the board of the Genealogical Society decided, as part of a larger administrative change, that the work being done by the women should be subdivided and that the Women's Committee itself should be superseded by six committees. The new committees were named, but the Women's Committee remained active until its work was absorbed by the Relief Society in 1912.[29]

Relief Society Sponsorship

Members of the Women's Committee were eager to transfer classes from the Genealogical Society to the Relief Society, seeing such a move as a giant step toward achieving their goal of genuine Churchwide participation. The transition took time, not because of any resistance by Relief Society leaders to genealogy, but simply because some of them questioned whether their organization should adopt any uniform course of study, feeling it inappropriate to interfere with the local autonomy of ward Relief Societies. Discussions began as early as 1906, but not until the end of 1907 did the board finally compromise by deciding to have lesson outlines prepared for genealogical classes. However, their use by the stakes was to be optional.[30]

Even the President of the Church could not force the issue when it was first discussed. On one occasion, President Joseph F. Smith overheard an interesting conversation about genealogy classes among his wife Julina (a member of the Relief Society General Board), Relief Society president Bathsheba W. Smith, Isabel W. Sears, and Susa Young Gates. He injected himself into the conversation, remarking, "Why Sisters, you ought to put that work into the Relief Society." The women laughingly assured him that such a "Herculean task" was not possible even for them. He repeated his suggestion twice more, but when the women made a tentative effort to introduce the idea to the Relief Society, they met with no success.[31]

The Relief Society General Board continued to resist expanding the Relief Society's role in genealogical instruction, but after 1911 things began to change. Susa Young Gates and Elizabeth McCune were appointed as board members. In addition, some local organizations began taking the initiative. The Relief Societies of Ogden joined together in October 1911 in asking the Genealogical

Society to provide instruction for their members. Then, early in 1912, the Women's Committee of the Genealogical Society wrote the Relief Society officially requesting that it sponsor genealogical classwork, and the board agreed.[32] On 20 April 1912, the Relief Society sponsored its first genealogical class in Ogden. Fifty people attended. Susa Young Gates organized the class, and Annie Lynch, secretary of the Women's Committee, taught it. Only ten people continued for the full sixteen lessons, but three years later, in mid-1915, the Ogden Stake reported that 369 people were actively working in genealogy, a total of 5,939 genealogical visits had been made, and 30,777 names had been collected.[33]

In December 1912, the Women's Committee of the Genealogical Society proposed sending a corps of genealogical teachers throughout the Church to provide instruction in addition to the lessons sponsored by the Relief Society. Gates and McCune could afford to travel. Carrying letters of recommendation signed by Anthon H. Lund and Joseph Fielding Smith, they began to stump the Church. During the summer of 1913, they visited all the Church communities in Canada and traveled throughout southern Utah. They preached the message of genealogy, held classes, and wrote back urging the Genealogical Society to open even more classes.[34]

All genealogical classes were optional, but Gates and her friends still hoped the Relief Society board would require them as a regular part of the Relief Society program. In the meantime, Gates urged the women of other stakes to write to the Genealogical Society requesting help. She anticipated that eventually the Society would communicate with every stake in the Church.[35] By the fall of 1913, classes had extended to several additional stakes. In Salt Lake City, special genealogical classes were held for the general boards of the Relief Society and the YLMIA.

The effort to promote required genealogical classes for all Relief Societies in the Church was part of a larger movement. The precedent was set in 1909, when the priesthood became the first organization to adopt regular Churchwide lesson manuals. A correlation committee under the direction of Elder David O. McKay attempted to correlate the programs of the various organizations, and representatives from the Relief Society were on that committee.[36] In 1914 the Relief Society became the last Church auxiliary to inaugurate uniform Churchwide lessons. That year the *Relief Society Magazine* began publication and carried outlines for monthly lessons on four different topics. The auxiliary devoted the second weekly meeting of each month to genealogy, fulfilling at long last one of Susa Young Gates's ambitions. For the next seven years, the women of the Relief Society received at least one lesson each month on genealogical techniques.

By 1915 nearly seven hundred ward organizations and over thirty thousand women were studying genealogy. The Society recommended that special committees be appointed in each ward, and the 1915 reports listed many wards with fully organized genealogical activities. Only a few wards gave completely negative or discouraging reports. One ward clerk reported sarcastically, "Everybody asleep in Beaver."[37]

These figures did not mean that everything ran smoothly. In November 1917, Sister Gates informed the board of the Genealogical Society that some branches of the Relief Society "felt discouraged concerning the difficult and technical lessons given on surnames for the past two years . . . [and] others have felt almost justified in setting aside these lessons for the more attractive and really essential work which we are now doing for the Red Cross." She had also discovered that the Relief Societies in Utah Stake had "gathered the impression that they were to drop their own genealogical lessons and confine their genealogical studies to the outlines just prepared by your society." She asked the Genealogical Society board what to do: "Will you kindly indicate by letter just what you would like . . . to be undone? We are quite willing to continue our lessons or discontinue them." On behalf of the Society, Joseph Fielding Smith answered in no uncertain terms: "We feel that it would be a deplorable thing should you, for any cause, discontinue the work in this direction." Gates published his reply in the *Relief Society Magazine,* asking the sisters to "resume your studies with renewed zeal and determination."[38] The classes went on.

A natural outgrowth of the lessons sponsored by the Genealogical Society's Women's Committee was the preparation of the first genealogical lesson manual. Gates and others saw a need for a well-organized, step-by-step printed research guide. Gates prepared most of the material, and the Society published the first lessons in the *Utah Genealogical and Historical Magazine,* beginning in October 1911. The Women's Committee, however, wanted them published as a book. The Relief Society board was unwilling, because of limited finances, to gamble on a publication venture, so the committee raised the money independently. The lessons, edited by Nephi Anderson, were published in 1912 as a forty-five-page book, *Lessons in Genealogy.* Within a year, the first edition was sold, expenses were met, and a second edition was issued.[39]

The Relief Society also published, with the approval of the Genealogical Society, Susa Young Gates's *Surname Book and Racial History.* Three thousand copies were printed. It was used by students in genealogical classes and in the Relief Society. A copy was also sent to every known genealogical and historical library in America and Europe.[40]

Encouraged by the success of these publications, the Relief Society General Board expanded its activities to include semiannual genealogical conventions in Salt Lake City. In the board meeting of 4 September 1913, Jeanette Hyde proposed that a series of genealogical lessons be given for interested people attending the forthcoming October general conference of the Church. It was too late to plan such an activity, but the board liked the idea and during the conference held a special genealogical reception for stake representatives.

By April 1914, the women were ready with a full-scale, three-day convention to follow the regular general conference meetings. Five hundred delegates from sixty-five stakes attended. After President Anthon H. Lund, representing the First Presidency of the Church, opened the conference, the women conducted all the sessions. Two meetings were held each day, consisting of instruction on genealogical methods and temple work. Emmeline B. Wells, president of the Relief Society, made a significant observation when she noted, "The work of the Relief Society is so closely connected with that of the Genealogical Society that membership in the one practically implies interest in the other."[41] For the rest of the decade, the two societies continued to cooperate in sponsoring genealogical conferences or lectures at general conference time.

Joseph Fielding Smith

One of the most energetic young Church genealogists in the early twentieth century was Joseph Fielding Smith, son of the President of the Church. After his return from missionary service in 1901, he went to work in the Church Historian's Office, paying particular attention to genealogy. On special assignment, he traveled to Massachusetts to gather data on the Smith family. His research resulted in his first book, *Asahel Smith of Topsfield, Massachusetts,* published in 1902.

Joseph Fielding Smith's leadership in the Society spanned more than half a century. Appointed as secretary in March 1907, he became librarian the following year and treasurer a year after that—holding all these positions concurrently. Although he was called as an Apostle in 1910, he served as secretary of the Society until 1922, vice president from 1925 to 1934, and president from 1934 until 1961. Following in the steps of his father, he eventually served as President of the Church.

Elder Smith was one of the major driving forces in the progress of the Genealogical Society. According to Society Superintendent L. Garrett Myers, "President Smith was the power, the motivator behind the development of the Genealogical Society. . . . For more than sixty years he was the moving spirit."[42] During the half century that the Society was not funded by the Church, Elder Smith donated generously from his own pocket to support its activities and help pay employee wages. He even turned over to the Society all the royalties from his widely sold book *The Way to Perfection.*[43] He expanded the services offered at the library and promoted the publication of a genealogical quarterly. He envisioned the day when genealogy would assume a status equal to all other major Church programs.

The leaders of the Society, especially Joseph Fielding Smith, were acutely aware that they lacked the expertise needed to fulfill their ambitious goals. They needed more information on record keeping and genealogical techniques. They also hoped to publish a genealogical and historical magazine and needed suggestions on publishing programs. Part of the solution, they decided in 1909, was to send Joseph Fielding Smith and Joseph Christenson, former secretary of the Society, on a tour of eastern genealogical libraries.

Elder Joseph Fielding Smith, ca. 1910, a Genealogical Society worker for nearly six decades, 1907–61. Elder Smith served as its president, 1934–61. Courtesy LDS Church Archives.

The trip would cost money, and the Society was not subsidized by the Church. The only funds available were the small amounts coming from dues and research fees, and these were needed to pay wages. Obtaining funds was "like squeezing a dry sponge," Elder Smith reported later.[44] The Society finally appropriated $500. The frugal twosome avoided all frills and underspent their budget by $200.

The two men visited many leading genealogical and historical libraries, including the Newberry Public Library in Chicago, the Library of Congress, the Historical Society of Pennsylvania in Philadelphia, and the New England Historic Genealogical Society in Boston. They examined card catalogues, filing systems, index systems, and preservation methods. They also asked for suggestions about publishing. When they returned, they made several recommendations designed to improve library procedures as well as to educate Church members about genealogy. In addition, they urged the publication of a quarterly, the *Utah Genealogical and Historical Magazine.* The proposal for the quarterly was approved. President Anthon H. Lund was named editor. Most of the work, however, fell on the shoulders of associate editor Joseph Fielding Smith. The first issue came out in January 1910.[45]

The editors conceived a broad role for the new publication. The first editorial noted there was no other publication such as this in the western United States. "We are not publishing the Magazine with the idea of furnishing the general public something to while away a few idle hours," the editor noted. Rather, the magazine was intended to provide valuable genealogical and historical data and also instruct readers on the gathering of ancestral records so they could prepare to do temple work for the dead. As in the case of the Society itself, the major purpose of the magazine was religious, although the editors felt it would be useful to anyone interested in genealogical work.

Each issue of the magazine contained forty-eight pages. It was well balanced, with personal and family histories; pedigrees of particular families; helpful information on how to do research; articles on various kinds of records and record collections; historical articles of general interest, though mainly with reference to Church history; theological articles, particularly pertaining to salvation for the dead; and other articles of interest to genealogists and historians. It was an ambitious and well-designed journal. There were 368 subscribers to the first edition.[46]

While the Society had carved a permanent niche for itself in the Church's program, the leaders were dissatisfied with what they perceived as a continued lack of enthusiasm among the members in general. Joseph Fielding Smith tended to feel Church leaders were not doing all they should to promote the work. Little wonder, he felt, that the members were not well informed, when the Church itself was not providing the vigorous leadership it should.

When Joseph Fielding Smith became a member of the Quorum of the Twelve in 1910, it became necessary to find someone to take over his responsibilities as secretary, librarian, and editor for the Genealogical Society. Elder Smith wanted to hire a full-time replacement, paying him a good salary. His irritation became intense when he could not seem to find enthusiastic support for his proposal. When Apostles Heber J. Grant and Anthony W. Ivins failed to attend an important board meeting where the matter was to be discussed, Elder Smith sent a strongly worded letter to Elder Grant that was clearly intended to create more enthusiasm for the next meeting.

In the letter, Elder Smith observed that despite the Prophet Joseph Smith's declaration that salvation for the dead was the most important work in which they could engage, Church efforts seemed focused elsewhere. Church schools, boards of the Church auxiliaries, missionary work, a museum, and many other things were taking up both time and money. No stake or ward genealogical organizations were functioning. He pointedly commented that the Society's directors met only once a month, and even then two or three were usually absent in favor of other meetings of "minor importance," such as bank directorships. The burden of genealogical work was really left to only one or two of the seven directors. "Now," he chided,

> if we can afford to do all this in the other organizations, which we are forced to admit are not of superior importance, why should we not be able and willing to choose an efficient brother filled with the spirit of the work to look after the interests of this Society . . . ? Why should we not be willing to pay him what his labors are worth?

The new Apostle then outlined his vision of what the Society ought to be doing:

> I hope to see the time when we can have an organization looking after the salvation of the dead, that will be as important in the eyes of the Saints as are the auxiliary organizations today. When we can have our officers in each Stake and Ward, properly organized and filled with zeal for the work. I hope to see the day when we can secure the records that are being published in the world that ought to be in our possession, without considering, as we have to do now, whether we will have the means to pay for them or not. I am convinced that we are not doing what we ought to do in this regard, and feel that we are even now under condemnation for the lack of interest and diligence given to this work.[47]

Evidently Elder Smith's pleading had some influence. At the urging of the board, the First Presidency soon authorized hiring Nephi Anderson, who was at that time in Independence, Missouri, editing the *Liahona, the Elders Journal.* Joseph Fielding Smith continued as secretary and treasurer of the Society, and Anderson became assistant secretary, assistant treasurer, and associate editor of the magazine.[48]

Elders Smith and Christenson used the ideas gathered on their eastern tour to begin upgrading the genealogical collection and services. Though the budget was limited, they gathered genealogical books from many parts of the United States and Europe, and by 1919 the library could boast over 5,000 volumes.[49] Near the end of that year, the library received another large shipment of books that had been accumulating in England during World War I. This made the English division of the library the largest collection in the building.[50]

The fact that members of the Society had exclusive library privileges sometimes caused complaints. In February 1908, for example, Susa Young Gates asked the library to allow certain women to search out information for those who were not Society members but had requested information through correspondence. Her petition was turned down, but she persisted, and by the end of the year she got her wish. Women record searchers were appointed to work under the direction of the assistant librarian and received a certain percentage of the fees charged by the library. Eventually the library provided part-time clerks who responded to mail requests by copying the desired information from books. In 1919 the library charged members of the Society at the rate of forty cents an hour, while nonmembers were charged fifty cents.[51] The library had only two full-time salaried employees: Nephi Anderson, the secretary and librarian; and Lillian Cameron, the assistant librarian.[52] The part-time clerks received modest wages according to the work they did.

The library was for research, but with limited financial and human resources, its staff had difficulty providing all the help that patrons requested. Susa Young Gates constantly urged the Society to open the library in the late afternoon or evenings. In 1910 the library was opened on Friday evenings, but after five months there was so little evening attendance that it was closed again.[53] But Gates persisted, and in 1917 she got certain Relief Society sisters to prepare a memorandum requesting that the library be opened from 9 A.M. to 9 P.M. six days a week. In return, "as good tithe payers," the women pledged to secure new members and to help each other learn the proper use of the books.[54] In this case, however, the pleading of the women did not succeed. The library continued with only a daytime schedule.

Expanding into the Stakes and Wards

Between 1910 and 1920, the Society expanded its efforts Churchwide. Exactly when it began to foster genealogical committees in the wards and stakes is not clear, but by 1911 local committees were being organized in some areas. Early that year, President Anthon H. Lund complained in a letter to stake presidents that nothing was being done in some stakes, and he proceeded to outline the responsibilities of ward and stake committees. After all, he observed, the Church had two thousand missionaries devoting time to deliver the gospel to the living, so why not do more for the dead? He urged every stake genealogical representative, stake president, high council member, and ward bishopric to join the Society. Stake genealogical representatives were to give personal attention to the matter of helping people, and if necessary, ward representatives should also be called. President Lund also asked all members of the Society to

Anthon H. Lund, member of the First Presidency, was also president of the Society, 1900–21. Courtesy LDS Church Archives.

subscribe to the magazine. He gently scolded some stake leaders for appointing genealogical representatives who were too old to meet with others or promote membership. Some had sent in no reports at all, so the Society simply did not know what was happening in those places.[55]

Gradually, ward and stake committees became part of the local administrative structure. In 1912 the Society circulated forms asking for reports from the stake representatives. Some reports were encouraging. In Provo, for example, many people were attending genealogical classes at Brigham Young University (BYU), as well as some adult classes, and Relief Societies were devising ways to assist people in doing their temple work.[56] Another stake was encouraging young girls in the Mutual Improvement Association to listen to older people tell their stories and write these down along with their genealogies.[57] In contrast, many stake representatives were doing nothing. In 1913, therefore, Nephi Anderson urged the board to either take action to "awaken these representatives to activity" or ask that the stake presidents replace them.[58]

In 1913 the Society issued printed instructions and suggestions for stake and ward representatives. The suggestions stressed the need for local authorities to assert the importance of their genealogical committees: "The Genealogical Society is one of the regular organizations of the Church," they were reminded, "and as such its officers—general, stake, and ward—should be recognized and have equal standing with other similar officers."[59] The instructions then listed all the responsibilities of the committees, including holding monthly meetings between ward and stake leaders, promoting membership in the Society as well as magazine subscriptions, and arranging for genealogical classes.

At the same time, the Society began its own outreach classes, independent from, though not in competition with, the Relief Society. In 1909 the Genealogical Society had been successful in getting genealogy into the curriculum of Church academics. Susa Young Gates was one of the prime movers behind this program and helped prepare the lesson outlines.[60] Classes were also conducted at BYU, with Gates as one of the initial teachers. Anticipating the Churchwide "four generation program" of later years, BYU genealogical classes required by 1920 that each student complete a family record that went back to his great-great-grandparents.[61]

The Society's promotional campaign also included visits to ward meetings and encouragement for wards and stakes to open other genealogical classes. By 1913 a number of stakes were holding their own genealogical classes, in addition to whatever the Relief Society was doing. Some of these classes were taught by representatives of the Society while others, apparently, were conducted by locally appointed experts.[62] In addition to the treks of Susa Young Gates and Elizabeth McCune into Canada and southern Utah in 1913, Society leaders taught elsewhere in Utah and in Idaho during the next few years.

In all their activities, the leaders of the Society worked through the regularly organized channels of Church administration. The best way to obtain success, Nephi Anderson observed, was to go through the established line of authority—from stake presidents, to bishops, to the ward representatives. In this way, he was convinced, the full Church organization would be involved, and people would not view genealogy as simply a fad being promoted by a few unofficial individuals.[63] In addition to the work in the stakes, in 1914 the Society began to send genealogical information to presidents of missions, who, in turn, were to disseminate it to interested Church members.[64] In 1915 the Church committee assigned to outline priesthood quorum lessons for the Church asked for a course of study on genealogy.[65]

By the end of the decade, priesthood leaders in some stakes were beginning to take genealogical activity more seriously. In 1917, for example, the president of the Granite Stake assigned two members of the high council to head a general stake committee and to coordinate the activities of priesthood genealogical committees in the wards. The following year, President Anthon H. Lund wrote to all stake presidents reminding them that the Society was one of the regular departments of the Church and that its officers should have equal standing with those of other departments. He urged all stake and ward committees to be fully organized in preparation for the new study outline being issued by the Society. The Society was also preparing a list of instructions for these committees.[66]

Moreover, the Genealogical Society found other ways to promote its interests throughout the Church. It held special meetings in Salt Lake City at general conference time for Society members. It cooperated with the Relief Society when that organization also began to hold genealogical conventions at conference time. Another program instigated by the Genealogical Society was "Genealogy Sunday." In 1912, Susa Young Gates suggested that one day a year be set aside for all Church members to receive genealogical instruction. The First Presidency approved the idea, and the Society designated the Sunday nearest 21 September—the anniversary of the angel Moroni's first appearance to Joseph Smith in 1823, when the coming of Elijah was prophesied (D&C 2:1–3). For a number of years, genealogy and salvation for the dead were the special topics of discussion on that particular Sunday throughout the Church.[67]

The International Congress of Genealogy, 1915

The highlight of the decade for the Church genealogical program was the International Congress of Genealogy in July 1915, held in connection with the world's fair in San Francisco. The women of the Relief Society began planning for it at least a year in advance, although Church leaders at first questioned whether their participation would help the Genealogical Society.[68] But Susa Young Gates felt differently, and her committee was very much involved in both the planning and the advertising.

Both the Relief Society and the Genealogical Society of Utah were invited to send delegates. The Relief Society made big plans. Gates invited every stake genealogical committee in the Church to send one or more delegates to California. She made plans to charter a special train from Salt Lake City. Circulars were printed and sent out. The *Relief Society Magazine* zealously promoted the conference, telling the women that if they were frugal they could finance the entire week's excursion for fifty dollars.[69]

The women responded enthusiastically, and on 22 July, a special Oregon Short Line train of fourteen cars left Salt Lake City with nearly 250 excursionists aboard. They reached San Francisco the next day. On Saturday, 24 July, they attended a special Utah day at the fairgrounds. The preconference highlight, however, was the daylong meeting hosted by the Genealogical Society of Utah on 27 July, the day before the three-day International Congress met. Considerable outside interest was expressed in the Church's activities, and the meetings were well attended.[70]

When the International Congress of Genealogy met the following three days, Latter-day Saints played a prominent role. Of the 106 official delegates from forty-six invited organizations, twenty-two were from the Genealogical Society of Utah and twenty-six from the Genealogical Extension Division of the Women's Relief Society.[71] In addition, many Church participants, especially women from the intermountain states, swelled the attendance. As if to emphasize the growing significance of the Church in genealogical work, the Congress appointed Joseph Fielding Smith and Susa Young Gates to a number of permanent committees. It also authorized the *Utah Genealogical and Historical Magazine* to publish proceedings of the Congress in its October 1915 and January 1916 issues. Special bronze medals were presented to Anthon H. Lund as president of the Genealogical Society of Utah and to Emmeline B. Wells as president of the Relief Society.[72] LDS Church genealogists were making their influence felt.

Transition

The Relief Society and the Genealogical Society continued to promote genealogical activity during the second decade of the century, but the Genealogical Society began to reassume the leadership role. While the women of the Church, largely through the Relief Society, led the effort to popularize genealogy and carried the major burden of research and temple work for many years, by 1920 the Genealogical Society, governed directly by the priesthood, began to take full responsibility for the genealogical program of the Church.

Some of the LDS Church representatives to the World Congress on Genealogy in San Francisco, 1915. Front (left to right): Romania B. Penrose, Charles W. Penrose, Anthon H. Lund, Joseph F. Smith, Mary S. Smith, Emmeline B. Wells. Center: Susa Young Gates, Heber J. Grant, Augusta Winters Grant, Charles W. Nibley, Jeanette A. Hyde, Elizabeth C. McCune. Back: James Blake, Joseph Fielding Smith, Annie Wells Cannon, Mark Austin, Lewis Anderson. Photographer P. Cardinell Vincent Co., San Francisco. Courtesy LDS Church Archives.

The last major genealogical initiative of the Relief Society was the sponsorship of temple excursions. By 1916 the women of the Church were encouraged to spend at least one day a year doing temple work for those people on the Relief Society "charity lists"—lists of names furnished to the Genealogical Committee by those who were unable to travel to the temples themselves. Arrangements were also made for women who lived long distances from the temples to donate money for the purpose of paying a gratuity to elderly patrons to do temple work. In addition, the Relief Society encouraged those far from temples to organize annual temple excursions.[73]

By 1920 the overlap between Relief Society activities and those of the Genealogical Society became problematic. The Genealogical Society was organizing committees in all the wards and stakes. It proposed, therefore, to assume complete responsibility for assisting in research, giving genealogical lessons, and collecting index cards in local Church units. The Relief Society was asked to continue promoting annual temple days and excursions for women and to teach genealogical lessons that were theological in nature. The Relief Society agreed to the plan, and for one year (1921) the women conducted classes on the theological basis of temple ordinances for the dead.[74] While these changes were taking place, Susa Young Gates asked the women not to "slacken your efforts . . . but hold up the hands of the brethren and continue in the good work of filling the temples."[75]

That year Clarrisa Smith Williams became General President of the Relief Society, and the general board was reorganized. Although Gates was retained on the board, she was removed from the lessons committee. Consequently, she did not have as much influence on decisions affecting Relief Society classwork.[76] Soon, the classes on genealogy were phased out completely.

The ease with which Susa Young Gates abandoned her genealogical classes and related projects to which she had given years of effort may be explained partially by the fact that she saw her administrative involvement in genealogy as a temporary assignment. She started the genealogical classes to remedy what she saw as a lack of knowledge within the Church. With the support of the priesthood leaders, she taught classes to both men and women, but she felt more comfortable working directly with the women, and she moved in that direction whenever possible. She depended upon the Genealogical Society for support and gave her full assistance to its plans even when it meant abandoning her own. Throughout all her years of service, she saw genealogy as a priesthood assignment.

Nevertheless, Gates continued to support and to be involved in genealogy. In 1921 the Genealogical Society officers asked her to serve on the activities and studies committee, directed by her son-in-law, John A. Widtsoe. She accepted the call but suggested, "If you wish some active work and help for women in the Genealogical movement, I would suggest that you create again the Women's Committee."[77] She explained that the sisters she had worked with previously were trained genealogists who had developed study programs and activities for the Relief Society, the Young Ladies, the Primary Association, and the Genealogical Society.[78] The Women's Committee was not formed again, but a number of women served with Gates on the Society's activities committee, which was responsible for the genealogical conventions sponsored Churchwide. The women's duties, however, were limited, and the Society organized no new activities exclusively for women.

Although by the end of 1920 genealogical programs for the Latter-day Saints were again fully under the auspices of the Genealogical Society of Utah, it was often the women, such as Susa Young Gates, to whom priesthood leaders wrote for advice on how to improve their organization and activities. Female genealogists traveled throughout the Church giving short courses and preaching the importance of ancestral research, and they staffed the library of the Genealogical Society. The Relief Society trained the women, and the women took their responsibility seriously. They tried valiantly to provoke the priesthood brethren to good works in genealogy, but in the meantime, they carried the major burden themselves. In the end, the women's work of more than a decade had provided the Genealogical Society with much new expertise and a vast new clientele.

The First Quarter Century

At the end of its first quarter century, the Society's accomplishments were still modest. Though exact figures are not available, by 1920 the Society had approximately 2,000 members.[79] In 1919, members made 275 "searches" in the library, as compared with only thirty searches ten years earlier. The library added 627 volumes during the year preceding its April 1919 meeting, making a total of 5,027 books. Financially, the Society seemed to be in good shape. For the year ending 1 April 1918, for example, it had an income from dues, library fees, book sales, dividends, donations, and stock sales of $11,553. Total disbursements, including $7,000 for the purchase of seventy shares of ZCMI stock, amounted to $12,177. Society assets also included $38,329 worth of stock in various Utah-based corporations.[80]

No visible image symbolized the expanded activities of the Society more than its new office complex. In 1917 the Church completed the magnificent new Church Office Building at 47 East South Temple Street in Salt Lake City. The first two floors housed the offices of the General Authorities of the Church. The Genealogical Society was given the entire fourth floor for its exclusive use. For the first time, Society facilities were physically separated from those of the Church Historian's Office. The accommodations included a large room for the library collection, several offices, and a large classroom. The quarters were spacious and, for the time being, adequate. The move from the former location was completed on 17 March 1917, although for the entire previous month, staff members had been busy ordering and arranging the books and research facilities for the formal opening. Research work began on 11 April, and the first genealogical class in the new building was held on 26 June 1917.[81]

As the decade drew to a close, the leaders of the Society could express both discouragement and optimism. Genealogical work was more widespread in the Church than ever before, although activities within wards and stakes still varied widely. Priesthood leaders were beginning to assume greater responsibility. Classes were being conducted throughout the Church, but attendance tended to drop off as the enthusiasm of members often

Church Administration Building, 1917, at 47 East South Temple, Salt Lake City, location of the Genealogical Society, 1917–33.

Reading room of the Genealogical Society Library, ca. 1921, located in the Church Administration Building. Susa Young Gates sits on the left at the first table, and Joseph Fielding Smith is seated on the left at the second table. Courtesy Utah State Historical Society.

waned quickly. Nevertheless, the Society had a rapidly growing membership, good leadership, excellent research facilities, and important contacts throughout the world. In 1918 a Boston bookseller, F. J. Wilder, wrote to the Society with high praise and optimism for the future:

> Within the next ten years your Society is destined to become the largest and the strongest in the world for the reason that it is founded on a more substantial basis than any other society of its kind. You will see in years to come people from all parts of the West and the East flocking to your city to spend days and weeks studying because of the advantages that can be had with your Society.
>
> Not only will people of the Mormon faith come to you, but the outsider as well may become interested in your faith because of the treatment he will receive at your hands.[82]

While it is debatable whether all of Wilder's prediction was fulfilled within ten years, his statement embodied Church genealogists' vision of what the Society would become.

NOTES

[1]Susa Young Gates, untitled manuscript in folder entitled "Women and Genealogy," Susa Young Gates papers, Utah State Historical Society, Salt Lake City, 29-31. For brief biographies of Susa Young Gates, see Carolyn W. D. Pearson, "Susa Young Gates," in *Mormon Sisters,* ed. Claudia L. Bushman (Cambridge: Emmeline Press, 1976): 199-223; Rebecca Foster Cornwall, "Susa Young Gates: The Thirteenth Apostle," in *Sister Saints,* Vicky Burgess-Olsen ed. (Provo: Brigham Young University Press, 1978): 61-93. The material in this chapter relating to Susa Young Gates and the Relief Society is based on James B. Allen and Jessie L. Embry, "'Provoking the Brethren to Good Works': Susa Young Gates, the Relief Society, and Genealogy Work," *BYU Studies* 31 (Spring 1991): 115-38.

[2]"Susa Young Gates," *Utah Genealogical and Historical Magazine* 24 (July 1933): 98-99 (hereafter cited as *UGHM*); Pearson, "Susa Young Gates," 213.

[3]"Susa Young Gates," 98-99.

[4]See John A. Widtsoe, "The Opening of Our New Home," *UGHM* 25 (April 1934): 56; Pearson, "Susa Young Gates," 97-100, 212; Andrew Jenson, *Latter-day Saint Biographical Encyclopedia,* 4 vols. (Salt Lake City: Andrew Jenson History, 1901-36), 2: 628.

[5]Undated and untitled manuscript in Relief Society Genealogical Programs folder, Susa Young Gates collection, Archives Division, Historical Department, The Church of Jesus Christ of Latter-day Saints, Salt Lake City (hereafter cited as LDS Church Archives), folder 1.

[6] Undated and untitled manuscript in Relief Society Genealogical Programs, folder 2.

[7] "Susa Young Gates," 99.

[8] Gates, "Women and Genealogy," 11. This manuscript says that the column began in 1905, but the date given above is correct.

[9] Susa Young Gates to Pierson W. Banning, 27 March 1916, Susa Young Gates papers, LDS Church Archives.

[10] *Deseret Evening News,* 8 August 1908.

[11] *Deseret Evening News,* 8 August 1908. Joseph Fielding Smith (1876–1972) was the son of Joseph Fielding Smith (1838–1918), who was President of the Church at this time. The father was usually identified as Joseph F. Smith and the son as Joseph F. Smith Jr. Later, however, the son adopted the convention of being called Joseph Fielding Smith, and he is usually identified that way today. Though the early records dealt with here identify him as Joseph F. Smith Jr., we have adopted the more well-known convention.

[12] *Deseret News,* 8 August 1908.

[13] Untitled manuscript, Susa Young Gates papers, LDS Church Archives, 4.

[14] Gates, "Women and Genealogy"; Susa Young Gates, "Report of the Genealogical Extension Work of the Relief Society," Susa Young Gates papers, LDS Church Archives.

[15] Susa Young Gates circular letter, addressed "Dear Sister," 26 August 1918; Susa Young Gates to Joseph Fielding Smith, 17 October 1918, Susa Young Gates papers, LDS Church Archives.

[16] *Deseret Evening News* to Elwood Ward Relief Society (Utah), 30 September 1918, Susa Young Gates papers, LDS Church Archives.

[17] Gates to Smith, 17 October 1918.

[18] Gates to Smith, 17 October 1918.

[19] Susa Young Gates to the President and Board, Genealogical Society of Utah, 29 August 1918, Susa Young Gates papers, LDS Church Archives.

[20] Though Susa suggested on 29 August 1918 that Joseph Fielding Smith become the editor, in the same letter she also suggested Anderson.

[21] Gates, "Report of the Genealogical Extension Work of the Relief Society"; Gates, "Women and Genealogy," 12.

[22] Gates, "Women and Genealogy," 12–14.

[23] Gates, "Women and Genealogy," 12–14.

[24] Gates, "Women and Genealogy," 14.

[25] Genealogical Society Minutes, 17 November 1908, Family History Department of the Church (hereafter cited as FHD).

[26] Following through on what some women wanted to accomplish through the DUP, for example, they memorialized certain events and movements in Church history in a series of public meetings in 1911 and 1912. See list in an announcement in *Deseret Evening News,* 16 September 1911. The list included pioneers from Zion's Camp, from various immigrant pioneer groups, and from various periods in Church history.

[27] "The Genealogical Society of Utah," *UGHM* 1 (January 1910): 40.

[28] "Tribute to the Genealogical Society of Utah," *UGHM* 5 (January 1914): 42, from "A Christmas Salutation," *Deseret Evening News,* 20 December 1913.

[29]See report, "The Biennial Meeting of the Genealogical Society of Utah," *UGHM* 1 (July 1910): 137–40; *Deseret Evening News,* 6 April 1910; Genealogical Society Minutes, 15 March 1910. Five of the committees were on (1) memberships and magazine subscriptions, Benjamin Goddard, chair; (2) meetings and social gatherings, C. S. Martin, chair; (3) historical and genealogical papers, Osborne J. P. Widtsoe, chair; (4) town and family histories, Joseph S. Peery, chair; and (5) published records and relics, Thomas A. Clawson, chair. The sixth was an executive committee consisting of Heber J. Grant, Joseph Fielding Smith, and Joseph Christenson.

[30]Relief Society General Board Minutes, 19 October, and 2 November 1906, and 6 December 1907, LDS Church Archives.

[31]Undated and untitled seven-page manuscript, Susa Young Gates papers, LDS Church Archives. This manuscript, written about 1916, is a draft of an article by Susa Young Gates, "Genealogy in the Relief Society," which appeared in *UGHM* 7 (January 1916): 41–45. The above story did not appear in the final publication. In Gates, "Women in Genealogy," an allusion is made to this meeting. In the first manuscript, the meeting is dated 1908, while here it is dated 1910.

[32]Relief Society General Board Minutes, 1 February, and 15 February, 1912.

[33]"Genealogical Activity in Ogden Stake," *UGHM* 7 (January 1916): 46–47. This article indicates that the class began on 20 March, but it is clear from the Relief Society General Board Minutes and from early references in *UGHM* that it did not begin until 20 April.

[34]"Genealogists Abroad," *UGHM* 5 (July 1914): 125–33.

[35]Relief Society General Board Minutes, 13 April 1913, 44–45.

[36]Thomas G. Alexander, *Mormonism in Transition: A History of the Latter-day Saints, 1890–1930* (Urbana: University of Illinois Press, 1986), 152.

[37]Report filed in Susa Young Gates papers, LDS Church Archives. The 1915 date is inferred from internal evidence.

[38]Susa Young Gates to Anthon H. Lund and the Genealogical Society, 20 November 1917, Susa Young Gates papers, LDS Church Archives; Susa Young Gates, "Genealogy," *Relief Society Magazine* 5 (August 1918): 475; Joseph Fielding Smith to Susa Young Gates and members of the Genealogical Committee, General Board of the Relief Society, reproduced in Gates, "Genealogy," 475–76.

[39]The manual contained lessons on the following topics: Material and Sources of Information; Approximating Dates; Methods of Recording; Heirship in Temple Work; Numbering; Work in the Library; Some Standard Books; What the Country Genealogist Can Do; Family Organizations; Pedigrees and Family Groups; Instructions concerning Temple Work; and Making Out Temple Sheets. See Gates, "Women and Genealogy," 17–18; and "Susa Young Gates," 99. The publication of this little book evoked some interesting commentary in a German magazine devoted to women's suffrage. The author, Peter Von Gebhardt, made various favorable observations about the Church and its practices, then praised the "excellent little book" in glowing terms. "We ask if the German woman also could not become active in the field of practical genealogy," he continued, "and it would be well if the American Lesson Book could find imitation among us." Gates, "Women in Genealogy," 18–19, apparently quoting a translated version of the article.

[40]Gates, "Women and Genealogy," 23.

[41]*Deseret Evening News,* 7 April 1914.

[42]L. Garrett Myers, oral history interview by Bruce Blumell, 1976, typescript, James Moyle Oral History Program, LDS Church Archives, 40.

[43]Paul F. Royall to Jessie Evans Smith, 2 January 1968, LDS Church Archives; George H. Fudge, oral history interview by Bruce Blumell, 1976, typescript, James Moyle Oral History Program, LDS Church Archives, 28.

[44]Myers, interview, 15.

[45]Joseph Fielding Smith and Joseph Christenson to the Board of Directors of the Genealogical Society of Utah, 15 November 1909, Genealogical Society correspondence, FHD; *Deseret Evening News,* 18 December 1909; Genealogical Society Minutes, 18 November 1909; "Joseph Fielding Smith," *UGHM* 16 (April 1925): 50–51.

[46]Genealogical Society Minutes, 12 January 1910.

[47]Joseph Fielding Smith to Heber J. Grant, 7 June 1910, Genealogical Society Minutes.

[48]Genealogical Society Minutes, 23 June, 7 July, 20 September, 18 October 1910, and 19 April 1912.

[49]See description in "The Library of the Genealogical Society of Utah," *UGHM* 10 (July 1919): 114–19.

[50]*Deseret Evening News,* 19 December 1919.

[51]Genealogical Society Minutes, 18 February, and 15 December 1908; "Library of the Genealogical Society," 115.

[52]Genealogical Society Minutes, 15 March 1915.

[53]Genealogical Society Minutes, 18 October 1910, and 17 March 1911.

[54]Susa Young Gates to Anthon H. Lund, 20 March 1917, Susa Young Gates papers, LDS Church Archives.

[55]Anthon H. Lund to stake presidents, 15 May 1911, Genealogical Society circular letters, LDS Church Archives.

[56]"Genealogical Work in Provo," *UGHM* 3 (July 1912): 133–35.

[57]"Summer Work for Mutual Girls," *UGHM* 3 (July 1912): 138–39.

[58]Genealogical Society Minutes, 20 January 1913.

[59]*Instructions for the Stake and Ward Representatives of the Genealogical Society,* pamphlet issued by the Board of Directors of the Genealogical Society, 1913.

[60]Genealogical Society Minutes, 20 July, 23 August 1909; and *Deseret Evening News,* 8 January 1910.

[61]"Genealogical and Temple Notes," *UGHM* 11 (January 1920): 45–46.

[62]Genealogical Society Minutes, 20 June, and 21 November 1913; "Genealogical and Historical Notes," *UGHM* 3 (April 1912): 90; and 3 (October 1912): 195.

[63]Nephi Anderson to N. L. Morris, 8 August 1913, Genealogical Society circular letters, LDS Church Archives.

[64]Genealogical Society Minutes, 28 December 1914, and 15 January 1915.

[65]Genealogical Society Minutes, 21 May 1915.

[66]"The Society's Conference Meeting," *UGHM* 8 (July 1917): 117; *Deseret Evening News,* 14 April; Genealogical Society Minutes, 20 July 1917; "Outlines of Studies and Activities for the Genealogical Society for the Season of 1918," *UGHM* 9 (January 1918): 44–48; and "Outlines of Studies

and Activities for the Genealogical Society for the Season of 1919-1920," *UGHM* 10 (October 1919): 163-69.

[67]Genealogical Society Minutes, 19 January, 20 February, and 21 June 1912; "Minutes of the Meetings of the Committee on Preparation of Genealogy and Historical Papers," 13 June, 3 October 1912, Archibald F. Bennett papers, FHD.

[68]Joseph Fielding Smith to Susa Young Gates, 22 July 1914, Susa Young Gates papers, LDS Church Archives.

[69]*Relief Society Magazine* 2 (May 1915): 239. See also various documents in Susa Young Gates papers, LDS Church Archives; Relief Society General Board Minutes, 9 March, 9 June, and 1 July 1915, LDS Church Archives; and "Women and Genealogy," 24-25.

[70]James Adam Barr, "International Congress of Genealogy," *UGHM* 6 (October 1915): 157-64.

[71]Barr, "International Congress of Genealogy," 157-64.

[72]Barr, "International Congress of Genealogy," 157-64.

[73]See the genealogy sections in the *Relief Society Magazine* 2 (December 1915): 550-52; and 3 (February-March 1916): 113-14, 171-72.

[74]"Theology and Testimony," *Relief Society Magazine* 8 (January 1921): 55-57; and (February 1921): 114-19.

[75]"Notice to Genealogical Committees, Both Stake and Ward," *Relief Society Magazine* 7 (December 1920): 731.

[76]Cornwall, "Susa Young Gates," 79.

[77]Susa Young Gates to Anthon H. Lund and General Board of the Genealogical Society, 14 October 1920, Susa Young Gates papers, LDS Church Archives.

[78]Gates to Lund, 14 October 1920.

[79]Estimate based on an examination of membership figures given in the minutes for 1908-20. Usually, though not always, the figures separated life memberships from annual membership fees. Apparently during this period at least 1,300 life memberships were issued, and in 1919 some 500 annual memberships were issued.

[80]Genealogical Society Minutes, 8 April 1918.

[81]Andrew Jenson, "The Historian's Office," *UGHM* 8 (April 1917): 61. This issue of the magazine had a major section devoted to the new Church Office Building and included pictures of the facilities.

[82]Genealogical Society Minutes, 15 February 1918.

Chapter 3

The Pleasures and Problems of Growth, 1920–1940

By 1920 the twenty-six-year-old Genealogical Society had won a permanent and prominent place in the official programs of the Church. Nearly every ward and stake had a genealogical organization. Temple attendance was increasing, and the expertise of the Society staff was always in demand by people who came to do research. Genealogical leaders were continually quoting the Prophet Joseph Smith's statement that "the greatest responsibility in this world that God has laid upon us is to seek after our dead," and they seemed determined to emblazon that attitude upon the conscience of every Latter-day Saint. Nevertheless, only a handful of Saints in most wards were devoting much time to genealogical research, although the number of members heeding the persistent call for genealogical work was growing gradually.

The next two decades saw tremendous growth, the inauguration of several new programs, and the emergence of some important new leaders. Susa Young Gates reminisced in 1927:

> We who have seen this organization develop from . . . a dozen founders in 1894 . . . with headquarters in a little upper room in the Historian's Office, to a lively membership of 4,724 with spacious and luxurious library and offices in the Church Office Building, contemplate with wonder the daily renewed miracle.[1]

Growth of the Society

By the end of 1937, the library contained over 19,200 books, including several thousand volumes from Scandinavia, Germany, and the British Isles obtained by John A. Widtsoe while he was president of the European Mission. The Society planned to spend $2,500 annually on new books. Only four genealogical libraries in the country were more extensive: the Library of Congress in Washington, the New England Historic Genealogical Society Library in Boston, the Newberry Library in Chicago, and the New York Genealogical and Biographical Society Library in New York City. In 1928 one well-known genealogist from Chicago remarked that although some libraries had more books, the indexing system of the Utah library was the finest he had ever seen.[2] The library served an average of seventy-five patrons each day.[3]

By 1934 the Society had nearly 6,000 lifetime members and hundreds of annual members. That year it moved into new headquarters in the Joseph F. Smith Memorial Building, with expanded research facilities that could accommodate 300 researchers. Twenty trained researchers worked for the research bureau, and the new Temple Index Bureau had a card file of over six million names.[4]

During this era, genealogy became highly institutionalized in the Church through home teachers, classes for various age groups, handbooks, numerous new committees, and an increasing amount of official endorsement and emphasis from Church leaders at all levels. In the 1920s, the Patriarch to the Church, Hyrum G. Smith, headed a "Committee on Activities and Lesson Work" intended to promote both conviction and activity among Church members. Working with priesthood leaders, auxiliary officers, and Church schools, the committee promoted publications, sponsored conventions, erected memorials, promoted family organizations, and urged temple excursions.

The Great Depression of the 1930s provided, in one respect, an unexpected stimulus to genealogical work; many who were out of work took the opportunity to do some long-neglected family research. One Society staff member later noted that there was probably more work done in this period than at any previous time, with the library often filled to capacity.[5]

As might be expected, all this expansion was accompanied by intensive discussions, some differences over policy, and a few misunderstandings. Several thorny questions were debated in these two decades. Their resolutions had important consequences for the future.

New Leaders

During these years of expansion, the Society was led by four different presidents. The first three were all members of the First Presidency of the Church during their tenure as president of the Society—Anthon H. Lund, who served as president after the death of Franklin D. Richards in 1899 until his own death in 1921; Charles W. Penrose, who died in 1925; and Anthony W. Ivins, who

Society officials, 1923, in front of the Church Administration Building. Shown are (left to right) Church President Heber J. Grant, board member; Joseph Christenson, librarian; Elder Charles W. Penrose, president; Elder Anthony W. Ivins, vice president; William A. Morton, secretary; Elder Joseph Fielding Smith, treasurer; Elder John A. Widtsoe, board member; Patriarch Hyrum G. Smith, board member. Courtesy Utah State Historical Society.

Officers and staff of the Society, 1923, in front of the Church Administration Building. Courtesy Utah State Historical Society.

held the position until 1934. At that point, Elder Joseph Fielding Smith of the Council of the Twelve was appointed president. Elder Smith had been a member of the board since 1907. He had also served as librarian, editor, secretary, treasurer, and vice president. By the time he was released in 1961, he had led the Society longer than any other president.

Elder John A. Widtsoe, also of the Council of the Twelve, was appointed to the board of the Society soon after being called as an Apostle in 1921. A respected scholar and academician, Widtsoe brought broad perspective and foresight into guiding the direction of the Society for the thirty years he served on the board. He helped create support for the establishment of a Temple Index Bureau. He also promoted such significant projects as microfilming and propounded views that anticipated future programs such as the name-extraction program.

The position in the Society that demanded the most time was that of secretary. Since the president was always a General Authority of the Church and therefore able to devote only part of his time to the Society, the secretary became the full-time manager. In 1928 this position went to Archibald F. Bennett, who devoted the rest of his career to the Society and became one of the most well-known genealogists in the Church and in the genealogical world. He was the author of numerous books and articles; his best-known work was *Saviors on Mount Zion,* a genealogical instruction manual published for the Sunday Schools in 1950. His

Archibald F. Bennett, ca. 1938, author, teacher, publicist, genealogical enthusiast, and Society secretary, 1928–1961. He was popularly known in the Church as "Mr. Genealogy."

writings, public addresses, classes at Brigham Young University, and willingness to help people at the Society endeared him to many. An avid researcher, he became particularly interested in the family of Joseph Smith. Through some clever genealogical sleuthing, he discovered a previously unknown daughter, who died in infancy, in the family of Joseph Smith Sr.[6]

After Elder Smith became president in 1934, he employed L. Garrett Myers, a banker by profession, as the superintendent of research and as assistant treasurer. Myers later became superintendent of the Society. Working behind the scenes and receiving little recognition, he directed the day-to-day work of the Society for twenty-five years.

"Grass Roots" Inspiration: The Temple Index Bureau

The upsurge in genealogical activity and temple work among Church members inevitably resulted in duplication of effort, incomplete and inaccurate records, and serious discussions about solving such problems. Leaders became increasingly concerned over the fact that overlap in research by unacquainted branches of the same family frequently led to duplication of temple work, because no effective cross-referencing existed between the temples. Further, the demand for names to accommodate temple patrons sometimes led to the performance of vicarious ordinances before the deceased person had been accurately identified or the family relationships clearly proven.

Beginning at least as early as the 1890s, various unsuccessful attempts were made to eliminate duplication of research and temple work. Some families experimented with their own card-indexing system. The Society developed a rudimentary surname index to families submitting names for temple work, but it was not an adequate reference to individuals.[7] Another effort to avoid duplication would be eschewed by modern librarians, although it seemed to be a practical solution at the time: "When a name is taken from the books," researchers were instructed in 1919, "a check mark should be placed opposite that name, to the end that no one else shall take that name again for purposes of temple work."[8] This policy continued until 1927. Various other solutions were tried, but none were adequate.

Harry H. Russell, ca. 1937, founder and director of the Temple Index Bureau.

Harry Russell was one of those people most concerned about research and temple ordinance duplication. His efforts eventually resulted in the establishment of an important new approach to the problem. Converted to the Church in 1912 at age forty-three, Russell moved to Utah and became actively engaged in temple work and genealogical research. From 1914 to 1918, he served as a missionary on the Temple Block in Salt Lake City, and for twenty years, he was an officiator in the Salt Lake Temple.

One of Harry Russell's research sources was a book of the genealogy of the Abbott family. After spending some 360 days in the temple performing proxy ordinances for his ancestors listed in the book, he learned that certain relatives were also doing Abbott names in the St. George Temple. He went south to visit them. To his dismay, he discovered that they had the same book and had been doing work for the same names he had done in the Salt Lake Temple. His training as an accountant and businessman led him to quickly calculate the hours lost if such duplications were taking place in all the Church's temples (five were operating in 1920, and the Alberta Temple was nearing completion). The results greatly offended his business sense, for he saw untold loss of both time and money, most of which could be avoided by an effective coordinating system. He was so dismayed with the situation that, even though he continued to work as a temple officiator, he refused, at least for the time being, to perform endowments for his own progenitors.[9] But he did not let the matter drop. Rather, he began to press for the establishment of a clearinghouse that would index all names for which temple ordinances had been performed, identify them properly to avoid duplication, and incorporate all past ordinances into the index.

Harry Russell had embarked on a difficult campaign. Several obstacles stood in his way, including some officers of the Society who, even though they recognized the problem, had objections to the kind of bureau he was proposing. Joseph Fielding Smith, for example, was initially reluctant to plunge into new water.[10] One of his concerns, apparently, was the high cost involved, since it would take considerable manpower to go through all the records, transfer them to index cards, then keep the system up-to-date. But Russell found support from other leaders, including Elder John A. Widtsoe and President Heber J. Grant.

Harry Russell's unyielding tenacity was one of the major factors in establishing the Temple Index Bureau. He always called it his "baby," quipping that getting it approved was just like having labor pains.[11] Yet it would not have been born without the help of others. At least by 1921, all the temple presidents had joined the chorus of voices calling for something to be done. At the time of April 1921 general conference, Elder Widtsoe met with the temple presidents and recorders. After much discussion, they decided that a committee should be formed, consisting of representatives from each temple, to formulate a plan.[12] At a similar meeting during the October conference, the committee presented a plan which the temple officials approved. On 3 November, Elder Widtsoe reported this progress to the directors of the Society, who then instructed the activities and programs committee, chaired by Elder Widtsoe, to continue working on the project and to bring some definite recommendations and cost estimates to the board and to the First Presidency. Joseph Fielding Smith—apparently more supportive of the project by this time—and Joseph Christenson were members of this committee. By the following April, their plans were in order, and the new Temple Index Bureau was established. Officially, the Index Bureau became an adjunct to the Church Historian's Office, because it was considered part of the record-keeping system of the Church. The Index Bureau was not transferred to the Society until 1942. Harry Russell received a fitting recognition for all his efforts when he was appointed the first superintendent of the new bureau.

Russell had the momentous task of providing an index of all the names that had ever been endowed. The Executive Committee of the Society, and Joseph Fielding Smith in particular, gave wholehearted support. The Society quickly ordered 200,000 cards that had been specially designed by Russell. Within two years, another 200,000 were needed. Eventually the index would consist of millions of cards.

This new program led to a new kind of Church missionary call. In each community where a temple stood, except Laie, Hawaii, women with typing skills were called as missionaries to transfer names from temple records to index cards. In August of 1922, twelve missionary typists were busily engaged at the Salt Lake Temple, five in Logan, four in Manti, and three in St. George. Russell supervised the work, insisting that special attention be paid to accuracy. After nearly five months, the typists in the Logan Temple had completed 126,000 index cards, and all but 44,000 had been checked against the original records and sent to Salt Lake City.[13] By 1924 the Church had authorized placing five typists, in addition to Russell himself, on full-time salary.

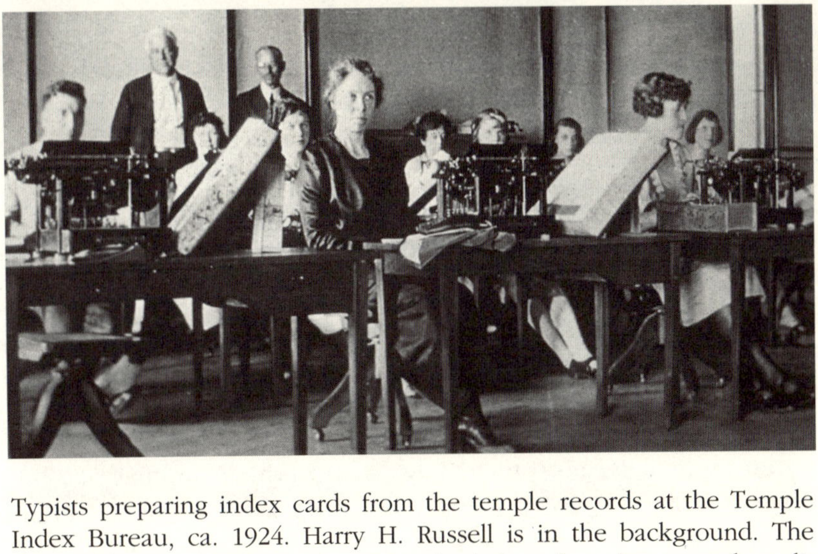

Typists preparing index cards from the temple records at the Temple Index Bureau, ca. 1924. Harry H. Russell is in the background. The index was used to eliminate name submissions for whom temple ordinances had already been performed.

The bureau took four and one-half years to get the index in order so that it could begin functioning as a clearinghouse for vicarious endowments. In the meantime, several problems had to be solved. Some were purely functional, such as what kind of material should be used in index cards. Not content with just any index card, Russell conducted elaborate durability tests on various cards before approving which to use. As the work progressed, the question arose whether the index could be used by researchers before it was complete. In October 1925, the Bureau decided to allow families, when properly supervised, to use the partially completed index as a check for duplication in their own research.[14]

Russell's most complicated problem was devising an efficient system of filing—one that would facilitate name finding as quickly and accurately as possible. Because of variant surname spellings, a patron could expend considerable time searching in dozens of places for a single surname. Russell noted, for instance, that there were thirty-eight different ways to spell *Smith*. To solve the problem, he devised a phonetic filing system so that all names that sounded alike would be located together. "Auxiliary" cards guided researchers from alternate spellings to the standard spelling for each name. Patronymic prefixes were ignored; hence, names beginning with such prefixes as *von* or *Mac* were filed under the first letter following the prefix.

Despite Russell's painstaking work, his system was neither flawless nor problem free. Even though he prepared detailed instructions for his filers, some of them did not follow instructions, and the system "fell down in the execution," as he put it. When he discovered the flaws, he began immediately to have the cards rearranged, but after five years the job was still not complete. With a task so monumental and filled with so much potential for human error, understandably the bureau continued to be plagued with problems and never completely solved the dilemma of duplication.[15]

Harry Russell's frustrations were complicated by the fact that he was creating a new system with which others might disagree—for example, Elder Joseph Fielding Smith. "I think you made a *very great blunder* in ignoring all *prefixes,*" the Apostle had written him when he first devised the plan. While Russell worried about countering authority, he did not change his mind. In 1932, Elder Smith urged Russell to adopt a phonetic filing for given names similar to the one used for surnames. In Russell's mind, this was a patent impossibility. The task of rearranging and making adequate "headers" (cross-reference cards) was so gigantic as to be unthinkable. The surname problem was complicated enough, but to try to file phonetically the thousands of given names such as *Niels, Nels, Nils, Ann, Anna, Anne, Annie,* "and so on ad infinitum," was, he said, "ridiculous to even consider it at all." Such a departure from the system of locating given names according to spelling "would mean disaster, loss of money, and ruin in the files. Remember that cards are going into the files at the rate of almost half a million a year. We are distracted with the complexities that we now have, to say nothing of adding more," he wrote in 1932. Three years later, still miffed at Elder Smith's continued pressures to change the system, he gently reminded his superior of the value of practical experience in the business of filing. He had already tried the proposed system and found it unworkable:

> It's easy for people to stand off and say, 'Why don't you do, thus and so?' when they have no practical experience in the matter in question, and when the matter has been tried, found wanting and abandoned long ago. If we do not know more about our own problem than any one else, we should be arrested and sent to Provo.[16]

Whatever else may be said for Harry Russell, it will never be said that he was afraid to speak his mind. Symbolic of his ultimate commitment, he often signed such letters, "Yours for the Dead."

By 1925 most of the indexing was complete, and Harry Russell was ready to begin what he called "the stupendous task of arranging the cards in the files so as to be 'get-at-able.'" To do this, he estimated, would require his staff to handle about three million cards, five to ten times each. The files were nearly complete by October 1926. On 12 October, Russell was assigned to prepare a notice for the *Deseret News* that would make the announcement he had long awaited: beginning 1 January 1927, all temple sheets prepared for endowments must pass through the Temple Index Bureau. This would apply to all except the Hawaii Temple, which would keep its own index system.[17] The job of clearing names through the Temple Index Bureau then became a prominent aspect of the work of the Genealogical Society for the next sixty years.

Harry Russell had one final difference of opinion with Joseph Fielding Smith. The index cards reflected endowments that had been performed, but not the sealing ordinances. Complete accuracy, Russell felt, demanded that the sealing records also be indexed. He began to work toward this end and apparently was able to file at least some sealing cards. Joseph Fielding Smith, however, disagreed with Russell's plan. In Elder Smith's opinion, the number of duplications prevented by adding the sealing records would be minimal and hardly worth the tremendous cost in time and money. But Russell persisted, and on 18 April 1935, went over Elder Smith's head by writing to President Heber J. Grant. President Grant forwarded the letter to Elder Smith, asking for more information. Elder Smith immediately wrote a long explanation of his view to the Church President, then drafted a reprimand to Russell. "When are you going to quit annoying President Heber J. Grant?" he asked, asserting that less than one-fourth of one percent of the index cards contained insufficient information.

> Now, please, let President Grant alone and quit bothering him with this kind of matter. . . . It is not becoming in you to constantly try to place me in a hole by appealing to President Grant and stating that it is with difficulty that you can get anything accomplished. We have decided that the Bureau shall be an Index Bureau and not a Bureau of Records.[18]

Harry Russell could hardly contain himself. "You are off on the wrong foot," he told Elder Smith. "You are wrong exactly 99 $^{9}/_{10}$%," for instead of "*some* cards with a lack of necessary information," all cards containing records of endowments up to 1928 were incomplete. The recording of endowments up to that point, he said, was "disgracefully deficient and defective"—it omitted names of fathers, mothers, husbands, and wives. The only solution was to put sealing cards, at least pertaining to sealings for the dead, in the files for the period before 1928. Then, with a touch of humor, Russell wrote, "After you have the SEALING CARDS UP TO JANUARY 1928, I will be perfectly willing to hold my peace, quit saying mean things about your defective temple records, and be a real good little boy from that time on."[19]

One complicating factor, only hinted at in this correspondence, was the irregularity in the sealing records that grew out of the nineteenth-century practice of "adoption."[20] Elder Smith felt it would be unwise for such information to be made generally available to families whose ancestors had been adopted into other families, and he was disturbed whenever it was discovered that workers in the Index Bureau had given out such information. He believed this practice could only cause needless confusion and misunderstanding. Eventually, Elder Smith requested that the record of all sealings not connected with actual family relationships be made unavailable.[21]

Despite all the challenges, the Temple Index Bureau made a laudable record for itself. A name could be cleared for temple work in an average of thirty-five seconds. During the first five years of operation, a total of 4,246,668 names were checked, resulting in the prevention of 264,334 duplications (about 6 percent). By 1 January 1936, the number of names checked had reached 6,833,371, with 561,535 duplications avoided. One month later, on 2 February, Harry Russell died, hopefully well satisfied with how his "baby" had matured. In time the percentage of duplicate rejection increased. By the end of 1959, the Bureau housed nearly 21,800,000 cards, had checked over 29,000,000, and avoided nearly 6,000,000 duplications (about 20 percent).[22]

Society staff sorting Temple Index Bureau index cards, ca. 1935. Harry H. Russell sits on the right side of the table. Courtesy Delbert and Barbara Roach.

Research Assistance

While indexing and avoiding duplication in temple work was important, promoting genealogical research was still the primary function of the Society. Research activity increased dramatically in the 1920s and 1930s, along with the development of several new programs within the Society and accelerated efforts to generate enthusiasm at stake and ward levels.

Beginning in the early 1920s, the Society no longer appointed field agents on an official basis. Apparently, it did not want to be held officially responsible for the work of professional researchers. Still, the Society continued to recommend competent professionals to its patrons and even transmitted funds from Utah patrons to foreign researchers. These included some former agents of the Society.[23]

The Society made every effort to expose research scams. In 1935, for example, it issued a strong warning in the *Deseret News* against "certain individuals, styling themselves genealogists [who] are resorting to an attractive type of advertising and thereby inducing many members to place orders with them for genealogical research." According to the warning, such people simply gathered names indiscriminately, with no proof of family connection. These names could not be used for temple work under the rules of that time.[24] The following year, the Society called attention to a group known as the Media Research Bureau that was advertising compiled genealogies for sale "which in reality are brief compilations of very general information already in print and of very little use to those who purchase copies."[25]

While the library encouraged research, it attempted to avoid duplication of research effort by restricting patrons to pursuit of only four surname lines of their own ancestors. As stated in the *Temple and Genealogical Handbook* of 1924: "limiting the performance of temple ordinances in behalf of those who are the kindred of the individuals engaging in that sacred work, is intended to prevent the endless confusion and repetition that would result if there was no limitation."[26] Patrons were supposed to indicate which line they were working on to Lillian Cameron, who was placed in charge of library research in 1920. Work on additional lines was permitted only after a further request was approved. Cameron could also employ workers to do research for patrons at a cost of fifty cents per hour for members and sixty cents for nonmembers of the Society. The researchers received forty cents, and the Society kept the rest as a service fee.[27]

Lillian Cameron's work in assisting research was in addition to her other duties as librarian because the position of research supervisor was not established until 1923. Susa Young Gates accepted the first appointment, but within a few months the executive committee decided that a man should have the assignment.[28] In 1924 the Society established the Research Bureau, headed by Andrew K. Smith.

The recommendation to establish a research bureau came from board member John A. Widtsoe. During an extensive Scandinavian tour on Church business, Elder Widstoe observed genealogical researchers doing work for Utah members, and he became convinced the Society should supervise their labors. He recommended that this objective be accomplished through a central research bureau established by the Church.

The Society did not adopt the worldwide supervisory program Elder Widtsoe had in mind, but it did establish the Research Bureau, which supervised all research done at the library, hired researchers, made contacts with foreign researchers, transferred money to foreign countries when needed, conducted classes in genealogical research, assisted in obtaining information not available in the library, and acted as a general clearinghouse in coordinating research activities. As in the case of many such innovations, the new bureau did not escape criticism. The Logan Temple recorder complained, for example, that the Society was attempting to "corral" all genealogical research. The Society replied, "Our research work is optional with the people, as to whether they accept it or not."[29]

The Research Bureau expanded rapidly, employing at least twenty full-time researchers as well as several part-time people in 1932. The Bureau was organized into three major divisions. The first division, the Research Department, provided research help in several languages and offered to "undertake any kind of service connected with the searching and compiling of records."

Research staff of the Genealogical Society, 1938. Staff members compiled genealogies for a nominal fee, 1924–65. Left to right, standing: Areta S. Blake, Leah Y. Phelps, Jeannette S. Lunt, Ada W. Chace, Margaret Hoyer, Elizabeth N. Jones, Mary Peterson, Mabel Y. Sanborn, Ernst Koehler, Ovena J. Ockey (supervisor of researchers), Friedericka W. Hofer, Gertrude L. Baird; left to right, seated: Grace R. Reynolds, Edna Alley, Ralphena Hacking, Reva Baker, Gwen Bryner, Ellen M. Alley, Marie J. Heninger, Ida A. Taylor, Kathryn C. Stayner, Edith M. Coray. Courtesy Delbert and Barbara Roach.

Staff members looked for overlapping research, filled out family group sheets and temple sheets as research was completed, had the temple sheets checked with the Temple Index Bureau, and later recorded completed temple ordinances. A subdivision known as the Correspondence Department sought information in other parts of America and in Europe when requested by patrons.

The second division, the Instruction Department, organized classes in genealogical research, published lessons, and offered instructional services to all the stakes and wards of the Church. For those who were too far away from the library, the department offered personal help and instruction by correspondence.

A third division, the Research Clearing House, aided people who were doing their own research and wished to cooperate with an elaborate plan for avoiding duplication of research. One of the Research Clearing House subdivisions, the Information Bureau, kept a mailing list of all patrons with a known relationship to any particular surname, a progress sheet for each researcher, and a book of pedigree charts with an index to those who had contributed each pedigree. The Information Bureau endeavored to provide preliminary reports to those who requested information by correspondence, though it became immediately evident that the demand exceeded the bureau's ability to respond quickly.

The Genealogical Archive was another subdivision of the Research Clearing House. To the extent that genealogists were willing to cooperate with this archive, their completed genealogical research was filed in a series of "surname books." By 1928 the Archive had accumulated 13,000 surnames. Researchers wishing to deposit copies of their records in the archives were charged a nominal fee for copying and indexing; for dedicated genealogists the advantages of building up a major file of completed work was well worth the cost.[30] In 1928 a new file, the Patrons' Section, was created which consisted of family group sheets submitted by patrons. The Clearing House also housed Church census records, pedigree charts, and an index to a variety of Church historical records known as the Early Church Records Index. The Research Clearing House was renamed the Church Genealogical Archives in 1929 and renamed again as the Church Records Archives in 1942, as part of the new names-processing procedures that are discussed in more detail below.[31]

Genealogical Archives record room, 1937. Left to right: Esther C. Naylor, Marcella Collett, W. Henry Chase, Ellen O'Brien, Olive Davis. The Archive solicited family group sheets and pedigree charts from Society members. Courtesy Delbert and Barbara Roach.

Several problems plagued the Research Bureau, including serious financial deficits. The Bureau was lenient in collecting unpaid accounts, and the supervision charges did not meet the department's overhead expenses. In March 1935, the deficit amounted to $3,000. A large number of inactive accounts were carried on the books (that is, open accounts of patrons who had not come back for some time). The bureau attempted to rectify the problems by placing a 10-percent supervision fee on all funds deposited; by instituting more rigid accounting, collecting, and auditing procedures; and by closing inactive accounts. By mid-1936 such financial difficulties were apparently subsiding.[32] The Society continued to assist in research through 1966, when the increase in Church membership made it impossible to provide this service to all members of the Church.

As genealogical activity quickened throughout the Church in the 1930s, a number of stakes proposed the creation of local or branch genealogical libraries. The Society, however, officially discouraged such suggestions. The directors felt that small branches could not provide adequate research facilities under any circumstance—a better policy would be to spend all available resources in building the central library in Salt Lake City. In 1934 a genealogical archive was established in the British mission without serious objection from Salt Lake City, but the general preference for centralization remained.[33] Decentralization was an idea ahead of its time—the concept was revived thirty years later when it became feasible to create effective branch libraries.

Despite all the programs and activities, and what appears to be an amazing surge of genealogical activity and success, the directors of the Society were not fully satisfied. Nor, apparently, would they be until they felt that all Church members were doing their genealogical duty. In connection with a plea for more funds in 1939, the editors of the Society's magazine wondered aloud why more members of the Church were not as enthusiastic as they: "We wonder at times if the membership of our Church understand the real function of the Genealogical Society."[34]

Apparently one reason for lack of participation in genealogical research was financial. People did minimal research in the 1930s simply because they could not afford even the small fees charged at the library. The Society itself sometimes provided research help for certain "worthy" poor who could obtain recommendations from their bishops. Some patrons were permitted to pay with produce. In the eyes of at least one researcher, this practice tended to get out of hand. As she told one of her supervisors, she refused to accept any more dried apples or prunes. She had eaten them all winter and could hardly bear to look at another.[35]

In the meantime, the Society continued to seek ways to help Church members improve their research skills and avoid duplication. One way was to encourage surname and family organizations.[36] Surname organizations consisted of people doing research on particular surname lines, regardless of direct family relationships; family organizations were composed of people doing research connected with particular family lines. Such organizations could help avoid duplication and thus facilitate more effective, less expensive research.[37] The Society seemed to give some preference to researchers who were members of such groups.

Correcting Slipshod Research

The 1894 revelation received by Wilford Woodruff regarding the importance of researching one's own ancestors became, in the early twentieth century, the justification for restricting one's research to his or her direct ancestral lines. The fact that this rule was not always followed is evinced in a 1929 letter from the Society's board of directors to President Heber J. Grant complaining that "a certain laxity has grown up in some of our methods." A great deal of temple work was being done for individuals not identifiable either as direct ancestors or as members of any family group. As a result, some genealogists had molded their methods to that attitude, "and devices are used by them to obtain numerous names of the dead, with just barely sufficient personal identification to get past the rules of the temples." These rules were so lax, they protested, that some "family group genealogies" were not really family groups in the spirit of true genealogical research. "The very success of research has come to be judged by the quantitative output of names, and by the cheapness or the speed of copying names from sources readily available."[38]

In the minds of the directors of the Society, such slipshod methods were unjustifiable, even if more careful research would mean a decrease in temple work: "Such an attitude, if unchecked, would soon demoralize the whole system of research, and destroy the truth and sanctity of our temple records. It would deliberately teach our people to forget the necessity for making lineal connections with their ancestors."[39] The Society urged, therefore, that people do research first on their own direct family lines, and recommended that if they were to do research on related families, they should do it in connection with representatives from those families. Only as a last resort should permission be given for any other kind of name gathering and then only with the understanding that every effort would be made to connect the names within family groups.[40]

The problem did not abate, however, partly because some Saints were so anxious to collect names for temple work that they would accept even the most tenuous proof of family connections, and partly because the limited supply of names provided by the research process threatened to close down or limit the operation of some temples. In 1935 one professional researcher, who was also a member of the Los Angeles Stake genealogical board, exacerbated the debate when he solicited work by pointedly criticizing the Church policy of doing temple work only for names with identifiable family relationships. "Experienced genealogists know this cannot be done beyond a few generations," he argued, "and experienced temple workers know that it would be only a matter of a short time until temple work would be retarded as a result of this misguided effort. That time has now arrived." He claimed that his stake had received instructions to gather "not only the much maligned locality names, but surnames wherever they can be found." When this attitude was reported to the board of the Society, they quickly disapproved such counsel as "inconsistent with and contrary to the revealed word of the Lord on our responsibility in temple work and the established policy of the Church as to our responsibility."[41]

The next year it was discovered that a member of the Mesa Temple presidency had been promoting genealogical research in California, claiming that the current policy had almost stopped the flow of names from the California Mission. Without consulting the mission presidency, he arranged genealogical meetings in various branches, took with him various books, and encouraged the people to begin by extracting names, regardless of family relationship. When the mission president brought this to the attention of the Society, Elder Joseph Fielding Smith, on behalf of the Society, fired back a strongly worded letter roundly condemning the attitude of the Arizona genealogist and reiterating the policy of the Society:

> We have given instructions repeatedly . . . that members of the Church should confine their activities to their own lines. . . . We are taught that the work is not complete until parents are sealed and their children are also sealed to the parents. This makes it necessary that the family units be maintained. When names are gathered at random without any thought of family order and the baptisms and endowments are done, then what about the sealings? Our greatest difficulty in the genealogical work is in trying to unravel work of this nature for members of the Church. They too frequently gather names and go to the temple feeling that they are accomplishing something, and then find themselves in a tangle. We are unable, in many cases, to unravel the tangle. . . . Temple work must be orderly

> and when it is not, it leads to endless confusion. We who are at the head of the genealogical work have protested, and do now protest, against the procuring of names at random and without due knowledge of relationship.[42]

The solution to the problem in the eyes of the Society was to be found in "more and continuous research."[43] But the problem would not be solved so simply. It would persist for several decades until a new procedure known as "extraction" would reduce the requirement for research to generate the volume of names needed by the temples.

Stake and Ward Genealogical Organization

The growth of genealogical work was unavoidably accompanied by greater institutionalization in Salt Lake City and at the local level. "This organization . . . is not an auxiliary," Joseph Fielding Smith emphasized to an Idaho Falls genealogical convention in 1922:

> Get that firmly fixed in your minds. The Sunday School, Primary, Religion Class, Mutual and Relief Society, these are auxiliary organizations, but this organization is a part of the great Temple work system of the Church. . . . It has a place which is unique—peculiar to itself. It has a position which is absolutely necessary in this Church and Kingdom.[44]

With this attitude, the officers of the Society set about to strengthen local organizations and enlarge their sphere of activity. They organized a kind of correlation committee headed by John A. Widtsoe and including representatives from the Sunday School, Young Men's and Young Women's Mutual Improvement Associations, Church education, the Primary, and Brigham Young University. One objective was to place all Church organizations in close touch with the Society.[45] Over the next two decades, even though many, if not most, Church members still were not regularly doing genealogical work, apparently very few in the Church escaped being touched at least in some way by the influence of the Society.

In 1920 the Society made new recommendations for strengthening stake and ward genealogical committees. Each stake was to appoint a genealogical representative with two assistants, and each ward was to organize a similar committee. These committees were to meet regularly, supervise genealogical activities within their stakes or wards, give assistance to families, conduct classwork, and organize temple excursions.[46] By 1932 committees were organized, most according to the "official plan," in every stake as well as in many missions.[47]

The recommended plan for stake and ward organizations had become highly elaborate by 1937. Each committee consisted of a genealogical representative and two counselors (each of whom had charge of various subcommittees or departments), a secretary, endowment committee, sealing committee, baptism committee, temple project committee, senior class committee, junior class committee, research and records groups, home teaching committee, finance committee, social committee, and magazine and Society membership workers. Genealogy was highly visible, which was exactly what the Society had in mind.[48] The ideal plan, according to the lessons presented by the Society in 1934, would be to have one ward committee member for every twelve families. The hypothetical "Salt Lake City Ward" with 1,680 people and 400 family units was to have a committee consisting of thirty-six members, including the representative and his two counselors.[49] If the ideal plan were followed, everyone in the ward above the age of thirteen would soon be involved in some phase of genealogical work.

Presumably no stake achieved the ideal, but according to the reports a number of stakes showed some impressive activity. In the last quarter of 1937, for example, Ensign Stake in Salt Lake City reported 3,070 families in the stake. Of these, 1,140 were active in genealogical research. Eight wards were holding senior genealogical classes, and three were holding junior classes. A total of 1,299 people had attended the temple, performing 9,889 baptisms for the dead, 8,172 endowments for the dead, 2,486 proxy sealings of wives to husbands, and 5,850 proxy sealings of children to parents. Thirty-one families subscribed to the genealogical magazine. At the other end of the scale, many stakes had only a small number of families engaged in research and did little temple work, even if they were relatively close to temples. Some stakes did not report at all.[50]

The directors of the Society were concerned that Church members in the missions have the same instructions and challenges as those in the stakes. Church programs in the missions, however, were usually less organized than those in the stakes. Members in the missions were more scattered and in areas where temples and the facilities of the Society were not readily accessible. Elder John A. Widtsoe, president of the European Mission from 1927 to 1933, attempted to organize genealogical work on that continent. His plan was used and met with some success in a few branches. Later the directors of the Society attempted to organize all the missions along the same lines as the stakes, wherever it was feasible.[51]

Some satisfying success stories emerged as members outside the United States became more and more involved. In 1935, after working for one and one-half years, a committee in the Czecho-Slovak Mission presented its first group of names for temple work. They sent the names of eighty-two relatives to Salt Lake City in what they proudly dubbed "The First Czecho-Slovak Temple Excursion." In 1936 some Saints in the Joinville Brazil Branch organized the first Church genealogical society in that country, began to hold classes, and set up correspondence with Europe, particularly Germany. The fifty-nine members in the branch had an average attendance of thirteen in the eleven classes held that year—probably a better average than most wards in Utah.[52]

The success of the Church's genealogical program depended greatly on local genealogical leaders. They led the way in getting Church members involved in seeking out their ancestors and performing temple work. They were responsible for genealogical classwork. They recruited new members of the Society; sold subscriptions to the magazine; promoted various fund-raising activities, including a book fund for the genealogical library in Salt Lake City; organized research excursions to the library, especially when it appeared that names for temple work were running short; arranged for volunteers to help copy records, such as cemetery files; and helped index vital records. Their assigned activities included taking surveys of all ward families to ascertain what records the families had, whether they were converted to genealogy, and whether they were temple attenders. They were then to assist families that needed help in any respect.[53] Committee members also functioned as genealogical home teachers, spending at least one night a week visiting homes and instructing families in genealogical methods. The results of all this activity did not meet the Society's expectations, for while some committees took their responsibilities seriously, others simply did not follow through.[54]

Promotion of Local Activity

The Society supported the work of its local committees with a variety of programs and initiatives. These included regional genealogical conventions, genealogical classes in cooperation with the Mutual Improvement Association, separate genealogical classes on Mondays, genealogical Sunday, junior genealogical classes, and more. This program was designed to make genealogy as much a part of everyday Church activity as any other Church work.

At first, apparently, regional genealogical conventions consisted merely of meetings for stake representatives held in connection with general conferences in Salt Lake City. Then in the 1920s, the Society began to hold special conventions in the stakes, often with two or three stakes in combination. These conventions added to the demands placed on the time of Church members, but in the view of the Society, it was the most important time a person could contribute.[55] About half the stakes participated.[56]

The problem of financing the stake conventions came up for serious discussion in 1928. The directors of the Society decided to ask all genealogical workers in each stake to donate $.25 annually to a special fund to pay convention costs. Soon the Society established the policy of holding conventions only in those stakes that so contributed. In addition, the travel expenses of the representatives from Salt Lake City were kept at modest figures. In 1929, for example, fifty-four conventions were held at a total cost of $745.25, or $13.80 each. In 1934 sixty-three conventions cost about the same on average, and $179.87 was spent for a trip through several missions. Clearly, the dedicated representatives of the Society had no tendency toward padded expense accounts.[57]

At the suggestion of Elder John A. Widtsoe, the Society began to develop standardized programs for these stake conventions. Earlier programs emphasized doctrine, but eventually the standard programs also included practical instructions. Members of the board insisted that convention representatives be prepared to "give efficient, practical help and instructions, and not spend the time of the convention sermonizing on general doctrinal themes."[58]

The Society entrenched itself even more firmly into established local programs through the expansion of classwork in the wards. Some conflict was probably unavoidable, as the Society appeared to be encroaching on the grounds of other organizations. In the 1920s, the Church priesthood quorum meetings were held on Tuesday evening, after which the Mutual Improvement Association (MIA) held its classes. In 1928 the president of the MIA, George Albert Smith, invited the Society to conduct a genealogical class as part of the Mutual program. The Society readily agreed, although some misunderstanding arose when the MIA left the impression in its handbook that the genealogical class was a division of MIA, whereas the Society wanted it made clear that the class was under the direction of the Society and the ward bishop. Some people felt the class should be taught once or twice a month, while the Society wanted it taught at least three times. Such disagreements naturally irritated the leaders of the Church, who were already having difficulty enough attempting to correlate the various burgeoning Church programs.

In October 1931, Elder Melvin J. Ballard, general secretary of the MIA, and Elder Joseph Fielding Smith, president of the Society, both spoke out. "There should be no spirit of rivalry between members of the two groups, nor any thought that the success of one group is a corresponding detriment to the other," Elder Ballard read from a statement prepared by the leaders of the MIA. "Surely we can cooperate in attaining the same grand objective, the saving of souls." "There should be no rivalry, no petty jealousy," Elder Smith affirmed. "It is the same Church, the same Gospel, and all work towards the same ends."[59] The solution in this period was simply, as originally planned, for the ward MIA to have two classes for adults, one of which was genealogy, making the choice of which to attend optional. It was also agreed that, if the bishop saw fit, the genealogical class could be held on a night other than Tuesday.[60]

The general trend in the 1930s moved toward setting aside a special night for genealogical work in lieu of the Tuesday night class. In 1932, Monday night was designated as the regular night Churchwide for genealogical classes.[61] This schedule, too, did not work entirely smoothly. In 1936, for example, one stake president tried to persuade the genealogical committees to return to meeting with the MIA on Tuesday, so that Monday could be set side as "Home Night" in the stake. A long discussion among the board of directors ensued, and a kind letter was sent from Joseph Fielding Smith to the presumably erring stake president: "It was reported that in your stake there was a move on foot to make Monday evening 'Home Night,' thus taking away from the genealogical workers the night on which they meet," he wrote. He then reported that the Council of the Twelve had recently decided to suggest that Saturday night be designated "Home Night" throughout the Church. This, they felt, would be good preparation for the Sabbath and also would "put a stop to Saturday night parties and dances, which interfere so materially with the Sunday Schools the following morning." He further reminded the stake president that they had already tried meeting with the MIA—unsuccessfully. "We hope," he said, "that the workers in the genealogical work will not be deprived of the night which they have chosen."[62]

By the end of the 1930s, Monday night was generally accepted as genealogy night throughout the Church. While only a small percent of the ward members attended this class, those who did constituted a genealogical teaching force that was supposed to keep everyone else involved at least to some degree. The fourth Monday of each month was genealogical home teaching night, and the genealogical class was responsible to make the visits. "After the opening prayer," said the instructions from Church headquarters,

> the members should go out to their appointed districts for home teaching, two by two, and make short but helpful visits. Ascertain something about the person you are going to visit beforehand, and find where he needs your help. Give that help in the most efficient way you can, and be ready to report your visit at the next meeting of the committee.[63]

In the 1930s, the Society also established the fifth Sunday of any month that had five Sundays as "Genealogy Sunday." Local genealogical leaders planned and presented ward sacrament meeting programs on that day.

Even after all this activity, many local leaders were concerned that their ward members were not attending the temple often enough. As a result of this concern, some wards started a temple missionary program. Working with the ward genealogical committees, bishops called ward members on special missions to attend the temple at least once a week. In the Hillcrest Ward in Salt Lake City, for example, Bishop Oscar J. Harline in 1928 began to call groups of about twenty people on three-month temple missions. Later the time was reduced to two months. The results, the bishop reported, were greater spirituality, temple attendance, and temple worthiness. Many other wards had similar programs, sometimes involving especially the elderly or the unemployed in these callings.[64]

In 1934, however, Elder Joseph Fielding Smith objected to such mission calls. It would be like calling people on missions to attend sacrament meeting or to pay tithing, he said; these were things that members were supposed to do without special calls. Even though Joseph Christenson pointed out that this practice had been going on for years and that its discontinuance would "be detrimental to temple work and would leave the temples almost empty," Elder Smith took the matter to the First Presidency and the Twelve. The decision as announced to the board in February 1935 was that bishops and stake presidents could instruct, advise, persuade, and encourage temple attendance in every other way, but that formal mission calls were not to be issued. As a result, temple attendance decreased after the temple mission calls ceased. Years later, in 1949, the Society learned that some stakes were again issuing regular calls for temple missions, and Elder Smith again instructed the board that such calls were inappropriate.[65]

Another type of expansion occurred that the officers of the Society found undesirable. Apparently some missionaries were using genealogy as an approach to missionary work, and in 1939, President David O. McKay of the First Presidency questioned the advisability of this practice. Archibald F. Bennett, secretary of the Society, fully agreed and made efforts to so instruct the proper missionary officials.[66]

Genealogy and the Youth

The youth were not exempt from the work of the Genealogical Society. As early as 1922, the Primary Association of the Church, with the support and encouragement of the Society, sponsored temple excursions for children over eight to perform baptisms in behalf of the dead.[67] Nearly fifty thousand proxy baptisms were performed by Primary children in 1923.[68]

In addition, the young men (at that time, between the ages of twelve and twenty-one) and young women of similar age were urged to take a greater interest in genealogical work. Predictably, some zealous ward committeemembers soon suggested a junior genealogical class. One such person was Karl Weiss of the Salt Lake City Third Ward in the Liberty Stake. After accompanying the youth to the temple for baptisms, Weiss discovered that none of them kept records of the names for whom they had been baptized and they did not seem to understand the full importance of what they were doing. He was soon made chairman of his ward committee, and under his direction, the first junior genealogical class in his ward was held on 5 February 1929. Other wards followed suit. "There is a vast field here being now hardly touched," the Society noted with satisfaction at the end of the year.[69]

The board seized the opening quickly, and in October 1930, they officially approved a plan for junior genealogical classes Churchwide. Joseph Fielding Smith prepared the lesson material, which consisted of twelve lessons. Young men studied it as part of their weekly Aaronic Priesthood lessons, taking one lesson each month, and the young women participated though the weekly meetings of the MIA. The "Book of Remembrance" project received its start in these junior genealogical classes. As a place to record important personal experiences and collect genealogical records, the "Book of Remembrance" became an important tradition in households throughout the Church.[70]

By 1935, due to the fact that genealogical instruction in the priesthood quorums was only partially successful, the Society was encouraging the formulation of junior genealogical classes separate from other activities. A full course of study was prepared. The Society also proposed that the Sunday Schools and seminaries be encouraged to present genealogical lessons.[71] In at least one case, a bishop issued written "calls" to young people to attend the class. For a time in the early 1930s, even the Primary Association began to give genealogical and record-keeping instruction to children between the ages of eight and twelve.[72]

Although some people objected to requiring additional activity from young people, success stories poured in from various places in the Church. In 1940, for example, Weber Stake reported that 103 students received certificates for completing a junior genealogy course, and thirteen received fourth-year certificates. Cache Stake reported that many of its young people found more interest in the genealogy lessons than any other subject. From the mission field, the Columbia South Carolina Branch reported ten "Books of Remembrance" completed within the year.[73]

Not everyone, however, was convinced. Some stake and ward leaders were dismayed at the way such expanding programs were eating away at the time of the young people. Church activity on Sunday, MIA on Tuesday, the encouragement of at least one night a week as home night, along with studies and other school and social activities all combined to make enough activity. To take another night each week for a genealogical class seemed to go too far. So strong was the feeling among twelve stake presidents that, late in 1936, they wrote a combined letter to the First Presidency. It expressed the sentiments of all those who were concerned with the cumulative demands of the Church programs, as well as certain frustrations of Church leadership:

> In recent years there has been a marked tendency to multiply the calls made upon the time of our people, both old and young, until it is next to impossible to find a time when we can meet our children in the home circle.
>
> Our immediate problem has to do with the call made upon us to hold weekly junior genealogical classes for boys and girls. We recognize that there is great value in such training, but cannot a place be found for it in one of the organizations which is already functioning?

> In addition to all the Church organizations and activities we now have, and besides the school work and school socials and other functions that our young people are expected to participate in, it appears to us too much to lay it upon them as a duty to attend still another weekly class. We find that in many cases we cannot consistently ask attendance at these new classes on the part of our own children in addition to what they are already doing, and yet if we cannot ask it of our own, how can we consistently urge it upon others?
>
> If we demur to giving these new classes enthusiastic support, we are told by our genealogical workers that the movement is prescribed by the General Authorities of the Church, and we are thus placed in the light of being out of harmony with our leaders. We are, therefore, taking this opportunity to state our case to you in the hope that some way may be found to put this instruction in one of our present youth organizations, or if it may not at least be left optional with ward bishoprics depending upon local conditions and the kind of leadership available for such work.

Commenting on one bishop's practice of officially calling certain boys and girls to fulfill genealogical assignments, the presidents observed that these young people were usually the most active in other organizations and that parents felt they may well be overburdened "so that instead of finding pleasure in it, they will find it burdensome and distasteful. Yet parents are placed in the embarrassing position of having their children decline the bishop's call if the new activity is not undertaken. Such a situation appears to us very unfortunate."[74]

On December 22, that letter stimulated a lengthy discussion among the directors of the Society. Joseph Fielding Smith insisted that such an attitude was a blow at one of the most important activities ever instituted among young people. Not convinced by the stake presidents, the directors ended their meeting with a unanimous decision to emphasize junior genealogical work in the forthcoming conventions "more than ever before!"

The board also decided to send letters to forty-eight stake presidents in whose stakes junior classes had been conducted in order to obtain a wider sampling of opinion. Signed by Joseph Fielding Smith, the letter asked four basic questions: (1) What was the value of the junior genealogical program? (2) Had compulsory means been used to obtain attendance? (3) Were junior classes requiring too much time? (4): "In view of the vital character of the training afforded," what other ward organizations require youth attendance at night, and how much time do they demand?

Most stake presidents polled were highly supportive, agreed that junior genealogy should not be combined with MIA, thought it not too much to ask the youth to meet on Monday night, and assured Elder Smith that no compulsory means were used. The president of Cache Stake, for example, reported an enrollment of about 260 in the genealogical classes, mostly young people from sixteen to twenty-five years of age, and a 70 percent attendance record. "There is so much social activity among our high school and college students," he observed, "that we think no harm can come if we persuade them to miss a social in order to spend an hour in learning something of their ancestors." A few stake presidents, nevertheless, expressed mild reservations, mostly because they felt that the young people were already too busy and that taking another night for a Church program was a little too much. "I believe if this class could be made part of the Sunday School classes," wrote the president of the Oakland Stake, "then all the youth of the Church would get the benefit."[75]

The Society used these results to make an even stronger case for junior genealogy. On 18 January 1937, Elder Smith sent a circular to all stake presidents and bishops, reminding them of the importance of temple work in general and junior genealogical work in particular. "Strange as it may appear," he reported, "we have met with opposition, and there is a great deal of indifference shown by many officers in stakes and wards." He enclosed a list of twenty "invaluable and permanent benefits directly resulting from Junior Genealogical Classes" that had been "recently pointed out by a number of stake presidents." These were compiled from the responses to his earlier letter. He also included several impressive quotations from the supportive letters that had been received.[76]

Although concerns continued to be expressed from time to time, junior genealogical classes continued for another twenty years or more. Many young people received awards and certificates for work completed, and it became an important Church tradition for them to make temple excursions to perform baptisms. Some young people completed special genealogical projects, compiled personal pedigrees, and frequented cemeteries to copy information from tombstones for later compilation into genealogical records. Many people who later became prominent in genealogical work were first introduced to genealogy through the junior classes.

Other Genealogical Activities

The Society found many other ways to promote its interests. Genealogical conventions continued, speeches were sometimes broadcast over radio, and other genealogical programs of various sorts were presented whenever possible. Considerable energy was spent on pageants and other public productions. One of the earliest productions occurred in connection with the centennial of the first visit of the Angel Moroni to young Joseph Smith. It was celebrated on 6 October 1923 during general conference with the performance of an oratorio composed by B. Cecil Gates entitled *Salvation for the Dead.* The oratorio was prepared for performance under the auspices of Elder John A. Widtsoe and B. Cecil Gates and was sung by the Tabernacle Choir. Other pageants were presented on such themes as the ancestry of George Washington, Joseph Smith, Brigham Young, and prominent political and Church leaders. In 1936 a pageant marked the one hundredth anniversary of the visitation of Elijah to Joseph Smith. A few years later, the Old Testament prophet was also honored in a Tabernacle Choir production of Mendelssohn's *Elijah.*

With all this activity, the rooms provided for the Society at the Church Office Building on South Temple Street became cramped. The Society moved to larger quarters in the Joseph F. Smith Memorial Building, part of a complex recently vacated by the LDS College. The new headquarters occupied three floors of the newly renovated building, just north of the Hotel Utah. On the first floor was a two-hundred-seat classroom and the Temple Index Bureau. The archives, the business department, and the research department were given ample space on the second floor, and the third floor was devoted to a public reading room with a capacity for three hundred persons. This move was far more complicated than earlier moves. The Temple Index Bureau alone had six million name cards and was acquiring more at the rate of 400,000 per year, the library contained some 16,000

Joseph F. Smith Memorial Building, December 1933, at 80 North Main, Salt Lake City, location of the Genealogical Society, 1934–62.

volumes as well as an elaborate index, and the Society had a large staff of men and women serving the public.

Formal opening of the new quarters came with an open house on 17 January 1934. It was attended by nearly 5,000 people, some 2,000 of whom stayed for the public meeting in the fourth floor auditorium at 8:00 P.M. and heard several General Authorities remind them of the importance of the work in which they were engaged. The Spirit of the Lord, remarked Elder David O. McKay, had been felt not only by the Saints, but also by many others, causing them to collect their genealogies. "These have been made available to the Latter-day Saints, and proves to us conclusively that this is the time of fulfillment of the prophecy of Elijah."[77]

NOTES

[1]*Deseret News,* 17 December 1927.

[2]*Deseret News,* 27 March 1928.

[3]*Deseret News,* 11 November 1931, 18 December 1937.

[4]*Salt Lake Tribune,* 14 January 1934.

[5]L. Garrett Myers, oral history interviews by Bruce Blumell, 1976, typescript, James Moyle Oral History Program, interview 3, 2–3, Archives Division, Historical Department, The Church of Jesus Christ of Latter-day Saints, Salt Lake City (cited hereafter as LDS Church Archives). Also L. Garrett Myers, telephone interview by Jessie Embry, 20 January 1977. See also James M. Black, oral history interview by Bruce Blumell, 1975, typescript, James Moyle Oral History Program, interview 4, LDS Church Archives. Black says he did a lot of genealogy during this period because it was hard for him to get a job.

[6]Archibald F. Bennett, "Research Finds 'Lost Girl,'" *Instructor* 91 (December 1956): 384.

[7]This seems to be one implication of a speech given by Benjamin F. Cummings at the Granite Stake Genealogical Convention, 11 June 1917, though the intent of his comments was to encourage genealogical researchers to consult the index, then communicate with the people working on the line before they continued. B. F. Cummings, "Research Work and the Genealogical Society of Utah," *Utah Genealogical and Historical Magazine* 8 (July 1917): 135; 11 (January 1920): 44 (hereafter cited as *UGHM*).

[8]"The Library of the Genealogical Society of Utah," *UGHM* 10 (1919): 119.

[9]Mary Camenish, interview by James B. Allen, 3 March 1977, Provo, Utah, tape recording, LDS Church Archives.

[10]Camenish, interview.

[11]Camenish, interview.

[12]Genealogical Society Minutes, 22 April 1921, Family History Department of the Church (hereafter cited as FHD).

[13]Genealogical Society Minutes, 16 June 1922; Joseph Fielding Smith to Joseph R. Shepherd, 28 October 1922, Joseph Fielding Smith papers, LDS Church Archives; Joseph R. Shepherd to Joseph Fielding Smith, 27 October 1922, Joseph Fielding Smith papers, LDS Church Archives.

[14]Archibald F. Bennett, "The Growth of the Temple Index Bureau—a Worldwide Clearing House," *Improvement Era* 39 (April 1936): 219–20.

[15]Harry H. Russell to Genealogical Committee, 31 July 1932, Joseph Fielding Smith papers, LDS Church Archives.

[16]Harry H. Russell statement, dated 5 January 1932, Joseph Fielding Smith papers, LDS Church Archives; Harry H. Russell to Joseph Fielding Smith, 15 May 1932, Joseph Fielding Smith papers, LDS Church Archives. The mention of Provo is an allusion to the state mental hospital in Provo.

[17]Genealogical Society Minutes, 12 October 1926; Joseph Fielding Smith to President Heber J. Grant and counselors, 1 November 1926, as reported in Genealogical Society Minutes, 19 November 1926.

[18]Heber J. Grant to Joseph Fielding Smith, 1 June 1935, Joseph Fielding Smith papers, LDS Church Archives; Joseph Fielding Smith to Harry H. Russell, 3 June 1935.

[19]Harry H. Russell to Joseph Fielding Smith, 4 June 1935, Joseph Fielding Smith papers, LDS Church Archives.

[20]See discussion of "adoption" in chapter 1.

[21]Myers, interview 5, 1-2.

[22]*Handbook for Genealogy and Temple Work* (Salt Lake City: Genealogical Society of Utah, 1949), 13; Bennett, "The Growth of the Temple Index Bureau," 221; Archibald F. Bennett, *Saviors on Mount Zion* (Salt Lake City: Deseret News Press, 1960), 176.

[23]Genealogical Society Minutes, 23 November 1928, 22 March 1932; "Notice concerning the Gathering of Genealogy," *UGHM* 15 (July 1924): 144; "Questions Asked and Answered at the Inter-Stake Genealogical Convention, Idaho Falls, 12-13 December 1922," *UGHM* 14 (April 1923): 70; John A. Widtsoe, "Obtaining Scandinavian Genealogies," *UGHM* 19 (January 1928): 1; Clara J. Fargergren, "Ella Hecksher and Her Work," *UGHM* 19 (January 1928): 9; "Hans N. Ogaard and His Work: Genealogical Research in Denmark," *UGHM* 19 (January 1928): 12.

[24]*Deseret News,* 23 March 1935.

[25]Genealogical Society Minutes, 14 April 1936.

[26]*Handbook for Genealogy and Temple Work* (Salt Lake City: Genealogical Society of Utah, 1924), 318. There were numerous subsequent editions.

[27]Joseph Fielding Smith, and others, to Lillian Cameron, 1 July 1920, Genealogical Society correspondence, FHD.

[28]Genealogical Society Minutes, 10 April and 8 November 1923; *Deseret News,* 24 April 1923.

[29]Genealogical Society Minutes, 14 September 1924, 9 April 1928.

[30]Andrew K. Smith, "The Genealogical Research Bureau: Its Organization and How to Cooperate with It," *UGHM* 19 (July 1928): 114-23. Andrew K. Smith, "Extending the Benefits of the Research Clearing House to Those Compiling Their Own Genealogy," *UGHM* 18 (October 1927): 151-53; Andrew K. Smith, "Vicarious Offerings: The Research Clearing House," *UGHM* 18 (January 1927): 9-16.

[31]*Handbook for Genealogy and Temple Work,* 1949 ed., 13, 67-69.

[32]Genealogical Society Minutes, 20 December 1929, 11 April 1932, 9 April 1934, 26 March 1935, 21 January, 25 February 1936.

[33]Genealogical Society Minutes, 19 November 1931, 18 December 1934, 17 September 1935, 14 April 1937, 15 March, 20 November 1938, 7 November 1939.

[34]"Memberships," *UGHM* 30 (January 1939): 25.

[35]Genealogical Society Minutes, 22 March 1929; Myers, interview 3, 17.

[36]Archibald F. Bennett to Heber J. Grant in Genealogical Society Minutes, 25 September 1928.

[37]See, for example, Genealogical Society Minutes, 26 June 1926.

[38]Genealogical Society Minutes, 25 September 1928. Many other minutes in this period of time suggest the same concern, and some disapproval of the name gathering process. See also, "Our 'Responsibility' in Research and Temple Work," *UGHM* 20 (January 1929): 46-48.

[39]Genealogical Society Minutes, 25 September 1928.

[40]Genealogical Society Minutes, 25 September 1928.

[41]Genealogical Society Minutes, 2 July 1935. See also, minutes for 17 September 1935, where the board discussed the problem of the same researcher providing that kind of data for Saints in Idaho.

[42]Genealogical Society Minutes, 19 March 1939, which include a copy of the letter from Joseph Fielding Smith to Nicholas G. Smith, 6 March 1936.

[43]Minutes of the Board of Directors, 21 April 1942, 5:72, FHD.

[44]Joseph Fielding Smith, "The Genealogical Society, Its Purpose and Mission," an address to the Idaho Falls Genealogical Convention, 17-18 January 1922, *UGHM* 13 (April 1922): 75.

[45]*Deseret News,* 18 December 1920.

[46]One set of instructions clearly suggested the Society's negative attitude toward the lack of genealogical activity of many Church members. The ward committees, it said, were "to assist and supplement the work of the ward teachers in converting the negligent or the unconverted to the need of so living that they may become worthy of entering the House of the Lord." "Instructions for Stake and Ward Genealogical Workers," *UGHM* 14 (January 1923): 29. See also Genealogical Society Minutes, 18 June and 16 July 1920; *Handbook for Genealogy and Temple Work,* 1924 ed., 237-47.

[47]Genealogical Society Minutes, 11 April 1932.

[48]"Organization Chart for Stakes and Wards Recommended by the Genealogical Society of Utah," *UGHM* 28 (October 1937): 167.

[49]"Lesson Five: The Wise Appointment of Responsibilities," *UGHM* 25 (October 1934): 174.

[50]"Stake Genealogical Activities, 1 October, to 31 December 1937," *UGHM* 29 (April 1938): 82-83.

[51]Genealogical Society Minutes, 22 March 1929, 14 April 1931, 18 October 1932; *Millennial Star,* 19 September 1929; John A. Widtsoe, "European Program for Genealogical Study, Research and Exchange," *UGHM* 21 (January 1930): 33-34; John A. Widtsoe, "Genealogical Activities in Europe," *UGHM* 22 (July 1931): 97-106.

[52]Spencer L. Taggert, "The First Czecho-Slovak Temple Excursion," *UGHM* 26 (October 1935): 183; *Deseret News,* 23 January 1937.

[53]Nephi Anderson, "Duties of Ward Committees," in report of Idaho Falls Genealogical Convention, *UGHM* 13 (April 1922): 59-62.

[54]Genealogical Society Minutes, 21 May 1926; Richard B. Summerhays to stake representatives, 11 August 1926, Genealogical Society circular letters, LDS Church Archives; "Field Notes for Genealogical Committeemen: Home Teaching," *UGHM* 24 (July 1933): 112-18; Part II of a lesson outline, "The Art of Home Teaching," *UGHM* 26 (January 1935): 17-48; "Senior Classwork Department: Teaching One Another, Lessons 31-38," *UGHM* 31 (January 1940): 40-45; home teaching department in various issues of *UGHM,* 1930s especially.

[55]Genealogical Society Minutes, 15 November 1924, 14 April 1936; George D. Pyper to Archibald F. Bennett, 16 October 1936, copy in Joseph Fielding Smith papers, LDS Church Archives.

[56]In 1930, for example, there were 104 stakes. Sixty-four had contributed to the convention fund and sixty conventions were held. In 1935 there were 115 stakes and seventy-nine conventions were held. Genealogical Society Minutes, 23 January 1931, 21 January 1936.

[57]Genealogical Society Minutes, 30 October and 23 November 1928, 20 December 1929, 23 January 1931, 28 January 1933, 9 April 1934, 5 February 1935, 21 January 1936; Letter from Archibald F. Bennett to stake representatives, 7 December 1928, Genealogical Society circular letters, LDS Church Archives.

[58]Genealogical Society Minutes, 2 April 1935. See also the program for one of the early conventions as outlined in *Deseret News,* 25 November 1922, and compare with later programs as outlined in *Deseret News,* 14 January 1933, and "Convention Program for 1939," *UGHM* 30 (January 1939): 23–24.

[59]*Deseret News,* 5 October 1931.

[60]*Deseret News,* 5 October 1931; "Weekly Genealogical Classes," *UGHM* 19 (October 1928): 181–82; "Weekly Genealogical Classes," Lesson Department, *UGHM* 20 (January 1929): 45–46; Ethel I. Bird, "A Successful Class in Genealogy," *UGHM* 20 (April 1929): 86–87; "Genealogical Classes in the MIA," *UGHM* 21 (January 1930): 31–33; *Deseret News,* 15 November 1930; Joseph Fielding Smith to ward bishoprics, 30 August 1928, Genealogical Society circular letters, LDS Church Archives; Genealogical Society Minutes, 21 September 1928, 10 June 1930.

[61]Archibald F. Bennett to stake representatives, 1 June 1932, Genealogical Society circular letters, LDS Church Archives.

[62]Genealogical Society Minutes, 7, 14 April 1936. The lessons offered by the Society were not limited to the "how-to" aspects of genealogy. In 1924 the Society published its *Handbook for Genealogy and Temple Work,* prepared by Susa Young Gates. Its twenty-nine chapters contained both doctrinal and practical instruction. The lessons for 1928 were based on the text *Seeking after Our Dead,* much of which was doctrinal in nature. In 1931, Joseph Fielding Smith's *The Way to Perfection* was published. This series of purely doctrinal essays provided lesson material for nearly a year and a half. Lesson outlines, based on the forty-nine chapters in the book, were published in the genealogical magazine. Then came a three-year instruction program in which the first year (1933) consisted of doctrinally oriented lessons entitled *Our Lineage* and the second was a practical series of administrative lessons, *Church Service on Genealogical Committees.* The rotation began again in 1937 with *The Way to Perfection,* then in 1939–40 a new manual, *Teaching One Another,* was added. Written like a story, each lesson centered around an episode in the life of the fictional George Brown, who became a genealogical worker and, finally, chairman of the genealogical committee in his ward. It contained a mixture of doctrinal and practical lessons.

[63]Genealogical Society of Utah, *Teaching One Another* (Salt Lake City: Genealogical Society of Utah, 1938), 24.

[64]Oscar J. Harline, "What Temple Work Did for Our Ward," *UGHM* 25 (October 1934): 150–51; Walter M. Everton, "Devices for Increasing Temple Attendance," *UGHM* 24 (April 1933): 72–73; Joseph Christenson and Archibald F. Bennett to Joseph Fielding Smith, 18 December 1934, Genealogical Society correspondence, FHD; Myers, interview 3, 2–3.

[65]Genealogical Society Minutes, 18 December 1934, 5 February 1935, 19 May 1936, 15 March 1949.

[66]Archibald F. Bennett to David O. McKay, 3 November 1939, David O. McKay papers, LDS Church Archives.

[67]Schedule accompanying letter from Genealogical Society to stake representatives, 31 October 1924, Genealogical Society circular letters, LDS Church Archives.

[68]Clara W. Beebe, "Temple Work," *Children's Friend* 23 (November 1924): 342.

[69]Harold Lundstrom, "Silver Jubilee . . . for Junior Genealogists," *Church News,* 6 February 1954; Genealogical Society Minutes, 20 December 1929.

[70]Genealogical Society Minutes, 10 October 1930, 11 November 1930; "Instructions on Junior Baptismal Work for Stakes within the Salt Lake Temple District, 1 January 1931," *UGHM* 22 (April 1931): 72-73; "Genealogical Activities for the Lesser Priesthood," *UGHM* 22 (July 1931): 111-12; *Deseret News,* 31 October 1931.

[71]Genealogical Society Minutes, 27 May 1932, 5 February, 8 and 22 October 1935, 20 October and 3 November 1936; "Field Notes for Genealogical Committeemen," *UGHM* 24 (April 1933): 65-72.

[72]Genealogical Society Minutes, 25 November 1932; *Deseret News,* 3 December 1932.

[73]Lloyd T. Kidd, "Junior Classes in the Southern States," *UGHM* 31 (January 1940): 46-47; "Our Slogan," *UGHM* 31 (January 1940): 47.

[74]Genealogical Society Minutes, 22 December 1936. Interestingly two future General Authorities were among the signers of the letter: Marvin O. Ashton and Harold B. Lee.

[75]Elder Smith's letter plus many of the replies, and some excerpts from the replies, are found in the Joseph Fielding Smith papers, LDS Church Archives.

[76]Joseph Fielding Smith to presidents of stakes and bishops of wards, 18 January 1937, Joseph Fielding Smith papers, LDS Church Archives.

[77]Genealogical Society Minutes, 27 February 1932, 28 January 1933; *Deseret News,* 19 August and 29 September 1933, 6, 16 and 18 January 1934; Journal History 21 July 1933; Widtsoe, "Opening of Our New Home," *UGHM* 25 (April 1934): 51-60.

Society staff, 1954. Courtesy Frank Smith.

Chapter 4

Quest for Effectiveness, 1940–1960

Even though most Latter-day Saints were unforgettably aware of the importance of seeking out their ancestors, not all were involved in doing so. Only a small percentage, in fact, were actively engaged in research. Nevertheless, most were directly affected by the Church's commitment to genealogy. Genealogical classes for all age groups, genealogy home teachers, temple excursions, genealogy conventions, genealogy sermons in worship services, the genealogical magazine, and sermons on the doctrinal commitment of the Church were all basic elements of the LDS mosaic. In combination, these highly visible activities regularly pricked the conscience of every member.

Genealogical research took time and patience, and many Church members seemed not to have enough of either. Often they could point with pride to some family member, usually a sister, a cousin, or an aunt, who was the official or unofficial family genealogist, and who, in effect, was doing all the research for the entire family. They squirmed uncomfortably when asked about their own genealogical activity, but they were convinced of its importance, willing to work in the temple, and usually ready to contribute money for family research.

Between 1940 and 1960, the Society moved in some significant new directions. The major quest at midcentury was for more effectiveness, which meant striving for better classwork, more thorough correlation with other Church organizations, more efficient record-gathering and research programs, improved public relations with Church members, and greater progress toward eliminating duplication and error. The major challenge was achieving a suitable balance between the needs and capacities of the central facilities of the Society in Salt Lake City and the desires and limited opportunities of Church members outside of Utah.

Correlation, 1940

One important achievement was the integration of genealogical instruction into the Sunday Schools—something the Society had attempted previously but could not accomplish until Church leaders themselves began to press for consolidation of the Church's growing programs. The vested interests of the various organizations made earlier attempts at correlation extremely difficult. The late 1930s saw a renewal of the effort to correlate activities. By 1940 the Church had established a Church Union Board consisting of representatives from the Relief Society, Sunday School, Young Men's and Young Women's Mutual Improvement Associations, the Primary, and the Genealogical Society. One of the major purposes of the Union Board was to attempt to correlate study programs.[1]

The Society had been criticized for holding weekday classes that added to the already heavy meeting schedule for members. Society leaders continually proposed that genealogical instruction be incorporated into other organizations, particularly the Sunday School. As early as 1937, Archibald F. Bennett began negotiating with the Sunday School board regarding that possibility.[2] By mid-June 1940, they finally agreed that genealogical instruction should be incorporated into Sunday School lessons at the ten- and eleven-year-old level, the fifteen- and sixteen-year-old level, the missionary training course, the adult gospel doctrine class, "and in other courses as often as occasion is offered for emphasis upon the application of subjects of genealogical interest."[3]

The First Presidency quickly approved the plan. The Society had gained nearly everything it had been striving for with respect to genealogical instruction in the Sunday School. Moreover, representatives of the Society were officially placed on the Sunday School board.[4]

At the same time, the Society suffered the disappointment of losing its magazine. In May 1940, a subcommittee of the Union Board was formed to review the Church's publications program and to make recommendations to the First Presidency.[5] J. Reuben Clark Jr., a member of the First Presidency, had previously suggested that the *Improvement Era,* the *Instructor* (the Sunday School magazine), the *Weekday Religious Education* (a magazine for seminary and institute teachers), and the *Utah Genealogical and Historical Magazine* be combined. The Union Board made the same recommendation. The officers of the Society were distressed, not only because they would no longer have their own magazine, but also because the Society would lose about $1,000 per year in subscriptions. Joseph Fielding Smith suggested that if the *Era* became the combined Church magazine, the Society should ask to share in its profits. This idea was never seriously considered, and the decision was made to discontinue the genealogical magazine. In its place, the *Improvement Era* incorporated a genealogical section that began in 1940 and continued until 1954.[6]

Nevertheless, the magazines were not fully consolidated. The genealogy and religious education magazines were both discontinued, but the *Instructor* continued for another thirty years. This situation did not sit well with some genealogical leaders, who made sporadic, but unsuccessful, attempts to get their magazine reinstated. As late as 1961, Joseph Fielding Smith was still complaining that even though the Society was required to give up its magazine, "virtually all the others still continue to publish their separate magazines."[7]

One goal of the correlation effort was to reduce the number of meetings members were expected to attend, and the Society cooperated fully. As soon as the Sunday School plan was announced, the Society canceled all local genealogical conventions, including those already scheduled. It also eliminated weekday classes. In October 1941, the genealogical meeting usually held in connection with general conference was also canceled. Eight years later, Archibald F. Bennett wanted to reinstitute a meeting at conference time, but Joseph Fielding Smith quickly vetoed the idea because of the continuing concern among Church leaders that too many meetings were being held.[8]

In August 1940, the Society board announced its plans for implementing the new program in the stake and ward genealogical committees. Genealogical home teaching was scaled down, so that these specialized home teachers would no longer be expected to visit and instruct every family. Instead, help would be given only to those who requested it. The board saw in the new program a chance to give Melchizedek Priesthood quorums more direct responsibility for temple work. Stake and ward committees, therefore, were each to have a chairman who was a high priest and two assistants, one of whom was a seventy[9] and the other an elder.

In October 1940, Elder John A. Widtsoe commented on these changes in an address to the last genealogical conference held in connection with a general conference. Referring to the genealogical class in Sunday School, he declared, "I am really thrilled, for here is not only the opportunity for a few to receive technical instruction in genealogy, but the possibility for every member of the Church to receive such instruction." Then, alluding to problems still perceived by the Society, Elder Widtsoe reminded his listeners that "we have had some difficulty in bringing about the establishment of classes in genealogy" and, further, that "only a small number of the membership of the Church [are] engaged in this work." With careful preparation, wise organization, good teaching, and cooperation between the boards of the Sunday School and the Society, the problems could be solved and all members, both young and old, could be taught the principles of genealogy.[10]

Retreat from Retrenchment

Retrenchment did not last long, however. Despite the 1940 decision that local committees would no longer visit every home in the ward, when the officers of the Society perceived activity languishing, they renewed their efforts to get every Church member involved. By 1945 the Society had approved the enlargement of ward committees to enable them to do more effective home teaching.[11] The 1949 handbook outlined an elaborate training program and specified that, eventually, "every family in the ward should be visited by [genealogical] home teachers."[12]

Not all wards fully followed the Society's instructions—probably only a minority even came close. Many had difficulty simply staffing their committees, and it was a common complaint that bishops used the best people in other organizations. But regardless of such grievances, the expanded view of the mission of the genealogical committee had been officially reestablished.

Just as it was impossible to retrench for long in home teaching, it was also impossible to eliminate genealogical conventions. In spite of the official announcement, as early as 19 November 1940 the officers of the Society were discussing the possibility of again holding conventions,[13] though not at general conference and not as extensively as before. In less than a year after the conventions were officially canceled, the president of the Rexburg stake expressed concern over a decline in temple work. The board of directors agreed to hold a regional convention in Rexburg, as well as other places, if necessary. By September 1941, genealogical conventions had been held in a number of stakes.[14] The attitude, it appears, was one of general cooperation with the original retrenchment idea, but only so long as it did not seriously retard genealogical activity.

In December 1941, the United States entered World War II, and the Church had to curtail travel and other expenses. Stake genealogical conventions were again discontinued, as were excursions to temples outside one's own district.[15] When it became apparent that the Society was losing touch with its stake workers, it assigned Joseph Christenson to visit as many stakes as possible during the wartime emergency. He was not to hold conventions, but he was to maintain personal ties between the Society and local workers.[16]

The Society also found other ways to promote its interests during the war. In 1942 Church leaders allowed local genealogical committees to present ward sacrament meeting programs on the Sunday evening of stake conferences, although the committees were encouraged to cooperate with the Sunday School in doing so. The Relief Society, the Sunday School, the Mutual Improvement Associations, the Primary Association, and the Genealogical Society were also authorized to hold special meetings on the evening of "Fast Sunday"—the first Sunday of each month, when no other meetings were normally held in the wards.

The Society officers realized that another genealogical meeting would not be universally popular. In preparation for the meeting of 3 January 1943, therefore, they instructed local workers to announce the topic in such a way that it did not appear to be simply another genealogy meeting. The announced theme for the evening meeting was "Who am I and What is my Mission?" In a letter, Archibald Bennett advised the stake chairmen to "let the appeal of the question be the attraction. Some folks, you know, would absent themselves if they knew it was to be a genealogy program regardless of how interesting the message."[17] These special Fast Sunday evening meetings continued for many years after the war.

Before the war was over, pressures were building to begin genealogical conventions anew. The Sunday School, MIA, and Primary were holding what amounted to conventions—so why not the Society? In November 1944, Elder John A. Widtsoe reported to the board that in his visits among the stakes he found little genealogical work being done, and he stressed the need for conventions as a remedy. A few stake conventions were held early in 1945. By December the board was approving them on a regional basis and had even appointed a convention committee. In August 1945, after wartime gasoline rationing had been lifted, the First Presidency officially authorized the resumption of regional meetings for all auxiliaries, including the Genealogical Society. The Society immediately drew up a schedule and proposed a budget for the 1946 conventions. Additional people were appointed to assist the officers of the Society in visiting conventions, which were held in most of the stakes or regions of the Church in 1947. That year the official convention slogan was "Trace the Forefathers of the Pioneers and Gather their records with our might from every land."[18]

The program for genealogical conventions was always outlined by the board. The 1959 conventions, for example, began with a stake leadership meeting emphasizing home teaching and planning for research and temple work, followed by a general assembly in which a filmstrip on the new microfilming program was presented.[19] Sometimes conventions would cover two days—Saturday and Sunday. In general, officers of the Society believed the conventions were among their most effective activities; they motivated local leaders, involved large numbers of people in special training sessions, and provided opportunities for the presentation of special Church-produced filmstrips and movies. The first movie, "The Hearts of the Children," was produced in 1959 and shown at all the 1960 conventions.[20]

By the 1950s, the Society and its local committees were engaged in a wide range of activities. They were conducting classes, promoting research and temple activity, holding local socials, participating in various special programs and pageants, checking records, and doing whatever else seemed necessary to stimulate those who had not yet caught the vision. The Society also sponsored a project to copy information from gravestones for the library collection. Every stake was asked to check the cemeteries within its boundaries, and, if the Society did not have the cemetery records, to make arrangements to copy the sexton's records and the gravestones.[21] In August 1949, an article in the *American Cemetery Magazine* caught the flavor of this activity by reporting the avocation of Gertrude Jones of Buffalo, New York. Entitled "Tombstone Detective," the article noted that Jones had visited over one hundred old cemeteries in western New York and western Pennsylvania and had prepared over 10,000 records. "She takes her lunch basket, crowbar, trench shovel, wooden support and pads of paper and does a good deal of hill climbing in the pursuit which is not for the sedentary mind." As a member of the Church, Jones explained to the reporter the doctrinal basis for her interest and indicated that many volunteers as well as paid workers were collecting such data.[22]

Cooperation with the Sunday School

Meanwhile, the correlation effort of 1940 gave the Society high hopes for the genealogical training class in Sunday School, which would use a text entitled *Out of the Books.* Originally designed as a one-year course for people over eighteen, within a year it was modified to be a two-year course. However, the Sunday School class could not sustain a high enough level of interest to hold many people for a two-year period; in 1944 only 48 percent of the Sunday Schools in the Church were holding genealogical classes.[23] Many might be surprised to see nearly half the wards of the Church sponsoring regular genealogical instruction, yet the response was disappointing to the Society leaders, who felt genealogical classes by then should have saturated the Church.

In February 1945, Archibald F. Bennett reported that local Sunday School superintendencies were "lukewarm and half-hearted" in their support for the class and that they eagerly seized upon any pretext to discontinue it. Lack of space, repetition, and the elective nature of the course were all frequent excuses. The solution, Bennett believed, was to "promote" people automatically to the genealogical class after two years in the Gospel Message class, to design a better two-year course, and to press for "more authoritative Official Endorsement." George R. Hill, general superintendent of the Sunday School, agreed with some of his suggestions but objected that a two-year course competed with the adult's Gospel Doctrine class.[24]

Whatever the problem, clearly the class was not overwhelmingly popular in most wards, and complaints poured in during the late 1940s and the 1950s.[25] In 1945 a stake genealogical supervisor protested that the text was uninteresting and noted that some successful teachers were using alternate course materials. A. William Lund, chairman of the Sunday School's genealogical training program, replied that others had found the text to be very good. He reminded the local leader that the first qualification of any supervisor or teacher was to be loyal to the prescribed course.[26]

There were other complaints: people were not interested, the same textbooks were used too frequently, there was not enough advanced material for people who had already been in the class for a year, and the course was not practical enough in its orientation. Nevertheless, the class continued, and the General Authorities gave it their full blessing and support. Considering the fact that the class remained elective in nature, it attracted a fair number of people, both young and old, throughout the Church.

Revival of Independent Classwork

Another step toward the near nullification of correlation and retrenchment was the reinauguration of junior genealogical classes independent of the Sunday School, albeit not directly under the supervision of the Society. Archibald F. Bennett pressed for junior classes as early as February 1945, but Elder Joseph Fielding Smith, remembering the problems of the 1930s, simply replied that it would not be wise to attempt to hold such classes on a week night. In August another member of the board of directors, James M. Kirkham, raised the issue again, and Elder Smith advised that they be patient for a while.[27] By December 1947, however, Elder Smith apparently had been patient long enough. Bennett raised the issue again, and Elder Smith agreed to have plans made for junior classes. A year later, he gave his support to both junior genealogical classes and regular classes for the ward committee. He did so, he said, because of "lack of enthusiastic support being given the classes in the Sunday School."[28] But the First Presidency rejected the idea, explaining that they did not think the juniors would be willing to meet either during the week or on Sunday afternoon and suggesting that the Society work out some adjustments with the Sunday School. The Society immediately set up meetings with the Sunday School superintendency, but with no results.

Dissatisfied with the progress being made, the Society began to branch out again beyond the Sunday School. In February 1949, Archibald F. Bennett and L. Garrett Myers, who had been appointed as a classwork committee, proposed new senior and junior genealogical classes to be held on Sunday afternoons at 3 P.M.[29] Three days later, Joseph Fielding Smith officially wrote the First Presidency of the Church urging a new look at the classwork program. After listing several compelling reasons,[30] he recommended a weekly class for genealogical leaders, a four-year course for youth ages twelve and over and asked that both these classes be held either Sunday afternoon or on a week night. After considerable discussion, however, the First Presidency decided not to adopt the plan.[31] In 1952 the board of directors was still making proposals for sponsoring junior classes outside the Sunday School.[32]

Many local wards, meanwhile, began holding their own junior genealogical classes outside the official auspices of either the Sunday School or the Society, although with the knowledge of both. Conducted under the direction of the ward genealogical committees and approved by the bishops, the classes were not bound by Sunday School time constraints and were not dependent upon the Sunday School for teachers. In the Mesa Arizona Stake, for example, the ward and stake committees agreed that Sunday School was not the place for junior genealogical class work. By 1957 the stake had at least one youth class in each ward. Some wards had three classes: a beginning, an advanced, and a special research class. They used the two-year course of study provided for the Sunday School. The genealogical leaders of that stake felt their program was so successful that they urged the Society to sponsor a similar program Churchwide.[33]

Many of these classes began with great enthusiasm. A total of 150 youth were enrolled in the Mesa Stake in 1952. The classes in some wards, however, were short-lived. Certain bishops, much to the consternation of local genealogical leaders, complained that the Church's youth program was already full and that the junior classes were not officially recommended.[34] Apparently, whatever happened on a local basis was strictly outside the auspices of the Society, but from such scattered places as Logan, Utah; Mesa, Arizona; Los Angeles, California; and Cowley, Wyoming came reports of more or less successful youth classes outside the Sunday School.

The Society also began to hold classes again, independent of the Sunday School, in the 1950s. An evening course of twenty-eight lessons was taught at the Society's library for any stake that would send thirty to seventy people.[35] In some cases, stakes held their own genealogical schools and workshops, which the Society approved. It disapproved, however, of individuals going outside their own stakes on their own initiative to offer courses of instruction.[36]

Junior genealogical instruction resurfaced as an issue at the Society board meeting on 1 November 1957. A committee was appointed to make a list of the stakes where independent classes were organized, with the idea in mind of again seeking permission from the First Presidency for the Society to resume full responsibility for the genealogical training of the youth.[37] Even with the support of some Sunday School board members, however, nothing was done officially to reinstate junior genealogy as part of the program of the Society. Church leaders still opposed holding weeknight classes, even though many wards were doing just that and even though it was becoming increasingly difficult to find a time on Sundays when chapels were not in use.[38]

Junior classes continued for a few years where there were enthusiastic leaders, but they had disappeared almost completely by the end of the 1960s. At the same time, the original Sunday School program for youth was gradually discontinued, although the special genealogical training class in Sunday School for all ages was retained. It is also noteworthy that in many university wards, particularly those for young married students, the genealogical class was well attended.[39]

Corporate Reorganization

The year 1944 marked the fiftieth anniversary of the organization of the Genealogical Society of Utah. It also marked the legal expiration of the original Articles of Incorporation. Church and Society leaders began to reconsider the organization of the Society and plan a major shift in its status.

As early as 1941, President J. Reuben Clark Jr. suggested that after 1944 the Society should be officially brought under the auspices of the Church. The board agreed. Even though the Society was incorporated under the laws of Utah as a separate entity, approximately 98 percent of its budget came from the Church. In 1943, for example, the Society had an income of only $2,400 beyond what it received from the Church, yet it spent $150,000.[40]

In March 1944, the members of the First Presidency officially advised the Society that they desired that it become "wholly a Church institution" and that all annual membership fees be dropped. With regard to people who had become life members, the First Presidency suggested that it would be better to repay their fees in full, if necessary, "so as to leave the library and records of the Society wholly under the control of the Church." This decision was made not only because the Church was footing the bills, but also because the Society housed certain confidential records that the First Presidency felt it important to control. As a public corporation, the Society would have a more difficult time restricting access to records, but as a Church institution, it could withhold or restrict the use of whatever seemed appropriate.[41] In November the Society became a Church corporation with a new name: the Genealogical Society of The Church of Jesus Christ of Latter-day Saints. The requirement for membership fees was rescinded.[42]

When the members of the Society voted to change the nature of the organization, they naturally recalled the struggles and concerns of those who founded it fifty years earlier. At the suggestion of John A. Widtsoe, Elder Mark E. Petersen composed a short statement of appreciation for those early stalwarts. The statement, along with their names, was placed in the minutes. Had any of the founders been at the 1944 meetings, they would have been astonished at what had happened to the organization they pioneered. The Society employed over one hundred people,[43] directed research in many parts of the world, housed an extensive library and research bureau, operated an impressive temple index bureau, and controlled $109,000 in financial assets that would be turned over to the Church.[44]

A few seasoned genealogical leaders may have been slightly dismayed that the Society was giving up the technically independent status it had enjoyed for half a century.[45] If such concerns were felt, however, they were soon set aside, for the work of the Society continued to expand. Beginning in 1945, a number of assistants were assigned to help with the growing number of genealogical conventions and instructional programs.[46]

The work of the Society grew so much that organizational refinements were needed. In 1951 the board of directors formed an executive committee that would meet weekly to consider all activities of the Society. The full board would meet monthly. The primary full-time managers were Archibald F. Bennett, executive secretary and librarian, and L. Garrett Myers, superintendent and personnel director.[47] In 1961, Myers's assignment was enlarged. He supervised an office manager, A. Phillip Cederlof; an administrator of the Microfilm Division, T. Harold Jacobson; and an assistant superintendent, George H. Fudge. Fudge supervised the Records Division, directed by Elwin W. Jensen; the Library Division, directed by Ellen Hill; the Research Division, directed by Henry E. Christiansen; and the information and public service program.[48]

The expanding work of the Society was dramatically reflected in its growing budgets. Like any Church organization, it was constantly being asked by the Church committee on expenditures to trim expenses and cut the annual requests. Nevertheless, the budget gradually expanded from $743,000 in 1948 to over $1 million in 1955 and nearly $2 million in 1960.[49] The increase in spending was due to an expanding library program, increasing temple attendance (which meant more time and expense to clear and process names), and the rapidly growing microfilm program. In 1957 it was reported that the amount of temple work had doubled in the previous four years alone.[50]

Name Submission Controls

A major innovation in the process of submitting names for temple work occurred in the early 1940s. Many submissions for temple work remained incomplete and inaccurate. In 1938 the Salt Lake Temple presidency grew deeply concerned and appointed a "censor committee" to double check the information on names submitted there. The presidency observed that the temple was censoring (that is, correcting) half the records it received. They proposed that the Church establish a central auditing committee within either the Society or the Temple Index Bureau. The presidency even expressed willingness to transfer their censors to the bureau, thus preventing extra expense for the Church.[51]

The Society was already checking submissions against the Temple Index Bureau file to avoid duplicate ordinance work, but it was not willing to assure the accuracy and completeness of the submissions. Joseph Fielding Smith was cautious. He argued that the proposed procedure would slow down the work at the Index Bureau and require the additional expense of hiring younger, more alert, people. He was not convinced that the number of errors then being made justified the amount of time and expense necessary to correct them. He preferred greater effort in teaching people in general how to submit information correctly in the first place.[52]

Finally, in November 1939, an extensive report was presented to the Society that eventually resulted in the implementation of an entirely new program to control the submission of names for temple work. The new program augmented the Temple Index Bureau objective of preventing duplication of ordinances with three new objectives: (1) to make it unnecessary to copy and recopy records, with the attendant problem of continual proofreading by patrons and temple staffs; (2) to avoid duplication of research; (3) to eliminate "promiscuous name-gathering regardless of relationship."[53] Two years were required to finalize plans and to acquire the needed supplies and equipment. On 1 January 1942, the new program was put into effect, and it remained in place for the next twenty-seven years until replaced by computerized names processing.

Under the new program, the Church Genealogical Archives was renamed the Church Records Archives and was merged with the Temple Index Bureau into the Record Department. A staff of record examiners was employed to review and correct all family group sheets submitted for temple work. This, in effect, was the censor committee that had been previously suggested. An elaborate procedure regulated the movement of family group sheets and Temple Index Bureau cards through censoring, indexing, correction, typing, and proofreading sections; to the temples for ordinance work; then back to the Society for permanent filing, with copies mailed to patrons for their records.[54]

The decision to use the family group sheets as the name submission form was an equally significant change in facilitating name processing for temple work. Prior to 1942, a deceased person's name would appear on many separate forms before all of his or her required temple ordinances were performed. An investigating committee discovered that sometimes a name was recorded up to sixty different times before the temple work was complete. The family group sheet consolidated and replaced all other submission sheets, providing significant savings for Church members preparing names for temple work. Revised from an early family group sheet, the new sheet had spaces for vital information, such as birth and death dates, and space for recording the dates of temple ordinances.[55] Thus, the family group sheet became a single reference point for both research results and temple ordinance data.

When the ordinance work was complete, the clerks placed the finalized group record into a newly created file called the Main Record Archive. This archive served as the primary source of information for temple work performed after 1942 until computers took over the function of recording temple work in 1969. In addition, the Society used the Main Record Archive to provide

Staff checking the Temple Index Bureau card index, ca. 1960. Each name submission was checked against this index of temple endowments.

a new service known as the "research survey." For $2.50, the Society offered the services of a skilled researcher to compare information on a patron's pedigree chart against the compiled records of the Record Department and to provide guidance from the library catalog on original sources for continued research.[56] This new program was a giant step toward the continuing goals of keeping better records, promoting more efficient research, and offering improved service from the Society.

As a result of the increasing demand for temple names and the revamped name submission procedures, Society resources were strained. In the first five months of the new names submission program, 70,000 family group sheets were sent to the Index Bureau for checking. The Record Department found it impossible to handle the volume, and a massive backlog developed. This, in turn, led to a concern that there would not be enough names available for temple patrons. In this mild crisis, the Society decided to close the library to the public while the Salt Lake Temple was closed for vacation in July 1942. Employees of both the temple and the Society could then help catch up on the work. The Society also suggested that all the Utah temples temporarily decrease the number of temple sessions and that all temple typists who could be spared be sent to work in Salt Lake City.[57]

The process required to clear names for temple ordinances continued to move more slowly than the demand for names at the temple. In a lengthy response to a 1944 letter from Joseph Fielding Smith inquiring why the temple index file was not up to date, L. Garrett Myers rehearsed a litany of problems. Temple work had already been done for many of the names being submitted (320,000 out of the 781,500 submitted in 1943, for example). Many records submitted were incomplete and inaccurate, making it difficult to clear them. Poor record keeping had resulted in proxy ordinances for some individuals having been performed under as many as thirteen different names. Adding to these complications were the numerous "emergency" requests from people traveling through Utah who wanted temple work done immediately—often in behalf of young men who had been killed in military action. At times fourteen to twenty-five Society workers were engaged in such emergency service. Myers was sympathetic with these requests but less sympathetic with people who were gathering names and not doing genealogy. Some members simply wanted to do temple work for celebrities, even though such indiscriminate name gathering was strictly against the rules of the Society. Myers was particularly displeased with those who had what he called a "Royalty complex" and who delighted in trying to "effect a connection with and to perform temple work for every king and potentate of record."[58]

By midcentury the Record Department was a beehive of activity as family group sheets poured in. In 1944 the archives added a total of 105,938 family group sheets to its holdings.[59] At one time in 1952, the archives were so heavily used by patrons that the recording work fell into arrears. Joseph Fielding Smith ordered the archives closed to the public for three months in order to catch up.[60]

The typing department maintained a staff of skilled employees qualified to type in English, Scandinavian, German, French, Swiss, and Dutch. At the beginning of 1944, the Society kept thirty typists busy on two shifts. They were capable of turning out nearly 3,000 record sheets a day. The proofreading department also kept busy, with its staff of linguistically competent people double-checking on the typists. Finally, the censor

Family Group Records Archive, ca. 1960, in the Joseph F. Smith Memorial Building. Family group sheets were prepared by the Society from names submitted for temple work, 1942–69.

department provided a final check on the accuracy of records, either clearing them for temple work or returning them to the patron for further research and verification.[61]

Clearing names for temple work was vastly more complicated than anyone had anticipated, and the reasons for the slowdown at the index bureau went beyond those outlined in Myers's letter. Its employees were highly transient, due, in part, to low wages as well as the policy of not allowing young women to work for the Church after they married. Training new workers slowed the pace of activity.[62] Moreover, people with the necessary research and linguistic skills who would work for the modest salaries paid by the Church were not always easy to find.

The complexities of the new procedures also necessitated the publication of a revised handbook that would draw instructions together in concise, easy-to-find form. The previous handbook had been issued twenty-five years earlier. Prepared by Henry Christiansen, the new handbook was published in 1949. It was bound in loose-leaf form so that deletions and additions could readily be made. The *Handbook for Genealogical and Temple Work* became an important guide to Church genealogical research for many years to come.

Because the work of the Society was so closely related to the work of the temples, the Society often established or modified policies that affected the processing of records for temple work. The "heirship" policy was one example. Until the 1950s, a family group sheet presented for temple work had to contain the name of the "heir," defined as the oldest member of the family, living or dead, who had been baptized while living. Temple work was indexed according to this heirship system. But the process became cumbersome, for it was often difficult to determine the heir, especially in large families where relationships were frequently very remote. Eventually a new recording and indexing system eliminated the need for an heir. The rule was dropped in 1952.[63]

The pressure to provide names for the temples was temporarily assuaged in 1954 by the creation of the temple file. Before that date, it was assumed that the members of a particular family would perform the temple work for ancestors whose names they submitted unless they made other arrangements. When the people doing the temple work died or discontinued their efforts, names for whom the temple work was not complete remained on file awaiting the attention of other descendants. In the late 1940s, names still waited in the files for endowment and sealing, although the baptism had been performed twenty to thirty years earlier.

At the same time, those living far from temples were permitted to request that proxies be provided for the names they submitted. The list of names received in this way were known as "community" or "mission" lists. It was also considered appropriate for persons submitting these names to send in a donation that could be used to reimburse the proxies, who were paid moderate fees ranging from fifty cents to a dollar.[64] However, this recommendation did not preclude accepting names from those who could provide no reimbursement.

This situation changed with the creation of temple and family files in each temple. The names that had been in the pending files for years, the old mission lists, and any new names submitted after April 1954 were automatically assigned to a temple file. This file was used to provide names for those who came to do proxy work but who did not have their own family names at the temple. Those submitting names needed to specify that they wanted the names kept in the family file at a particular temple if they desired to do the proxy work themselves.[65]

Research Difficulties

The Research Department also experienced growing pains during these years. Established to assist those who could not do their own research, the department charged a fee for the services of trained researchers. The department maintained contacts with researchers throughout the United States and in many foreign countries. After 1948 Church members were urged to submit their genealogical research orders for Europe through the Society. These requests were then channeled through the missions to reputable researchers, whose work was returned to the patron after scrutiny by the department. The Society did not claim responsibility for those researchers, but it did try to make certain that patrons received responsible assistance.[66]

The Research Department had particular problems in the early 1940s due to the effects of World War II. Contact with most European researchers was cut off, except with those in the British Isles. Many European archives were closed to research because of the war. Correspondence was lost—in one case some eighty letters, together with money for research, went down when a ship was sunk. Immediately after the war, Archibald F. Bennett traveled to Europe to reestablish research connections in several countries.[67]

Like the Record Department, the Research Department was plagued with frequent personnel turnover. In addition, the Research Department was supposed to be self-sustaining, with researchers being paid from funds deposited by patrons. Despite a healthy surplus in the mid-1940s, serious financial problems existed by the mid-1950s. Researchers were initially paid between $85 and $105 a month. Patrons were charged $.80 per hour, but salaries continued to rise as the work demanded more qualified researchers with special linguistic skills. By 1954 the Society was charging patrons $1.50 per hour, the former surplus was gone, and the deficit was growing.[68] By 1955 the deficit had reached nearly a thousand dollars a month,[69] and the Society was asking the Church for greater subsidization.[70] By 1960 the problem still was not solved, but Church leaders knew that many people who needed research assistance were already sacrificing to pay for genealogical research. The Church did all it could within reason to assist. Still, it could not afford to pay a major portion of the research expenses even for hardship cases.

Amid all this activity, the Society faced inevitable personnel problems. Three problems seemed to plague it most: the constant need for competent transcribers and typists with bilingual skills; the high turnover caused by the Church policies of not hiring married women and of dismissing young women once they married; and relatively low salaries, which made it difficult to keep the most highly skilled employees. In the first seven months of 1957, for example, the Society lost 72 employees: 19 because of marriage, 25 to other employment, 7 who were called on missions, 7 who moved away, and the rest for miscellaneous reasons.[71] Two months later, the total turnover for the year to date reached 137—a new record.[72] The Society continually petitioned for higher wages for its employees in order to alleviate the problem, but the personnel committee of the Church responded that current income and other budgetary requirements simply would not permit raising salaries. Elder Joseph Fielding Smith pressed the First Presidency to relax the restriction on women working after marriage. By 1960 they had relented somewhat; a young wife could work for six months after her marriage.[73] This policy, together with a new training program inaugurated in 1957, helped a little, but in 1960 the Society was still complaining of a great backlog of work and a shortage of skilled employees.

Even though Myers and other supervisors seemed very concerned about the morale and personal problems of the employees, the general personnel policies of the Society were sometimes rather stringent. Vacation policy, for example, insisted that an employee take both vacation weeks at the same time: he or she could not take a week off at one time of the year and another week off at another time, nor even take two or three days off and charge it to vacation allowance.[74] On the other hand, a hospitalization and surgery plan was adopted in 1944, an employee credit union was operating by 1955, and by 1958 employees were on the federal Social Security program. These benefits provided some inducements and helped the Society keep pace with the benefits offered by competing employers.

The rapidly expanding use of the library and archives exemplify the mounting work load of the Society. In 1944 approximately 13,766 patrons used the library, which then housed 42,000 volumes. Three thousand books, 10,637 rolls of microfilm, and 125 manuscripts were added that year alone. The addition of books, films, and manuscripts as well as the number of patrons mounted dramatically each year. In 1960 a total of 85,381 patrons (an average of 291 per day) registered at the library and 24,607 at the archives. Including Society employees, one thousand persons were using the facilities of the Society each working day.[75]

During this period, library patrons were almost exclusively Church members. A 1955 survey by a graduate student in library science at the University of Chicago indicated that the majority of patrons—52 percent—came from Salt Lake City and vicinity. Another 30.9 percent, including BYU students, were from the Provo and Ogden areas. The rest were largely from other parts of Utah, and only a few were from out of state. Fully 99 percent of the users were Church members.[76] This ratio changed in later decades when interest in genealogy dramatically expanded outside the Church.

While the Society assisted thousands of patrons, some requests caused frustrations. In his 20 October 1944 letter to Joseph Fielding Smith, L. Garrett Myers commented on some of these problems. Now that the Society was so well known, some people apparently expected it to perform vast amounts of free service. "Some of our people who would not think of asking the Presiding Bishop's Office or some other department of the Church for special favors, have no hesitancy in asking us to give them, free of charge, from $5.00 to $5,000 of free service," Myers complained. He was also concerned with a certain overzealousness on the part of some people who perhaps should not have been doing genealogical research in the first place. "We do not mean to infer that their motives are not correct," he explained, "but they are actually not mentally qualified to do the research work. They bombard us with thousands of sheets which we cannot accept; they drive our workers to distraction and sour their own relatives on genealogy and temple work." Finally, Myers commented on the "fallacy prevalent in the Church" that genealogical research was mainly for elderly people. They could be engaged in no finer service than temple work, "but it is not proper to begin training an individual for research work after he or she has reached seventy or seventy-five years of age. Poor eyesight, and above all, lack of technical training disqualify them for this type of work."

To Branch or Not to Branch

As interest in genealogy grew, numerous requests were made for the establishment of branch genealogical libraries or, at least, for some kind of lending service from the Salt Lake City library. In 1941, for instance, a member of the Hawaii Temple presidency inquired about a branch library in Hawaii. The board was reluctant to approve such expanded responsibilities, though it did agree to provide Hawaiian Saints with microfilm copies of records obtained in Hawaii.[77]

The question of branch libraries continued to recur and to precipitate serious policy discussions among the officers of the Society. In 1944, Joseph Fielding Smith suggested that a branch library be established in the Idaho Falls area, but L. Garrett Myers objected. First, he argued, a library was not really the key to research, for it contained only a few of the necessary research tools. Other sources, such as parish records, had not been published and therefore were not available in libraries. Furthermore, the expense of opening a branch seemed prohibitive. A good library needed many sources, and even if the local library could afford to get them, the cost of cataloging and indexing the books was too high. The Society had a budget that year of $160,000, and Myers wryly asked if a stake could afford such a thing. His main objection, however, was that branching would lead to duplication of research. He evidently felt that, even if people did some research locally, they must eventually get help from the library in Salt Lake City and that whomever they hired to help them would simply do much of the work over again.[78]

The Society had definitely established the policy of not approving branch libraries. Their objective was to have a large central library for the benefit of all Church members, although they had no objection to local civic funds being used for local genealogical library purposes.[79] But requests continued to arrive, and Myers frequently had to defend the policy.[80] In 1952 the president of the Phoenix Arizona Stake proposed that the library in the Arizona Temple become a branch of the Society library and that it secure copies of microfilms from the central library as well as book loan privileges. A blue-ribbon committee appointed to evaluate this request rejected the proposal. Besides the problem of cost, the committee was fearful that approving a library in Arizona might set a precedent that the Los Angeles area would soon want to follow. The Society simply could not afford it.[81] Nevertheless, more requests came from such places as St. George, Utah; the Florida Stake; the Santaquin-Tintic Stake; and even Holland. The policy remained firm, although in 1960 the Society had seriously considered the possibility of lending books to local genealogical organizations. Private genealogical groups had been established in Provo, Logan, St. George, and Mesa, as well as Northern California. The Society still did not officially encourage them, but by this time Joseph Fielding Smith was suggesting that the time might come when the Society would establish branch libraries.[82] It would not be long before this possibility would materialize.

Outreach

Although the Society still had no official branches outside Salt Lake City, it was nevertheless deeply involved in encouraging genealogical research in other parts of the world. The Church asked all missions, particularly those in Europe, to establish mission and branch genealogical organizations similar to those in the stakes.[83] By 1960 new European mission presidents were given instructions in genealogical organization as part of their orientation program.[84] The Society prepared a course of study especially for the European missions. It was translated into German in 1956. In 1960 the Society had 169 research correspondents in Western Europe (that is, people who worked either full- or part-time filling orders for the Society, though they were not necessarily official employees of the Society). In February alone, the Society's research staff exchanged 1,268 letters and sent 307 money orders to Europe for research.[85] The Society even had its own small research staff in England, under the direction of Elder Frank Smith (which was phased out in the early 1960s).[86]

The Society promoted the message of genealogy among Latter-day Saints with missionary zeal, taking every reasonable opportunity to integrate genealogy into other Church programs. The annual Leadership Week (later called Education Week) held in the late summer at Brigham Young University (BYU) offered a perfect opportunity. Genealogical sessions, conducted by official representatives of the Society, were designed at first for stake genealogical committees only, but in 1953 they were expanded so that anyone attending Education Week could participate. Archibald F. Bennett, who conducted many of the classes, noted with pleasure that the participants in Education Week that year rated genealogy as the third most valuable program. Beginning in 1960, the offering included special classes for youth.[87]

As Education Week expanded beyond the Provo campus, the Society went with it. The first Education Week program in the Los Angeles Area was held in 1958. Archibald F. Bennett conducted two genealogical classes each day. In 1958 and 1959, Education Week programs were held also in Salt Lake City, Ogden, Idaho, Arizona, and Northern California, with the Society participating in all of them. However, by the early 1960s, it became apparent that the Society simply did not have a staff large enough to give Society employees time off to keep up with the burgeoning BYU program. In 1964 the Society officially provided faculty for the last time. Genealogical training continued in Education Week programs, but the faculty was obtained independently by Education Week officials.[88]

Genealogy also found its way into the curriculum of other Church educational programs without the administrative involvement of the Society but always with its cooperation. In the early 1950s, Archibald F. Bennett taught classes both at BYU and in the Church's Institute of Religion adjacent to the University of Utah. Genealogical classes became a permanent part of the BYU curriculum, which, in 1960, began offering a two-year technical genealogical degree. BYU's extension program also provided classes in various Utah cities, taught by representatives of the Society. It even offered an "Ancestral Research Certificate" upon completion of a specified series of courses. In the fall of 1953, fifteen lessons on genealogy were introduced into the curriculum of the early morning seminaries for high school students in Southern California, as part of a three-week genealogical project. Seminaries distributed thirty thousand genealogical forms to the students, who were each encouraged to complete a book of remembrance consisting of a pedigree chart, four family group sheets, various personal records, and a life story. Those who completed the requirements received a genealogical award. A thousand books had been turned in by 7 December. Although genealogy did not become a permanent part of the seminary curriculum, projects such as these reflected the broadening interest in genealogy throughout the Church.[89]

The Society also found other ways to reach the public with its message. Television presented a golden opportunity. Beginning in January 1954, Brigham Young University and the Society jointly sponsored a series of twenty programs on KDYL-TV. Hosted by the popular Archibald F. Bennett, a series called "What's Your Name?" was aired on Sundays from 1:00 to 1:30 P.M. Each program featured the lineage of some prominent person (U.S. president Dwight D. Eisenhower was first), followed by an informal discussion on genealogical concerns. Joseph Fielding Smith publicized the series by writing to all the stakes within the broadcast area, asking the genealogical chairman to announce the program in stake and ward meetings and to encourage people to get together in groups to watch it. The program was successful enough that it continued into 1955.[90]

Flourishing of Ethnic Genealogical Groups

As the emphasis on genealogy and temple work became increasingly significant in the LDS consciousness, the special genealogical concerns of ethnic groups within the Church spawned at least three ethnic genealogical organizations.[91]

Native Americans. The Lamanite Society was organized in 1919 to help Native American Church members gather their own ancestral records and prepare them for temple work. Although it did not officially come under the direction of the Society, the Church took an interest in it, and Melvin J. Ballard of the Council of the Twelve was appointed to act as advisor. By 1926 the Lamanite Society no longer existed, but during its short life it succeeded in gathering numerous family names and in performing a considerable amount of temple work.

Polynesians. The Polynesian people had genealogical traditions that made it impossible to collect and prepare their records for temple work in the same way European genealogies were compiled. Much of the information concerning Polynesian families had to be gathered from oral traditions that did not provide the precise documentation required by the Temple Index Bureau in order to clear names for temple work.

Before the Society's Polynesian Department was organized, missionaries from the United States did much to assist in compiling Polynesian genealogies. In 1933, William A. Cole, an experienced genealogist, was called to serve a second mission in New Zealand. During his years there, he spent much of his time working on Maori genealogies, gathering over 60,000 names and compiling them into thirteen volumes. On his way home in April 1936, he showed a copy of his work to Edward L. Clissold, president of the Hawaiian Temple. A year later, Elder Cole and his wife were called on a third mission—this time to serve in the Hawaii Temple. As might be expected, they spent their spare time preparing Maori genealogies for temple ordinance work.[92]

Other Church members interested in the Polynesian people saw the need to compile and record their genealogical research more efficiently. Early in 1937, William M. Waddoups, president of the Samoan mission, proposed to the First Presidency that a genealogical association, something like the genealogy committees in the stakes, and a genealogical clearinghouse be established in each of the South Seas missions. The officers of the Society agreed that it would be beneficial to have an association in each mission under the direct supervision of the mission president. They opposed, however, the establishment of a clearinghouse in each mission. The Hawaii Temple already had a clearinghouse for Polynesian names and any additional clearinghouses would each require the employment of trained genealogists who were skilled in record keeping and typing. A better plan, they suggested, would be to improve the organization of the Hawaiian clearinghouse.[93]

Still not satisfied, Church leaders in the Pacific began to discuss the possibility of organizing a Polynesian Genealogical Society. Again the officers of the Society disapproved, primarily on the basis of cost. Disappointed, in 1937 the Pacific leaders complained to President David O. McKay that the North Americans simply did not understand the genealogical problems of the Polynesian people.

The champions of the Polynesian proposal did not easily give up. As soon as William M. Waddoups was released as president of the Samoan Mission, he returned to Salt Lake City prepared to argue the case in person and to present another plan. Each Polynesian mission, he proposed, should have a genealogical organization similar to those in the stakes, a filing system similar to that at the Index Bureau, and a plan to generate interest and enthusiasm among the members. An archives and a research bureau for all Polynesian missions should be established at some place considered mutually favorable and accessible. Waddoups urged that the Polynesian archives be established at Laie, Hawaii, rather than in Salt Lake City. After all, he observed, the temple for the Polynesian people was at Laie, and any complications that might arise for members traveling to do temple ordinances for their ancestors could be quickly solved if the archives were near by.[94]

On 28 September 1937, the Society board met, approved the plan, and sent it to the First Presidency with the recommendation that the central index bureau and library be established at the temple in Laie.[95] The plan was not approved—possibly for economic reasons. Instead, a Polynesian Research Department was organized as part of the Society, headquartered in Salt Lake City. William W. Waddoups was appointed as supervisor.[96] Although Waddoups and the Church leaders in Hawaii were undoubtedly disappointed with the compromise, nevertheless, they saw one advantage: Waddoups had the full and enthusiastic support of Archibald F. Bennett and access to all the facilities and support of the Society.

By 1940 the department had received information on over five thousand family groups from Hawaii, Samoa, New Zealand, Tonga, and Tahiti and had arranged them on proper sheets. All of the names had been indexed, many had been sent to the Hawaii Temple for ordinances, and efforts were being made to complete all the appropriate temple work as soon as possible. Approximately ninety volumes dealing with Polynesian genealogy and history had been collected for the library, and various articles and lessons in genealogy were being published in the official periodical of the New Zealand Mission, *Te Karere*.[97]

The Polynesian Department encountered problems, but they accomplished many things with the continuing support of Society leaders and the dedicated work of Waddoups, Cole, and others.

On 26 January 1957, L. Garrett Myers wrote the First Presidency of the Church pointing out the need for a clearinghouse exclusively for Polynesian records and recommending the employment of William Cole and M. V. Coombs.[98] In July 1957, President David O. McKay interviewed William Cole. They reviewed the earlier proposals for establishing a series of clearinghouses in various Polynesian islands. They discussed microfilming Polynesian records, organizing a new Polynesian Department in the Society, and establishing a library in the Polynesian area. In August, Cole was appointed chairman of the Polynesian Committee and hired by the Society as head of the Polynesian Department.

Cole went to work eagerly. First, he had all the Polynesian genealogical sheets in the archives copied in triplicate: one for his department, one for the clearinghouse being planned in New Zealand, and one for the appropriate Polynesian mission in preparation for the eventual establishment of clearinghouses within each mission. In March 1958, just a month before the dedication of the New Zealand Temple, Cole arrived in New Zealand and began making preparations for the clearinghouse. Soon it became a small research center with a small reading area and donated books. Cole started microfilming Polynesian records and obtained microfilm readers. Before he returned to Utah in 1957, Cole and other genealogical workers toured New Zealand instructing the Saints in genealogical techniques. Finally, in 1961 he and Elwin W. Jensen published a book, *Israel in the Pacific,* that was intended for use in genealogical classes in the South Pacific.

The Polynesian Department at the Society, meanwhile, continued to expand its work as it obtained permission not only to check the temple sheets, but also to process them for temple work, thus almost completely bypassing the regular Index Bureau. At its height, the department employed eight people.

In 1961 a major reorganization of the Society took place, and several programs were reassessed, including the Polynesian Department. Eventually, the department became the Pacific Isles Processing Section of the Records Adjustment Department, and in 1965 it became a small unit within another section.

Germans. Another ethnic organization, the German Genealogical Society, was founded in 1926 by a group of German Saints living in Utah. The group consisted largely of first-generation

German immigrants and met once or twice a month in Salt Lake City. By 1930 it had received the commendation of the Genealogical Society for their "most excellent work" in performing 5,613 baptisms, 5,485 endowments, and 469 sealings in 1930.[99] Seven years later, the German society reported that since 1926 it had been responsible for over 140,000 baptisms, nearly 49,000 endowments, and over 32,000 sealing ordinances. In addition, 284 people had attended eleven genealogical classes sponsored by the German society during the year.[100]

The German Genealogical Society cooperated closely with the Genealogical Society of Utah. In the early 1930s, it conducted various fund-raising activities in order to purchase German genealogical books for the library.[101] After the Society moved to the Joseph F. Smith Memorial Building in the 1930s, a special room was given to the German society where it could keep its records and hold committee meetings. The German society also submitted annual reports to the Society. After the major reorganization of 1961, however, the German society, like the Polynesian organization, was absorbed by the Genealogical Society, and was no longer identified as a separate entity.

There may have been other genealogical associations organized for the sake of various ethnic or other special interest groups, though historical records identifying them are missing. The history of these three groups, however, is an impressive illustration of the variety of activities resulting from the Church's emphasis on genealogy.

Summary

The two decades between 1940 and 1960 were decades of rapid growth in genealogical research, increasing visibility for the Society, and greater effectiveness in research and recording. The Society operated between two poles, being drawn inexorably into the center of Church organization, correlation, and consolidation on the one hand and reaching outward to the proliferating stakes, branches, and ethnic groups of the expanding Church on the other hand. Two new temples were dedicated in the United States, two in Europe, and another in New Zealand, contributing to even greater genealogical interest abroad among the Saints in the areas they served. In addition, the Society's vast microfilming program discussed in chapter 6 began to have a powerful impact on the nature and effectiveness of research.

NOTES

[1]A. Hamer Reiser to Archibald F. Bennett, 3 May 1940, Genealogical Society correspondence, Family History Department of the Church (hereafter cited as FHD). See also Genealogical Society Minutes, 4 May 1937, FHD, for a discussion of the function of the Genealogical Society in connection with the proposed General Priesthood Activity Board.

[2]See Genealogical Society Minutes, 7 December 1937, 1 February, and 29 January 1938; Archibald F. Bennett to Joseph Fielding Smith, 21 January 1938, Joseph Fielding Smith papers, Archives Division, Historical Department, The Church of Jesus Christ of Latter-day Saints (hereafter cited as LDS Church Archives). The latter includes a resolution adopted by the Genealogical Committee of Taylor Stake in Alberta, Canada, urging the Society to put genealogical classes in the Sunday School because of the difficulties involved in meeting at other times.

[3]See Archibald F. Bennett papers for summary of decisions reached by the Church Union Board in 1940; Genealogical Society Minutes, 15 May, and 18 June 1940; George Q. Morris to the First Presidency, 20 June 1940, in Archibald F. Bennett papers, LDS Church Archives; Genealogical Society Minutes, 18 June 1940.

[4]Archibald F. Bennett to stake genealogical representatives, 3 June 1940, Genealogical Society correspondence, FHD; *Deseret News,* 5 and 6 July 1940; Genealogical Society Minutes, 13 August 1940, which include a letter from Archibald F. Bennett to stake presidents. A. Hamer Reiser, oral history interview by William G. Hartley, 1974, vol. 1, 209–10, LDS Church Archives. Eventually, according to Reiser, A. William Lund, Joseph Christenson, Archibald F. Bennett, and Joseph Fielding Smith were all placed on the Sunday School Board.

[5]A. Hamer Reiser to Archibald F. Bennett, 6 May 1940, Genealogical Society correspondence, FHD.

[6]Genealogical Society Minutes, 16 July, 10 September, and 31 December 1940, 14 January, and 4 February 1941.

[7]Genealogical Society Minutes, 16 January 1951, 16 June 1961.

[8]Archibald F. Bennett to stake representatives, 3 July 1940, Genealogical Society correspondence, FHD; Genealogical Society Minutes, 9 September 1941, 14 March 1949; *Deseret News,* 6 July 1940.

[9]Traditionally, stake seventies quorums were responsible for missionary work in the stakes. They were eliminated from Church organization in the 1980s, however.

[10]*Deseret News,* 26 October 1940.

[11]Genealogical Society Minutes, 15 February 1945.

[12]Genealogical Society, *Handbook for Genealogy and Temple Work* (Salt Lake City: Genealogical Society of Utah, 1949), 35-36. The Society published many editions of this handbook.

[13]Genealogical Society Minutes, 19 November 1940.

[14]Genealogical Society Minutes, 25 March, 6 May, and 9 September 1941.

[15]Joseph Fielding Smith and Archibald F. Bennett to stake genealogical chairmen, Genealogical Society circular letters, 6 March, and 15 April 1942, LDS Church Archives. Genealogical Society Minutes, 3 March 1942, which include a letter to stake chairmen, dated 2 February 1942.

[16]Genealogical Society Minutes, 1 December 1942.

[17]Genealogical Society Minutes, 16 March, 5 May, and 1 December 1942; Archibald F. Bennett to stake chairmen, 10 June, and 7 December 1942, 18 January 1943, Archibald F. Bennett papers, FHD.

[18]Genealogical Society Minutes, 26 September, 21 November, and 5 December 1944, 9 January, 12 June, 14 August, and 23 October 1945, 14 January 1947; Joseph Fielding Smith and Archibald F. Bennett, "Letter No. 51" 1947, Genealogical Society circular letters, LDS Church Archives; Joseph Fielding Smith and Archibald F. Bennett to stake chairmen, 23 August, and 10 January 1945, Genealogical Society circular letters, LDS Church Archives.

[19]Archibald F. Bennett to stake presidents and genealogy chairmen, 1 December 1958, Genealogical Society circular letters.

[20]Henry E. Christiansen, oral history interviews by Bruce Blumell, 1975-76, typescript, James Moyle Oral History Program, LDS Church Archives; James M. Black, oral history interview by Bruce Blumell, 1975, typescript, James Moyle Oral History Program, LDS Church Archives; George H. Fudge, oral history interview by Bruce Blumell, 1976, typescript, James Moyle Oral History Program, LDS Church Archives; L. Garrett Myers, oral history interview by Bruce Blumell, 1976, typescript, James Moyle Oral History Program, LDS Church Archives; notes in Archibald F. Bennett papers, LDS Church Archives.

[21]Joseph F. Smith and Archibald F. Bennett to stake chairmen, 9 January 1950, Genealogical Society circular letters, LDS Church Archives.

[22]Copy of article in David O. McKay papers, LDS Church Archives.

[23]Genealogical Society Minutes, 21 November 1944.

[24]A. William Lund to A. Hamer Reiser, 10 December 1940, Genealogical Society correspondence, FHD; Genealogical Society Minutes, 27 September 1941, 15 February 1945.

[25]The Archibald F. Bennett papers contain several such letters.

[26]Myrtle R. Zundel to A. William Lund, n.d.; A. William Lund to Myrtle R. Zundel, 7 December 1945, Genealogical Society correspondence, FHD.

[27]Genealogical Society Minutes, 15 February, and 14 August 1945.

[28]Genealogical Society Minutes, 9 December 1947, 21 December 1948.

[29]Genealogical Society Minutes, 8 February 1949.

[30]It was necessary to provide supplements to the Sunday School, he argued, for (1) many Sunday Schools did not have classes, (2) the classes were too short anyway, (3) many people lacked the devotion necessary to insure success in the classes, (4) the Sunday School wanted a new text every year, and (5) many young people were simply not receiving the training.

[31]Joseph Fielding Smith to the First Presidency, 11 February, 17 March, and 22 April 1949, Genealogical Society correspondence, FHD.

[32]Genealogical Society Minutes, 8 February, and 24 May 1949, 13 February, and 12 March 1952.

[33]E. E. Brundage to Archibald F. Bennett, 3 March 1957, Archibald F. Bennett papers, FHD.

[34]Mrs. W. Howard Millett to Archibald F. Bennett, 26 January 1957, Archibald F. Bennett papers.

[35]Archibald F. Bennett to stake chairmen, 22 January 1953, Genealogical Society circular letters, LDS Church Archives; Genealogical Society Minutes, 27 March 1951.

[36]Genealogical Society Minutes, 21 April 1954.

[37]Genealogical Society Minutes, 1 November 1957.

[38]See L. Garrett Myers to Mark E. Petersen, 13 December 1957, Genealogical Society correspondence, FHD, for more statements on the problems of Sunday School instruction, attempts to hold instruction at other times, and Myers's views as to what should be done.

[39]This conclusion is based on our personal observations in the 1970s and 1980s.

[40]Genealogical Society Minutes, 29 September 1941; Archibald F. Bennett to J. Reuben Clark Jr., 6 November 1941, Genealogical Society correspondence, FHD; Myers, interview; Genealogical Society Minutes, 18 April 1941.

[41]The letter from the First Presidency to the Genealogical Society is incorporated in the Genealogical Society Minutes, 21 March 1944.

[42]Genealogical Society Minutes, 18 April, and 20 November 1944; Articles of Incorporation in Genealogical Society papers, FHD; Joseph Fielding Smith to the First Presidency, 8 June 1944, Joseph Fielding Smith papers, LDS Church Archives. In his letter to the First Presidency, Elder Smith says that the members voted in a meeting on 11 April, but the minutes of the Genealogical Society in which this vote took place are dated 18 April.

[43]In 1943 there were 106 employees at the Society. Genealogical Society Minutes, 27 September 1943.

[44]The assets are appended to the letter from Joseph Fielding Smith to the First Presidency, 8 June 1944, Joseph Fielding Smith papers, LDS Church Archives. They included the following: assets of the Society and the magazine (cash, stocks, and first mortgage loans), $40,000; assets of the Genealogical Research Association, $7,000; restricted bequests to be used for specified purposes (consisting of cash, real estate, stocks, and first mortgage loans), $20,000; monies belonging to patrons to be used for researchers at home or abroad (consisting of cash and some U.S. government bonds), $42,000.

[45]This seems apparent from oblique comments in Genealogical Society Minutes, 16 June 1961, and Fudge, interview. These comments suggest that Joseph Fielding Smith may have had some slight misgiving, though not serious enough to create an issue.

[46]Christiansen, interview; Joseph Fielding Smith to the First Presidency, 12 December 1945, Genealogical Society correspondence, FHD. The assistants appointed in 1945, according to this letter, were Benjamin L. Bowring, Harold A. Dent, Henry E. Christiansen, and W. Henry Chase. They met often with the board, though they had no voting power.

[47]Genealogical Society Minutes, 16 January 1951; Myers, interview.

[48]Genealogical Society Minutes, 24 February 1961.

[49]First Presidency to Joseph Fielding Smith, 13 April 1948, Genealogical Society correspondence, FHD; L. Garrett Myers to Joseph Fielding Smith, 16 November 1955, Genealogical Society correspondence; Genealogical Society Minutes, 30 October, and 9 December 1959. The Society requested a budget of $2,095,000 for 1960 but was required to reduce it by $150,000.

[50]L. Garrett Myers to Joseph Fielding Smith, 30 October 1957, Genealogical Society correspondence, FHD.

[51]Salt Lake Temple Presidency to Joseph Fielding Smith, 3 June 1938. Genealogical Society correspondence. Genealogical Society Minutes, 7 June 1938. The discussion on this letter went unresolved for so long that the Society did not reply to the temple presidency for some time. On 31 October, the presidency again wrote the Society, noting that no reply had been received and asking for consideration of their plan.

[52]Genealogical Society Minutes, 7 June 1938.

[53]Genealogical Society miscellaneous minutes, 7 December 1938, FHD; Joseph Christenson, A. William Lund, Archibald F. Bennett, James M. Kirkham, George F. Richards Jr., and Orson Rega Card to the Board of Directors of the Genealogical Society, 28 December 1938, Genealogical Society papers, FHD; Genealogical Society miscellaneous minutes, FHD, 21 November 1939; Genealogical Society Minutes, 28 November, and 8 December 1939.

[54]*Handbook for Genealogy and Temple Work,* 1949 ed., 72.

[55]See L. Garrett Myers and O. Henry Christiansen, interviews, for comments on the significance of this change.

[56]*Handbook for Genealogy and Temple Work,* 1949 ed., 74–80.

[57]Meeting of the Temple Archives Committee, 3 June 1942, in Genealogical Society miscellaneous minutes, FHD.

[58]L. Garrett Myers to Joseph Fielding Smith, 24 April 1944, Genealogical Society correspondence, FHD.

[59]Genealogical Society Minutes, 5 February, and 24 May 1960.

[60]Genealogical Society Minutes, 25 April 1952.

[61]Genealogical Society Minutes, 11 January 1944.

[62]Genealogical Society Minutes, 26 February 1958.

[63]Genealogical Society Minutes, 19 December 1947, 25 April, 11 June, and 8 December 1952; Joseph Fielding Smith to First Presidency, 8 December 1952, Genealogical Society correspondence, FHD; Joseph Fielding Smith to Stake Presidents and Genealogical Chairmen, 28 April 1954, Genealogical Society circular letters, LDS Church Archives.

[64]Edna B. Allen, former assistant recorder, Logan Temple, telephone interview by James B. Allen, 5 January 1995. This policy is referred to in Genealogical Society Minutes, 5 November 1940. The people who accepted these donations were usually retired people who were devoted to temple work and who needed a little extra income.

[65]*Handbook for Genealogy and Temple Work,* 1956 ed., 113–23.

[66]See Christiansen, interview; and Frank Smith, oral history interview by Bruce Blumell, 1976, typescript, James Moyle Oral History Program, LDS Church Archives. See also *Handbook for Genealogy and Temple Work,* 1949 ed., 71–73.

[67]Myers, interview.

[68]Genealogical Society Minutes, 11 January 1944, 9 January 1945.

[69]Genealogical Society Minutes, 25 April 1952.

[70]Genealogical Society Minutes, 11 January 1944. See also Robert Peterson, oral history interview by Jessie Embry, 1977, typescript, LDS Church Archives. Peterson became supervisor of the typing department in 1952.

[71]L. Garrett Myers to Committee on Personnel, 6 August 1957, Genealogical Society correspondence. For example of concern over low wages and the inability to compete with outside employers, see Genealogical Society Minutes, 11 March 1947, 19 February, and 24 March 1960.

[72]L. Garrett Myers to Joseph Fielding Smith, 19 October 1957, Genealogical Society correspondence, FHD.

[73]Genealogical Society Minutes, 5 February, and 24 May 1960.

[74]Genealogical Society Minutes, 9 March 1948.

[75]Genealogical Society Minutes, 9 January 1945, 9 January 1951, 20 January 1961; Memorandum by L. Garrett Myers, 23 January 1961, Genealogical Society correspondence, FHD.

[76]William Raymond Brace, "The Utah Genealogical Society" (master's thesis, University of Chicago, 1956), 45–52. Of the users, 56.7 percent were fifty years of age or older, and 73 percent had found what they were looking for in the library.

[77]Genealogical Society Minutes, 29 September 1941, 21 April, and 1 December 1942.

[78]L. Garrett Myers to Joseph Fielding Smith, 20 October 1944, Genealogical Society correspondence, FHD.

[79]Genealogical Society Minutes, 6 August 1946.

[80]For example, in response to a complaint that people in lower income brackets needed the local service, Myers argued that the Society could still help them and that with proper desire and faith even the poorest people could obtain the names they needed. L. Garrett Myers to Philinda Keeler Naegle, 26 August 1949, Genealogical Society correspondence, FHD. See also L. Garrett Myers to Joseph Fielding Smith, 15 September 1950, Genealogical Society correspondence.

[81]Genealogical Society Minutes, 25 April, and 11 June 1952. The investigating committee consisted of Mark E. Petersen, A. William Lund, Archibald F. Bennett, James M. Kirkham, and L. Garrett Myers. In a later letter to Joseph Fielding Smith, Myers commented that one proposal had been to film all books in the library and make copies of all microfilms for distribution on request. This, he said, would take ten years, the cost of filming the books would be $425,883.76, and the increased salary costs for branch library services would be $300,000 per year. See Myers to Joseph Fielding Smith, 4 November 1952, Genealogical Society correspondence, FHD.

[82]L. Garrett Myers to Santaquin-Tintic Stake Presidency, Attn. Max E. Nelson, clerk, 28 January 1958, Genealogical Society correspondence, FHD; Genealogical Society Minutes, 22 March 1960.

[83]Genealogical Society Minutes, 9 March 1948.

[84]First Presidency to Archibald F. Bennett, 8 February 1954, Archibald F. Bennett papers, FHD; Alvin R. Dyer to Archibald F. Bennett, 5 August 1959, Archibald F. Bennett papers; Genealogical Society Minutes, 19 February, and 24 May 1960, 20 January 1961.

[85]"Memorandum to the First Presidency," prepared by L. Garrett Myers, 25 March 1960, LDS Church Archives, 2.

[86]See Genealogical Society Minutes, 14 August 1945; Junius M. Jackson to Hugh B. Brown, 3 August 1961, Genealogical Society correspondence, FHD; Smith, interview.

[87] The most valuable was "Improvement of Teaching," and number two was a class on the bible by W. Cleon Skousen.

[88]Archibald F. Bennett papers, FHD, boxes 1 and 2, contain various programs, notes, and correspondence dealing with BYU education weeks. Bennett himself was apparently a very popular drawing card in these programs.

[89]Genealogical Society Minutes, 26 August, 28 October, and 9 December 1953; Ray L. Jones, "A Successful Book of Remembrance Project," *Improvement Era* 57 (July 1954): 503. See also Archibald F. Bennett papers, FHD, box 3, for information on BYU technical and extension programs.

[90]*Church News,* 23 January, and 30 January 1954, 19 February, and 26 February 1955; Joseph Fielding Smith to stake genealogical chairmen, 11 January 1954, Genealogical Society circular letters, FHD; Joseph Fielding Smith to stake presidents and genealogical chairmen, 11 March 1954, Genealogical Society circular letters.

[91]These organizations are not discussed at length here because they did not become a permanent, integral part of the Genealogical Society. However, some extended information about them may be found in chapter 8 of James B. Allen and Jessie L. Embry, "Hearts Turned to the Fathers: A History of the Genealogical Society of The Church of Jesus Christ of Latter-day Saints, to 1975," on file in the Family History Department and in the LDS Church Archives.

[92]William A. Cole, "Brief History of the Polynesian Department," typescript, 1966, copy located in files of Henry Christiansen, FHD. This history is basically the reflection of Cole, and his personal disappointments and biases are clearly evident in it.

[93]First Presidency to Joseph Fielding Smith, 24 March 1937, Joseph Fielding Smith papers, LDS Church Archives; Joseph Fielding Smith to President Heber J. Grant and counselors, 26 March 1937, Joseph Fielding Smith papers.

[94]William W. Waddoups to Joseph Fielding Smith, 24 September 1937, Joseph Fielding Smith papers.

[95]Genealogical Society Minutes, 28 November 1937.

[96]Genealogical Society Minutes, 9 November 1937. See also Cole, "Brief History of the Polynesian Department," but note that his dates are slightly different than those reflected in the correspondence.

[97]William W. Waddoups, "Genealogical and Temple Work in Polynesia," *Utah Genealogical and Historical Magazine* 31 (July 1940): 161–63.

[98]L. Garrett Myers to the First Presidency of the Church, 26 January 1957, Genealogical Society correspondence, FHD.

[99]*Deseret News,* 1 November 1930.

[100]*Deseret News,* 23 October 1937.

[101]Genealogical Society Minutes, 10 June 1930; *Deseret News,* "Genealogy" section, 1 November 1930.

Elder Howard W. Hunter, president of the Society, and Elder Theodore M. Burton, Society vice president, review sheets submitted as part of the three-generation program, ca. 1965.

Chapter 5

New Directions, 1961–1975

The Genealogical Society experienced more far-reaching changes between 1961 and 1975 than in any previous period. In many ways, these changes reflected the broad changes in the Church that resulted from correlating its programs and establishing the priesthood line of authority as the primary channel for communicating the directives of Church leaders to each member. New leaders significantly changed the focus of the work of the Society. They permitted names to be taken from record sources and submitted directly for vicarious temple ordinances. The Records Tabulation Program, enhanced by computer technology, provided the flow of names required to keep up with increased temple attendance. General Authorities such as N. Eldon Tanner, Howard W. Hunter, and Theodore M. Burton instigated farsighted programs to encourage widespread genealogical activity, including a branch library system and promulgation of a program encouraging members to submit four generations of genealogical information.[1] The Society expanded its library services, moved into new facilities, changed its research policy from hiring professional researchers to simply providing better assistance for patrons, and hosted the 1969 World Conference on Records.

Changes in Administration

The first of the three major reorganizations during this period came in 1961. Board members were surprised when, during a 22 June meeting with Presidents David O. McKay and Henry D. Moyle, they were told that the Society was to be reorganized and that all of them were being released. Even Joseph Fielding Smith, who had served as president for twenty-seven years and as a member of the board for twenty-seven years before that, was released, along with his two primary administrators, Archibald F. Bennett and L. Garrett Myers. General Authorities of the Church, the First Presidency explained, must be relieved from such heavy administrative responsibilities.[1]

The 1961 reorganization was actually part of a renewed Churchwide correlation movement. In 1960, Elder Harold B. Lee, as chairman of the Melchizedek Priesthood Committee, was assigned to reexamine Church curriculum. He appointed Antone K. Romney, dean of the College of Education at Brigham Young University, to head a committee to do a historical survey of Church programs. The committee focused particularly on the way programs may or may not have been integrated, or correlated, effectively within the larger structure. After reviewing the committee's final report, the First Presidency announced the new correlation plans on 30 September 1961. Genealogy became one of the four functions of the priesthood.[2]

Although the Genealogical Society was restructured just prior to the announcement,[3] the correlation effort prompted the reorganization. However, certain administrative problems that had become apparent may also have played a role in the change.[4]

The reorganization took place quietly, surprising many staff members and unavoidably hurting some feelings. L. Garrett Myers, for example, who was in charge of personnel and had devoted his life to the Society, was out of town when the change was announced and was undoubtedly stunned when he learned he had been relieved of all his responsibilities. George Fudge, who had only recently been made assistant superintendent to Myers, was asked by President Henry D. Moyle to direct the operations of the Society until the First Presidency appointed a new president.[5]

The new leaders were announced on 6 July 1961. Junius M. Jackson, former president of the New England Mission, became president—the first time this office was held by someone other than a General Authority. Jackson was given two assistants, Lamont B.

Presidency of the Genealogical Association, 1961: (left to right) President Junius M. Jackson with his assistants George H. Fudge and LaMont B. Gundersen. The Genealogical Society was directed by business leaders in 1961–62.

Gunderson and George H. Fudge, as well as a new six-person board of directors.[6] Neither Junius Jackson nor his first assistant had previously been employed by the Society, but George Fudge had worked fifteen years for the Society in Salt Lake City and had helped pioneer microfilming in England. Fudge remained in charge of the Society's daily activities, while Jackson worked with other matters and directed the convention staff.[7] Paul Royall and Roy Brown became, respectively, secretary and treasurer.[8] Archibald F. Bennett, who had been "Mr. Genealogy" in the Church, remained as director of education and was also placed in charge of the Genealogical Library.[9]

The new officers began their work with a major discussion on the nature of the Society—Should it continue as an incorporated body under the laws of the state of Utah, or should it disincorporate and become strictly a Church organization, functioning as a Church auxiliary? Most board members, including Junius Jackson, thought that it could function better as an auxiliary. Exactly why they preferred auxiliary status is not clear, although they may have felt it would give them greater opportunity to attend stake conferences as official visitors and thus promote genealogy more effectively. For whatever reasons, they voted on 27 July to propose that the Society be discontinued as a corporation. They also began to refer to the Society as the "Genealogical Association"[10] (a name that sounded more like other auxiliaries). The term "association" was used until the end of Jackson's administration but never caught on generally.

This new auxiliary status was fully in line with Church policy. It was a novelty, nevertheless, for long-time staff members to suddenly see board members going out on stake conference assignments with General Authorities.[11] The new status only emphasized, however, the increasingly significant role of genealogy in the minds of Church leaders.

The Society that Junius Jackson took over was a large, complex organization with difficult problems of administration and coordination. It encompassed a huge genealogical library, a vast international microfilming program, a rapidly growing index bureau, a $2 million budget[12], and hundreds of employees as well as hundreds of volunteer workers in the wards and stakes. The responsibility for supervising a unique combination of paid professionals and volunteer Church service workers proved challenging.

Society staff, 1962, in front of the Joseph F. Smith Memorial Building. Courtesy Frank Smith.

The professionals were tightly controlled by the administrative system and procedures of the Society itself, but the Church service workers, scattered in wards and branches throughout the world, were in the difficult position of taking direction both from their local ecclesiastical leaders and from the Society. These local volunteers were appointed by the local leaders, were responsible to them for genealogical classes, and were dependent upon them for promoting the classes and supporting genealogical work generally. At the same time, they were responsible for submitting activity reports required by the Society and coordinating all research and temple work through the Society.

Jackson's administration was short lived but vigorous. His reports to the First Presidency pointed with pride to the new board's efforts "to bring genealogical work out of its hiding place and into the limelight of responsibility with the membership of the Church."[13] In the first six months, he and his staff worked with architects and the Church Building Committee on finalizing plans for a new genealogical building, instituted a study of personnel and work flow, discontinued overtime work in order to save money, studied purchasing procedures and in the process effected substantial savings, developed a motion picture for the 1962 conventions, improved other convention materials, received permission from the First Presidency for Society representatives to hold conventions in the missions within the United States, and planned a monthly bulletin that began publication in 1962. The Society staff also created new monthly report forms for stake and ward workers, developed a new family group sheet that was more readily adaptable for typewriter use, established a committee to approve what records were to be microfilmed throughout the world, studied new electronic technology and its adaptation for genealogical work, and began writing new lesson materials and instruction manuals. But the most significant change in this period was a policy of extracting names from genealogical sources and submitting them directly to the temples (the Records Tabulation program discussed below), which helped solve the increasingly difficult problem of keeping the temples supplied with names.

The year 1962 saw a significant expansion of all the Society's programs, including more local conventions. There was also a major genealogical convention, attended by 7,000 people, in connection with the general conference of the Church in October. At the same time, the General Authorities felt the need for direct administrative involvement with this rapidly growing Church unit.[14] On 4 December 1962, the First Presidency announced the release of Jackson and his board, and appointed Elder N. Eldon Tanner of the Council of the Twelve as president. The *Church News* commented on the vast programs and new direction of the Society as a result of advanced technology. Elder Tanner, the paper reported, would have full supervision "of all educational, public service, library, research, and microfilming activities of the Society, the index bureau and the storage vaults for microfilm records now nearing completing underground in Little Cottonwood Canyon. He will work closely with the Church advance planning committee in the field of electronic recording."[15]

Like the 1961 reorganization, this change was also part of the continuing correlation movement within the Church. In January 1963, the correlation committee divided the responsibilities of the priesthood into four major categories: missionary work, welfare, home teaching, and genealogy. A General Authority was assigned to direct each of these areas. Rather than continuing as an auxiliary function, genealogical work became a basic priesthood assignment. The head of the Genealogical Society also became a member of a Church coordinating committee.[16]

Elder N. Eldon Tanner brought a new administrative style to the Society. His managerial skills had earned him a well-deserved reputation as a leader, both inside and outside the Church. His respect for individuals, nonauthoritarian style of leadership, willingness to listen, personal humility, and obvious ability to make well-reasoned decisions created a warm regard for him within the Society. Elder Tanner dealt openly with complaints and attempted to correct whatever problems caused them. When patrons protested that the library was not open on Saturday evening, for example, he changed the policy. He required employees to take complaints directly to the parties they felt were doing something wrong. He effectively delegated responsibilities to employees and made them feel a part of the Society's program. Microfilmer James Black described him as "one of the greatest leaders we have had

Elder Nathan Eldon Tanner, president of the Society, 1963. He was released from this position when he was called to the First Presidency of the Church.

in the Genealogical Society. I think everybody developed a real love for him. He seemed to be a person who liked to make use of the people who were in the Society to the fullest extent. He made the employees feel as if they were close, trusted friends," Black recalled. "And I think he got results. There wasn't anything I wouldn't do for him."[17]

Elder Tanner remained as president for only a year, but during that time he made some significant changes. When he took over, he found forty-seven departments that, at least in his view, were not working together as well as they should. He quickly streamlined the operation, reducing the number of major administrative units to nine.[18] He attempted to separate public service functions from internal programs. He hired professional librarians, reduced the size of the research division, worked on the development of a computer program, and moved ward genealogical classes to the MIA. Under his direction, the Society was again reincorporated under Utah state law as the Genealogical Society of the Church of Jesus Christ of Latter-day Saints, Inc. Under the new charter issued in November 1963, the First Presidency continued to select the Society's officers.[19]

In October 1963, Elder Tanner became a Counselor in the First Presidency of the Church. In December the First Presidency appointed Theodore M. Burton as vice president and general manager of the Society, and he served as chief administrative officer until 1977. Paul Royall, secretary of the Society under Junius Jackson, also retained his major administrative responsibilities.

Elder Burton, an Assistant to the Council of the Twelve, had been presiding over the European missions of the Church. His only previous experience in the genealogy program was as a stake chairman for genealogy. Years later he good-naturedly recalled that as a young man he thought of genealogists as fanatics "with one foot in the grave." He imagined that he was being assigned to an organization that spent a lot of money heedlessly, but he learned quickly how wrong he was. Before leaving Europe, he began his new assignment by visiting several microfilming projects.[20]

In the reorganization, President Tanner allowed George Fudge to choose between directing microfilm operations or directing systems and improvements. Having worked with systems since 1959, he elected to take charge of that program and to organize a name extraction department.[21] Fudge molded the activities of the Society and the Family History Department for the next twenty years, eventually serving as the Department's managing director, the chief executive officer under the General Authorities.

On 21 January 1964, President Tanner was succeeded as president of the Society by Elder Howard W. Hunter of the Council of the Twelve. Elder Hunter exerted a quiet, but pivotal, influence on Society work for many years. He had served on the board of directors from 1960 to 1961. Reappointed in late 1963, he had served only one month of his second term on the board when he was appointed to replace Elder Tanner. He remained president of the Society for eight years. (From 24 January 1970 until 25 May 1972, he also served as Church historian.[22]) In 1972, the First Presidency divested itself and the Council of the Twelve of all direct administrative responsibilities within the various Church departments. Accordingly Elder Theodore M. Burton, Society vice president, replaced Elder Hunter as president. Elder Hunter continued to serve on the board of directors until 14 February 1975.[23]

Needed: A Change in Policy

An acute shortage of names continued to plague the Society's efforts to keep the temples supplied, but two important developments, occurring almost simultaneously, helped solve the problem: computer technology was adapted to the genealogical and temple program of the Church and policy was changed regarding name submission for temple work. The Genealogical Society and, consequently, the temples moved with solemn deliberation into the computer age.

In the 1950s, Church policy still required that all names submitted for vicarious ordinances be identified on family group sheets, which were submitted by a family representative, checked by the Genealogical Society, then sent to the temples. People submitting names could reserve them for their own families to use when attending the temple, or they could put them in the "temple file," introduced in 1954, as a source of names available to patrons who had no family names for which to do the work. Most people who attended the temple were dependent upon the temple file. Exceptions to the established program were sometimes allowed in order to keep the temples running, but the policies of the Society did little to solve the problem of name shortages.[24]

A factor that contributed to the shortage of names was the time-consuming process the Society required to clear names. Early in 1960, L. Garrett Myers told the Personnel Committee of the Church that his employees were working overtime because of the shortage of names at the temples and that more part-time help was needed.[25] In 1957, for example, the Society forwarded 780,464 names to the temples, but during the year, 950,379 endowments had been performed.[26]

Another problem arose because women consistently attended the temple in greater numbers than men, and the supply of female names diminished much faster than male names. Special priesthood sessions were held at some temples in order to catch up on the completion of male ordinances. For several years, the Logan Temple held priesthood sessions on George Washington's birthday. In 1953 the president of the Logan Temple instructed all stake presidents in his district that women should not come to the temple at all unless they had their own family names for which to perform ordinances—the supply of female names was completely exhausted.[27] Also, as another temporary solution, families were urged to put their names in the regular temple file rather than the restricted family file, so that all patrons could have access to them.[28] These measures, however, provided no permanent relief.

Genealogical leaders faced a crisis as efforts to persuade Church members to increase their personal research met with little response. In 1958 ten temples were in operation, and temple activity had increased 29 percent that year, but the Society was unable to keep pace. Pleas by Society representatives at local conventions went unheeded. Members who were doing research continued to submit incorrect forms that could not be cleared. In 1961 some 42 percent were rejected, and another 26 percent were found to be duplicates. Name shortages required cutbacks in the number of daily temple sessions. In 1959 most temples eliminated two sessions per day. By 1960 the supply of names was precarious—only a six week's supply was on hand at most temples, and only a month's supply was at the Salt Lake Temple. The Society tried to compensate by increasing its output with overtime, night shifts, and holiday shifts.[29] In Salt Lake City, Society workers were literally running back and forth each day carrying names to the temple to keep it open.

This crisis led to a number of urgent, but perhaps unrealistic, proposals to local Church leaders. In 1958, for example, Joseph Fielding Smith and Archibald F. Bennett asked stake genealogical chairmen to increase the size of ward genealogy committees to sixteen or more, to contact every family at least once every two months, to encourage better attendance at genealogical classes, to promote home-study courses, and to ask members to set aside two days each month as research days, keeping track of the number of hours spent on research. In practical terms, however, most members of the Church were not research-oriented, and they did not have the time, skill, money, and motivation to keep up the steady pace needed to supply the temples.[30]

Genealogical leaders faced a dilemma. On one hand, Church policy regarding the submission and clearance of names made it impossible for the supply of names cleared for temple work to keep pace with increasing temple attendance. On the other hand, the Church had stepped up its emphasis on regular temple attendance, making the name shortage even more acute. Clearly, something had to be done, and soon.[31] The only answer was to introduce a new system.

As early as the 1940s, several genealogical leaders had begun to soften their previously inflexible position on the process of submitting names. On 16 April 1943, for example, the board discussed the issue. Elder Joseph Fielding Smith said he would like to see the day when a staff of experts under the jurisdiction of the Society would do research and prepare names for temple work. With a touch of hyperbole, he estimated that "95% of those working on their own lines bungle the records in compiling them, leading to confusion comparable to a tangled ball of string. . . . Is it not the responsibility of the Church to prepare these records?" he asked. He also suggested that the Society had been a little too strict in requiring individuals to submit only their own family lines, though he still insisted that whatever names were submitted must be in connection with family group units. While he continued to oppose "haphazard" work, Elder Smith nevertheless observed that "we will shortly receive millions of names from Europe. Won't we have to broaden out?" Elder John A. Widtsoe concurred, commenting that "we had been limiting ourselves unduly from a fear of promiscuous name gathering and in part had forgotten our obligation to the dead."[32] Archibald F. Bennett remarked one month later that, in the long run, there were really no families "of exclusive private ownership," for all ultimately were interrelated. Other members of the board agreed that it would be a "shortsighted policy" to spend money for the building of temples without providing an adequate supply of names.[33]

In September 1943, Elder Widtsoe anticipated the policy that eventually developed when he declared that the Society ought to obtain all published manuscript and microfilm records as fast as possible and use the names for temple work. "Why don't we use the names for temple work which cannot be tied to any Church families?" he asked. "The Lord has provided these names by inspiring genealogists to compile and publish them. In an extremity like the present, why not use the names from such records? . . . For what purpose have these books been compiled, if not to make the names available for temple work?"[34] Three years later, Bennett made a similar appeal. A large number of Danish records were coming in, and he believed the Society should organize them into family groups for the use of people attending the temples without their own family names. Elder Smith agreed, predicting that eventually family records for temple work would be prepared by genealogical experts. "Is it not the business of the Church to prepare names for temple work?" he asked again. The minutes and correspondence of the Society during this period are filled with such discussions, and at least two committees were appointed to study the problem.[35] The only real solution, however, was a wholly new approach to the philosophy of name submission.

Over the next several years, many suggestions were made for the use of electronic devices to speed up processing. George Fudge put the problem succinctly to the board in June 1961. The only alternatives were either not to worry if the temples ran out of names or to initiate a new program to produce names in addition to those provided by the public.[36] But drastic changes do not come easily, nor do they come overnight. Church leaders proceeded quietly and cautiously, as they listened to suggestions for new programs that the marvels of computer technology were beginning to make possible.[37]

Changing Role and Policies: Computers and the Controlled Extraction Program

The Society began investigating the use of mechanical data processing methods as early as 1941 and decided they were not suitable for Society purposes, especially because of the problems that would be involved in completely changing the old filing system. But investigation continued into the possibility of transferring information from the Temple Index Bureau (TIB) cards to magnetic tape and finding a way to index and classify it electronically. Sixteen years later, after the Society began seriously to consider the use of computer technology, the idea of manually copying the TIB to magnetic tape still seemed so enormous as to be impractical, though the possible perfection of an acceptable optical scanner seemed to offer some hope.[38]

Computer programming was a new and highly technical field. Most people were not only unaware of its potential, but also somewhat apprehensive of investing in something they did not understand. No one within the Society had the technical qualifications to develop or work with a computer program, though a number of people, including Myers, Bennett, and Fudge, were eager to see what computers could do.

Just as the Church was reaching a serious crisis in providing enough names to the temples, many young Latter-day Saints began to carve out careers in computer technology and programming. Impressed with what recent technological improvements could do for the Church, particularly its genealogical program, they eagerly discussed it among themselves. One group of young men in the Los Angeles area began meeting together informally in the late 1950s and eventually decided to make some positive suggestions to the Church. After discussing some of the possibilities with certain Church leaders in Salt Lake City, the group wrote a small demonstration program. With the approval of Church leaders and the cooperation of the Society, raw data was obtained from microfilm copies of christening records from the British Isles. The data was entered into a computer, which, in turn, sorted the names into family groups at the rate of some forty thousand groups per hour.[39]

In the meantime, the Financial Planning Department of the Church was adapting new technology to Church needs. Alfonzo Pia, director of the Financial Department's mechanized data processing and related functions, began to counsel with Myers, who also met from time to time with the California group. A new system for keeping the temples supplied with names was eventually devised through the cooperation of these groups.[40]

Many who had been involved in genealogical leadership for years questioned the wholesale application of computer technology. They hesitated not just about the mystery of advanced technology, but also the implications for policy. If computerized methods resulted in the gathering of an almost unlimited supply of names and if those names were submitted to the temple for ordinances by the Society rather than by family representatives, would not this procedure diminish the feeling of responsibility of the members toward their own family research? And since computers could keep track of each different ordinance separately, would it be permissible for vicarious temple work to be done for people out of the traditional order—that is, could a regular proxy endowment for the dead be performed before the preliminary ordinances and by a different person? These issues were carefully discussed, but in the long run, when compared with all the positive factors, they seemed much less significant than the need to keep the temples open and have vicarious work performed for all the dead, no matter what the family relationship.[41]

The spirit of the transition from the old to the new was beautifully demonstrated during this period in a presentation given by the California group to the Council of the Twelve. Elder Joseph Fielding Smith, the venerable president of the Council, was there. Well over eighty years old, this stalwart of the Genealogical Society for over fifty years seemed to represent traditional programs and policies, and he was a bulwark against too rapid or irresponsible change. When Gary Carlson, barely over thirty, stood to make his presentation on the grand possibilities of computers, he was naturally apprehensive as to whether President Smith would understand what he was talking about—especially since it appeared to him that the elderly Church leader kept falling asleep. As Carlson later recalled:

> I remember I got up to give my presentation and I looked right at President Smith and I tried to talk very slow and distinct right to him. He sat in his chair with his head bowed and eyes closed as though totally sound asleep. So I changed the inflection of my voice and I'd pause and I'd almost yell and I would do everything that I could to try to wake him up, because I so wanted him to understand the concept that we were talking about. . . .
>
> We finished up and several of the Brethren came up and said that was fine and they appreciated the information. I got to President Smith and I said, "I hope you understand what we were trying to say. Is there anything I can answer or any question I can help you with?" He looked me straight in the eye and he said, "Now, Brother Carlson, you may think I was asleep. I'm an old man and my eyes are tired and my body is tired and I have to rest whenever I can." I felt smaller and smaller. He said, "But I heard what you said. I don't understand it, but I have the feeling that you young men know what you are talking about and I have confidence in you."[42]

That instance represented the willingness of Church leaders to make the transition. "I practically flew home without the airplane," Carlson recalled later. "He didn't understand it, he knew he wasn't going to, but he could feel that we understood the technology that we were talking about, and he had confidence in us. That was a humbling experience."[43]

Church leaders took the new possibilities so seriously that some members of the California group were officially called as consultants. At the request of the First Presidency, they were released from all other Church service assignments.[44] In January 1961, the First Presidency approved the utilization of electronic records processing, the employment of computer experts, and the purchase of a computer.[45] The Society soon organized an electronic processing committee, and by 1962 the move toward computer use was underway.

However, even the members of this group were disheartened by the thought of transferring the old TIB information to magnetic tape. If only the TIB had initially been done on punch cards, they moaned, the modern Church could have saved millions of dollars.[46] Little did they realize the obstacles Harry Russell had to surmount in the 1920s to even get the TIB launched. On Russell's limited budget, the additional expense of punch cards, proper typewriters, and a training program might have kept him from implementing his project. Ultimately, the Society decided not to attempt to transfer the TIB wholesale to computers, but rather to check the names processed under the new system against the TIB and when they appeared in both places to transfer the TIB data into the new system.[47]

The California group met each Sunday and sometimes made special trips to Salt Lake City, at Church expense, to consult and to work with data. At the October conference of the Genealogical Association, several General Authorities of the Church urged the genealogists to take full advantage of the new technology. Elder Mark E. Petersen, however, cautioned the Society that the computer did not relieve Church members of their personal family responsibilities.[48]

Nevertheless, the General Authorities clearly recognized that the Society was now responsible for supplying the temples with names, even before providing direct research assistance or training to individuals. President David O. McKay made it clear that the temples were not to run out of names and that the Society was responsible to see that they did not.[49] As a result, George Fudge marshaled the development of the R-Tab (Records Tabulation) program, which was the predecessor to the electronic name extraction program. Under R-Tab, names were taken from microfilm copies of British parish registers and prepared for temple work. In the first R-Tab effort, Fudge experimented with the records of the Bolden, England, parish by having one of his assistants, Queenie Mead, extract names and place them on family group sheets. The work was too time consuming to provide the temples with enough to keep them open doing proxy baptisms and endowments. They quickly turned to simply extracting names.[50]

Nevertheless, concurrent with extracting single names through R-Tab, the Society continued to experiment with compiling names on group sheets so that sealings could be performed. Between February 1961 and January 1964, the records filmed in 1948 by James Black in northwestern Italy were extracted, and the names placed on family group sheets.[51] The issue arose as to who should be listed as the family representative when the sheets were prepared for temple work. In a letter to President Hugh B. Brown on 17 August 1961, George Fudge explained the problem and asked for advice. If family representatives must be listed, then the Society must set up a training program, he explained. Four months later, on 14 December, he reported to the board, in strict confidence, that the First Presidency had authorized the Society to begin compiling names for the temple without listing a family representative. The implications of this new policy were tremendous, and the reasons for the initial confidentiality were obvious. Church leaders wanted the members to hear about this major change in policy from official sources and not by way of rumor. Also the expanding role of the Society in pursuing such a name extraction program would require a greater budget, and at that point, the money was not available.[52]

In 1962 the R-Tab program was underway, even though the Society did not own a computer. Instead, the Church organized the Advanced Planning Department, headed by Kendall Wright, who was a member of the California consulting group. All Church computers were located in this department, and all the other Church departments used its services.

Under the original Records Tabulation Program, names were all typed on index cards. In 1961, after consulting with Alfonzo Pia, the Society began to use flexowriters—typewriters that

Staff using flexowriters, ca. 1965. The flexowriter produced a punched paper tape. The data from this tape was transferred to a magnetic tape and then fed into a computer.

produced punched paper tapes. By June 1962, a computer was available, and the flexowriter data was sent to it. Two typists copied the same data from the same microfilms; then the data from the paper tapes was converted to magnetic tapes and fed into the computer for comparison. If everything matched—an indication that the two sets of data had been copied accurately—a new "C" tape was created that contained all the correctly copied information. When discrepancies arose, they were reconciled, and a corrected record sent through for further processing. The system was soon refined so that data could be entered directly on magnetic discs, and the corrected names were sent directly to the temple without being put on family group sheets.[53]

In 1962 the Church began to call people on missions to work in the name extraction program, beginning with certain English parish records on microfilm. Initially, seventy-five men and women from ten stakes were called to work eight hours a week for two years. Some worked at microfilm readers extracting names in longhand, while others learned to use flexowriters. As the electronic R-Tab system grew, the unit cost of clearing names for temple work dropped from a high of $1.37 in 1967–68 to $.64 in 1973. Before long, flexowriters, which were comparatively noisy and awkward, were eliminated, and the program was designed for regular computer terminals.[54]

The computer had changed the nature of the genealogical program of the Church. However, Church members were still reminded that they were responsible for their own families and must become acquainted with their ancestry. "It doesn't matter whether your computer is able to compile all the family group sheets for every one that ever lived on the earth," President Joseph Fielding Smith told Alfonzo Pia. "It remains the responsibility of each individual to know his kindred dead. . . . Even if the work is done, then it is still each person's responsibility to study and become acquainted with his ancestors."[55] The new policies allowed the Church to keep the temples open, provide the living with the blessing of regular temple attendance, and do vicarious temple work for all the dead whose records were available, regardless of family relationships. Leaders were concerned, however, that the computer would replace the Spirit of Elijah and that the hearts of the children would not be turned to their personal forebears. But for many Church members that problem did not materialize; families throughout the Church continued to submit family group sheets.

The Society still had not solved the problem of processing all the group sheets promptly. Clearing names for temple work sometimes took as long as two years. Checking was a very slow, manual process, which seemed incongruous when compared with the rapid computer process used for other temple work. The Society decided to change the forms necessary for submitting names to the temple. Instead of using the old family group sheets, the Society would have the names for temple work submitted on new single-entry forms. This way, patrons would not have to wait until they had a complete family group sheet before submitting names for ordinance work. July 1969 was set as the date to begin submitting names for temple work on the new forms.[56] That year the Society introduced the Genealogical Information and Name Tabulation (GIANT) program, inviting Church members to submit the individual names they had been keeping in their files for years because they could not link them to family groups. George Fudge later said that people emptied their cupboards of such names.[57]

Research Division

The Genealogical Society did not forget its obligation to help members with their own research. By 1961, however, the research division seemed hopelessly flooded with requests, and researchers were complaining that they were both overworked and underpaid. The board of trustees was reluctant to raise the fees charged to patrons, but at the same time the cost to the Church for continuing this research was high. In 1965 the board decided to eliminate the research division and redirect the Society's activities to educating patrons in research methods rather than doing the research for them. In January 1966, the board announced that it would accept no new research accounts. All custom research was eliminated before the end of the year.[58]

The alternative was a program decided on by the board earlier, in 1963, to recommend private researchers to patrons and to develop a testing program for accrediting researchers. The first accreditation examinations for professional researchers in the sources of Denmark and Scotland were complete by 1964. Becoming accredited was not an easy process. Candidates had to (1) have access to the collection, (2) complete a thousand hours of research in the area of specialty, (3) possess a working knowledge of the language for the area of specialty, and (4) pass a comprehensive exam.[59] The written examination administered by the Society could take as long as eight hours. In addition, the candidate was required to defend, before a committee, a pedigree he or she had prepared. In 1976 the accreditation list included 131 researchers. The list was updated quarterly.[60]

The Society assumed no responsibility for furnishing clients with an accredited genealogist or for certifying the work accomplished by the researcher. However, the genealogists signed an agreement promising to abide by certain conditions. They agreed to reply promptly to all correspondence connected with their employment; to clearly inform clients about fees, deposits, other agents used, reporting methods, and areas of accreditation; to make regular written reports to clients explaining all aspects of their work, including any reasons for delay; to maintain accurate accounting; and to adhere to "The Genealogist's Code" prepared by the Board of Certification of Genealogists.

While it no longer accepted private research accounts, the Society provided general research assistance. Research papers describing the main genealogical sources in different countries were prepared by the Society's professional staff and published. The Society also offered to do certain kinds of selected research projects. It would, for a nominal fee, check the Temple Index Bureau and copy appropriate index cards for patrons. It would also make brief searches of the library sources for surnames and localities.[61]

Library

As the Society phased out doing research for patrons, it gradually expanded its library services. In 1961 the Society's president, Junius Jackson, encouraged the staff to improve its approach to serving the public. "We need to be missionaries," he declared, "and patrons should get excellent attention from everyone in this building." Nevertheless, when Delbert Roach became head of the library in 1963, he found considerable criticism of its operation. Book and microfilm stacks were closed to the public. Patrons could check out only one roll of film at a time, which slowed service since the staff were constantly on the run trying to provide the books and films requested.[62] Gradually the library changed these policies. In January 1965, after an extensive reclassification and recording process, it became an open-stack library. Access to the microfilm collection remained restricted until November 1969, when a better humidity control process was installed in the library, and a new, simplified classification system was developed for easy patron retrieval of the films.[63]

Even with open stacks, the limited library staff had difficulty serving all its patrons. Between 1961 and 1969, the average number of daily users increased from 301 to over 600. The staffing problem was partially solved with the establishment of a volunteer program; Church members from the Salt Lake Valley received training and worked at the service desk in the evenings and on Saturdays.

The open-stack system created some new concerns about the use of certain microfilmed records of temple ordinances. These films were still restricted. Patrons were required to show temple recommends before they could use the microfilm and were asked to work only on their own family lines. In 1974, however, when a book was published containing information from the restricted microfilmed records, the policy for accessing such sensitive records was tightened even further.[64]

Branch Libraries

During all this time, the Society continued to receive requests for the establishment of branch libraries. The first step toward a major policy change came in 1961, when residents of Logan, Utah, organized their own genealogical library in connection with the public library and asked the Genealogical Society in Salt Lake City for help in expanding their resources. At the 2 November meeting of the board, members were urged to support such regional

Reading room of the Cache Valley, Utah, Branch Library, 1967. Microfilms from the Society can be ordered by the branch libraries. This service provides worldwide access to the Society's collection.

libraries. They would provide researchers with preliminary sources although the more advanced sources would remain in Salt Lake City. Establishing branches in local areas, George Fudge argued, would help patrons avoid needless expenditures of time, effort, and money. The board agreed with him. Later that year, the Los Angeles Temple supervisors asked for permission to establish a library at the Bureau of Information near the temple. Permission was granted two months later,[65] but like the one at Logan, this library was not a completely official branch of the Genealogical Society.

Some resistance to establishing branch libraries continued, partly because of the expense involved and partly because of the fear they would diminish the resources of the main library. When N. Eldon Tanner became president of the Society, he reconsidered the concept and appointed a committee, chaired by Delbert Roach, to investigate it. As a result, Elder Tanner announced in the October 1963 general conference that four branch libraries would be established in Mesa, Oakland, Logan, and Cardston. Actually, the first official branch library was established in May 1964 in the library of Brigham Young University as a pilot project. The trained librarians available, the number of students and community residents available as patrons, and the proximity to Salt Lake City all made BYU a natural choice for the new experiment. In June 1964, the Logan library became an official branch. In October the branch program was turned over to Archibald F. Bennett, who vigorously promoted it.[66] By the end of the next year, there were branches at twenty-one locations, and the number doubled to forty by the end of 1966.[67] The seventy-fifth branch library, in Moses Lake, Washington, was founded in 1968. Clearly, the availability of microfilming and other technologies had provided an important basis for the rapid expansion of genealogical research opportunities in many parts of the Church.[68]

The Society soon developed guidelines for establishing branches. A group of stakes could request permission to set up a library or, in isolated areas, an individual stake could do so. Minimal facilities included an adequate room, good lighting sources, and access to rest rooms. Once the branch was established, a revolving fund was set up at the Genealogical Society to help finance the orders for films by patrons. The library district was to contribute one cent per capita to this fund. The local stake was responsible for branch library operations, and staff members included volunteers called to fill this Church service assignment. At first libraries were set up in either Church or public buildings. However, some residents of Logan complained about the Church genealogical library being located in the public library building. The Logan branch library was moved to the basement of the Logan Tabernacle. It soon became policy that all libraries should be set up on Church property.[69]

Initially branches could not be located within a sixty-mile radius of each other. In October 1971, however, Theodore M. Burton asked the Society trustees to eliminate that rule, for it seemed impractical. A more feasible plan, he suggested, would be to establish branch genealogical libraries in stake centers, rather than to build additional physical facilities in public buildings. The board agreed, and with this significant change in policy, branch genealogical libraries could be established in stake centers throughout the Church.[70]

Each branch library had a basic set of microfilms, books, and other materials. It could order additional microfilms from the Society in Salt Lake City. In 1964 branch libraries ordered 1,295 rolls of film; the following year they ordered 9,676 rolls, and in 1966 the number reached 22,691. By 1968 between 170,000 and 200,000 patrons were using the branch libraries each year, with an estimated monthly attendance of between 200 and 250 people per library. By 1973, with the computerizing of the branch library system, requests for films were handled with increasing efficiency.[71]

Publications

During this era, the Society issued a number of publications designed to encourage research as well as motivate its employees. In 1962 it initiated an in-house publication called the *Genealogical Researcher,* which was sent to ward and stake genealogical committees. The following year, however, Church leaders asked that the information be included in the *Improvement Era* rather than in a separate publication. In 1964 the *Church News* also added a section on genealogy. The following year, Douglas D. Palmer started a weekly genealogical column, "What's Your Line," that continued for three years in the *Church News.* In January 1965, the Society began issuing *News and Reviews for Branch Libraries,* which contained reports from various branch libraries and information on books and other materials that the branches might want to purchase. The same year, it also inaugurated the *Genealogical Society Observer* for the benefit of employees and branch libraries. In 1973 the *Observer* became a single-page bulletin for priesthood leaders and branch libraries, and the newsletter for employees was renamed the *Record.* The *Observer* continued for four more years, and the *Record* for one.[72]

Special Classes and Seminars

The correlation program resulted in changes to long-standing programs of the Society, causing unavoidable discomfort for some. In 1964, for example, Archibald F. Bennett saw one of his cherished responsibilities disappear. The Society was no longer responsible for genealogical instruction programs throughout the Church. Because genealogy had become one of the four functions of the priesthood, its teaching responsibility also became a priesthood function. Therefore, the Society was no longer directly responsible for classes and course outlines, although it still cooperated with the educational efforts of the other organizations of the Church. As its main work, it now provided facilities and resources for research, direct assistance to patrons when possible, and a continuing supply of names to the temples. The Society's staff did not do research for other people or conduct regular genealogical classes as part of its responsibility.[73]

Nevertheless, certain specialized classes and seminars on how to do genealogy continued. For example, the library still taught classes on the use of library files, films, and research books and on "analyzing your own research problems." They were conducted by Archibald F. Bennett and the library staff.[74] In 1968 and 1969, the workload of the Society was so heavy that special orientation classes were held daily for the benefit of those interested in learning how to use the library. The library also had audio-taped tours, and volunteers gave tours of the facilities. "Locality lectures" were held so that patrons could learn what sources were available for particular countries. So many people attended a series called "Spotlight on English Research" in January 1968, that it had to be repeated. For one week during the 1969 World Conference on Records (see below), the library held classes in German on "Library Procedures and Genealogical Sources for Research in Germany." Classes were also held on genealogical programs developed by the Society, such as Records Tabulation.[75]

In addition, the Society planned various seminars. The first genealogical seminar at Brigham Young University was held in 1966, and 483 people attended. By 1975 nearly 3,000 people, including a number of genealogists not affiliated with the Church, attended the meetings. Many had traveled great distances. As these week-long seminars grew, a number of features were added. A General Authority of the Church gave a motivating address on genealogy each day. Beginning, intermediate, and advanced subseminars were added in 1970; the next year, special subseminars were held for branch librarians; and in 1972 classes were added for stake and ward genealogical leaders. By 1974 classes were taught in fundamental research methods for the British Isles, continental Europe, Scandinavia, the United States, and Canada. A session for

General Assembly of the World Conference on Records, 1969. This conference gave the Society international recognition as a leader in genealogical endeavors.

youth was added in 1975. In 1976 approximately 3,000 people attended the annual seminar.

Leaders of the Society began to recognize that even with such good attendance, continuing the seminar program would not meet the needs of all the members of the Church. Some, in fact, believed it was becoming a program only for Church members in Utah. The Society made the decision to discontinue its involvement in the seminars in favor of encouraging priesthood leaders to hold stake genealogical seminars. However, beginning in the summer of 1978, annual seminars were sponsored at Brigham Young University by the Family and Local History Program.[76]

World Conference on Records, 1969

Of all the classes, seminars, and other public programs held during this period, the most significant was the World Conference on Records, 3–8 August 1969. That year marked the Genealogical Society's seventy-fifth anniversary. The board felt nothing could provide a more appropriate celebration than a worldwide convention for genealogists and genealogical organizations.

Detailed planning for the conference began after a planning committee was organized in December 1967. They adopted the theme of "Records Protection in an Uncertain World." With Frank Smith as program chairman, the committee planned an ambitious program on research and record keeping. The Society invited genealogists, archivists, librarians, historians, computer experts, microfilm technologists, and civic leaders from around the world to take part. [77]

The Society was not disappointed. People from many nations flocked to Salt Lake City for the conference. Those who came were well served. Five thousand participants, including some who arrived just in time on a charter flight from Frankfurt, Germany, attended the opening session in the Salt Lake Tabernacle on the evening of 3 August. They heard General Authorities of the Church explain the reasons for the Church's commitment to records preservation and genealogical work and were treated to a musical program by the Mormon Tabernacle Choir.

The program included various general sessions in which participants heard about UNESCO's archival work from Dr. Alfred Wagner; the role of newspapers in preserving history and genealogy from Lord Thompson of Fleet, owner of the *London Times* and 180 other newspapers; archives of the future from United States Archivist James B. Rhoads; the Genealogical Society's microfilm program from Elder Howard W. Hunter; the preservation and use of records from Dr. Felix Hull, County Archivist for Kent, England; "Records Preservation in an Uncertain World" from U.S. Senator Wallace F. Bennett; and records preservation in the U.S.S.R. from Genadii Alexandrovich Belov, Director General of Archives, Moscow. Participants could also choose from over 230 sessions dealing with the creation, storage, and preservation of records; retrieval of records; written history of the British Isles as well as the Germanic, Slavic, Scandinavian, and Romance countries; written, oral, and traditional history in the Pacific, South Asia, Africa, Middle East, United States, and Canada; history and records of East Asia; heraldry; genealogical and hereditary societies; publication of genealogical material; and family organization. They enjoyed tours of the facilities of the Genealogical Society, including the famous Granite Mountain Record Vault. Many participants stayed in the homes of local Church members, which gave them a chance to observe some personal aspects of family life in Salt Lake City.[78]

The conference was also the occasion for some awards to the Society. On 5 August, Agfa-Gevaert, Inc., of Antwerp, Belgium, the world's major microfilm supplier, presented an award to the Society for "valuable contributions to the state of the art of visual communications and records preservation." Dr. Ken Stryker-Rodda, president of the American Society of Genealogists, also gave a certificate of appreciation to the Society. Later in the year, it received an award of excellence in microfilming from the 3-M company, a certificate of award in a graphics arts competition sponsored by the Printing Industries of America, Inc., for the brochure on the world conference, and an award of merit for the success of the conference from the American Association for State and Local History.[79]

The conference was considered a huge success by the Society, but there were some disappointments. Early estimates anticipated the possibility of 20,000 visitors to Salt Lake City during the conference, but the actual number attending was 6,000.

The Society estimated that the income from and cost of the convention would balance at $456,000. In the end, however, revenue from registration and other fees came to only $134,918.48, while expenditures amounted to $383,861.34, resulting in a net loss of $248,942.86. Some Church leaders worried about the losses, but Society officials, including Theodore M. Burton and Frank Smith, maintained that the positive effects of the conference outweighed the costs.[80] The conference legitimized the Society in the eyes of many archivists worldwide and opened the way for microfilming in previously untouched realms on the globe. It was, according to Howard W. Hunter, president of the Society at that date, one of the great successes of the Church.[81]

Personnel

During the early 1960s, the Society was responsible for hiring its own employees and sometimes had difficulty retaining well-trained personnel. In 1960 the employee turnover reached 77 percent, but in 1961, after the rules allowed women to work for six months after their marriage (see chapter 4), it dropped to 57 percent.[82] In the 1970s, Church policy was modified to allow married women to continue to work in Church offices indefinitely.

The Society also worked to promote high morale among its employees. It developed an orientation manual and various training programs, and Society personnel were encouraged to attend professional conferences and schools in order to improve their skills. In 1973 the Society held a major seminar for its employees, where division leaders discussed the history and the future of the Society and where various staff members presented musical numbers. The number of employees was becoming so large that their relationship to the Society could become impersonal. The leaders hoped that motivational programs would help employees feel they were important in the genealogical work of the Church.[83]

Physical Facilities

The rapidly expanding programs, library resources, and staff continued to create a need for larger and better facilities. In December 1933, the Society had moved into the basement and first two floors of the Joseph F. Smith Memorial Building. By 1949, Elder Joseph Fielding Smith was appealing to the First Presidency for more space. In 1955 the third floor, previously a ballroom, was remodeled, and the Society's microfilm readers, some offices, and the library reading room were moved to that floor.[84]

The added space met the needs of the Society only temporarily. What the board really wanted was a new library building located near the Salt Lake Temple. The First Presidency approved the concept in 1949, but nothing was done at the time. In 1960 there was still much discussion about the location of an archive building. Church leaders went to the Huntington Library and other archives in order to get ideas about what might be done, but more than two decades passed before the Society obtained its own library building.[85] In the meantime, the Society leased extra commercial property in Salt Lake City for additional space.

The need for new facilities became acute in 1960, when the city announced plans to widen the street where the Joseph F. Smith Memorial building was located. The plans meant that the

Montgomery Ward Building, ca. 1962, at 107 South Main, Salt Lake City, location of the Genealogical Society, 1962–72.

building would have to be razed. The Church promised the State of Utah that the Society would be out of the building within two years. Various suggestions were made for a new location, such as an old munitions plant on Redwood Road or some alternate sites on the east side of Salt Lake City. The Society had high hopes for the possibility of building on a fifteen-acre plot on Foothill Boulevard near Twenty-first East, but in the end, none of these locations were approved. In 1962 the Society moved into the abandoned Montgomery Ward building at 107 South Main Street. As the need for more room became critical, the Society also took over space in the Beehive Bank Building. These facilities were considered only temporary, since the Redwood Road site was still being considered. Officials of the Society were adamant, however, that they did not want to move to Redwood Road. It was in an industrial area; it was too far from downtown; there was inadequate parking available; and access to the area for patrons was very indirect. As late as 1969, Elder Theodore M. Burton was seriously discussing possible plans for remodeling the Montgomery Ward building in order to utilize that space more effectively.[86]

In the meantime, the Church erected a new twenty-six-floor office building on North Temple Street, which was ready for occupancy in November 1972. The four floors of the west wing and considerable space in the central tower were allocated to the Society.

Stake and Ward Organizations

The Genealogical Society was concerned not only with improving its central facilities, but also with maintaining viable genealogical organizations at the stake and ward levels. When genealogy became a central priesthood responsibility, local high-council members and high-priests group leaders were made directly responsible for stake and ward genealogical activities. These included teaching genealogical classes and examining records compiled by local Church members for submission to the Society. Unfortunately, the Society found that many of the family group sheets submitted contained the same types of errors that had always plagued the program. In January 1964, a new examination program was set up in an effort to eliminate some of the mistakes

Church Office Building, ca. 1972. The Genealogical Society was located in the west wing, 1972–85.

before they reached the Society. All records submitted were to be checked by two ward "examiners," who presumably had studied a training manual designed to help them locate errors on the forms. The Society stressed the fact that examiners should be teachers who helped ward members learn correct procedures, not censors.[87]

Genealogical Society leaders undoubtedly remembered the mixed success of earlier efforts to conduct genealogical classwork in the wards. Nevertheless, plans were soon made to once again have a genealogical class taught in the Sunday School, and a new lesson manual was written. The Society also planned to teach an adult genealogical class in connection with the MIA and encouraged priesthood quorums to study genealogy. Junior classes were begun in 1964 in five pilot stakes. Plans were made to expand them to the entire Church in 1965.[88]

There was still some debate, however, over where genealogy should be taught—that is, to what age group and in what organization. On 18 February 1964, Elder Burton commented candidly on the problem in a reply to an inquiry from Elder A. Theodore Tuttle. The Society really did not know where the classes would be most effective, he said. The junior classes for teenagers in the pilot stakes were a success, but, because of the manual being used, the adult Sunday School classes were ineffective. The courses in the MIA had been successful in some stakes, but due to the haste of the Society in getting the classes into the MIA, there had not been enough preparation, and the program had not worked well. Elder Burton suggested that until more information could be obtained, the genealogical program at the ward level should be confined to encouraging Church members to gather pedigrees, make family group sheets, and write personal histories. In subsequent letters, Elder Burton pointed to some additional problems, especially with the MIA classes. The number of family group sheets being submitted for temple work were not increasing as a result of the classes, because, he felt, there was too much emphasis on why genealogy should be done and not enough on the practical, how-to-do-it lessons. "We can talk about genealogy from now until dooms-day," he commented, "and not get any work out of our people unless we begin to do actual research."[89]

A new genealogy manual for the MIA class, entitled *Genealogy in Action,* was prepared for 1964. Its emphasis was not on doctrine and theory, but on organization, research, and submission of information. It outlined a thirteen-week course of instruction. The Genealogical Society stated that the class could also be taught in Sunday School if a local stake president or bishop felt that was a more appropriate place. The Society also suggested that stake and ward leaders take the course together and that it also be presented in priesthood quorums. Unfortunately, the genealogical class became a cause for some mild tensions within the Church as some wards began to hold it on Sundays, along with a workshop, at the same time as Sunday School opening exercises and classes. Complaints were registered about a policy that would allow this, and in April even Elder Burton objected to it. He wrote to the First Presidency stating his feelings that genealogical workshops should not be held on Sundays; he also did not feel that he had the authority to give such instructions to stake presidents and bishops. The policy was soon defined in such a way that wards could teach the genealogical classes at any time. The Society reported that the most successful classes were those held during Sunday School time. A new manual, *Family Exaltation and You,* was prepared for the course in 1973. It contained twelve lessons.[90]

Two stake and ward programs were eliminated during the 1960s. One was the practice of sending out genealogical home teachers to ward families, along with lessons and monthly study guides. This program had been reinstated under President Junius Jackson but was canceled when N. Eldon Tanner assumed Society leadership. Regular home teachers, however, were told to ask how much genealogical research was being done by the families, and MIA classes were to take over the lesson materials.[91]

The convention program was the other program to be discontinued, though not until after it had seen some significant expansion. When Jackson became president of the Society in 1961, he enlarged the convention staff to twenty-eight, because of the increasing number of stakes to visit. Some of the new people were volunteers, not Society employees, who had received the assignment as a Church calling and were trained by the Society.[92] To increase interest in the conventions, the Society produced various film and slide presentations. It also took programs to the missions of the Church. In 1962, for example, the Society explained its operations to two hundred international stake leaders. It also held a special genealogical meeting for stake presidents, stake genealogical chairmen, and bishoprics on the day before the opening of the October 1962 general conference of the Church.[93]

It was not long, however, before conventions were eliminated as a function of the Society. In 1963, as part of the general correlation program, the convention staff was transferred to the Church's new priesthood genealogical committee. In the stakes of the Church, one of the quarterly conferences each year was devoted to genealogical and welfare topics. A genealogical representative accompanied the General Authority visiting a stake conference and might be asked to speak three or four times during the weekend, as well as hold a genealogical workshop on Sunday afternoon. During the regular conference sessions on Sunday, the genealogical workers were given fifteen minutes, during which they emphasized genealogy as a priesthood responsibility.[94]

Eventually, the priesthood genealogy committee was reduced to Thomas Daniels as executive secretary and Elder Burton. The convention staff was eliminated. In 1967 the First Presidency began calling Regional Representatives of the Twelve, and one of their charges was to encourage genealogical work. By this time, the Society no longer had the responsibility for working directly with the wards and stakes.[95]

Promoting Genealogy

The Genealogical Society continued to find various ways and means to promote research in the Church and, at the same time, to avoid duplication of research efforts. One effort to prevent duplication was the development of the Pedigree Referral Service (PRS). Through this service, genealogists could register family surnames they were working on and receive information from others who were researching the same family names. The PRS used a computer to classify data by surname, town, county, country, and dates. Interested people could register for the service at no cost, but patrons requesting information would be charged a nominal fee for finding people working on the same surname in the same locality. George Fudge, manager of research and development, was initially placed in charge of the program, but in 1965, it was transferred to Delbert Roach and the Genealogical Library, where it became a patron service.[96]

The Society announced the beginning of the Pedigree Referral Service through priesthood authorities. In addition, articles appeared in the *Church News* and the *Genealogical Observer* inviting anyone doing genealogical research to register. The Society also encouraged people who were not members of the Church to register for the service. Articles explaining the PRS appeared in an El Paso newspaper as well as in *Family Weekly* and *Reader's Digest.*[97]

The Society had great hopes for the PRS, even anticipating two million names on the system. At first the officers of the Society planned to subsidize the program, hoping it would pay for itself once it got started. They were disappointed in the initial responses from members of the Church. After three years, the PRS still had only 800,000 names, and the Society was paying about five thousand dollars a month to subsidize the program. The Society made every effort to keep the PRS alive, even raising the membership fee from two dollars to four. Anyone who submitted a request to the service was required to register with the PRS, but when this policy failed to produce any more names, the requirement was eliminated.

The experience with the PRS demonstrated how few Church members were actually doing genealogical research. The Society thought that 20 to 25 percent of the Latter-day Saints were actively involved, but the results of the PRS experiment suggested that the figure was only about 2 percent. Some revisions in the program in 1968 failed to improve participation, and the PRS was finally abandoned in 1969. The names already on the computer were printed and microfilmed so they could be used by patrons.[98] Nevertheless, the need to coordinate research remained and in time would be addressed in new programs, such as the Family Registry and Ancestral File (see chapter 8).

The Society also made other efforts to encourage research and cooperation among members, including a three-generation and then a four-generation genealogical program. In 1965, following a suggestion by Paul Royall, the Society began to ask all Church members to submit three generations of family group sheets. Through this program, the Society hoped to teach members how to fill out the forms properly by giving them experience and having them receive help from ward examiners. Families were also encouraged to form family organizations. In addition, the three-generation program was seen as an opportunity to help train high priests group leaders and ward examiners in their genealogical responsibilities. The Society planned to microfilm the three-generation sheets so they could be used for research. By the end of 1966, approximately 20 percent of Church members had participated in the three-generation program.[99]

In 1966 the priesthood genealogy committee introduced a four-generation program at the stake conferences of the Church. The three-generation program was to continue, but members were asked to submit one more generation. In support of both the three- and the four-generation programs, the Society sent stake presidents, bishops, and other priesthood leaders a packet of information explaining how the programs should operate. The material was for use in the stake conferences devoted to genealogy. In 1967 the two programs were combined. The Society also encouraged Church members to submit two additional family group sheets, to keep books of remembrance, to attend the temple, to take part in the MIA genealogical workshops, to submit information to the PRS, and to be active in family organizations.[100]

In the meantime, the Church was expanding globally, and the Genealogical Society became concerned about how to promote its message and provide research assistance outside the English-speaking world. Until the 1960s, all Genealogical Society manuals were produced in English, but Theodore M. Burton began to encourage the Church to translate the materials. Eventually arrangements were made to have translations done. In 1962 plans were also made to form a genealogical society in Mexico, and the following year a genealogical library was set up there.[101]

In still another effort to be of service, the Society began a stake indexing program in the 1960s. In 1945 a patron had donated some Icelandic records to the Society, but a number of mistakes were found in the records. Henry Christiansen was asked to work with them. In 1967 a member of a stake high council in Springville, Utah, offered the services of members of his stake to index those records. The offer was accepted, and members of the stakes donated over 4,000 hours of work to index 1,251 pages. The success of this program gave the Society the confidence needed to begin similar indexing programs in other stakes.[102]

The period between 1961 and 1975 was one of constant change. The Genealogical Society's status moved from a brief stint as an auxiliary to one of the four basic priesthood programs of the Church. The Society stopped doing research for individuals but began to provide more effective assistance in the main library as well as in a network of branch libraries. It also began a name extraction program designed to keep the temples open regardless of whether or not Church members were providing enough names through their own research. Nevertheless, Latter-day Saints were not excused from doing their own ancestral research, putting family groups together, and performing sealings in the temples. During the April 1975 general conference of the Church, Elder Theodore M. Burton told priesthood bearers that the Society was furnishing 77 percent of all the names presented for vicarious ordinances in the temples but that it could not do the work of establishing family lines. "It is your personal, individual missionary responsibility," he reminded them, "to see that your direct-line ancestors have been baptized, endowed, and sealed in proper family order."[103]

NOTES

[1]Genealogical Society Minutes, 22 June 1961, Family History Department of the Church (hereafter cited as FHD).

[2]James B. Allen and Glen M. Leonard, *The Story of the Latter-day Saints,* 2d ed., rev. and enl. (Salt Lake City: Deseret Book, 1992), 596.

[3]Actually, there was some confusion about how to initiate the reorganization. According to the charter, the president was to be appointed by the First Presidency, but the rest of the officers were to be elected by the Society's membership. Since the Society had not accepted paying members since the charter was filed with the State of Utah in the 1940s, the only known members were General Authorities, temple presidencies, and former life members. An attorney suggested a meeting be called of this group, but the General Authorities decided to make the changes internally and not follow the terms of the charter. Lorin F. Pace to the First Presidency, 1 August 1961, Genealogical Society correspondence, FHD; Henry Christiansen files, July 1961, FHD.

[4]The reasons are not all clear, but apparently general administrative procedure had been rather loosely handled, and among other things, there may have been some concern about possible inappropriate use of funds and poor accounting. Theodore M. Burton, who later became vice president and then managing director of the Society, emphasized, however, that the problems were the result of carelessness rather than dishonesty. See Theodore M. Burton, oral history interview by Bruce Blumell, 1976, typescript, James Moyle Oral History Program (hereafter cited as JMOHP), Archives Division, Historical Department, The Church of Jesus Christ of Latter-day Saints, Salt Lake City (hereafter cited as LDS Church Archives), 8; George H. Fudge, oral history interview by Bruce Blumell, 1976, typescript, JMOHP, 39–40.

[5]Fudge, interview, 39–40.

[6]The new board consisted of G. Eugene England, Lorin F. Pace, Zelph Y. Erekson, Edward H. Sorensen, Irvin Fox, and Howard S. Bennion. Genealogical Society Minutes, 6 July 1961.

[7]Fudge, interview, 39–40.

[8]Genealogical Society Minutes, 10 October 1961.

[9]Bennett's work at Brigham Young University and in other educational capacities had made him well known as a teacher. He was delighted to continue working in the educational department of the Society, for he felt it was "an important and highly attractive division of the work." Archibald F. Bennett to Daniel H. Ludlow, 31 August 1961, Archibald F. Bennett collection, FHD; Genealogical Society Minutes, 10 August 1961.

[10]Genealogical Society Minutes, 14 December 1961.

[11]Henry E. Christiansen, oral history interview by Bruce Blumell, 1975 and 1976, typescript, JMOHP, 45; Burton, interview, 10.

[12]Mark E. Petersen to the Budget Committee, 19 December 1960, David O. McKay papers, LDS Church Archives. In this letter, Elder Peterson recommends, on behalf of the Society, that the Society's 1961 budget request be reduced from $2,413,864 to an exact $2 million dollars.

[13]Genealogical Society Minutes, 19 November 1962.

[14]There was also a suggestion that the management of the Society in the Jackson administration was not effective, in spite of the accomplishments listed above. Reportedly, Jackson, Gunderson, and some of the new board members were inexperienced and spent little time at the Society. It was said, for example, that Gunderson spent only a few hours a week at the Society talking with employees and that Jackson himself was not a good administrator. See Burton, interview, 8; Frank Smith, oral history interview by Bruce Blumell, 1976, typescript, JMOHP, 25–26.

[15]*Church News,* 19 January 1963.

[16]See Richard O. Cowan, *The Church in the Twentieth Century* (Salt Lake City: Bookcraft, 1985): 306–10, including chart on p. 309.

[17]James M. Black, oral history interview by Bruce Blumell, 1975, typescript, JMOHP, 1–2; Smith, interview, 26–27.

[18]Burton, interview, 8.

[19]Initially, N. Eldon Tanner was listed as president, Theodore M. Burton as vice president, and Paul Royall as secretary. N. Eldon Tanner to Secretary of State

of the State of Utah, 1 October 1963, Genealogical Society correspondence, FHD; Genealogical Society Minutes, 8 November 1963; Certificate of Incorporation of The Genealogical Society of The Church of Jesus Christ of Latter-day Saints, Inc., with foregoing minutes.

[20]Burton, interview, 3, 7, 8.

[21]Genealogical Society Minutes, 8 April, and 22 October 1963, 14 December 1964; Fudge, 1976 interview, 46.

[22]Fudge, interview, 46.

[23]Genealogical Society Minutes, 28 January, and 15 July 1964, 25 May 1972; *Deseret News,* 26 May 1972.

[24]At least as early as 1939, for example, the Hawaiian Temple was not in use much of the time because of lack of names. Elder John A. Widtsoe suggested that the Hawaiian Saints might be allowed to submit names for temple work even if they were not of their own direct lineage. Genealogical Society Minutes, 28 February 1939. The Logan, St. George, and Manti Temples likewise experienced shortages. When the president of the St. George Temple brought this matter to the attention of the Society in 1941, Archibald F. Bennett simply replied that "the function of our Society is to gather names for individual patrons" and to encourage members to do their own research. He urged that something be done to stimulate research in the temple district but offered no further help so far as providing a constant supply of names was concerned. Archibald F. Bennett to Harold S. Snow, 29 December 1941, Temple correspondence files, FHD.

[25]L. Garrett Myers to Committee on Personnel, 19 January, and 19 February 1960, Genealogical Society correspondence, FHD.

[26]L. Garrett Myers to Church Budget Committee, 18 January 1958, Genealogical Society correspondence.

[27]A. George Raymond, President of the Logan Temple, to All Stake Presidents, 15 April 1953, Genealogical Society correspondence.

[28]A discussion of these problems was held in a meeting of temple presidents, 4 April 1958, as recorded in minutes filed in Archibald F. Bennett papers, FHD.

[29]L. Garrett Myers to Committee on Personnel, 19 February 1960, Genealogical Society correspondence, FHD.

[30]Joseph Fielding Smith and Archibald F. Bennett to Stake Presidents and Stake Genealogical Chairmen, 18 February 1958, Genealogical Society Correspondence, FHD.

[31]Fudge, interview, 9–11, 15–16; Memo from George H. Fudge to President Hugh B. Brown, 17 August 1961, Genealogical Society correspondence, FHD; Joseph Fielding Smith and Archibald F. Bennett to Stake Presidents and Genealogical Representatives, 18 February 1958, Genealogical Society circular letters, LDS Church Archives; Robert Petersen, oral history interview by Jessee Embry, 1977, rough draft, LDS Church Archives, 6; Smith, interview, 14.

[32]Genealogical Society Minutes, 16 April 1943.

[33]Genealogical Society Minutes, 22 June 1943.

[34]Genealogical Society Minutes, 27 September 1943.

[35]Genealogical Society Minutes, 16 April 1946; Myers, interview 7, p. 13. In June 1943, Myers and Archibald F. Bennett were appointed to a committee to look into the whole problem, and in April 1946, Myers, Bennett, and Harold A.

Dent were appointed as a committee to make recommendations specifically with regard to the incoming Danish records.

[36]Genealogical Society Minutes, 2 June 1961.

[37]For some thoughts on the early impact of technology, including computer technology, on various Church programs, see James B. Allen, "Testimony and Technology: A Phase of the Modernization of Mormonism since 1950," in *After 150 Years: The Latter-day Saints in Sesquicentennial Perspective,* ed. Thomas G. Alexander and Jessie L. Embry, Charles Redd Monographs in Western History, no. 13 ([Provo, Utah]: Charles Redd Center for Western Studies, 1983), 173–207.

[38]Fudge, interview, 15; L. Garrett Myers to Joseph Fielding Smith, Genealogical Society Minutes, 10 October 1957; Genealogical Society Minutes, 24 May 1960.

[39]Gary Carlson, oral history interview by James B. Allen, 15 January 1980, typescript, JMOHP, 5.

[40]See Alfonzo Pia, oral history interview by James B. Allen, 1979, typescript, JMOHP, 2–16.

[41]See Carlson, interview, 20–22, for comments on this from the viewpoint of one of the computer experts.

[42]Carlson, interview, 9–10.

[43]Carlson, interview, 9–10.

[44]Carlson, interview, 7.

[45]Genealogical Society Minutes, 27 September 1960, 20 January 1961; L. Garrett Myers to the First Presidency, 4 October 1960, Genealogical Society correspondence, FHD.

[46]Carlson, interview, 19–20. See chapter 3 above for a discussion of the origin of the Temple Index Bureau.

[47]Lyle J. Gardner, "A Computer System for the Genealogist, Part I: Introduction to the Giant System" (paper presented at the World Conference on Records, 1969), 7. Copy in possession of Kahlile Mehr.

[48]*Salt Lake Tribune,* 5 October 1962; *Church News,* 13 October 1952.

[49]Fudge, interview, 15–16; Peterson, interview, 6.

[50]George H. Fudge, oral history interviews by George D. Durrant and John C. Jarman, 31 May–31 July 1984, 18. Copy in possession of Kahlile Mehr.

[51]Hugh Toner Law, "Biographical Sketch," June 1989, unpublished typescript, 4. Copy in possession of Kahlile Mehr.

[52]George H. Fudge to President Hugh B. Brown, 17 August 1961, Genealogical Society correspondence, FHD; Genealogical Society Minutes, 14 December 1961.

[53]Pia, interview, 8–12.

[54]See Burton, interview, 11–12; Fudge, 1976 interview, 16; Peterson, interview, 6–7, 17; George H. Fudge to Hugh B. Brown, 25 May 1962, Genealogical Society correspondence, FHD; Genealogical Society Minutes, 30 June 1962 (where the permission to extend missions calls is reported); form letter dated 18 September 1962, calling genealogical missionaries, to which the names of the first missionaries are attached, David O. McKay papers, LDS Church Archives; *Church News,* 15 September, and 27 October 1962; George H. Fudge to James E. Faust, 12 March 1963, Genealogical Society correspondence, FHD;

other miscellaneous letters in Genealogical Society correspondence about various aspects of the R-Tab and missionary program; "The Records Tabulation Program," *Improvement Era* 69 (October 1966): 872-73; various discussions reported in the Genealogical Society Minutes, 1962-73.

[55]Pia, interview, 12.

[56]Peterson, interview, 3-6, 14-16; Fudge, 1976 interview, 17-19; "A New System in Genealogy," *Church News,* 25 January 1969; "The New GIANT System in Genealogy," *Improvement Era* 72 (January 1969): 48-49; Christiansen, interview, 69-70.

[57]Fudge, 1976 interview, 20.

[58]Genealogical Society Minutes, 19 October, and 12 December 1961, 16 October 1962, 29 March 1963, 17 June 1964, 13 April, and 31 March 1966; L. Garrett Myers to Sidney C. Mayr Jr., 24 March 1961, Genealogical Society correspondence, FHD; Fudge 1976 interview, 25-26; Smith, interview, 29-30; Theodore M. Burton to the Patrons of the Research Department of the Genealogical Society, 17 January 1966, David O. McKay papers, LDS Church Archives.

[59]"Requirements for Becoming an Accredited Genealogist," mimeographed handout provided by the department in 1976.

[60]Personal interview with Roy Spjut, Research Specialist, Priesthood Genealogy Division, by Jessie Embry, 19 August 1976. Notes in possession of the authors.

[61]Genealogical Society Minutes, 17 June 1964; Theodore M. Burton, "How to Obtain Information from the Genealogical Society," *Fourth Annual Priesthood Genealogical Seminar Manual* (Salt Lake City: Genealogical Society, 1969), 27, 31-32.

[62]Genealogical Society Minutes, 7 December 1961, 1 May, and 3 September 1963.

[63]Genealogical Society Minutes, 1 May, 3 September, and 19 November 1963; Delbert E. Roach to Theodore M. Burton, 18 March 1974, Henry Christiansen files, FHD; Ted Powell, oral history interview by Jessie Embry, 1977, typescript, JMOHP, 10.

[64]Genealogical Society Minutes, 17 August 1961; Library Statistical Report, 1961-62, 1969; Henry Christiansen files, 1970, 1974, FHD.

[65]Fudge, 1976 interview, 34; Genealogical Society Minutes, 2 and 28 November 1961, 13 February 1962.

[66]Genealogical Society Minutes, 27 October 1964, FHD.

[67] Memorandum, May 1988, FHD.

[68]Genealogical Society Minutes, 2 and 31 July 1963, 28 January, and 3 March 1964; "Report on Branch Libraries," Henry Christiansen files, 1964, FHD; *The Genealogical Society Observer* 5 (March 1969): 5.

[69]Henry Christiansen files, 1964, FHD; Archibald F. Bennett, "The Day of Branch Genealogical Libraries Is Here," *Instructor* 100 (July 1965): 193; "Branch Genealogical Libraries," *Improvement Era* 69 (September 1966): 790-91; Theodore M. Burton to Lloyd A. Hamilton, 25 November 1964, Genealogical Society correspondence, FHD; Orson Cannon, oral history interview by Jessie Embry, 1977, typescript, JMOHP; Fudge, 1976 interview.

[70]Theodore M. Burton to Board of Trustees, 13 October 1971, included in the Genealogical Society Minutes, 27 October 1971.

[71]*The Genealogical Society Observer* 3 (January 1967): 9; 5 (September 1969): 14; Genealogical Society Minutes, 23 May 1973.

[72]Henry Christiansen files, 1962, 1965, 1973, FHD; Genealogical Society Minutes, 10 March 1964; George H. Fudge to Ronald G. Polland, 3 April 1963, Genealogical Society correspondence, FHD; Theodore M. Burton to All Stake Presidents, 14 April 1964, Genealogical Society circular letter, LDS Church Archives; Fudge, 1976 interview, 44; Theodore M. Burton to Paul Royall, 31 August 1964, Genealogical Society correspondence, FHD; Douglas D. Palmer, "What's Your Line," *Church News,* 1 May 1965.

[73]See Archibald F. Bennett papers, FHD, various memos and notes in 1964, for some insight into the frustrations Bennett was facing during the time of these changes. As late as June 1964, he still perceived his own duties as being directly related to teaching at BYU and supervising genealogical instruction in the Church.

[74]See material related to these classes in the Archibald F. Bennett files, FHD.

[75]*The Genealogical Society Observer* 4 (February 1968): 4; 5 (September 1969): 3; Genealogical Society Management Meeting, 6 January 1970, Central files, FHD.

[76]Burton, interview, 25–40; Genealogical Society Minutes, 11 April 1973; Priesthood Genealogical Seminar Syllabi, 1969–76; Smith, interview; Fudge, interview. The Family and Local History program, which was then under the direction of V. Ben Bloxham, was already doing an effective job of teaching genealogical classes and promoting genealogical studies on the BYU campus, and faculty members in that program had been regularly involved with the annual seminars. Therefore, taking over the seminars when the Genealogical Society stopped sponsoring them was a natural extension of the Family and Local History program. The Family and Local History program became part of the Department of History in 1977. For some historical background on Family and Local History at BYU, see V. Ben Bloxham, "Some Aspects of the Contribution of Local History Studies in England to the Establishment and Development of a Family and Local History Program at Brigham Young University, Provo, Utah, U.S.A." (Ph.D. diss., University of Southampton, 1980), chapter 4; Norman Edgar Wright, "History of the Genealogical Research Technology Program at Brigham Young University, 1960–1980," manuscript in possession of Norman E. Wright and a copy in possession of James B. Allen.

[77]Burton, interview, 49–50; Genealogical Society Minutes, 5 December 1967, 30 August, and 5 September 1968; "The World Conference on Records," *Improvement Era* 72 (January 1969): 22–24; Smith, interview, 37–38.

[78]*Deseret News,* 4 and 5 August 1969; Genealogical Society Minutes, 5 September 1968; *The Genealogical Society Observer* 5 (December 1969): 4–5; list of papers at the World Conference on Records provided by FHD.

[79]*The Genealogical Society Observer* 5 (December 1969): 4–5; *Deseret News,* 6 August 1969; Burton, interview, 49–50.

[80]The minutes of the Genealogical Society contain a balance sheet of the contents of the convention, dated 18 September 1969; Burton, interview, 49–50; Smith, interview, 37–38.

[81]Genealogical Society Minutes, 18 September 1969, FHD.

[82]Genealogical Society Minutes, 17 August, 28 September, 2, 9, and 16 November, and 5 December 1961, 25 January 1962, 26 November 1963, Fudge, 1976

interview, 30; Genealogical Society to Personnel Committee, 28 December 1961, Genealogical Society correspondence, FHD.

[83]Genealogical Society Minutes, 3 July 1962, 29 March 1963, 17 March 1964; Theodore M. Burton to Howard W. Hunter, 9 June 1964, Genealogical Society correspondence, FHD; Henry Christiansen files, 1955-60, FHD; Burton, interview, 64-65.

[84]Joseph Fielding Smith to First Presidency, 29 April 1949, Genealogical Society correspondence, FHD; *Deseret News Church Section,* 9 July 1955; L. Garrett Myers to Joseph Fielding Smith, 4 November 1955, Genealogical Society correspondence.

[85]Genealogical Society Minutes, 25 October, and 30 December 1949, 21 February 1957, 21 March 1958, 13 March, and 30 October 1959, 19 February 1960; L. Garrett Myers to Howard Barker, 21 February 1957, Genealogical Society correspondence, FHD.

[86]The minutes and correspondence of the Genealogical Society are filled, in this period, with concerns for space and with various proposals. For examples from the correspondence, see L. Garrett Myers to Church Building Committee, 9 August 1957; L. Garrett Myers to Wendell J. Mendenhall, 5 July 1960; Council of the Twelve Committee to the First Presidency, 30 December 1960; George H. Fudge to L. Garrett Myers, 25 May 1961; Genealogical Association to the First Presidency, 12 April 1962; George H. Fudge to Richard C. Miller, 8 March 1962; Junius M. Jackson, Lamont B. Gunderson, and George H. Fudge to Hugh B. Brown, 20 July 1962; George H. Fudge to N. Eldon Tanner, 10 July 1963; N. Eldon Tanner to Graham Doxey, 9 September 1963; George H. Fudge to N. Eldon Tanner, 21 November 1963. For examples from the minutes see Genealogical Society Minutes, 13 March 1959, 24 May 1960, 20 January, 3, 17 February 1961, 5 April 1962, 13 April 1966, 29 May 1969. All the above sources are located in the FHD. See also *Church News,* 30 June 1962.

[87]N. Eldon Tanner to Hugh B. Brown, 29 March 1963, Genealogical Society correspondence; Theodore M. Burton, "The Four Key Men," *Fourth Annual Priesthood Genealogical Research Seminar, 1969* (Salt Lake City: Genealogical Society, 1969), 4-6; "Family Group Sheet Examiners," 1964, Archibald F. Bennett collection, FHD; "The Ward Examination Program," *Improvement Era* 69 (June 1966): 484-85.

[88]Genealogical Society Minutes, 28 December, and 10 August 1961; N. Eldon Tanner to Executive Secretary of the Coordinating Committee, 10 April 1963, Genealogical Society correspondence, FHD; Archibald F. Bennett to N. Eldon Tanner, 13 September 1963, Archibald F. Bennett collection, FHD; "Popular Education in Genealogy," *Improvement Era* 67 (February 1964): 104-5.

[89]Theodore M. Burton to A. Theodore Tuttle, 18 February 1964, Genealogical Society correspondence, FHD; Theodore M. Burton to S. Dilworth Young, 12 June 1964, Genealogical Society correspondence; Theodore M. Burton to Edmond F. Woods, 9 June 1964, Genealogical Society correspondence.

[90]Derek Harland, *Genealogy in Action* (Salt Lake City: Genealogical Society, 1964); *A Continuing Program for Genealogy* (Salt Lake City: The First Presidency, 1968); Burton, "The Four Key Men," 18; Theodore M. Burton to the Quorum of the Twelve, 2 April 1964, Genealogical Society correspondence, FHD; Henry E. Christiansen, "Priesthood Leadership: How the Class Fits into the

Program," *Eighth Annual Priesthood Genealogical Research Seminar* (Salt Lake City: Genealogical Society, 1973); *Family Exaltation and You* (Salt Lake City: The First Presidency, 1973).

[91]Junius M. Jackson to Richard O. Grant, 23 February 1962, Genealogical Society correspondence, FHD; Genealogical Society Minutes, 19 April, and 31 May 1962; Junius M. Jackson, Lamont B. Gunderson, and George H. Fudge to All Stake Presidents and Counselors, 19 July 1962, Genealogical Society circular letters, LDS Church Archives; Home Teaching Lesson Guides, LDS Church Library; Presiding Bishopric to All Stake Presidents, 22 January 1963, Archibald F. Bennett collection, FHD; Archibald F. Bennett to N. Eldon Tanner, 8 March 1963, Archibald F. Bennett collection; N. Eldon Tanner to Dale G. Olson, 18 September 1963, Genealogical Society correspondence; Junius M. Jackson to A. L. Tidlund, 12 March 1962, Genealogical Society correspondence.

[92]Fudge, 1976 interview, 14; *Church News,* 29 December 1962, 11; Genealogical Society Minutes, 26 November 1962.

[93]Fudge, 1976 interview, 14; *Church News,* 29 December 1962, 11; Genealogical Society Minutes, 26 November 1962; Archibald F. Bennett to David O. McKay, 2 February 1961, David O. McKay papers, LDS Church Archives; Junius M. Jackson and Henry E. Christiansen, Report of the New England Mission Convention, 16 April 1962, FHD; Genealogical Society Minutes, 29 March, 9 April 1962, 21 December, and 24 August 1961; Junius M. Jackson, Lamont B. Gunderson, and George H. Fudge to All Stake Presidents, 17 September 1962, Genealogical Society correspondence, FHD.

[94]Fudge, 1976 interview, 52.

[95]Smith, interview, 29; Genealogical Society Minutes, 21 November, and 30 November 1961, 1 March, 9 October, and 9 November 1962; Theodore M. Burton to General Authorities, 1 June 1965, Genealogical Society circular letters, LDS Church Archives; Fudge, 1976 interview, 52; Thomas Daniels, oral history interview by James B. Allen, 1976, typescript, JMOHP, 2, 4–5.

[96]Burton, interview, 15–16; Fudge, 1976 interview, 21; Theodore M. Burton to Harold B. Lee, 18 September 1968, Genealogical Society circular letters, LDS Church Archives; Theodore M. Burton to Geraldine Bowen, 27 August 1964, Genealogical Society correspondence, FHD; Genealogical Society Minutes, 19 January 1965.

[97]Douglas D. Palmer, "Computer Tells You," *Church News,* 7 November 1964; Douglas D. Palmer, "Research Can Be Real Team Work," *Church News,* 23 October 1965; Douglas D. Palmer, "What's Your Line," *Church News,* 11 December 1965; Alvaretta K. Register to Genealogical Library, 23 February 1965, Archibald F. Bennett collection, FHD; *The Genealogical Society Observer* 4 (February 1968): 3; John J. Steward, "Try Climbing Your Family Tree," *Reader's Digest* 91 (September 1967), 103–7.

[98]Burton, interview, 15–16; "PRS Revisions in Force," *Church News,* 27 January 1968; Genealogical Society Minutes, 15 December 1964, 5 December 1967.

[99]Burton, interview, 24; Fudge, 1976 interview, 21–23; Douglas D. Palmer, "Three Generations: Each Family to Submit Initial Group Sheets," *Church News,* 13 March 1965; Douglas D. Palmer, "What's Your Line," *Church News,* 18 December 1965, 14; Jack E. Jarrard, "What's Your Line," *Church News,* 14 January 1967, 14.

[100]"Stake Conference Program for 1966," Henry Christiansen files, 1966, FHD; Jack E. Jarrard, "What's Your Line," *Church News,* 11 February 1967; "Priesthood Genealogy Program for 1966," *Improvement Era* 69 (March 1966): 190-91; "The Book of Remembrance," *Improvement Era* 69 (April 1966): 194-95; "The 1967 Challenge," *Improvement Era* 69 (September 1966): 820-21; *Continuing Program for Priesthood Genealogy.*

[101]Genealogical Society Minutes, 31 May, and 3 July 1962, 20 March 1963.

[102]Christiansen, interview, 21; *The Genealogical Society Observer* 4 (June 1968): 5.

[103]Theodore M. Burton, "Salvation for the Dead—a Missionary Activity," *Ensign* 5 (May 1975): 71.

Chapter 6

Gathering the Records

Of all the activities of the Genealogical Society, probably none has captured the attention of the world at large as much as its vast microfilming program—an effort to gather into one place the public, church, and private records of value to genealogical researchers. Started as a small project during the Great Depression, the microfilm program eventually became a sophisticated mainstay for the genealogical programs of the entire Church. Archivists, concerned over the loss of documents during World War II, were interested in assuring the preservation of their records, and the willingness of the Church to fund microfilming projects offered the means to do so. The program was initially undertaken in countries where Church members had the most ancestry, but eventually burgeoned worldwide.

Managing such an expansive effort was not an easy task. Producing quality films under a wide variety of circumstances continually challenged Society technicians. Adequate funding was a persistent problem. The filming effort was often accompanied by suspicions of the Society's religious motives and adverse publicity, although the appreciative comments of many who benefited from the microfilmed records were equally, if not more abundantly evident in the press. The vast numbers of genealogical sources necessitated making difficult decisions to define the scope of the filming project. Control from Salt Lake City worked for a few decades, but eventually, as the project expanded, supervision had to be decentralized.

Delbert Roach, 1947, observes the operation of a microfilm printer manufactured by Ernst Koehler. The printer copied a print master's images onto undeveloped film.

As the film collection grew, providing a means of storing and preserving the camera masters became a pressing issue. The solution was a vault blasted from the interior of a granite mountain, providing ideal storage conditions. Also, experiments in centralized film processing, contract filming, and high-reduction filming were conducted in an effort to increase efficiency.

The acquisition program expanded tremendously in both size and scope after the beginning of microfilming in 1938. The Society experimented with gathering new resources such as oral interviews. In 1975 approximately eighty microfilm operators produced 40 thousand rolls of film containing about 34 million exposures. In 1990 over two hundred operators produced 70 thousand rolls containing about 110 million exposures.[1] While filming opportunity was originally restricted in certain countries, political and social changes in the 1980s and 1990s made possible acquisition projects on every continent and in almost every nation.

The Need for Microfilm

By the mid-1930s, better methods were clearly needed for acquiring and handling the vast numbers of records potentially available to genealogical researchers. The Genealogical Library contained only printed records and handwritten manuscripts, and such resources provided just the tiniest fraction of the materials needed by most families. In 1943 the Church had practically exhausted its research facilities and poor record keeping was causing an unacceptable level of duplication in temple work. The Society board reported to the First Presidency:

> The needs of the Temples have far outstripped the research facilities of the Church. Until this is more evenly balanced, considerable time and money will be wasted and great duplication of effort will ensue. We have more or less concentrated our attention toward the building of temples and the performance of ordinances therein and have relatively neglected the acquirement of genealogies. It would be unwise to permit this situation to continue.
>
> . . . Many of the records which are now on the shelves of the Genealogical Library have been exhausted as far as names for temple work are concerned. Through the first six months of this year more than 546,000 names were checked at the Index Bureau and of this

> number 211,000 had previously been endowed. This is the highest percentage we have ever noted and we are hopeful that it can be reduced.
>
> . . . However, unless the Genealogical Society can provide a greater number of records secured from original sources, duplication of research work will remain at a high level.[2]

Securing information from original sources was time consuming and expensive. Tracing their ancestry as far as possible required many Latter-day Saints either to travel extensively or to hire professional genealogists. In many places, such as the Scandinavian countries, vital records were not even published. They were available only in manuscript form in government depositories.[3] Moreover, efforts to acquire more genealogical materials for the library were becoming complicated. In 1936, for example, an arrangement was made with the North Carolina Historical Commission to allow the Society to type cards of marriage records, with three copies going to the Society and three to North Carolina.[4]

That same year, Elder John A. Widtsoe urged the Society to begin copying or photographing European parish records, if permission could be obtained. With war threatening to engulf Europe, Elder Widtsoe warned of the danger such a tragedy could pose to government depositories where so many valuable records were housed. The Society quickly voted to appoint a committee to investigate the genealogical situation in Europe. Two years later, European Church members were hard at work copying parish records in some countries, such as Holland.[5] Such unsupervised manual labor was obviously inefficient, however, as well as fraught with possibilities for error. The need for something like the microfilm program was becoming obvious.

The Beginning of Church Microfilming

Ernst Koehler, a German immigrant, first brought the possibility of microfilming to the attention of the Society. A photographer in his homeland, Koehler had actually microfilmed some German books on genealogy before he emigrated to the United States. The Society authorized Koehler to investigate equipment, conduct experiments, and make recommendations. James M. Black was assigned to work with him.[6] Among other things, Black and Koehler soon discovered that many genealogical materials were already on microfilm and were available for purchase from governments and other agencies.

Before the Society acquired its first camera, it began to raise money to purchase records already on film, especially in Europe where an international crisis was imminent. A program to develop their own microfilming project was first presented to Church genealogists as an emergency measure because of the possibility of war. On 12 May 1938, Archibald F. Bennett wrote to stake genealogical representatives praising the new technology:

> Almost priceless original records containing genealogical data . . . can now be reproduced accurately and in completeness at a very nominal cost. . . . In view of the perilous state of world affairs, it seems that we must not delay in availing ourselves of every reasonable opportunity for securing the precious records so necessary in our work.[7]

In the same letter, in an attempt to raise funds, Bennett asked the stakes to solicit new memberships in the Genealogical Society or direct donations to a book fund from those who were already members. In December the appeal was renewed with even more urgency. Bennett wrote to the stakes:

> With a world trembling on the brink of wholesale war and devastation, there is every possibility that unless we act swiftly and decisively the records of millions upon millions of our ancestors will be destroyed beyond all recovery. Apparently the Lord has granted us a lull to seize this opportunity to rescue the records before it is too late. At the same time he has inspired the development of microphotography, by which records can be copied quickly, accurately, and so cheaply that it is almost unbelievable. It us up to us to act NOW![8]

Bennett was delighted with the enthusiastic response. By April, some stakes had subscribed over 200 percent of their quotas.[9]

At the same time, possibilities for microfilming were encouraging, for the Society had already received permission to photograph nearly two and one-half million pages of Danish parish records and a similar opportunity seemed likely in Germany and England.[10] In addition, the Society began to purchase United States records on film, as well as other genealogical records from various other organizations.[11] Nevertheless, problems with purchasing microfilms of records soon became evident. In 1939, for example, the Cannon family agreed to pay the cost to produce a microfilm copy of parish registers from the Isle of Man. The Society placed an order with University Microfilms at Ann Arbor, Michigan, to do this work. After several months, University Microfilms reported that they were unable to do the job. The parish ministers were unwilling to have the records microfilmed for fear of losing the payments they received when people came to the parishes to do the research themselves.[12]

Meanwhile, in October 1938, the Society purchased its first microfilm camera, a Graflex Photorecord, for $265. In November, Ernst Koehler began filming the Nauvoo sealing records and indexes. By the end of the year, the Society had filmed thirty-one volumes, consisting of 9,913 pages on 12 rolls of microfilm. A small beginning, but the program would grow dramatically in a surprisingly short time. On 10 January 1939, Koehler became the Society's first full-time, salaried, microfilm photographer.[13]

After the Nauvoo project was complete, Koehler began investigating other potential filming projects. A Danish photographer offered to copy records in his homeland at a cost of $2,963.10 for 100,000 exposures. Koehler estimated he could do the same job for $1,444.80. The board decided to send its own photographer when and if funds became available.[14]

The board also showed an early interest in acquiring copies of the huge storehouse of German records. The German Bureau for Racial Research in Berlin, consistent with Adolph Hitler's racial

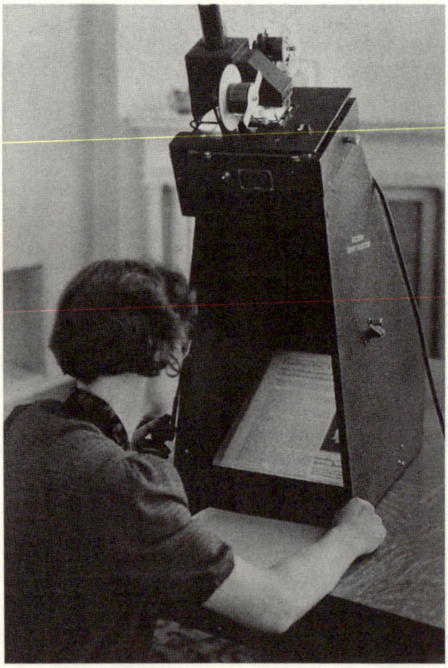

Recordak microfilm reader being used by Thelma Hill, head of cataloging in the Society Library, 1938. Courtesy Delbert and Barbara Roach.

theories, began during the 1930s to systematically gather and photograph old church parish records, encouraging the German people to trace their ancestry back at least to 1800. In the process, the Germans became pioneers in the photographic reproduction of records. By 1938 they had filmed 7,000 of the oldest, most dilapidated books of parish records. In 1939 the Genealogical Society wrote to German officials in an attempt to obtain copies of the films. In response, however, the Society was told that unperforated negative film was being used to photograph the records, and there was no printer available to make positive copies from such film. The Society replied that it had developed just such a printer and requested permission to send it to Germany to make the copies. Unfortunately, before that could happen all of Europe was engulfed in war.[15]

In addition to working with people in Denmark and Germany, the Society also sought an opportunity to secure records in Britain. The Church of England consisted of approximately 14,000 parishes, and the registers were usually in the custody of the parish priests. Hugh B. Brown, president of the British Mission, had attempted to get permission from the Society to begin microfilming those records, offering the Church of England positive prints of all records photographed. The Society suggested obtaining permission from each of the 43 diocesan bishops to approach the parish priests within their jurisdiction. After writing to the bishops, President Brown reported that he had received outright permission from some, "provisional permission by others, and curt refusals from still others." The majority of the bishops, nevertheless, were favorable to the idea. A British microfilming company, Micro-Security, Ltd., quickly offered its services to the Society. Some parish priests continued to resist the effort, however, fearing the loss of fees charged for the use of these records. Unfortunately, such continuing opposition as well as problems related to the outbreak of war prevented Micro-Security from photographing any parish records.[16] Most European microfilming had to wait until after the war.

In the United States, meanwhile, some significant projects got underway. One was in Tennessee, where the Works Projects Administration had sponsored the gathering and typing of county records, as it had in several states, in order to provide work for people with certain skills. In 1939 the Society exchanged copies of records in the Society's library for permission to film the entire Tennessee collection of several hundred volumes. L. Garrett Myers and Ernst Koehler began filming in Tennessee in October. They were also able to microfilm early LDS Church records in Kentucky. When the filming in Tennessee was partially finished, the Society received permission to have the balance of the records sent to Salt Lake City, where the work was completed. The records were then returned to Tennessee.[17]

Two key selling points of the microfilming program were established at the beginning of the project. First, the filming was done at no cost to the institution holding the records. Second, a free film-print copy of whatever records were filmed was returned to the institution. These were important considerations to archivists with overtaxed budgets. It gave them an opportunity to preserve their records at no cost.

In 1940 the Society received permission to film records available at the New York Genealogical and Biographical Society, where 53,718 pages of handwritten family histories were housed. Concerned about possible U.S. involvement in the European war, the New York society was planning to put the records away for safekeeping. Its leaders were willing, however, to let the Society microfilm the records first, and George Easter was hired to do the work on a part-time basis.[18]

The same year, the North Carolina Historical Commission gave the Society permission to photograph the Historical Commission collections. James M. Black was immediately transferred from the Society's library staff to a full-time position in the microfilm department in order to do the work. In May 1941, he was sent to North Carolina, where he remained until October 1943. He filmed not only the commission records, but also the records in several county courthouses. In a genealogical odyssey that Archibald F. Bennett called the "migratory course of our photographer from county to county," Black took his family into eighty-three North Carolina counties and copied nearly every record of genealogical value.[19]

James Black's North Carolina microfilming assignment inaugurated a career that would last, with only a short interruption during

World War II, for over thirty years. He was assigned to important supervisory positions that took him throughout the United States, Canada, South America, and Europe. Black's dedication to the Church and commitment to the microfilm program was exemplified in December 1945, when he was asked to return to the Society from his wartime job with the Union Pacific Railroad and continue his work in North Carolina. "Wages offered me were low in compari[s]on with those received at the Union Pacific Railroad," he later wrote, "but I considered the microfilming program of the Society the work of the Lord, and accepted re-employment."[20]

First Presidency Support

Despite the Society's success in Tennessee, New York, and North Carolina, the microfilming project was met with some reservations and initial restraint from Church officials. Some leaders had serious questions about the Church's financial involvement. In 1940, for example, Archibald F. Bennett proposed photographing a large collection of records at Raleigh, North Carolina. Although the price may not seem high by present standards, the estimated cost of $2,100 was too much for the Society's budget or the book fund gathered from members. The Society appealed to the First Presidency for funds, apparently believing that the obvious need for quickly obtaining more records would be persuasive.

The First Presidency did not approve the request. While they did not object to the Society continuing its program, they felt that genealogical research was an individual and not a Church responsibility. The First Presidency reasoned that Church financing would unwisely shift the responsibility for research from the members: "Once we begin this kind of work, we shall be involved into more and more expense until the amount would reach such proportions that we could not undertake to carry."[21]

The First Presidency's refusal to fund Society activities was not intended, nor interpreted by the Society, to be a restriction on Genealogical Society work. The Society continued to assume that its obligation was to gather all the records it could, using available membership funds. Elder Joseph Fielding Smith suggested that should the opportunity open up for gathering records from

England or Scandinavia, he would not object to again asking for help from the First Presidency. By this time, war had overrun all of Europe, causing Elder Smith great concern over the genealogical records. Nevertheless, he believed that the Lord would not only preserve the records, but would yet open up the way to obtain them.[22] The Society, meanwhile, put on an even more vigorous campaign for memberships and donations.

How long the First Presidency's official reticence lasted is unclear, but after the war, the official policy seemed to change quickly. L. Garrett Myers took a microfilm reader to the office of President J. Reuben Clark Jr., chairman of the Church finance committee, and spent hours showing him the possibilities. This demonstration apparently gave President Clark a clearer perspective on the importance of microfilming. He soon began using his influence to get money budgeted for the program.[23]

Church officials may also have been influenced by reports of a surprising amount of duplication in temple work and by the possibility that some of this duplication could be avoided by a better record-gathering system. Duplication was so prevalent that in some years the names eliminated because of previous endowments exceeded the number of endowments for the year. Acquiring more original source material would help prevent duplicating research. "It is with this thought in mind," one report said, "of making available to our people a maximum number of records in the least possible time with the least duplication, and the smallest outlay, that we have used the microfilm process in order to acquire millions of pages of genealogical data."[24]

Post World War II Expansion

Although microfilming was curtailed during the war years, the early projects provided an impressive beginning for the program and a base for further expansion. As soon as the war was over, the program grew dramatically particularly in Europe and Mexico. This growth is illustrated by the rapid rise in the amount of exposed film received. In 1944 and 1945, the Society received 24 and 69 rolls respectively. In 1946 the number went to 462, in 1947 it jumped to 4,501, and in 1948 it made another jump to 10,012.[25]

After the war, microfilming began again in Great Britain. In December 1945, the Society received permission to microfilm copies of parish registers located at the Newcastle Library in Durham. From a bank, James Cunningham, a local Latter-day Saint, obtained an old microfilm camera, which he and Frank Smith taught themselves to use. They finished the project in two weeks.[26]

Microfilming in Scandinavia began after the Society contracted with Arthur G. Hasso, an employee of the Danish National Archives and a former history professor at the University of Copenhagen, to film Scandinavian parish records. Hasso had offered to photograph the records seven years earlier, having obtained permission from the Danish Church Ministry. The Genealogical Society, however, felt the cost was too high, even after he offered a lower price. He filmed a number of records anyway and after the war, in 1945, contacted the Society again. This time they reached an agreement, and microfilming commenced in the Scandinavian countries in 1946.[27]

The next area outside the U.S. to be included in the microfilming program was Mexico. Work began there in 1952 after the mission president, Lucian M. Mecham Jr., witnessed the deplorable state of the nation's census records and pressed the Society for a year to do something about it. The records were stacked over six feet high, covered with dust, and soiled with droppings from pigeons roosting in the rafters of the abandoned church where they were stored. Other records were being lost through flooding, the hot climate, and neglect.

In August 1952, the Society sent Delbert Roach, a Spanish-speaking member of the Society staff, to begin microfilming in Mexico. With the help of President Mecham's influential friends and with a camera borrowed from UNESCO (United Nations Educational, Scientific, and Cultural Organization), he began filming at the National Archives in October. Roach continued to investigate record sources, finding vast quantities of desirable records and little opposition to them being filmed. After the Society began its filming, it received excellent cooperation from Catholic Church as well as civil officials.[28]

The history of early microfilming is filled with unusual, touching, and sometimes dramatic accounts of faith and devotion. None

Delbert Roach, surrounded by staff and records in the National Archives of Mexico when microfilming was initiated there in 1952. The Mexican film collection is the largest foreign collection of the Society.

illustrate this dedication better than the story of how a huge and important collection of German records came into the hands of the Church.[29]

In the 1930s, Paul Langheinrich, a German convert to the Church and an avid genealogist, was given access to all German archives and church record offices, and for a short time, did genealogical research for the government. In 1937 he moved to Berlin and did volunteer work in the Church's German Mission genealogical department. Near the end of the war, he became first counselor in the mission presidency.

During the war, as the allied armies advanced toward Germany, the German government began to take precautions with its genealogical records and other treasures, storing them away in places unlikely to be destroyed by bombs. Vast collections of documents and films were stored away in castles and mines located in eastern Germany, which eventually fell under Soviet control. Langheinrich was not willing to let such a priceless store of genealogical material escape the use of the Church. Immediately after the war, therefore, he and a few other German Saints began a personal crusade to find and recover this trove of information.

On 9 August 1945, Langheinrich wrote to the Russian commander in East Berlin, Field Marshal Zhukov, asking permission to provide food and clothing for Church members there and also to search for German genealogical materials. The chances of receiving a reply seemed remote,[30] but Zhukov passed the letter on to his successor, General Sokolovsky, who soon responded and gave Langheinrich approval to do everything possible for the Mormons in East Berlin and to keep any genealogical records that he could find. For the German Saints, this was clear evidence that the Spirit of Elijah was operating in their behalf.

At the same time, several young German Saints were called on missions. One of them was Rudolph K. Poecker, who left a wife and child at home and began his missionary work in January 1946. He was sent to lower Saxony, where many salt mines were located and which was under Russian control.

Elder Poecker, who had become fluent in Russian while serving in the German army, was soon called into the mission office, given a copy of General Sokolovsky's letter, and assigned to search for the hidden genealogical records. He went from one mining town to another, showing the letter to Russian officers and asking questions. He finally found an officer who knew that some of the records were in Stassfurt, in a salt mine 400 meters deep. The officer told Elder Poecker, however, that he must have a list of the records before he could grant permission to remove them. Elder Poecker then went to the Stassfurt mine, where he found that the man in charge had been worried about the disposition of the records and wanted to help. The two of them descended to a huge underground cavern, where they found a large cache of books, all containing genealogical records, stacked on the floor. They wrote down the origin of each collection, then measured the size of the stacks, taking care to overstate the measurements, rather than taking a chance of measuring short, so that nothing would be held back when the books were taken from the mine and checked by the Russians. Poecker took the list to the Russian officer, who gave him permission to remove the records.[31]

One problem in the effort to retrieve these and other records was finding enough money to cover the cost of transporting them from their various hiding places to Berlin. After considerable soul-searching, Langheinrich and other local Church leaders decided to use 10,000 marks from local Church funds, even though they had no official permission from Church headquarters in Salt Lake City. Such an opportunity simply should not be passed by, they reasoned. Later, after Langheinrich received 22,000 marks from the German government to establish an official archive, he returned the initial money to the Church.

Meanwhile, sixteen missionaries were assigned to help Paul Langheinrich retrieve records and transport them to Berlin. In February 1946, they went first to Rothenburg Castle on a mountain top in Thuringia. Having arranged with Russian officials for a railroad car, Langheinrich also rented a pickup truck and trailer to bring the records down from the mountain to the railroad. But the truck slipped and spun on the icy roads, and prospects for retrieving the records began to look bleak. Langheinrich and two missionaries stepped into the woods and prayed for help, then unhooked the trailer. The truck made the climb up the frozen road to the castle and the group was able to remove at least a few of the records. They would need a warm rain, however, one elder remarked, if they were to get all the records out in time to meet the railroad car. That night the warm rain came, making it possible for the truck with it trailer to make it to the castle. Langheinrich left some of the missionaries there to load the load the trailer while he and the others went on in the pickup to Castle Rathsfeld. There they obtained a huge store of Jewish records. Providentially, the railroad car arrived one day late, giving the missionaries time to acquire all the records in both castles, load them on the train, and send them to Berlin. That night it snowed, and by morning the mountain roads were frozen over once again. The missionaries were convinced that their prayers were answered and that God was watching over that important excursion.

The next year, Langheinrich and another missionary were arrested when they tried to retrieve the records from the mine in Stassfurt. The Russian commandant reluctantly cleared them and accompanied them to the mine. As he inspected some of the records, he picked up a document labeled "Letter of Frederick the Great to His Grandmother" and apparently thought the collection had strategic military significance. "Do you believe that we are going to begin a war with you with the old grandmother?" Langheinrich chided, at which point the angry general declared that the entire car was seized. Langheinrich, however, simply stepped forward and closed the railway car door. The general drove away in a rage, apparently still hoping to stop the shipment, but Langheinrich immediately seized the opportunity to use the mine office telephone and called the railroad station. "There is a loaded car here," he said with an air of authority, "which must be picked up immediately and taken to Berlin." The car arrived in Berlin even before Langheinrich.

None of these records could become the property of the Church, but Paul Langheinrich was soon funded by the German government to establish an archive.[32] As soon as the archive was established, Langheinrich set up a microfilming program and provided films to the Society. He later estimated that he put over one hundred million names on film. Largely, then, through Paul Langheinrich's tireless efforts as well as the dedication of the missionaries who worked with him so soon after the war, a vast treasure house of genealogical information was preserved for future generations.

Promoting and Managing the Program

The Society received welcome support and encouragement from Church leaders as the microfilming project expanded. Members of the Quorum of the Twelve demonstrated special interest in the program during their travels. In 1946, for example, while visiting members in war-torn Europe, Elders John A. Widtsoe and Ezra Taft Benson encouraged local leaders to look into microfilming possibilities.[33]

The Society soon sent representatives to negotiate contracts with governments, churches, and institutions. Archibald F. Bennett was the first. He spent six months in Europe in 1947, working with the mission presidents, investigating filming opportunities, and negotiating new projects. In 1950, L. Garrett Myers went to Europe to adjust microfilming contracts to meet the realities of recent devaluations in currency and to be a troubleshooter and diplomat for the program. In Switzerland, for example, he temporarily suspended operations after concluding that a man working for the Society had "a penchant for doing the wrong thing" and, among other things, had said things during an interview with the press that made it difficult to obtain permission to copy certain records.[34]

Clearly, the Genealogical Society was entering a new technological age that provided genealogists the miracle they had long awaited. James Black and his associates were the unsung heroes who created the standards and procedures which made the miracle happen.

As the microfilming program grew to major proportions, one of the many problems to appear was quality control. In August 1947, James Black was appointed microfilm editor of the Society. Before his appointment, there had been literally no control, and some of the film the Society received was very poor. Making acceptable films was a complicated process that involved several stages, each of which could affect the quality and usability of the film made available for research.

Black and his staff began inspecting the films at the Society, noting all the problems and finding solutions. Many of the records, they discovered, needed to be refilmed. As a result, Black had to travel to filming sites throughout the world to train camera operators.

In July 1948, Black went to Europe. Prior to that time, because of a shipment of poor quality film from England, Joseph Fielding Smith had ordered a halt to all microfilming operations until Black's arrival. Black began his work in Dewsbury, where he worked closely with George Fudge, an experienced microfilm operator, who had just been appointed microfilm inspector. Black eventually visited sites in the British Isles, Switzerland, Italy, France, Holland, Denmark, Norway, and Sweden. In each country, he trained personnel and established procedures necessary to improve the program.[35]

Building the Collection

As the microfilm program mushroomed, so did costs. In 1948, just ten years after the program began, the Society presented the leaders of the Church with a 1949 budget request of $749,599.88 for microfilm projects in Holland, Norway, Great Britain, Finland, Sweden, Belgium, France, Switzerland, Germany, Denmark, and the United States. The budget request had grown by more than $580,000 in two years. Joseph Fielding Smith, who may have had reservations in the early days of the program, was now one of its most enthusiastic advocates. He supported the budget and was determined to have the Society present all the facts to the budget committee. "I feel there is a real need for speeding up this work," he declared. "I think the Lord is willing that we should hurry in getting the microfilming done."[36] In January, after the budget was approved, Elder Smith expressed his amazement at the approval of such an extensive program, especially in contrast to "the small way in which the work began years ago."[37]

An opportunity to economize came in 1949, when the Du-Pont Film Company agreed to give the Society a film dealership which, it was estimated, would save about $170 per day in film costs alone.[38] Genealogical work not only used high technology, but had also become a significant business.

The microfilming record was impressive. At the end of 1938, the Society had acquired only twelve rolls (100 feet each) of microfilm; ten years later it owned 17,051 rolls; in another decade, the number had grown nine times to over 189,849 rolls.

By 1954, the films at Society headquarters contained approximately 150 million pages of records, or the equivalent of 500,000 volumes. L. Garrett Myers liked to describe the collection by noting that "if someone had the patience to unwind all the rolls of microfilm the Genealogical Society of the Church . . . has and place them end to end, he would make a trip from Salt Lake City to Edmonton, Canada, and return before running out of film."[39] In 1959 the production of microfilm by the Society peaked at 56,989 rolls, more than double that of any previous year.[40]

During this period of almost unbridled growth, the Society's requests for funds seemed to be always granted. Such leniency did not continue, however, for other Church programs were also expanding. The Church was building more meetinghouses, for example, to meet the additional needs of its rapidly growing membership around the world. When the Society's budget estimate for 1961 reached $2,413,864, the Church Budget Committee not only asked for reductions, but even asked if the whole microfilming program could be suspended during the next year. The Society board was aghast. The written response of L. Garrett Myers shows how deeply entrenched the Society was in projects that would be practically impossible to cancel. Thousands of films, he said, were still in labs and editing rooms and must be processed before the film spoiled or before it was too late for retakes. Also, certain contractual obligations required completion in thirty to ninety days. Canceling them would be disastrous for various reasons: some projects were nearly finished, several archivists had made special preparations for the Society's microfilmers, some microfilm was on advanced order, and replacing trained workers would be difficult when the program was renewed. In addition, the situation in the British Isles and Europe was very favorable to the program, and the Society had certain exchange agreements that should not be violated.[41] In spite of all these objections, however, the Society decreased its budget request, deciding to discontinue some projects and slow others.

Because of budget considerations, microfilming costs were closely scrutinized in 1961. Filming expenses varied from site to site. Costs ranged from two to nine cents per exposure in the United States and were higher in some other countries.[42]

Questions of contract filming with individuals or companies and reimbursement on an exposure basis rather a salary basis were intensively examined. The decision at the time was to continue on a salary basis and to implement a new expense accounting form. Operators in North America met in Salt Lake City in January 1962 to review the issues and changes. By the end of the year, the Society reported that great economies had been effected through a "frugal" approach and that the Society was now financially sound.[43]

Film production dropped from a high of 56,000 rolls per year in 1959 to only 25,000 in 1963. After that, production began to rise again until it reached a level of between 40 and 50 thousand rolls per year. By 1969 the film collection had grown to 660,000 rolls, and by 1975, it reached 862,770 rolls. When some 100-foot rolls were divided for cataloging purposes, the total stored in the Granite Mountain Records Vault came to well over a million. They included records from every state in the United States and more than forty other nations.[44] In 1977, George Fudge remarked, "We spent $10 million in 1976. We could easily be spending ten times that much. The task confronting us is monumental."[45]

The level of acquisitions dropped precipitously with the temporary decision in 1978 to film only extractable records. It remained below 40 thousand rolls until 1986. Late that year, the Temple and Genealogical Executive Council directed the Society to review the question of whether or not the Society was filming family history sources fast enough. Anomalous in times when budget cutting was the norm, the Council's acquisition initiative underlined their deep interest in providing the sources for research to the individual Church member. The Society proposed an increased budget for filming records threatened by destruction because of political turmoil or deterioration.[46]

A three-year plan was approved that targeted growth from 50 to 100 million exposures each year by 1989. As the Society entered the fiftieth anniversary of microfilming, it was significantly expanding its acquisition effort. Acquisitions rose from 70 million exposures in 1986, to 85 million in 1987, to 95 million in 1988, to 106 million in 1989. The impetus of the three-year effort continued as the rate of acquisitions rose to 130 million exposures in 1992, a three-fold increase over the period before 1985. Even with the increase in filming, Rick Ebert, the director of acquisitions, stated in 1991 that filming opportunities at that time still far exceeded the Society's ability to respond.[47] By 1994, the collection consisted of approximately 1.8 million microfilm rolls.

Public Relations

When James Black and others made contact with local authorities, they usually received enthusiastic cooperation. Many church and civic leaders were excited by the opportunity the microfilm program provided to preserve their records in permanent form at no expense to the community. In 1972, for example, Missouri's secretary of state publicly announced an agreement with the Genealogical Society to microfilm records in his state at a cost, over three or four years, of $500,000 to the Society. "The filming of more than 17 million pages of important genealogical records," he declared, "at no cost to the Missouri taxpayers, is an invaluable contribution to our state records management program. . . . Fires in courthouses and capitols have been our greatest enemy in preserving records. . . . With the microfilm on file, copies will always be available."[48] Such obvious mutual benefits were one of the factors in the success story of the microfilming enterprises.

Although reaction to the Church's microfilm projects around the world was generally positive and complimentary, there were exceptions. Some Catholic and Protestant church officials, for example, objected to the filming for various reasons. The Soviet Union even charged in 1953 that the program was tied to some kind of U.S. government effort to obtain detailed current population records.[49]

On the other hand, Genealogical Society representatives were frequently invited to speak to various public and private groups about the program. State and national governments enthusiastically supported microfilming because of what it could mean to their own record-keeping programs. In 1975, for example, the governor of the Commonwealth of Massachusetts issued an official proclamation praising the Church for its efforts and naming 15 July 1975 "Mormon Record Day."[50] In 1968 the Society received an award from Eastman Kodak Company for its "significant contribution to the advancement of the science of information technology." James M. Arnold, vice president of the company, noted that the Genealogical Society was the second largest organization to make use of Kodak products and the only organization making any significant use of microfilm for the preservation of genealogical records. He warmly commended the Society for its "unique storage, indexing and classification system."[51]

Deciding Where and What to Film

In the 1940s, after the Church began to assist in microfilming costs, Elder Joseph Fielding Smith insisted that the first priority was to search the records of countries where most of the ancestral records of Church members were located. If they had approval to obtain records from Europe, Elder Smith felt they should get them even if they cost a million dollars. This kind of commitment led to the policy of filming first the records that would be most valuable to Church members, beginning in areas where a large number of people joined the Church in the early days.[52]

Until 1961 camera operators, under the general guidance of the Society, decided what to film. The new board of directors, established in 1961, began to tighten this policy. Because they were not experts in genealogical records, the board formed a Records Approval Committee to decide what should be filmed.[53] At the same time, George Fudge toured operations in the United States. To his dismay, he found some filmers photographing inconsequential records such as full runs of newspapers.[54] To control the materials being filmed, Fudge recommended that a filming supervisor be appointed to implement the decision of the Committee.[55] The board appointed Fudge as temporary supervisor in 1962. In 1963, James Black was appointed to the newly created position of North American filming supervisor.[56]

With his appointment as Society vice president in 1964, Theodore Burton inquired where the First Presidency thought the Society should film. In response, the Presidency reaffirmed assumptions that had long guided the filming program: "The Society should continue as it has been doing, and concentrate its efforts in the records of the United States, British Isles, and northern

European countries and then spread into those areas in which there is the greatest number of new converts and where it can be done most economically and the data obtained most readily."[57]

Elder Burton also addressed the issue of what to film. In January 1964, he established the Microfilm Planning Committee (Records Selection Committee, 1967–70, then the Acquisitions Planning Committee through 1979, when the Directors Council assumed the responsibility) to succeed the Records Approval Committee, which had not functioned during the previous year. The Microfilm Planning Committee included representatives from all divisions in the Society and met on a regular basis. The various division representatives provided information based on their division's responsibility. For instance, Priesthood Genealogy informed the committee what records members of the Church needed and which areas were growing but were as yet unrepresented in the microfilm collection. Acquisitions identified what records were available. Temple Services was concerned about initiating filming in countries where temples were under construction, such as Japan and Brazil.[58]

A change in microfilming policy occurred as a result of the Society's focus on extraction programs in 1978–79. At that time, the Society decided to film "extractable" records only. This policy was rescinded in 1980, but the need to establish a long-term microfilming plan emerged from the discussions. A plan was developed in 1980–81 that required the gathering of a record mix that would provide not only for extraction, but also for tracing lineages. To apply this plan rigorously, the Society decided to write a profile for each country of the world and determine the records that needed to be filmed there in order to identify and link seventy-five percent of the families of the historic population.[59] During the next six-month period, Society staff members wrote record profiles for over one hundred countries.[60] In order to make decisions on what would be filmed even before cameras were in a country, these profiles were studied for information on record types, their value, and the estimated quantity yet to be filmed.

This program of consistent collection development was institutionalized in 1983 with the creation of a Collection Development Section.[61] This section was established to evaluate all proposed acquisitions against the profiles and the current Society collection in order to avoid duplicate or redundant acquisitions. The new organization provided for a separation of duties between collection specialists, who decided what to film, and negotiators, who decided when and where to film. It helped negotiators to know exactly what type of record should be filmed if permission were granted.

As an initial step in accomplishing their assignment, section staff began to review and rewrite the profiles—somewhat hastily compiled the year before—to make sure that no important source was overlooked. In 1984, the newly rewritten profiles began to be published. Over the next decade, sixty-two profiles were extensively revised and updated to identify exactly what sources could and could not be filmed. Once a profile was approved, new filming projects could go forward without further review.

Decentralization[62]

Until 1958 the microfilming program was administered from the headquarters of the Society in Salt Lake City. Two main problems arose from this situation: retake orders were not returned promptly to camera operators and the delivery of donor prints was delayed. In 1958, Arnold Seiler from Salt Lake City was appointed as supervisor of a newly expanded filming effort in West Germany. This was the first instance in which the Society maintained an official filming representative overseas. Because filmers in other countries began to consult with him, Seiler soon began to function as the de facto supervisor of all European filming.[63]

In 1960 responsibility for European filming was shifted to the European mission president—the Church representative responsible for all other Church programs and activities in Europe. This arrangement did not succeed because the mission president did not have the time or background to manage the complex filming program. As a result, the Society sent Harold Jacobsen to Scandinavia and England in 1961 and George Fudge to Europe in 1962 in behalf of the filming program. In 1963 the Society appointed another European representative, a native of Holland, Syger Hasenberg. This arrangement lasted for several years until supervision of the filming was returned to Salt Lake City. In 1967,

Elder Burton transferred staff from the Research Division—previously involved in doing patron research—to the Microfilm Division, giving its staff the responsibility of becoming experts on genealogical sources worldwide. They gradually began to negotiate for the sources they identified.[64]

In 1972 the Society decided once again to establish European-based supervision and sent Ralph Hughes to live in Europe. Although he was primarily responsible for resolving technical problems, he began to deal with personnel and administrative matters by default. In 1974, Thomas Lee Boam replaced Hughes. Under Boam the process of transferring responsibilities for personnel and payroll administration, quality control, negotiations, and project administration from Salt Lake City headquarters to foreign staff accelerated. Boam hired regional negotiators from the local population. They knew the languages and customs of the areas in which they worked and could resolve problems more quickly and efficiently.[65]

In the wake of Boam's work in Europe, other personnel from Salt Lake City were sent out to other areas of the world to provide decentralized administration of the filming program. In 1978, Dennis Neuenschwander was sent to Eastern Europe and Mel Thatcher to Asia. Jim Streeter was sent to Latin America in 1988. The filming program continues to operate with area managers working in the field and local staffs developing and absorbing a larger role in the microfilming program.

In the 1980s, in an attempt to control costs, the Society began to rely more on film purchases, joint ventures, contracts, and missionary couples, rather than salaried camera operators. In 1993 the Society employed the equivalent of two hundred cameras to acquire new sources from around the globe. This was three times the seventy-one cameras in operation in 1976.

Granite Mountain Records Vault

The massive influx of films to the library in Salt Lake City necessitated the construction of adequate storage facilities. Camera masters were first stored in the northeast corner of the Joseph F. Smith Memorial Building, which had housed the library

Fresh water reservoir in the Granite Mountain Records Vault. This water, used in film processing, comes from a spring inside the mountain.

since 1933. By 1950 there was no place to store film negatives; they were kept in packing boxes on top of the TIB card file cabinets.[66] The situation was temporarily resolved with the 1951 construction of a film-storage annex on the southeast side of the library. Within six years, that facility had become insufficient, and in 1957 the negatives were moved to the vault in the basement of the Joseph William Taylor Mortuary, just up the street from the library.[67]

Meanwhile, a long-term solution was under discussion. In 1954 the Society announced the proposed construction of a "buried vault," where proper humidity and temperature conditions could be maintained and the film would last for "hundreds and hundreds of years."[68] In 1956 the Genealogical Society and the Church Building

Central corridor and entrance into a record bay at the Granite Mountain Records Vault. The central corridor provides access to each of six bays where the camera masters of the microfilms are stored.

Committee agreed upon certain design requirements,[69] although a final decision on the specific location had not been made. Site surveys and debates continued. A site near the Salt Lake City police department's pistol range, close to Ensign Peak, was seriously considered and unanimously approved by the board of directors in February 1958. When geologists examined it in detail, however, they discovered that the rock formation there would require expensive and cumbersome reinforcement and that the rock would probably leak. The board of directors also considered caves and mines near Salt Lake City, as well as the possibility of building an underground concrete and steel vault in the heart of the city.[70]

In 1958 testing began in Little Cottonwood Canyon at the former granite quarry where the stone for the Salt Lake Temple had been hewn. Test drills, boring five hundred feet into the mountain, demonstrated that the area was solid granite and that excess moisture would not be a problem. Because of these advantages, the Society determined that the twenty-mile drive from Church headquarters was of little consequence. In 1959 final approval was given to build at this site. One million dollars were appropriated to begin construction of the facility, which would be called the Granite Mountain Records Vault.[71]

Construction work began in the summer of 1960. After active tunneling began, workers encountered a flow of clear, cold water, pure enough for drinking. This was the only water discovered in the vault area. Eventually, the water was directed to a concrete reservoir that could store some 33,000 gallons of water, which was used for the vault's huge laboratory as well as for culinary needs. By December 1963, the vault was ready to receive the films. The move was completed in the middle of January 1964.[72] The total cost approximately two million dollars.[73]

The completed Granite Mountain vault consists of four huge cross tunnels, each measuring 190 feet long, 25 feet wide, and 15 feet high. They are connected on either end and through the middle by three corridors. The water reservoir is in the rear, behind the fourth cross tunnel. The front tunnel houses the office and laboratory area. The other three tunnels, which lie under nearly 700 feet of granite, are the storage areas. Heavy bank vault doors at the front of each of the three corridors guard the storage area. The three storage tunnels have more than 65,000 square feet of floor space and are divided into six vault rooms. Each room can store 885,400 one-hundred-foot rolls of microfilm. Total vault capacity can reach the equivalent of 25 million 300-page books. The natural temperature in the storage area remains at 57 to 58 degrees year round, regardless of outside temperature. The natural humidity remains between 40 and 50 percent. Both conditions are ideal for film storage. An elaborate circulation and filtering system keeps fresh air moving through the storage area and eliminates dust, smoke, chemicals, and other air-borne particles.[74] An up-to-date film-processing laboratory in the vault provides the advantages of central processing, where quality control can be easily maintained and the film processing can be done efficiently and effectively.

Nature created some problems for the Granite Mountain vault in 1974, when unnaturally high amounts of moisture flowed through the rock and pooled in the cement floor below one of the vaults. The floor heaved upwards over a foot, and water began to seep into the vault. Micrographics staff donned work clothes and kept the water at bay until the problem was solved by drilling holes in the center of the floor. This measure permitted the water to flow into a floor drain and out of the vault.[75] In 1982 the water pressure built up again. Additional holes were drilled, and a permanent drain ditch installed to relieve the pressure.[76] By the flood

Granite Mountain Records Vault staff, 1966, in front of one of the portals.

year of 1983, the problem of water pressure had been resolved, and water buildup no longer threatened the vault.

In 1983 some blemishes were discovered on the films. In an audit of 17,228 rolls, half were found to have some form of blemish, none serious enough to make the film unusable. Most of the blemishes were traced to extended storage outside the vault without temperature and humidity controls or to poor washing in the development cycle. Eight years later the blemished films were reviewed. The blemishes had not worsened, indicating that vault storage appeared to have stopped blemish growth.

The process of print mastering was introduced in the 1980s. The printing process subjected films to temperature variations, humidity, and surface scratching. After numerous printings, some of the master films had begun to deteriorate. Experts decided to create a duplicate master for printing purposes after a master had been used five times. By May 1991, 37,445 rolls had been print mastered.[77]

As a repository for the huge investment of the Church in preserving records of the past, the Granite Mountain Records Vault, with its solid image, stands as a fitting symbol of the Genealogical Society's commitment to making these records available to future generations.

International Labs

In 1951 the Society decided, for the sake of efficiency, to decentralize some of its technical processes. To support European filming, a microfilm lab was established in The Hague. By inspecting, developing, and printing films on-site, the Society could save considerable expense that would be incurred if all these processes took place in Salt Lake City.[78] Filming errors were also inspected and corrected in Europe before the films arrived in Salt Lake City. By 1952 the laboratory was operational. Eventually it processed films not only from Holland, but also from other European countries, including East Germany, West Germany, Belgium, France, England, and Ireland. In 1958 the installation of additional equipment doubled the production capacity of the lab at The Hague.[79]

By 1956 production in Mexico warranted the installation of a lab. Four years passed, however, before the lab was approved and

The Society's first microfilm laboratory, ca. 1946. Ernst Koehler, the first microfilmer of the Society, sitting; his son, Richard, working at the developing sink. Courtesy Delbert and Barbara Roach.

constructed. Finally, in 1960, Lucian Mecham, who had been instrumental in starting microfilming in Mexico, returned to Mexico City at the request of L. Garrett Myers and supervised the lab installation. By that time, a three-year inventory (10,000 films) needed donor copies printed and the master films sent to Salt Lake City.[80]

In 1965, Elder Burton closed down all foreign labs, because they continued to be plagued with problems, and centralized all film processing at the Granite Mountain Records Vault. Unfortunately, centralization produced a four-month delay between a problem caused in filming and its discovery in processing.[81]

As a result, in the late 1970s, Church leaders approved reestablishing international labs. Frankfurt was chosen as the site of the first new lab. It was centrally located in Europe and was also the site of the Europe Area Office of the Church. The Frankfurt lab began to process German and Austrian films in 1978. By 1980 it was processing the films produced throughout Europe. Eventually, smaller labs were established in Japan and Brazil, and labs were set up under contract in Mexico and the Philippines.

Contract Filming

Elder Burton decided in 1967 to contract filming to a private organization. The plan was suggested by Van Neiswender, supervisor of the Microfilming Division. Supervising microfilmers around the world was becoming complicated, and quality control was still a problem. Dismissing people was difficult, even if their work was not satisfactory, because of the Society's desire to avoid ill feelings. Neiswender suggested making a contract with a commercial company that would hire people around the world, train them, and remove this burden from the shoulders of the Society. It seemed like a good idea at the time. The Society received a bid from Intrade, a branch of Trans-America Corporation, which organized a subsidiary, Reproduction Systems, to do the work. Reproductions Systems proposed to hire camera operators as independent contractors, rather than as salaried employees, and to pay them according to the number of exposures they took.[82]

The result for the microfilm operators was traumatic. In June all filmers in the United States received a letter from Elder Burton informing them that as of 15 July they would be released from their work for the Society. They were told that they would be hired by Reproduction Systems, according to terms worked out with that company, but otherwise their employment was terminated. Decidedly unhappy with the situation, some operators simply went to work elsewhere. Others reluctantly accepted employment with Reproduction Systems. To their surprise, they soon discovered that they made more money under the new system than they had made as salaried workers. They made better use of their time (obviously a result of the economic incentive), could hire help for themselves in order to work faster, and could work longer hours.[83] Meanwhile, Van Neiswender and other employees in the Society's processing lab went to work for Intrade, which set up its own lab in Salt Lake City.

In spite of its economic efficiency, however, the new program had its problems. Even though most operators continued to provide very good work, quality control in general declined, and more poor quality film began to show up. Some operators did only the records that were easy to film, skipping the difficult ones, and requests for retakes were sometimes ignored. In some cases the "easy" records were filmed beyond the dates needed. Consequently, the Society canceled its contract with Reproduction Systems in 1971 and then rehired full-time microfilm operators. Ted F. Powell, formerly supervisor of the Genealogical Library, was appointed manager of the newly created Microfilm Operations Division. Powell supervised the microfilm operators around the world as well as the processing and evaluation at the Granite Mountain vault.[84]

42x Camera

The cost of the microfilming program resulted in continual efforts to economize. In 1980 discussion centered on filming exclusively with 16 mm film. This move would permit cuts in the filming budget without necessitating cutbacks in filming. However, it would require a filming reduction greater than the traditional 14x–16x reduction used in 35 mm filming. Also, better readers would be needed to adequately retrieve the film image. In 1982 a 42x camera was manufactured that could deliver six times the exposure count on the same amount of microfilm, resulting in a large reduction in costs for film and film handling, processing, and storage. At a 42x reduction, documents with dimensions up 19 x 25 inches could be reduced to an image on a 16 mm film. The 42x camera did not fulfill its promise in all respects, but it did provide an important option in many filming situations.

Prior to the development of the 42x camera, filming at such a high reduction was normally relegated to labs where equipment and environment could be rigidly controlled. The Society wanted to produce a camera that could film in any location under difficult conditions. No adequate camera was available on the market, so the Society sponsored the development of one to meet its needs.

High-reduction filming required exacting lens and camera head quality in order to produce acceptable film at a 42x reduction. JML Optics in Rochester, New York, produced thirteen lenses in 1982. The Society accepted five.[85] Kodak produced thirty camera heads. Eleven were accepted.[86] The cameras were installed at headquarters and produced acceptable film. In 1983 cameras were sent to Italy, Minnesota, and Indonesia. The results were mixed. Filming went well in Italy and Minnesota, but in the primitive filming environment of Indonesia, the results were poor. The Society continued to promote the camera, and by the end of 1983, twenty-eight were being used in the field.[87] A decade later, they comprised approximately a third of the Society's total camera inventory.[88]

One significant problem with the new filming was returning the small image to its original size on a reader. The Society had to refit the readers at the library to handle the reduced image on the film. The Society received sixty-three zoom lenses in July 1983. Later, a 42x and even a 65x reading lens (which would return the image to larger than original size) were obtained from Northwest Microfilm. Readers at family history centers have been refitted as local circumstances permitted. In some countries, archivists would not accept the high-reduction filming because they did not want to buy new readers. Nevertheless, some archivists in other countries found that the small image was desirable, and they converted the film into microfiche format. Microfiche readers, unlike their microfilm cousins, were designed to handle high-reduction images.[89]

Oral Genealogy

For a decade and a half, the Society pursued an oral genealogy program intended to preserve ancestral information in countries where there were no written records. Mulivai Purcell conducted the first interviews in Samoa in 1968. Interviews in Tahiti began in 1972. In 1973 interviews were being conducted in American Samoa, Cook Islands, Tonga, and New Zealand.[90] The concept was simple—to tape the spoken memory of the living. In some societies, the memories of the older people extended back many generations. Their recollection often began with the most distant ancestor and continued a line of descent recounted to the present generation. The account would then begin with another distant ancestor and descend to the present. The final product was a pedigree in reverse—with the branches extending towards the present rather than back to the past.

In 1977 the program was taken to Taiwan and Indonesia. During 1978, changes were made in the technique of gathering oral histories. Instead of making a tape, the interviewer recorded the information on a form. The interviewers would travel by foot or boat to various locations, collect the information, then return that data to Salt Lake City.[91]

In 1978 the Society initiated the program in Africa—in Gambia, which was made famous by Alex Haley's novel, *Roots.* The Gambian project was threatened by an attempted government coup in 1981. The head of the program personally persuaded a mob of 400 to refrain from looting the offices that housed the oral genealogy interviews.[92]

The collection of oral histories presented a significant problem. It was very expensive to gather and record the information. Taping, transcribing, and typing pedigrees made the acquisitions process much more expensive per name than microfilming a manuscript. In 1981 Church leaders directed the Society to stop recording oral genealogies and pursue filming of written records where they were available. Some budget was left to finish outstanding projects, but at the end of 1982, all funding for recording oral genealogies was eliminated. Not until 1990 was the collection of oral genealogies reauthorized and revived on a smaller scale in Indonesia.

A Worldwide Program

During the last three decades, records have been microfilmed in every corner of the world, resulting in a collection in which three-quarters of the records come from countries outside the United States. The Quorum of the Twelve Apostles have approved or directed the initiation of filming in each new country. As of November 1994, filming projects have been mounted in 101 countries around the world (see appendix II).

The filming program in North America has continued uninterrupted from its beginning. Early filming began in the eastern United States. By 1950 extensive filming had been done in Connecticut, Delaware, Maryland, and North Carolina. Massive filming efforts were mounted in New Hampshire and Vermont during 1952 and in Maine during 1954. Eight filmers assisted in the Maine project, the only instance when the Society concentrated a large group of filmers in a single state in order to canvas all record locations and film all their genealogical records during a single summer. James Black contacted numerous town clerks, set up his camera in homes, tiny offices, stores, barns—wherever the records could be found and electricity accessed.[93] In 1956 filming began in the Southwest when the firm of Vance-Golightly of El Paso was contracted to film in New Mexico, Texas, Arizona, Colorado, and Northern Mexico.[94] Canadian filming began during 1957 with projects in Ontario. In Canada some of the most significant acquisitions were the films of Catholic records in Quebec and Ontario, where filming began in 1977 and 1979 respectively. In 1977, Elder Boyd K. Packer initiated an effort to fill a major gap in the collection by acquiring microfilms of the records of the Native Americans.[95] These records were filmed at federal records centers in Los Angeles, Fort Worth, Seattle, and Kansas City.

A wide range of record types have been filmed in the United States, unlike most other countries. In contrast with nations where civil registration or the records of a state church provide a single source for researching most of the population, the records of the United States are more diverse and each source less comprehensive. The most recent development in North America has been the filming of civil registration records. Vital record offices were generally unreceptive to Society initiatives until the 1990s—the only exception being Washington, which permitted the purchase of the state civil registration in 1959. Idaho deaths were filmed in 1990, and filming of civil registration records is now being conducted in North Carolina, Florida, Alabama, Kentucky, and Illinois, with more states to be done in the future. The civil registration of Ontario, Canada, for the nineteenth century was filmed in 1991-93.

Even with budget limitations since 1985, operations have expanded, primarily through the increased use of missionaries. Their role as filmers has been expanded into preparing documents for filming, an important, but arduous, task for large files of loose documents. After serving family history missions, many former missionaries have volunteered to film short-term projects. Contract operations and film purchases have also increased productivity.

Filming continued in Mexico during the 1960s. The Society did not move into other countries until 1965, when it initiated a project in Argentina. In Guatemala the Society began in 1970 to film notarial records of colonial Guatemala (which included what is now Honduras, El Salvador, Nicaragua, and Costa Rica). Filming in Panama began in 1972. In Chile, the program got underway in 1973, after a complicated series of negotiations with the Catholic Church regarding permissions and with the government regarding import duties (for cameras and film).[96] Beginning in 1975, the Society rapidly expanded microfilming into many countries of Latin America. Costa Rican filming began in 1975. Projects were initiated in Peru, Brazil, and El Salvador during 1976. Bolivia followed in 1977, and Honduras, Paraguay, and Ecuador in 1979. The Society held the first Latin American filming seminar in November 1979 to better train the new corps of camera operators. Sessions were held in Guatemala City and Lima. In 1981 Caribbean filming began in the Dominican Republic.

Political instability, geographic circumstances, and religious antagonisms hindered, but never completely stopped, the progress of projects in Latin America. Camera operators were regularly searched at gunpoint in El Salvador during 1979, prior to the temporary cessation of filming there in 1980.[97] Similar problems were encountered in Colombia and Peru in the early 1990s, as film operators on occasion encountered terrorists or drug traffickers. Geographic circumstances have also been daunting. Rudolfo Becerra, filming in Mexico in 1979, transferred his equipment from jeep to donkey in order to film a parish register in Amixtlan Puebla. While filming in Bolivia in 1980, Carlos Ferrari was halted by local citizens who objected to the filming and doused him with water as he scurried to leave.[98] Although filming of Brazilian civil records continues, filming of church records in Brazil was halted in 1983, when, in response to an inquiry from the bishops of Brazil, the Vatican objected to the program.[99]

In more recent years filming coverage has extended to virtually all Latin American countries. Filming began in Colombia during 1985. In 1991 no filming had been done in Venezuela. Then a Catholic bishop granted permission. Soon thereafter he became an archbishop, permitting him to influence other bishops favorably. The Society received the first films from Venezuela in 1992. Filming projects were completed in most of the Caribbean countries between 1990 and 1992.

Filming in the South Pacific began in 1959, when a few films were received from a small operation begun in New Zealand.[100] Two years later, a project was started in Australia. Polynesian filming began in 1970 on the island of Vanua Levu, Fiji. An arsonist set fire to the government office building on Rarotonga, Cook Islands, in May 1992. The records would have been lost had it not been possible to restore many of them with copies of microfilm in the Society's collection. Fifty-one films of government records were sent gratis to the Cook Islands.

Beginning in the early 1970s, the Society took the microfilming program into Asia, Africa, and the Middle East. This expansion represented a major departure from the policy of forty years—filming only in countries where many Church members had ancestors. The Society saw the necessity of filming records before they deteriorated in countries where climatic conditions rapidly destroy records. The Society was also aware of the growth of Church congregations in these countries, justifying a program to gather records in their behalf. Anticipating that the Church would eventually be established in all countries, the Society believed it prudent to begin filming even before many joined the LDS Church. The Society also realized that the cost of filming was less expensive in countries where the economy had not yet matured.

Filming in Korea commenced in 1972, in the Philippines in 1973, Taiwan in 1975, Japan in 1976, and Indonesia in 1977. Investigation into the records of India began in 1979. A record type unknown in the West was identified in Hardwar, a major Hindu pilgrimage center in Northern India. A clan of priests known as pandas function as registrars of vital statistics for families that come to holy cities for ritual bathing in the Ganges River. Filming of these records began in 1981. In Sri Lanka, filming began in 1979 with the country's civil registration records, a project that continues to the present. Unexpected circumstances often impeded filming in Sri Lanka, as in many other developing countries. For example, in the summer of 1981, a drought in Sri Lanka reduced the nation's electricity output. Consequently, the Society's cameras sat idle for two months.[101]

The most dramatic breakthrough in Asia occurred in mainland China. The opportunity to film there arose after the death of Mao

Tse-tung. The reinstatement of exiled professors, librarians, and archivists in their institutions coincided with the Society's preparations for the 1980 World Conference on Records. The State Archives Bureau of China accepted an invitation to attend the conference. The Chinese delegation was amazed at the public interest in genealogy demonstrated by the large attendance at the conference. That fall the Archives Bureau extended an invitation for Society representatives to visit Beijing.[102] Ted Powell, director of acquisitions, and Melvin Thatcher, regional manager of China and Southeast Asia, entered the "forbidden" city in April 1981. This was the first time foreigners had ever been allowed to see the archives.[103] A contract was signed in March 1983—the first formal microfilming agreement between a Chinese archive and a foreign institution. In June 1983, the filming began. In recognition of its cordial relationship, the Chinese archive invited the Society to attend the sixtieth anniversary celebration of the First Historical Archive in October 1985. On this occasion, the State Archive Bureau announced its intent to grant foreign scholars access to the archives and to encourage international cooperation and exchange.[104]

Political instability in the Philippines prompted a dramatic increase in the film production in that country during 1987. In a short time, the number of cameras increased from four to thirty-seven. The filmers ran the cameras on three shifts. At the zenith of the project in 1989, twenty million exposures were received on 13,500 rolls of film.

Filming in Africa began under the direction of Elder Boyd K. Packer, who had requested that the Society look into the possibility of filming in Rhodesia (later Zimbabwe). At the time, the change from white minority to black majority rule was imminent. The change could have imperiled the records of the previous regime. In November 1976, Ted Powell, director of acquisitions, successfully negotiated the filming of the records, and by 1978 the civil registration of that country had been filmed. While in Africa, Powell also successfully negotiated with South Africa, and filming started there in 1977.

Film acquisitions in the Middle East began in Israel. Elder Packer, along with Society officials, visited Jerusalem in 1977 and met a contingent of nine archivists and scholars. Elder Packer explained plainly that the Church wanted the records in order to provide Christian baptisms for their forebears. There was an immediate uproar until one rabbi, who taught comparative religion at Jerusalem University, asked for calm. He said, "You'll never make my grandfather, who is a rabbi, into a Mormon. . . . So why are we afraid? If we're afraid, we ought to join your Church. If we're not afraid we ought to let you use your money and help us preserve our records."[105] The request to acquire records was later granted.

In England the filming of parish registers in many localities was hindered by the concern of English church officials who did not agree with the religious basis of the LDS filming program. In 1952 the Society's filming effort was directed at obtaining civil records, and permission was received to copy the pre-1858 wills of Great Britain.[106] This proved to be a difficult project because the originals were rolled and coated with dirt and dust.[107] The project required a decade to complete.

The Society received a cable from England in 1951 announcing that official permission had been granted to film in Scotland.[108] The announcement was received with elation because negotiations had been underway for five years. Five cameras were installed in Edinburgh, and filming began of census records and parish registers.[109]

The British Isles was the focus of much filming activity during the 1960s. In January 1963, fifteen out of the forty-three cameras operating outside the U.S. were located in the British Isles. This number had decreased to three or four cameras by 1985. However, that year the Society was directed by the General Authorities to pursue a special invitation to film in Great Britain. Even though filmers had been scouring British archives for almost fifty years, permission had not been granted to film many records. Then in the early 1980s, many parish records were transferred into civil repositories, and the civil authorities were more responsive to negotiations with the Society than church authorities had been in the past. Additionally, interest in family history research was even more pervasive in Great Britain than in America. Archivists welcomed the opportunity to have frequently used collections filmed to preserve them for future generations. The Great Britain initiative lasted for seven years. At the end of the project in 1992, nearly sixty million new exposures on approximately 34,000 microfilm rolls had been acquired. Included in these were parish registers from 5,110 parishes and bishop's transcripts for 4,516 parishes.[110]

Many filming projects were completed in Scandinavia during the first half of the 1950s. Filming in Norway was completed in 1951.[111] In the following year, filming was completed in Finland. Swedish filming received such emphasis that in 1954, the Swedish collection had become the largest foreign film collection in the Salt Lake City library, a situation that would continue for another decade. The initial filming project in Denmark was concluded in 1952.[112]

Even though Scandinavian officials in general seemed highly supportive of the program, there was a certain amount of religious opposition, not unlike that experienced in England. In 1960, for example, an article entitled "Intrusion into Hosts of Lutheran Dead" was published in Denmark and circulated in that country and Germany. Certain Danish bishops and other church officials strenuously objected to the implications of the microfilming program. In Norway, too, the state church initially objected when the microfilming project began in 1948. The press reported the clergy's criticism of the filming project. Some positive publicity came in March 1963, when Alvin W. Fletcher presented a roll of film to Sweden's King Gustavus VI. The film represented the last in a series of some fifty million photos taken in the Swedish archives over a period of fifteen years at a cost of more than a million dollars.[113]

The filming program in Germany and the Netherlands spread southward during the 1960s and 1970s and moved eastward during the 1980s. Germany was recovering from the postwar deficit of equipment, film supplies, and trained personnel. In the early 1950s, filming was pursued vigorously in East Germany. The parish registers on deposit at the Berlin-Dahlem archives, which had been gathered by Paul Langheinrich, were transported to the East German mission home for filming and then returned to the archives. Langheinrich and his son also microfilmed the rest of the collection gathered from the salt mines and castles and temporarily deposited at Humboldt University in East Berlin. In West Germany from 1950–51, the Society sponsored a project to film the Prussian records at Goslar that had been taken out of the eastern provinces by the retreating German army.

The parish registers of the Netherlands had been filmed by 1955, and filming of other records continued in that country. In West Germany, the first projects—since the filming in Goslar—were initiated in 1956. Negotiation efforts in Germany were assisted by appeals made in behalf of the filming program by a Dr. Lampe, a German archivist previously involved in the filming at Goslar.[114] In 1957 the Society received permission to copy all church and vital records in Belgium. Filming was initiated in France in 1959.

In the decade that followed, the focus of filming in Europe moved south as projects in Scandinavia and the Netherlands diminished and those in West Germany, Belgium, and France increased. Luxembourg was filmed between 1961 and 1962. Italian filming began in 1972 as a joint venture between the Society and the Parma Diocese, with the University of Parma acting as intermediary. The decision was then made to film the Italian civil registration records before the church records. Throughout the 1980s, approximately fifteen cameras operated in the various archives in Italy. Beginning in 1975, the initial Spanish filming was conducted in Barcelona. The microfilming program was temporarily stalled when a convocation of Spanish bishops voted against it but was

The first two hundred rolls of microfilm were presented in 1948 by (left to right) Rinze Schippers (microfilmer), Cornelius Zappey (Netherlands Mission President), and Archibald Bennett to the National Archivist of the Netherlands, Dr. D. P. M. Graswinckel. Filming began in 1947 and continues to the present.

The first Italian filming contract was signed in Parma, Italy, in 1972. Ted Powell and John Jarman flank the archivist (center). During the 1980s, the Society operated about fifteen cameras in Italy.

resumed in 1979. More cameras operated in Spain and Italy during the 1980s than elsewhere in Europe. Filming in southern Europe was particularly important to the expanding membership of the Church in Latin America, whose ancestry traced back to the countries there. Political unrest in Portugal during the early 1970s made negotiations there impossible. In 1976 permission was granted to film in Madeira, a Portuguese island. By 1979 the political situation had stabilized, and filming began on the Portuguese mainland. A majority of the church records in Portugal were filmed by four to five cameras from 1979 to 1989.

Filming continued in the other countries of Europe, usually without fanfare. However, negative publicity would occasionally impede the program. In 1979 a jurist for the Lutheran Church issued a legal brief, addressed to all Protestant clergy in Germany, trying to persuade them that the microfilming program was illegal. Clergy in Bavaria and northern Germany believed the brief while clergy in other areas ignored it.[115] The Society also encountered negative publicity in Switzerland. Many Swiss archivists favored a microfilming agreement with the Society but hesitated because of the negative publicity that previously had accompanied filming in a particular canton. In spite of this reluctance, every few years the records of another canton are opened up for filming. Since 1975 the church records in the archives of Zürich, Ticino, Graubunden, Jura, and Solothurn have been added to the Society's collection.

In France opposition resulted from political circumstances. When the Socialist party came to power in 1982, a member of the Communist party was appointed as the minister of culture. He demanded the Society provide a second donor copy and pay additional fees to the departmental archives to cover all costs incurred by the filming. The Society could not meet his requests, shut down its cameras in the departmental archives, and began filming in church archives.[116] With a new administration, the impositions were lifted, and a new contract was signed in 1987.

The Iron Curtain was not impervious to the filming program. In 1957 the archivist of Hungary contacted the Society to discuss the feasibility of filming there. The revolution of 1956 had resulted in a loss of many archival records. The archivist had read about the Society's filming program in professional literature and saw it as a feasible and available method to ensure the security of Hungary's archival heritage.[117] Extensive filming of parish register copies in the Hungarian National Archives was conducted between 1960 and 1963. The national archivist of Poland also read an article about the program in *Archivum,* a professional archival journal. He wrote to the Society in 1961, asking if it would be willing to film in Poland.[118] After extensive negotiations, in 1968 the cameras began filming in the Society's second major project behind the Iron Curtain.

Gradually at first, but then very quickly, the filming program in Europe began to move east during the 1980s. Greek filming began in 1979 at Corfu, an Adriatic Island off the west coast of the country. East German archives opened their doors in 1981. Filming in Yugoslavia began in 1985. During the civil war between Croatia and Serbia in 1991, the archive of Osijek was bombed, and many of the records were destroyed. The church records from the archive had already been filmed and thus were preserved from destruction. In 1991, after decades of negotiation, a major hurdle was overcome in Austria, and the filming of church records commenced there. As in many other cases, the Society had patiently awaited the day when long-sought-for records would become available. Its persistence has usually borne good results.

One of the most significant filming opportunities occurred in the former Soviet Union. After the first World Conference on Records,

Society representatives repeatedly visited the archives administration in Moscow to initiate negotiations. The only result for twenty-two years was continued discussion. Soviet leaders had no interest in genealogical matters and suspected that the Society was a front for what they considered to be the omnipresent spying apparatus of the West. After the dissolution of the Soviet political structure in late 1990, the archival administration was freed from political bosses, and the archivists approached the Society. The dissolution of Soviet hegemony in 1991 freed archives not only within the Union, but also throughout Eastern Europe to negotiate with the Society. In 1991, Slovakia, Bulgaria, and Estonia signed contracts; Russia and Slovenia signed in 1992; Albania, Armenia, Belarus, and Ukraine in 1993; and Lithuania, Moldova, and Georgia in 1994. (For more information on microfilming projects and production, see appendixes II and III.)

The Filmed Record

Microfilm stored in the Granite Mountain Records Vault provides a safe haven for the archives of the world. Many Latter-day Saints believe this vast reservoir of material will provide the basis for a millennium of work in which families throughout the world will be identified and eternal family relationships established. In a quiet fashion, the Church has pursued a record-gathering effort unparalleled in the history of the world.

The timing of the microfilming project was perfect. World War II spurred the development of microfilm technology, demonstrated the need to protect records, and depleted the monetary resources of European archives. The Society brought the technology, offered to do what the archives wanted to have done, and offered to do it at no cost to the archives. The financial support of the First Presidency was crucial in enabling the Society to make such financially unprofitable contracts. Hesitant at first to fund a program whose cost appeared astronomical, the First Presidency supported it with unexpected generosity when later they saw its worth to the spiritual purposes of the Church. That support has been sustained for over fifty years.

Religious opposition might have abruptly terminated filming in many places, but civil control of many religious records made

In order to be filmed at Torre Pellice in 1948, the records from Pramol Parish, a Vaudois hamlet in northwestern Italy, were brought down the mountainside on a mule. Archibald Bennett stands in the background. Courtesy Delbert and Barbara Roach.

it possible for the Society to obtain permission to microfilm. To archivists, the benefit of preserving the record at no cost to them was significant. As important as these circumstances were, the success of the program was due to the vision and determination of committed individuals who worked more for a cause than for a salary. Underpinning the whole microfilming project was the religious goal shared by those involved in the work.

In a letter to Elder Mark E. Petersen in 1957, L. Garrett Myers summed up the progress of record gathering from the perspective of the Society:

> More than 20 years ago, President Joseph Fielding Smith instructed us to keep abreast of all the latest technical developments in record work. He stated that we should not only be informed of new accomplishments in this field, but that we should be leaders therein. He said that the Lord would provide ways and means to accomplish his purposes in the acquiring of records of the progenitors and kinsfolk of our people, so that the work for the salvation of the dead would go forward in an ever increasing tempo, and that custodians of great record repositories would be moved upon to make their collections available to us. This prediction has been most literally fulfilled.[119]

NOTES

[1]Statistical data presented here and elsewhere in this chapter comes from various internal reports compiled for administrative use and located in the Acquisitions Department, Family History Department, The Church of Jesus Christ of Latter-day Saints (hereafter cited as FHD). See also appendix III.

[2]Genealogical Society Minutes, 27 September 1943, FHD.

[3]Ovena Jorgensen Ockey, "Survey of Genealogical Conditions in Denmark, Norway and Sweden," *Utah Genealogical and Historical Magazine* 17 (July 1926): 220–22 (hereafter cited as *UGHM*).

[4]Genealogical Society Minutes, 6 October 1936.

[5]Genealogical Society Minutes, 27 October 1936, 15 March 1938.

[6]L. Garrett Myers, oral history interview by Bruce Blumell, 1976, typescript, James Moyle Oral History Program (hereafter cited as JMOHP), Archives Division, Historical Department, The Church of Jesus Christ of Latter-day Saints, Salt Lake City (hereafter cited as LDS Church Archives); L. Garrett Myers, telephone interview by Jessie Embry, 20 January 1977; James M. Black, "Microfilming Experiences of James M. Black, 1938–1972 in Service with the Genealogical Society," FHD, typescript (film 1313899), 1, 7–8. This manuscript is an excellent source of information on the microfilming program, and much of the following

material is based on this source. For some interesting background on Koehler and the origin of his interest in microfilming, see Archibald F. Bennett, *Saviors in Mount Zion* (Salt Lake City: Deseret News, 1960), 106–7.

[7]Archibald F. Bennett to Stake Genealogical Representatives, 12 May 1938, copy on file in Joseph Fielding Smith papers, LDS Church Archives.

[8]Archibald F. Bennett to Stake Genealogical Representatives, 17 December 1938, reproduced in *UGHM* 30 (July 1939): 190–91.

[9]Archibald F. Bennett to Stake Genealogical Representatives, 7 April 1939, copy on file in Joseph Fielding Smith papers, LDS Church Archives.

[10]Archibald F. Bennett to Stake Genealogical Representatives, 7 April 1939.

[11]In 1939, for example, permission was obtained to film the manuscript records of the early Dutch Churches of New York state as well as any records of genealogical value in the Tennessee State Library at Nashville. Negotiations were also in progress for filming certain records in Italy, as well as important manuscripts at the Bishop Museum and Archive in Hawaii. *UGHM* 30 (October 1939): 254–56.

[12]Genealogical Society Minutes, 28 November 1939, 9 April 1940.

[13]Black, "Microfilming Experiences," 3.

[14]Black, "Microfilming Experiences," 5.

[15]Bennett, *Saviors on Mount Zion,* 108; Kahlile Mehr, "Microfilming in the Lands of the North, 1938–1975," FHD, 1980, typescript, 2; Black, "Microfilming Experiences," 4–5.

[16]Genealogical Society Minutes, 6 February 1940.

[17]Genealogical Society Minutes, 19 September, and 7 November 1939; 9 January, and 15 May 1940; Myers, interview; Black, "Microfilming Experiences," 63.

[18]Genealogical Society Minutes, 31 December 1940, 5 May 1942.

[19]*Deseret News,* 4 September 1943; Black, "Microfilming Experiences," 8–15; Genealogical Society Minutes, 11 January 1944.

[20]Black, "Microfilming Experiences," 15.

[21]The First Presidency to Joseph Fielding Smith, 26 December 1940, Genealogical Society correspondence, FHD; Genealogical Society Minutes, 14 January 1941. These sources suggest that Joseph Fielding Smith himself, even though he was president of the Society, agreed with the First Presidency's reservations.

[22]Genealogical Society Minutes, 14 January 1941.

[23]Myers, interview.

[24]Genealogical Society Minutes, 27 August 1976.

[25]Black, "Microfilming Experiences," appendix.

[26]Genealogical Society Minutes, 15 February 1945; Frank Smith, oral history interview by Bruce Blumell, 1976, typescript, JMOHP; George Fudge, oral history interviews by George D. Durrant and John C. Jarman, 1984, typescript, copy in possession of Kahlile Mehr, 67–68; Black, "Microfilming Experiences," appendix.

[27]Myers, interview; Black, "Microfilming Experiences," 5, 15–19; Genealogical Society Minutes, 28 November 1939, 9 January, and 23 October 1940, 11 December 1945, 19 February, and 16 April 1946.

[28]See Lucien M. Mecham Jr., oral history interview by Gordon S. Irving, 1974, LDS Church Archives; Genealogical Society Minutes, 17 April, and 1 September 1953, 21 November 1956, 13 March 1959, 5 and 19 February 1960; L. Garrett Myers to Church Building Committee, 10 September 1956, Genealogical Society correspondence, FHD; Myers, interview.

[29]The following account of the activities of Paul Langheinrich and his associates is based on Don C. Corbett, "Records from the Ruins," FHD, typescript; "Report of Procurement of Church Records, Films, and Photocopies," Europe Manuscript History, 16 August 1945, LDS Church Archives; Rudolph K. Poecker, oral history interview by James B. Allen, 18 February 1985, typescript in possession of James B. Allen; Frederick W. Babbel, *On Wings of Faith* (Salt Lake City: Bookcraft, 1972): 57-60.

[30]At least that is how it was interpreted by some of the German Saints who were involved at the time. Poecker, interview.

[31]Elder Poecker had another interesting experience in a small town on the border of East and West Germany. There he found many records behind the altar of a Lutheran church, along with a famous painting of the Last Supper. He thought he was going to be able to "rescue" the painting along with the records, but somehow the Russians arrived before his truck got there and made away with it. He did, however, save the genealogical records. Poecker, interview.

[32]At first the archive was set up at Wolfsgrün, and literally tons of records were transferred from Berlin, but in 1948 it was moved back to Berlin. Langheinrich later had an interesting tale to tell about some of the problems involved in transferring records from Berlin to Wolfsgrün. On one occasion, he and some others were taking a large truck and trailer full of books to Wolfsgrün when they were stopped by some armed Russians whose car was stalled. The Russians wanted to be towed into Leipzig, but Langheinrich suspected something was "fishy" and simply did not trust them. He looped a rope around their bumper, however, then climbed on the back of the trailer and held the rope himself (presumably looping it around some support). As they came near the service station in Leipzig, he simply let go of one end of the rope so that it slipped loose from the bumper, freeing his party from the Russians. Later, not far from their destination, the group came to a Russian sentry station with the crossbar on the gate blocking the highway. The driver somehow did not brake properly, and the heavily loaded truck crashed through the gate. After the truck stopped, the Russians in the car caught up. In addition, the guard at the gate pulled the driver from the truck, smashing him in the face. Langheinrich soon calmed the guard down, however, then found a carpenter, went into the woods, and cut down a tree from which they fashioned another crossbar. They then proceeded on their way. Corbett, "Records from the Ruins," 16-17; "Langheinrich Report."

[33]Genealogical Society Minutes, 28 May, and 6 August 1946.

[34]The renegotiation of contracts on these trips, along with other economies, saved the Society an estimated $100,000. On three successive trips in the 1950s, Myers improved arrangements with the Danish National Archives, purchased some important collections in England, and obtained permission to film records in France. Genealogical Society Minutes, 17 May 1950; L. Garrett Myers to Joseph Fielding Smith, 23 February 1960, Genealogical Society correspondence, FHD. See also Myers, interview.

[35]Genealogical Society Minutes, 26 November 1946, 14 October 1947, 7 July 1948; Black, "Microfilming Experiences," 19-50.

[36]Genealogical Society Minutes, 26 November 1946, 9 November 1948; Archibald F. Bennett to Alma Sonne, 13 November 1948, Genealogical Society correspondence, FHD. The 1947 budget, as noted in the 1946 minutes above,

was $170,000.00. The breakdown of the 1949 budget by countries is Holland, $68,437.18; Norway, $41,898.70; Great Britain, $92,988.00; Finland and Sweden, $114,762.00; Belgium, $15,000.00; France, $15,000.00; Switzerland, $25,000.00; Germany, $150,000.00; United States, $184,514.00; and Denmark, $45,000.00.

[37]Genealogical Society Minutes, 11 January 1949.

[38]Genealogical Society Minutes, 30 December 1949.

[39]*Salt Lake Tribune,* 6 April 1954.

[40]Black, "Microfilming Experiences," appendix.

[41]Genealogical Society Minutes, 19 December 1960; L. Garrett Myers to the Budget Committee, 19 December 1960, Genealogical Society correspondence, FHD; L. Garrett Myers to Mark E. Petersen, 11 January 1961, Genealogical Society correspondence, FHD.

[42]Genealogical Society Minutes, 4 December 1962.

[43]Genealogical Society Minutes, 17 August 1961, 9 November 1961.

[44]James M. Black placed a huge and very interesting appendix at the end of his "Microfilming Experiences." The appendix includes copies of microfilming reports from 1938 to 1975. All of the statistics presented above and many of those given elsewhere in this chapter are taken from that source. Black listed the other nations and geographic areas represented by the vast microfilm holdings as Mexico, Great Britain (England, Ireland, Scotland, Wales, Isle of Man), Denmark, Sweden, The Netherlands, France, Germany, Belgium, Finland, Canada, Poland, Hungary, Norway, Austria, Guatemala, Argentina, Switzerland, Australia, Polynesia (Cook Island, Fiji, Samoa, French Polynesia), Italy, New Zealand (sources include Maori histories), Chile, Korea, Japan, Russia, Iceland, Caribbean (Guadeloupe, Puerto Rico, Martinique, Haiti), Bahamas, Philippines, Panama, Luxembourg, China, Costa Rica, Peru, Brazil, Portugal, Singapore, Czechoslovakia, Spain, and "miscellaneous" countries.

[45]Charles Hillinger, "The Mormon Files," *Sundancer* [Hughes Air West inflight magazine] (January 1977): 46.

[46]Managing Director's minutes, 7 April 1987, FHD.

[47]Rick Ebert, Presentation to Staff, 6 February 1991, FHD.

[48]*Deseret News,* 4 November 1972.

[49]*Salt Lake Tribune,* 26 November 1953; *Denver Post,* 26 November 1953. Archibald F. Bennett simply labeled the charge "ridiculous" and pointed out that "the practice of collecting genealogy of church members was started in 1840. . . . The procedure not only predates Communism, but certainly predates the current world situation."

[50]The proclamation actually provides a fitting summary of what the microfilm program did for various states. It reads:

> WHEREAS, The Church of Jesus Christ of Latter-Day Saints (Mormon) have now finished their project of microfilming the records of the towns, cities and courts of Massachusetts; and WHEREAS, These records are the irreplaceable early to the year 1850 records [*sic*]; and WHEREAS, The filming of these important records of the states' cities towns [*sic*] and courts was done at no expense to the state or the towns, cities and courts; and WHEREAS, Free copies of these microfilmed records have been given to the state, towns, cities and courts; and WHEREAS, Our own native son Robert J. Tarte of Ashland has been

> the Microfilm Coordinator of this great project for his Church; and WHEREAS, Our great Commonwealth would like to express a feeling of gratitude toward the Church of Jesus Christ of Latter-Day Saints (Mormon) and its microfilm coordinator Robert J. Tarte, NOW, THEREFORE, I, MICHAEL S. DUKAKIS, Governor of the Commonwealth of Massachusetts, do hereby proclaim July 15, 1975, as MORMON RECORD DAY and urge the citizens of the Commonwealth of Massachusetts to take cognizance of this event and to participate fittingly in its observance.

Copy on file at the FHD.

[51]*Deseret News,* 22 November 1968.

[52]See Genealogical Society Minutes, 18 February 1947, 5 October 1948; Myers, interview. According to the minutes, Elder Smith was convinced that the Church need not be as much concerned with countries such as Ireland, France, Spain, and Italy as with other European countries, for he did not think there were as many descendants of Israel in those countries. Certainly they did not provide the large numbers of early converts to Mormonism as did England, northern Germany, and the Scandinavian countries. Significantly it was in the latter areas that microfilming was done most extensively at first.

[53]Genealogical Society Minutes, 24 August 1961.

[54]George Fudge, oral history interview by Bruce Blumell, 1976, typescript, JMOHP.

[55]Genealogical Society Minutes, 2 January 1962.

[56]Black, "Microfilming Experiences," 80. This document is confusing at this point, for Black mistakenly penciled in the notation that Elder Tanner appointed him in 1962. However, Elder Tanner did not begin his administration of the Society until 1963.

[57]Genealogical Society Minutes, 21 January 1965.

[58]Information summarized from Acquisition Planning Committee Minutes, various dates from 1971 to 1979, FHD.

[59]"Ten-Year Genealogical Records Gathering Project Plan," typescript attached to Management Meeting Minutes, 14 September 1981, FHD; "Philosophy of Records Gathering," typescript attached to Micrographics Division Managers Council Meeting Minutes, 25 January 1982, FHD. The rule of 75 percent was later changed to 80 percent.

[60]Micrographics Standing Committee Minutes, 29 December 1981, FHD.

[61]The following information is based on the personal knowledge of Kahlile Mehr, who was involved in all these activities.

[62]Some information not specifically documented in this and later sections is based on the personal knowledge of Kahlile Mehr, who had discussions with various Genealogical Society administrators over time, who was personally involved in some of the events and programs discussed, and who has studied the various internal reports of the Department that are compiled for official use only.

[63]Genealogical Society Minutes, 18 September 1957, 26 February 1958, 28 June 1960.

[64]Genealogical Society Minutes, 19 February 1960, 26 April 1960, 24 May 1960, 3 February 1961; personal knowledge of Kahlile Mehr, based on discussions with various Genealogical Society administrators.

[65]Mark Bell, "Microfilm Acquisition of Genealogical Records in Europe, circa 1975–1984," FHD, typescript, 2.

[66]L. Garrett Myers to Joseph Fielding Smith, transcription of letter in Genealogical Society Minutes, 19 July 1950.

[67]Genealogical Society Minutes, 1 November 1957.

[68]*Deseret News* and *Salt Lake Telegram,* 1 February 1954.

[69]These requirements included the following:

> (1) The vault is to be within a 25 mile radius from the Church Administration Building. (2) The film storage area . . . is to have a minimum of 30,000 sq. ft. expandable to 58,000 sq. ft. and about 28,000 sq. ft. for offices, laboratories, mechanical equipment and service features. (3) Air temperatures are to be held within 65° to 72°, and relative humidity is to be held within 40 to 50 percent. (4) The air is to be filtered to remove any dust or chemicals. (5) The storage vault area is to have an overburden of soil or rock at least 250 feet in depth. (6) Other factors to be considered in evaluating a suitable site are: a) Accessibility from downtown Salt Lake City. b) Availability of water, sewer and electric power. c) Characteristics of earth or rock formation at the site which would have a direct bearing on first costs at time of construction, and upon maintenance and operation costs thereafter.

Handout provided by the Genealogical Society entitled "Church Records Vault," FHD.

[70]Myers, interview; Genealogical Society Minutes, 7 February 1958; Myers to Howard Barker, 10 February 1958, Genealogical Society correspondence, FHD; "The *Era* Asks: What Is the Granite Mountain Records Vault?" *Improvement Era* 69 (August 1966): 699 (interview with Elder Theodore M. Burton).

[71]Genealogical Society Minutes, 13 March 1959.

[72]Genealogical Society Minutes, 14 January 1964.

[73]*Church News,* 7 December 1963.

[74]See "Records Protection in an Uncertain World," pamphlet published and distributed by the Genealogical Society of the Church, 1975.

[75]Ted Powell, telephone conversation with Kahlile Mehr, 11 October 1993.

[76]Historical Report, April 1982, FHD.

[77]Memorandum, May 1991, FHD.

[78]Genealogical Society Minutes, 15 August 1952.

[79]Genealogical Society Minutes, 13 August 1958.

[80]Genealogical Society Minutes, 5 February 1960.

[81]Black, "Microfilming Experiences," 116–17.

[82]Burton, interview; Black, "Microfilming Experiences," 132.

[83]Black, "Microfilming Experiences," 133.

[84]Burton, interview; Fudge, 1976 and 1984 interviews; Ted F. Powell, oral history interview by Jessie Embry, 7 March 1977, LDS Church Archives.

[85]Micrographics Division Historical Report, September 1982, FHD.

[86]Historical Report, January 1983, FHD.

[87]Micrographics Division Historical Report, December 1983, FHD.

[88]Rick Laxman, telephone conversation with Kahlile Mehr, 14 January 1994.

[89]The small screen size of a microfiche reader does require that a large document be read in pieces when the image is returned to its original dimensions.

[90]These interviews are part of the Family History Library collection.

[91]Historical Report, July 1979, FHD.

[92]Micrographics Division Historical Report, August 1981, FHD.

[93]Black, "Microfilming Experiences," 64.

[94]Black, "Microfilming Experiences," 73.

[95]Historical Report, August 1976, FHD.

[96]References scattered throughout the Genealogical Society correspondence, and a summary of some of the negotiations found in "History of Microfilming Project, Chile" (n.d.), Henry Christiansen files, FHD, typescript; Black, "Microfilming Experiences," 143-55.

[97]Historical Report, November 1979, FHD.

[98]Historical Report, June 1980.

[99]Historical Report, June 1983.

[100]Genealogical Society Minutes, 13 March 1959.

[101]Micrographics Standing Committee Minutes, 15 August 1981, FHD.

[102]Mel Thatcher, "An Overview of Genealogical Acquisitions in the People's Republic of China," 1-3, Genealogical Society Minutes, 10 April 1986.

[103]Historical Report, May 1981, FHD.

[104]Thatcher, "An Overview of Genealogical Acquisitions in the People's Republic of China," 3, 4, 5, 6.

[105]Ted Powell, oral history interview by Ron Watt, 24 May 1982, 8-9, LDS Church Archives.

[106]Genealogical Society Minutes, 25 April 1952.

[107]Genealogical Society Minutes, 10 September 1952.

[108]Genealogical Society Minutes, 24 April 1951.

[109]Genealogical Society Minutes, 18 January 1952.

[110]Dean Hunter, "Summary of Filming—Great Britain—1986 to 1992," FHD, typescript, 1, 4; Genealogical Society Minutes, 11 February 1993.

[111]Genealogical Society Minutes, 15 August 1951.

[112]Genealogical Society Minutes, 12 August 1952.

[113]Genealogical Society Minutes, 26 February 1958, 5 February 1960; *Salt Lake Tribune,* 27 March 1963; Mehr, "Microfilming in the Lands of the North." Mehr's short essay provides a summary of what was happening in Europe, particularly the Scandinavian countries, in this period.

[114]Genealogical Society Minutes, 13 August 1958.

[115]Mark Bell, "Microform Acquisition of Genealogical Records in Europe, circa 1975 to 1984," FHD, typescript, 8.

[116]Management Meeting Minutes, 11 February 1982.

[117]Genealogical Society Minutes, 2 July 1957, 1 November 1957.

[118]Genealogical Society Minutes, 17 March 1961.

[119]L. Garrett Myers to Mark E. Petersen, 11 March 1957, Genealogical Society correspondence, FHD.

Chapter 7

Simplification, Decentralization, Cooperation, 1975–1994

In 1975 the Genealogical Society of Utah became the Genealogical Department of The Church of Jesus Christ of Latter-day Saints—a move that more fully integrated it into the central administrative structure of the Church. As part of this reorganization, a number of administrative changes were made. These included the creation of a new priesthood genealogy division and later a priesthood area support division intended to define member responsibility more clearly, teach members how to do genealogical work, and help priesthood leaders perform their family history duties. This chapter provides an overview of all these administrative changes and of various new programs and policies developed from 1975 to 1994. Each of these developments had important consequences for the genealogical work of the Church.

The work of the Genealogical Department in this era was influenced by a number of significant events in the history of the Church. Two revelations that concerned concepts central to family history were added to the canon of LDS scripture. Between 1975 and 1994, the number of temples in operation around the world grew from sixteen to forty-six, greatly expanding the opportunity for Latter-day Saints everywhere to perform proxy ordinances. Finally, in 1981, President Spencer W. Kimball placed family history research and temple work on a par with other aspects of Church activity when he clarified the three-fold mission of the Church as "to proclaim the gospel, to perfect the Saints, and to redeem the dead."[1]

Departmental Organization

Until 1975, the Genealogical Society existed apart from other units of the Church as a separately incorporated, tax-exempt body. While integrated in many ways into the structure of the Church, the Society's unique status presented some administrative difficulties. In addition, it was distinctively different from other genealogical societies, for it not only supported research, but also regulated the identification of deceased persons for whom temple ordinances could be performed. By making the Society part of the organization of the Church, Church leaders hoped to streamline its operation and make it more effective.[2]

On 18 November 1975, Elder Boyd K. Packer and other General Authorities met with the Society's staff to explain the change. Elder Packer noted that being a "department" of the Church rather than a "society" would expand the scope of the organization's responsibility. He also stated that the change was in accordance with the status of other Church administrative units:

> We've operated as the Genealogical Society for generations. *Department* just moves the boundaries out. There are a lot of things that the Genealogical Society does, but most of what we do really, we do here at Church headquarters, and we need to reach way out into the Church now in many ways that we haven't before, and we're just joining the other departments. . . . So we're just organizing just the way the whole rest of the Church is organized, only better.[3]

Elder Boyd K. Packer, 1975, ardent supporter of family history and temple work, served many years on the Temple and Family History Executive Council. Courtesy LDS Church Archives.

Beginning 10 December 1975, the Genealogical Society became the Genealogical Department of the Church, a fully integrated part of the central administration. The corporate entity of the Genealogical Society of Utah became another name under which the Church does business and is used principally for negotiating microfilming contracts.[4]

As a result of the reorganization, the title of the head of the Department changed from *president* to *executive director.* Nine people had served as president of the Society since its organization in 1894. The last one, Theodore M. Burton, became the first executive director of the Department. Since his release in 1978, there have been five other directors. The fourteen leaders of the Genealogical Society/Department during its first century are listed below. All except Junius Jackson were also General Authorities of the Church.

Franklin D. Richards	1894–1899
Anthon H. Lund	1900–1921
Charles W. Penrose	1921–1925
Anthony W. Ivins	1925–1934
Joseph Fielding Smith	1934–1961
Junius Jackson	1961–1962
Nathan Eldon Tanner	1963
Howard W. Hunter	1964–1972
Theodore M. Burton	1972–1978
J. Thomas Fyans	1978
Royden G. Derrick	1979–1984
Richard G. Scott	1984–1988
J. Richard Clarke	1988–1993
Monte J. Brough	1993–present

The new Department was charged with three main responsibilities: (1) to gather records that could be used for genealogical research, (2) to provide names for the temples and keep an official record of temple ordinances performed, and (3) to encourage Church members to do genealogical research as well as teach them how to do it.[5] Five divisions were created within the Department to achieve these purposes: Acquisitions and Field Operations, Library Services, Temple Services, Priesthood Genealogy, and Administrative Services.

Acquisitions and Field Operations was responsible for acquiring genealogical sources by gift, purchase, or microfilming. Records specialists in this division began negotiating microfilming contracts in countries outside the United States, supervising filmers, acquiring books and book catalogs, and, in some areas, arranging the recording of oral genealogies.

Library Services organized, described, and made these sources available for use. This division supervised cataloging, reference, and collection development. Cataloging described the materials, reference assisted patrons in the use of the materials, and record specialists identified what sources could be added to develop the collection.

Temple Services processed all the names for temple work and maintained the official temple ordinance record. It set up temple service centers in several temple areas outside North America. These centers extracted the microfilms containing local information, cleared the names, and submitted them to the temples for the ordinance work to be done by local members. Only the finalized records of ordinances performed were sent to Department headquarters in Salt Lake City. Temple Services worked directly with the temples in answering questions about ordinance policies until 1981, when this responsibility was transferred to the Temple Department (created in 1979). Temple Services was then renamed the Names Processing Division.

The fourth division, Priesthood Genealogy, was created to assist and encourage Church members in their own research.[6] It was asked to simplify the genealogical procedures and forms used by the Church so that members would find them less intimidating.[7] To accomplish this task, Priesthood Genealogy began to generate research and class materials, provide instruction, and otherwise assist Church members and the genealogical community at large in their research.

Administrative Services, the fifth division, handled hiring, budgeting, and other administrative tasks in support of the other divisions.[8] It began to hire more people with advanced degrees and special skills. Language background was an important consideration because of the international nature of the collection and clientele.[9]

Executive Directors of the Family History Department, 1976–1994

Theodore M. Burton, 1972–78

J. Thomas Fyans, 1978

Royden G. Derrick, 1979–84

Richard G. Scott, 1984–88

J. Richard Clarke, 1988–93

Monte J. Brough, 1993–

Photographs courtesy LDS Church Archives

The organization of the Department has continued to evolve. The Projects and Planning Division was created in 1981 to control the development of automation. The Priesthood Genealogy and Library Services Divisions were merged into the Member Services Division in 1985. In 1990 the Administrative Services and Projects and Planning Divisions were reconfigured into various support groups, leaving only three divisions—Member Services, Names Processing, and Acquisitions. In 1992, Member Services was renamed as Research Support Services. The same year a priesthood and area support division was organized to respond more effectively to the needs of priesthood leaders.[10]

Long-Range Planning

Another significant development after the creation of the Department was the integration of long-range planning into Department operations in 1976. Before that time, long-range planning was informal; department management dealt with issues singly rather than as part of an integrated plan that covered all facets of Department activity. The initial step towards the creation of a long-range plan was taken in 1974, when Elder Theodore M. Burton announced to Department leaders that he had been preparing data to show "long-range trends" and suggested a monthly meeting to consider the Department's course and the effect of the activities of one area on another. Elder Burton desired to introduce a program that would produce action rather than guilt. He observed that "for many years we have stressed genealogy with the result that people feel guilty but have not felt impelled to do this." Consequently, he proposed the expansion of extraction, the automation of temple ordinances, renewed emphasis on temple attendance, and support for family organizations, rather than individuals, to do family history research.[11]

Elder Burton's proposals were expanded over the next two years, and a plan was presented to the Quorum of the Twelve and the First Presidency in 1976. After its approval, the Department had a clear vision of what it sought to accomplish. Department leaders continue to use the long-range goals of the plan as a guide to measure Departmental accomplishments.

The plan anticipated many of the major accomplishments of the next two decades. These included the creation of multiple automated data files, such as those found in FamilySearch; the widespread distribution of genealogical information through personal computers; and the use of programs such as Family Record Extraction to involve a larger spectrum of Church members in family history activity; and other goals listed below.

The plan was updated regularly, milestones were identified by which progress could be measured, and annual status reports were made to higher management. New staff positions were also created

1976 Long-Range Goals

No.	**Summary of Goal**	**Current Implementation**
1	Develop and maintain a central genealogical file that shows family relationships and temple ordinance data for individuals	FamilySearch, Ancestral File
2	Design all name entry systems to place individuals in their proper family order	Ancestral File
3	Prepare a single index to all temple work for a given individual	International Genealogical Index
4	Make information in the central genealogical file available to Church members as a beginning point for their own genealogical research	FamilySearch
5	Establish genealogical service centers in temple districts, particularly overseas, and involve members in a records extraction program	Family History Service Centers, Family Record Extraction
6	Use modern technology in temple recording and enable service centers to process names locally	Ordinance Recording System, TempleReady
7	Transfer to families and local priesthood leaders the burden of determining the accuracy of name submission and responsibility for avoiding duplication of temple ordinances	TempleReady
8	Develop and maintain a family organization register to aid members in contacting other persons researching their same lines	Family Registry, Ancestral File
9	Provide a service to assist priesthood leaders in more difficult areas of genealogical research	Published research outlines
10	Continue the present program of gathering records of genealogical interest from around the world	Expansion of microfilm acquistions

to support planned projects. In each case, a project administrator and a project manager were assigned. Teams of programmers, user specialists, and other staff were assembled to develop the plan. The Projects and Planning Division was given responsibility for development. Planning continues to be part of the current effort to make family history an integral part of the work of the Church.

Member Responsibility: Individual and Collective

When the Church's regional representatives gathered in Salt Lake City in the fall of 1975, they were presented with some startling information: member involvement in genealogical activity was not keeping pace with Church growth. In 1972, 66 percent of the names submitted for temple work had been provided by members, but in 1975 only 26 percent came from that source. Moreover, only 7.5 percent of the Church membership had participated in the four-generation program.[12] The reason for this situation, said Elder Boyd K. Packer, was that many members thought genealogical research was simply too hard:

> Genealogical work in the Church for the most part is left to those few members who have taken a keen interest in it. . . . Genealogical work has, I fear, sometimes been made to appear too difficult, too involved, and too time-consuming to really be inviting. . . . We intend to streamline and simplify genealogical research and record clearance, to fit the needs and circumstances of the average member of the Church, rather than to accommodate the genealogical specialist.[13]

The Department attempted to reverse the trend by preparing materials for General Authorities to present in stake conferences held during 1977. They were to stress that member involvement in genealogy required little research expertise. Members were to be encouraged to (1) write personal histories, (2) establish or support family organizations, (3) complete the four-generation program, and (4) go to the temple regularly.[14] The Department hoped to introduce members to family history basics with the expectation that some would take the next step into the more demanding requirements of original research and the identification of new names for temple work.

Under the Church correlation program, the high priests in each ward were responsible for genealogical activity. In 1976, Priesthood

Genealogy developed a program to help the high priests in their work. The new program provided closer correlation for genealogical activity between the stake president, the high councilor in charge of genealogy, the bishop, and the high priests group leader. Whenever a General Authority attended a stake conference, he emphasized the role of the stake president and the high priests group leader in genealogy. George Fudge noted later that this new effort, stimulated by President Spencer W. Kimball's interest in genealogy, was the first united effort by all of the General Authorities in behalf of family history.[15]

Significantly, the religious importance of genealogy was emphasized in a powerful way during the April 1976 general conference. At that conference, the members of the Church voted to sustain the action of the First Presidency and Quorum of the Twelve in adding two important revelations to the canon of LDS scripture. One was a vision of the celestial kingdom, given to Joseph Smith in the Kirtland Temple in 1836 and concerning the salvation of those who die without a knowledge of the gospel (D&C 137). The other was President Joseph F. Smith's 1918 vision showing the Savior's visit to the spirit world and expounding the doctrine of redemption of the dead (D&C 138). As the first addition to scripture since the middle of the nineteenth century, this action was a dramatic reminder to Church members of the eternal significance of their family history labors.

The key objective of the Department in renewing the emphasis on genealogy was to "streamline and simplify." One tool for reaching this goal was a new program that involved members primarily in name extraction at the local level rather than in extended research. For almost two decades, name extraction had been done at Church headquarters, but in February 1978, stakes were asked to assume primary responsibility for this ongoing work. At the same time, Church members were told they were no longer required to submit family group sheets or to provide names for temple ordinances for ancestors beyond four generations.[16] Department employees were informed that name extraction was now the Department's highest priority.[17] They were directed to explain to Church members that pursuing extended research is a "privilege" rather than a "responsibility" and that the stake record extraction program would handle temple ordinances for ancestors in earlier generations.[18]

This simplified program eliminated the need for a complex research process to identify ancestors. Research was time consuming, required uncommon expertise, and was virtually impossible to coordinate so as to avoid one researcher duplicating the work of another. Under the new program, extended research was replaced by the one-time extraction of all names from a family history source. As Elder J. Thomas Fyans explained in October 1978, genealogical activity was to become a cooperative effort rather than continue to be an emphasis on individual research beyond four generations:

> It is apparent, then, that *ours* is a shared ancestry. . . [and] it has become apparent that genealogical research efforts are being duplicated. . . . It is for this basic reason that President Kimball has directed us that we should seek out our ancestors back four generations. After that we should work together as a Church through the records extraction program.[19]

President Ezra Taft Benson made a similar statement:

> A second major change [of the new program] is that original research beyond the four-generation level will be accepted but will no longer be required of individual members or individual families in the Church. Instead, the Church has assumed the responsibility to begin a massive record-gathering and extraction program in order to prepare names for temple work.[20]

This was a startling new message. Research had been the staple of family history programs from the inception of the Genealogical Society of Utah. While extraction was indisputably a quicker and more efficient method of providing names for the temples, it had not been so clear that the responsibility of Church members to seek after their own ancestors should be removed. The new policy was particularly devastating to private researchers, who soon lost legions of clients.

Church leaders soon became concerned that a vital link connecting generations was being overlooked in the new program. The feeling that something was not right crystallized in 1979, when the Department suggested filming and discarding the archive sheets that contained all names submitted for temple work between 1942 and 1969, prior to the time when name submission became computerized. The information would not be lost, but the elimination of the paper copy of the family group sheets seemed to represent the de-emphasis on research. In a letter to the Presidents of the First Quorum of the Seventy, the Council of the Twelve stated that they feared the Department "might be straying from some of the ancient moorings to which we should be anchored."[21] In council with the Presidents of the Seventy in February 1980, Elder Packer reiterated, "The name extraction program should be carefully managed so that it does not dominate the genealogical program of the Church." He recommended that the Department encourage a reemphasis of genealogical research among the members of the Church.[22]

These statements caught Department leadership by surprise. They were disquieted to see the reversal of a program that had been approved on every level and had been publicly endorsed. However, Church leaders had apparently felt that the implications of emphasizing collective rather than individual responsibility had warranted reappraisal. In the April 1980 general conference, President Spencer W. Kimball reaffirmed that research should continue past four generations in order for families to redeem their kindred dead.[23] At the same conference, Elder A. Theodore Tuttle announced in the priesthood session: "Once you complete your four generations, you are not finished. Continue to search out all of your ancestral lines."[24] The responsibility for extended research that the new program had lifted from the shoulders of the members was set gently back into place. Many members, however, missed the reversal and for years continued to think that four generations was the extent of their individual responsibility.

Aside from the temporary emphasis on extraction rather than extended research, the renewed call for four-generation sheets and the implementation of stake record extraction revived genealogical activity in the Church. The four-generation program was not only renewed, but also revamped. The Church requested that new sheets be submitted and that the accuracy of the data be checked before submission. Numerous discrepancies had been noted in sheets submitted under the old program, and the Department hoped to improve the quality of the information they received. Also, there had been numerous duplicate submissions under the old program. To eliminate this problem, the Department requested that sheets be submitted by families (adult brothers and sisters) rather than individuals. The new program also required compilation of a pedigree chart to accompany the sheets.[25] Consequently, everyone, even those who had submitted previously, had something to do. At the same time, stake record extraction provided a new opportunity for thousands to participate meaningfully in family history work.

Ancestral File submissions, 1981. A massive influx of family group sheets arrived in the two weeks preceding the perceived deadline for submissions. Shown are April Sams (left) and Lois Gardner (right).

Meanwhile, the rationale for the renewed four-generation program was expanded by the development of Ancestral File, a master file of completed research. The Council of the Twelve announced that submissions after 1 July 1979 would "become the foundation for a genealogical record of this dispensation."[26] Because of advancements in computer technology, Ancestral File is easily accessible to members trying to avoid duplication of effort.

The new emphasis on genealogy had a weak link, however. No one at the local level was primarily responsible for explaining the technical issues involved in compiling a family history. Correlation had placed the responsibility for promoting the program on the priesthood, but technical information was difficult to transmit. The need for expertise at the ward and branch level spurred the creation of a new Church position—ward genealogical consultant (later the ward family history consultant). This position replaced and expanded the former position of ward genealogical forms examiner.[27] The consultant helped members fulfill their family history responsibilities as defined by the priesthood.

Renewed emphasis was again placed on the need for extended research. Elder Mark E. Petersen wrote in the August 1981 *Ensign,* "We must trace our own ancestry back as far as we can. The four generations are not enough. We have the extraction program and it will help, but it does not relieve us of our own personal responsibility." This message was also sent out to stake conferences during the first half of 1982. The purpose was to reemphasize the importance of members doing their part in providing names for temple ordinances.[28]

In the last half of 1987, family history was again stressed in stake conferences in connection with the introduction of a new manual for members, *Come unto Christ through Temple Ordinances and Covenants.* James E. Faust, a member of the Temple and Genealogy Executive Council, stated the objective of these conferences: "It is hoped that in these stake conferences we can simplify the approach to genealogy, and demystify it so that every member, regardless of training, will find it doable."[29] Each member was asked to begin searching for at least one unendowed ancestor and to go to the temple for that person.

The stress on making genealogy "doable" led to a significant change in the name of the Department. Leaders felt that *genealogy* reflected the means rather than the purpose of the Department. A decade earlier Elder Theodore M. Burton had stated, "It is not genealogy which is our goal and we ought to stop using this word as frequently and indiscriminately as we have done in the past. Our work really is that of family exaltation and I suggest we use this expression."[30] In August 1987, the First Presidency announced that the Genealogical Department would be called the Family History Department, and the name of the Genealogical Library (in Salt Lake City) would be changed to the Family History Library. Church leaders hoped this change would remove the implication that professional training was needed to pursue one's ancestry.[31] The Department altered the names of subordinate divisions and departments to reflect this new approach. For example, branch genealogical libraries were renamed family history centers.

As the decade progressed, the opportunity for member involvement in family history activity was expanded by automation. In 1988, Family Record Extraction moved name extraction into members' homes and into members' home computers. FamilySearch, put into use in 1990, placed large automated research files at the disposal of members using computers at family history centers and local Church clerks' offices. In 1993, TempleReady made it possible for members to clear names for temple work. Automation expanded member participation as thousands of members contributed in ways not possible before the advent of the personal computer. (See chapter 8 for more information.)

Priesthood Administration

The Department's role in reaching all Church members with the family history program was aided by developments in the Church's administrative structure. In October 1975, the First Quorum of the Seventy was reestablished as the third presiding quorum of the Church. In subsequent years, a Second Quorum of the Seventy was added. Within the next few years, the Department came under the administration of the Seventy. Since 1978 the executive director of the Department has always been one of the Presidents of the First Quorum of the Seventy. Concurrent with this change, additional General Authorities from the Quorums of the Seventy have been appointed as assistant executive directors.

Changes also occurred at the next higher administrative level. In 1977 the Church created four executive committees (later called councils) among the members in the Quorum of the Twelve. These councils formalized the decision-making structure of the Quorum in administering the operations of the departments of the Church. One of these councils was the Temple and Genealogy Executive Committee,[32] now known as the Temple and Family History Executive Council. The Council oversees the Department and, under the direction of the First Presidency and the Council of the Twelve, promotes family history efforts Churchwide through the administrative framework of Area Presidencies, headed by members of the Quorum of the Seventy. The Department obtains guidance and direction from the general Church councils regarding developments in the family history program.

Area offices, established in the 1970s where large numbers of Church members exist, have developed as extension centers for the headquarters offices in Salt Lake City. For the areas in which they are located, these offices have gradually assumed the responsibilities of Church headquarters. Since area offices are closer to local members, they are more responsive to their needs.

In 1985 the Church gave Area Presidencies and offices total responsibility for training and motivating members in family history work, processing names, supervising family history centers, ordering microfilm, and supervising family history staff.[33] The most notable exception to this large-scale transfer of authority was the retention of the Department's acquisitions staff. The Department suggested that Area Presidencies appoint an adviser (a paid staff person, volunteer, or missionary) to supervise their newly acquired responsibilities. To keep the advisers and the Area Presidencies informed on technical issues, in 1986 the Department appointed a person to serve in headquarters as first-contact for each area.[34]

The responsiveness of area offices to their new role has varied greatly. In 1990 the Department learned that the Mexico/Central America Area had called an area adviser and was producing their own materials and training programs.[35] However, as of 1991, most Area Presidencies did not have trained family history personnel on their staff. Instead, they used either Church service personnel (that is, people willing to donate their time to Church callings) or full-time employees with limited background in family history.[36] In response, the Department began training area family history advisers brought to Salt Lake City during general conference.[37]

In 1992 the Department began to devote more resources to working with Area Presidencies. Five high-level staff members at Department headquarters were appointed as area coordinators. Through a newly created division, Priesthood and Area Support, the area coordinators began planning for the development of family history services in each area of the Church. They sent letters to Area Presidencies during 1992 requesting that family history plans be prepared by the Area Presidencies.[38] The objective of the plans was for areas to identify their needs and for the Department to respond to those needs as far as resources permitted.[39] Even though research guides and forms had been translated into a number of languages in previous years, one of the most pressing needs the areas identified was the cultural adaptation of these materials. In 1993 a pilot team was commissioned to design multicultural guides and forms.[40]

Currently, the administration of the Department is organized to promote the family history mission of the Church anywhere members live. The primary line of communication for family history policy is through the Temple and Family History Executive Council and Area Presidencies to local leaders. A network of family history centers and family history service centers (both discussed below) provide the technical assistance and resources patrons need to accomplish their family history work.

Branch Libraries/Family History Centers

In 1964 the Department began to establish branch libraries (later called family history centers)[41] at Church facilities in the United States and Canada. Eventually, other centers were established internationally. At the local centers, Church members had access to the Family History Department's microfilms. During 1977–80 the Department focused its resources on expanding the stake record extraction program. After that period, providing local centers with as many services as their circumstances permitted was emphasized in order to facilitate research locally. As a result of these efforts, in 1994 over 2,000 centers ordered approximately 75,000 microfilm rolls per month.[42]

Establishing and operating a center involved a number of problems that are illustrated by the history of the South Jordan Stake Genealogical Library. Established in 1976, the South Jordan center was the first in the Salt Lake Valley and was one of the first centers belonging to an individual stake in Utah. Local family historians struggled to acquire facilities in a building already used to the maximum, as well as to find competent staff members. The facilities were Spartan—the library was located in a classroom next to the regular meetinghouse library, and the classroom continued to be used for other Church programs. Microfilm readers and books were stored in cabinets which were locked when the center was not open so the room could be used by the three wards meeting in the building.

Marian Egbert, the librarian, had two assistants. One ordered the films, handled the finances, and took care of the microfilm reader. The other was in charge of the staff and gave individual assistance to patrons. The center also had a training supervisor, who held monthly meetings with the staff. Sixteen Church members, recommended by their bishops as among the most qualified and called by a member of the stake high council, worked three-hour shifts. The center was open from 9 A.M. to 9 P.M. on Fridays and 9 A.M. to 5 P.M. on Saturdays, though Egbert hoped to have longer hours when she could get a larger staff. The center could not advertise its services; it could not even have a sign on the door or a telephone. People learned about it from Church meeting talks and by word of mouth.[43]

Notwithstanding these and other obstacles, local centers have become a major component of the family history program of the Church. By 1977 about 50 percent of those using the central collection were accessing it from family history centers. By 1992 this figure had risen to 75 percent, with approximately 2,500,000 patrons using the centers in comparison to 800,000 using the Family History Library. The average center was open an average of thirty-two hours and had thirty-five visitors per week. The fact that these were primarily volunteer operations is underscored by the average annual local budget allocation of $567 per center.[44]

Efforts to decentralize and simplify family history programs in 1978 had a significant impact on Department support for family history centers. Jurisdiction for the centers was transferred from the Department to local Church leaders.[45] No longer extensions of the Department, they did not receive direct guidance from Salt Lake City. During this period, the Department also began promoting the concept of using the center facilities for extraction rather than research. Indeed, in late 1978, the Department decided that approval for new centers would be granted for extraction projects only.[46] The Department even sought to reduce circulation support in 1979, when it advised centers to direct orders for U.S. census films to Federal Regional Archive Centers.[47]

When the policy of giving priority to extraction was reversed in 1980, the research role of the centers was revived, and the Department began to improve support for them. David Mayfield, the director of the Department's library system, played a prominent role in providing resources for the centers. He obtained approval for distributing the microfiche version of the newly automated library catalog to the local centers. He appointed a branch library coordinator in 1981. In December, the coordinator published the first issue of a newsletter—*Branch Genealogical Libraries Memorandum* (later *Family History Centers Memorandum*)—to keep the centers advised of products and services they could receive.[48] In March 1982, prints of U.S. census films, restricted from circulation only three years earlier, were sent to large centers in Provo, Ogden, Mesa, and Los Angeles so that these films did not have to be ordered from Salt Lake City each time they were requested by a patron. In January 1983, a new *Branch Genealogical Library Operational Manual* was published. Beginning that year and lasting for the next four years, the library offered a semiannual introductory course in Salt Lake City for center staff. Many people responded, traveling to Salt Lake City at their own expense. In August 1984, over two hundred attended. In another support effort, the Department offered centers, at nominal cost, major research tools such as the International Genealogical Index (6,700 microfiche), the Accelerated Indexing Systems data base of U.S. census records (2,500 microfiche), and a selection of frequently used reference books (2,400 microfiche).[49]

With increased support from the Department, the number of centers began to grow. In October 1982, the 400th center was opened in Lake Oswego, Oregon, representing an increase of only 200 centers during the previous six years. During the next six years, this growth quadrupled—800 centers were added, making a total of 1,200. Approximately 25 percent of these centers were established outside the United States. In December 1994, 2,278 centers were in operation—39 percent of them outside the United States (U.S. and Canada 1,397,881 elsewhere).[50]

Over time, several centers in areas where there were temples or large concentrations of Church members developed extensive facilities. These included Mesa, Arizona; Idaho Falls and Rexburg (Ricks College) in Idaho; Ogden and Provo (Brigham Young University) in Utah; and Los Angeles, Oakland, and San Diego in California.

In 1985, the Department recognized that giving these large centers additional resources would greatly expand service to many members at minimum cost. Designated as multistake centers, they were given additional films, reference works, and computers.[51] In time a new center was built in Mesa, and the facilities in Oakland and Idaho Falls were remodeled. Additional multistake centers were established in Orange, California, and in Boise, Idaho.[52] With the additional material and with extended hours of service, these centers greatly increased the ability of the Society to serve Church members in their own areas.

Even though the centers were located in Church facilities, they were open to the family history community at large. Many people not affiliated with the Church made use of the research facilities in the centers. In some areas, as many as 80 percent of the patrons were not members of the LDS Church.[53] In return for the use of the facilities, they were asked to contribute copies of the results of their research to the Family History Library collection or to Ancestral File. Thus, the centers served as a point of cooperation between the Church and the many family history researchers outside the Church.

One of the unanticipated developments in the growth of the family history center network was the flourishing of centers at some penal institutions. The program, requested by inmates, involved any prisoners who found family history research to be a productive and fulfilling use of their time. For some it was therapeutic, helping them to reestablish family ties which had been severed by the events that led them to prison.[54]

Family history centers continue to make the huge collection amassed in Salt Lake City available throughout the world. However, they are not the only agents for decentralizing Department services. In addition, the Department has established family history service centers with a broader assignment to promote all family history programs in various areas of the Church.

Family History Service Centers

Establishment of service centers came in response to the need for decentralizing names processing. President Spencer W. Kimball explained the underlying concept in the Regional Representatives Seminar held September 30, 1976:

> Saints in every temple district must be taught to provide their own names. Japanese people should provide the names for their own Tokyo temple. South American people should provide the names for their own Sao Paulo temple. Likewise, the Mexico and Seattle and in every other established area. If they do so, then they will save their OWN dead. If they do not, and depend on Salt Lake City to send names from, they do not save their own dead, but instead work on other people's ancestry.[55]

Name extraction and names clearance would be performed at a temple service center (renamed Genealogical Service Center in 1981 and Family History Service Center in 1990) in the temple district where the temple ordinances were to be performed.

The first service center, supervised by Octaviano Tenorio, was established in Mexico City in January 1977.[56] Service centers were opened in Sao Paulo and Tokyo during 1978. New temples were being built in these cities, and the centers prepared for the opening of these temples by receiving names from members. Until the release of TempleReady in 1991, names for immediate family members were processed locally, while names for earlier generations were most often sent to Salt Lake City for duplication checking.

Along with names processing, film ordering also began to be decentralized in the late 1970s. Film circulation to countries other than the U.S. was hampered by shipping delays and insupportable import costs. Supplying a print sometimes cost more than making it in the first place. The solution to such problems came from Church leaders in Australia, who established a microfilm ordering center in 1973. For circulation to local family history centers, the ordering center obtained via long-term loans film prints of the most significant sources microfilmed in that area.[57] Other ordering centers were established in other countries during the next decade.

In 1980 the Department assumed responsibility for ordering centers and made them part of the genealogical service centers which it continued to establish. By the end of 1983, service centers were functioning in Mexico, Japan, Brazil, Great Britain, Australia, Germany, New Zealand, Tonga, Tahiti, Chile, and Samoa. In addition to names processing and microfilm ordering, the centers began to provide services such as reference assistance, equipment purchases, and photoduplication. More importantly, they began to train newly called family history center directors and priesthood leaders. Thus the service centers performed the essential functions of the Department for the areas in which they were established. Decentralization went one step further in 1985, when service centers were placed under the direct administration of Area Presidencies. The Department continued to help in an advisory capacity.[58]

At some centers, the film collection became substantial. In 1994 there were 124,023 films in Friedrichsdorf, Germany; 74,000 in Mexico City, Mexico; 74,000 in Sydney, Australia; 53,206 in Solihull, Great Britain; 59,704 in Auckland, New Zealand; and 48,100 films in Stockholm, Sweden. In addition, the service centers absorbed new functions such as Family Record Extraction and the implementation of FamilySearch. To reflect the expanding services of the centers, the name was changed in 1990 to family history service centers.[59] By that date, nineteen centers served 495 family history centers in fifty-five countries, territories, or colonies.[60] With the exception of acquisitions and cataloging, these centers performed all of the functions of the parent organization, substantially reducing reliance on resources in Salt Lake City.

Film Circulation

The demand for film circulation rose inexorably from 1975 to 1994. The Department was not prepared for the unexpected pressure. In time it took measures to reduce the long delay between the time a film was ordered and its arrival at a center.

The system for loaning films and other records to branch libraries was computerized in 1975, a change which greatly facilitated the circulation process. Since the films were more easily tracked by a computer, they could go to a branch library for a regular loan period of one month, for an extended period of six months, or for an indefinite loan if many users were expected to need the film over a long period of time. The six-month and indefinite loans were especially useful for outlying areas, such as Australia.

In March 1976, films circulated numbered 22,137, a 45 percent increase from March 1975. The following spring, circulation increased "far beyond . . . expectations" immediately after the U.S. broadcast of the television miniseries "Roots."[61] In 1978 circulation was double the 1975 figures. Additional staff members—one in 1976, eight in 1977, and fifteen in 1978—were employed to meet the demand. Still, the delay between film request and receipt lagged by as much as two to three months.[62]

To pay for the actual costs involved in circulating a film, in 1979 the Department raised the cost for a two-week loan from $.50 to $2.00, and a six-month loan from $2.00 to $3.00. This measure temporarily decreased demand by 50 percent.[63] However, the increase in the number of centers during the early 1980s increased circulation 80 percent—from 150,000 rolls per year in 1980 to 272,000 per year by 1984.[64] But the time lag involved in receiving ordered film continued, constituting the "single most dissatisfying" problem in local centers.[65]

The problem was finally resolved in 1987. Additional staff members were hired; the circulation function was changed from a single eight-hour shift to an around-the-clock, three-shift schedule; direct shipment from the vault via UPS was instituted; a new computer-based system known as the Microfilm Production Monitoring System was implemented to track film through all stages of production and handling; and circulation fees were raised again. The circulation lag dropped from four weeks to four days in some centers.[66] Other improvements followed as technology permitted. In 1989 orders could be faxed. Ordering by modem began to be implemented in 1993. By 1994 films were being circulated at the rate of 900,000 orders per year, or an average of about 3,500 a day.[67]

Publications/Videos

Circulating sources was not the only way the Department provided assistance to a worldwide audience; it also pursued a vigorous program of publication. In December 1976, the Department stopped sending representatives to stake family history seminars, making it increasingly important to publish information for distribution to the rapidly growing Church membership. The Department decided to produce a basic family history doctrine and research text for use in the Church's Sunday Schools. During 1977 two Department staff members, Glen Harris and Ed Platt, wrote *From You to Your Ancestors.* Other staff members worked on sixteen foreign language adaptations of the manual. In March 1978, 150,000 copies of the first English edition came off the press. The text was also published in other languages. By 1982, 518,000 copies had been sold.[68] *From You to Your Ancestors* served as the basic Sunday School genealogical manual for a decade.

To assist in the research process, the Department compiled research papers. Some of these short informational papers described sources and dates of material available in each country, and others dealt with a wide variety of genealogical topics such as paleography, emigration, research standards, and Department files and services. In July 1977, the Department published a list of 138 research papers.

In 1978 the Department publication program as well as all other Church publications came under the close scrutiny of Church leaders. They initiated a policy that Church publications be kept to a minimum, primarily in view of the increasing number of new members with insufficient background or literacy to read the huge amount of official Church material that had accumulated over the years. The watchwords were simplification and reduction.

This policy mitigated against specialized publications that attempted to clarify the complexities of family history research. As a result of the new guidelines, the publication of research papers ceased, but only temporarily.

In the 1980s, a new technology—videotape—came of age. In October 1982, the Church dropped 16 mm film in favor of videocassettes for the distribution of visual materials.[69] The Church soon established an Audio-visual Committee to control the production and distribution of videotapes. Working through this committee, the Department produced videos between 1985 and 1987 on how to use family history centers, how to research U.S. census records, and how to use the Family History Library catalog (available at family history centers).

After the focus on extraction shifted in the 1980s, the Department began to reemphasize the importance of individuals submitting names of their own ancestors. Three small manuals were developed over a three-year period and published in 1987 and 1988—one member guide, *Come unto Christ through Temple Ordinances and Covenants,* and two handbooks for local family history consultants, *Submitting Names for Temple Ordinances* and *Providing Temple Ordinances for Our Ancestors.* These manuals emphasized the identification of ancestors in recent generations rather than the distant past, an approach appropriate to the large number of new members who could readily identify ancestry in the recent past. This message also served as a reminder to older members to double-check their more recent ancestry to make sure that the temple work was complete. These publications introduced new forms and procedures, simplified to make a complex task as easy as possible. These aids included a basic task list for name submission, a letter-size family group sheet for name submission, a letter-size pedigree chart, and an ordinance pedigree chart that provided spaces to mark off when ordinances had been completed for all direct-line ancestors in the first eight generations.[70]

Along with new manuals, the Department obtained permission to distribute other new research aids. Reaffirming the need to support family history research with some degree of detailed information and guidance, in 1989 the Department published research outlines for each of the fifty states in the United States. Four years in process, these outlines distilled masses of information into digestible pieces to give family history center staff members, many of whom had limited genealogical experience, the information essential in aiding the novice researcher.[71] At the same time, some of the research papers published in the previous decade were reissued in new editions. Unlike many Church publications, these aids were intended for a specific rather than a general audience and were published in limited editions.

Further simplification and reduction occurred in 1992 and 1993, when the Church replaced the 1987 booklets with two new handbooks—one for leaders, *Temple and Family History Leadership Handbook,* and one for members, *A Member's Guide to Temple and Family History Work.* The First Presidency authorized distribution of the latter manual to the homes of every Church member.[72] These manuals identified the doctrinal basis of family history work and clearly identified leader and member responsibilities. The handbooks also explained ways in which automation had provided new tools to help members meet their family history responsibilities. Translations of these works are being produced to extend the information to members of the Church in many countries.

Name Submission

One of the primary goals of the Department has always been to assist Church members in obtaining and submitting names for temple work. Over the years, it has developed a number of name submission policies with the objective of reducing duplicate ordinance work. With the emphasis on simplification after 1975, however, the intricacies of name submission were gradually eliminated.

Name submission in the late 1970s was decreasing. Processing took four to six months for a name to be cleared for temple ordinances and returned to the submitter.[73] This lengthy process discouraged many members from submitting names. The de-emphasis of extended research during 1978 to 1979 also had a negative impact on name submissions, which dropped by approximately 20 percent during those years. With the renewed emphasis on extended research, name submission gradually increased from 1980 to 1987. Then the cumulative effects of family history automation efforts introduced during the 1980s began to bear fruit. Beginning in 1987, name submission increased precipitously. By 1990, 3.2 million names were being submitted annually as compared to approximately 700,000 in 1980. These names constituted 57 percent of those needed in the temples.[74] In 1993, 70 percent of the temple names were submitted by members.[75] This trend continues as family files in many temples are overwhelmed by a dramatic increase of members doing temple work for their own ancestors.

Submission rules were liberalized throughout this period. In November 1981, relationship restrictions on name submission were eliminated.[76] Previously, members were restricted to submitting only on their direct lines; now they could submit names regardless of relationship. The main exception was the rule of privacy, which required that work done for those born or married within the last ninety-five years be restricted to one's own relatives. In 1987 submission policies permitted the clearance of people with incomplete names, estimated dates, and place of birth or marriage unknown; this change meant that virtually any person known to have lived could be cleared for ordinance work. Even more dramatically, the role of clearing submitted names, absorbed by the Society in 1927 with the introduction of the Temple Index Bureau, was returned to Church members in the United States and Canada with the implementation of TempleReady in 1993—thereby fulfilling one of the long-range goals established in 1976.

Cooperation with the Genealogical Community

To promote family history work in general, the Department has sought the cooperation of many organizations outside the Church. This cooperation was aided by the widespread and growing popularity of genealogy as a favorite pastime.

Just after the Society became a Department in 1975, *Roots* by Alex Haley was published. The book was followed by numerous magazine and newspaper articles on genealogy, many of which referred to LDS genealogical efforts. These articles mentioned that the Church had the largest genealogical library in the world as

Alex Haley, 1980, author of *Roots,* popularized the cultural importance and traditions of genealogy. Haley credited the Society for its assistance in his research and spoke at the 1980 World Conference on Records.

well as a widespread system of family history centers.[77] However, genealogy still remained an obscure activity to the general public until the enormously successful television broadcast, of a miniseries based on Haley's book, in January 1977. When Alex Haley appeared on the "Tonight Show" with Johnny Carson, he shared some of the limelight with the Department by discussing its genealogical resources and projects. Immediately, news agencies flooded the Department with inquiries and requests for interviews. In the months that followed, correspondence to the library doubled, on one day peaking at 3,700 pieces of mail. The library was flooded with an average of 3,500 visitors daily during the summer of 1977, up from a high of 2,000 per day in the previous year. The *Church News* referred to the widespread interest as an "international genealogy mania."[78] After public attention cooled, a new host of genealogical enthusiasts remained, desiring to take advantage of the resources the Department had been accumulating for over eighty years.

In its continued effort to reach a worldwide audience, the Department hosted a second World Conference on Records in 1980. The first conference in 1969 had focused on the preservation of sources used in genealogy. The second highlighted the use of those sources to compile family pedigrees and histories. When the Conference convened 12 August 1980, approximately 11,500 participants representing thirty nations were present.[79] A full range of family history topics was treated in nearly three hundred presentations by experts from around the world. The central theme of the presentations was "Preserving Our Heritage," meaning the heritage of families. The stylized figure of a family served as the logo of the conference. At the second general assembly, Alex Haley highlighted this theme with his address, "Family: A Humanizing Force." Lord Teviot, a British genealogist, summarized his feelings about the conference in these words: "Absolutely marvelous. There isn't another genealogical or personal or family history conference in the world that can compare with the World Conference on Records."[80] While the first conference eleven years earlier had introduced the Department to the world, the second conference cemented its leadership role in promoting family history research in the international community.

To further its cooperative efforts with organizations outside the Church, the Department in 1976 decided to seek membership in the International Council on Archives. This body serves as the forum for coordinating worldwide archival activities. As an institution with extensive microfilming experience, the Department could offer training to nations just getting started in the process. The Department hoped that countries would establish record-preservation programs and share the filming burden, allowing the Department to purchase the microfilms it needed.[81] In the meantime, membership in the council promised the benefit of increased international visibility and the accompanying potential of extending the Department's microfilming project into new countries where a local record-preservation program was not imminent.

Prior to the Department's decision to join the international council, Dennis Neuenschwander, then the Department's acquisitions agent for Eastern Europe, had attended the 1975 roundtable of the council in Kiev. As the representative of a private institution in a council of nations, he was regarded with suspicion and distrust. The Department sent a large delegation of twelve representatives in distinctive blue suits to the 1976 congress of the council (held every fourth year, while roundtables are held in intervening years) in Washington, D.C., to staff a display about the Department and to answer questions about its goals and purposes. This effort began a process of making the Department's purpose and objectives clear to the rest of the genealogical world. As a result of their participation in the congress, department employees were appointed to positions on the automation and micrographics committees of the Council. The Department hosted another display at the 1980 congress held in London. In December 1980, Elder Neuenschwander was able to write, "From bare tolerance we now enjoy near full fellowship."[82]

In the years that followed, the Department continued to make important contributions to the Council. In 1984 the Department completed a microfilming manual entitled *A Guide to Micrographics* that was later used as the basis for the Council's new manual. Concurrently, microfilmers from around the world were trained by Department staff. In 1984, for example, trainees included operators from South America, the Middle East, and Asia. Membership was likewise beneficial to the Department. Contact with international archivists permitted the Department to initiate filming programs in countries such as Sri Lanka, India, and East Germany. In the 1988 and 1992 congresses, the Department demonstrated its automated databases of genealogical information in an effort to show the value of compiling and sharing this data worldwide.

By the mid-1970s, the Department was becoming increasingly visible to many people outside the Church who had many different kinds of interests. The *Los Angeles Times* carried a highly laudatory article, calling the collection a "genealogical gold mine."[83] Academicians in a variety of fields found the data available through the Department to be extremely useful in their research. In 1975, for example, Robert W. Fogel, a well-known American economic historian, working in the exacting field of cliometrics (quantitative history), reported on how he suddenly discovered what the Department was doing:

> The biggest breakthrough in our effort to collect a representative sample took place in Atlanta. There we learnt that the court records of every county in Georgia were available on microfilms at the state archives. Upon examining some of the reels we made the further discovery that they had been donated by the Genealogical Society of the Church of Jesus Christ of Latter-Day Saints, which was engaged in a Southwide microfilming project. And so it was that we learnt that the Mormons, for religious reasons, had photographed and stored in their archives near Salt Lake City microfilms of the very records that were so critical to us. With the assistance of Larry Wimmer and Clayne Pope, two faculty members of the Department of Economics at Brigham Young University, we established a team of

> students that is still at work in Utah and which has been able to retrieve data for scores of counties throughout the South at quite moderate cost.[84]

The desire of the Department to cooperate with governments, other organizations, and responsible scholars was featured by Ted F. Powell in an article published in *The American Archivist* in 1976:

> At present the society's collections are being used for study sponsored jointly by the American Cancer Society, the University of Utah, and the LDS Hospital endeavoring to determine whether cancer is hereditary and, if so, how we can predict it and warn living family members of the danger. The Yale University Medical School has spent many years in proving that twinning is based on heredity.
>
> The list of master's and doctor's candidates using our records for thesis preparation is too long to report. Their disciplines include anthropology, economic history, demography, population movement, and medieval family reconstitution. One scholar, who was trying to determine the economic status of typical English families during Shakespeare's time, was able to accomplish his task in less than a month in Salt Lake City, whereas it would have taken a year and a half to two years in England. The probates and wills are cataloged and readily available, without his having to wait or travel from shire to shire in order to gather information and record on his own.[85]

Powell concluded with a plea for continuing cooperation in the process of preserving the past: "We hope to continue to help archivists, government officials, and record custodians and preserve the irreplaceable records. . . . Through cooperation we can save the past for the future."[86]

The Department has been involved in the activities of many other genealogical societies. Department members have contributed substantially to the work of the National Genealogical Society; some members have been granted status as fellows of that institution. In an effort to keep other genealogical societies and genealogical periodicals informed of its activities and programs, the Department began to publish a newsletter, *News of the Family History Library,* in August 1989. The newsletter officially announces many of the Department's products and policies. Published quarterly, it is mailed to many genealogical and family history organizations in the United States. At the beginning of its second century, the Department is also developing initiatives to work closely with organizations that collect lineage-linked data, a primary result of family history research.[87]

Brigham Young University assisted the Department in its mission by introducing family history programs to students who could then serve as the future family history leaders in local church units. The Religion 261 course, Introduction to Family History, was revamped between 1987 and 1990 to accomplish this purpose. Students taking the course are involved in the extraction program and are introduced to FamilySearch at a newly completed computer lab in the Joseph Smith Building at BYU. It has become a popular course. In 1987, 250 students took the course each semester, and by 1993 this number had risen to an average of 900 students per semester. A new syllabus was introduced in January 1994, the result of a mutual effort of BYU and the Department. The new course was designed with the intent of motivating students to pursue family history work for a lifetime and not just for the duration of a semester.[88]

Genealogical Society Library, 1985, at 35 N. West Temple, Salt Lake City, was renamed the Family History Library in 1987.

Supporting the Work

Over the past two decades, the Department has initiated several significant changes to better support its worldwide programs. Service missionaries have enabled the Salt Lake City headquarters to expand services without greatly increasing expenses, and long-range planning has focused Department efforts. A new library and an automated database-searching facility have been built to provide better and more complete assistance to the genealogical community at large. While Department services have grown significantly, the increased responsibility has been met without major increases in staffing (approximately 700–750 staff positions were added over 1975–94).

In 1977 the Department began to discuss using volunteers to aid in its acquisitions program. The first effort, put into effect that year, was to have these volunteers help locate and analyze genealogical sources.[89] Eventually, however, they were made responsible for negotiating, microfilming, and teaching local members and priesthood leaders about genealogy. In 1980 the Department decided to have couple missionaries (that is, married couples called to full-time missionary service) rather than volunteers perform this work.[90] In 1981 sixteen missionary couples were serving in such diverse locations as Sri Lanka, India, Germany, Australia, Chile, Israel, New Zealand, and the United States. As the decade progressed, the functions performed by missionaries were expanded to include working in family history centers and family history service centers and participating in extraction projects. These couples usually served for eighteen months. In 1993 there were 400 family history missionaries serving outside Salt Lake City.[91]

At Department headquarters, meanwhile, part-time volunteers had served for many years, primarily on indexing projects. In October 1977, Benjamin L. Bowring was appointed to preside over the volunteers. He expanded the role of the volunteers the following year, making them fully responsible for a guide service created to provide new visitors an introduction to the library.[92] In 1981 an average of 351 volunteers served in the library, donating 103,484 hours of service.[93]

In 1981 the use of full-time Church service personnel was initiated at headquarters, starting with seven couples. Unlike the volunteer workers, Church service couples came not only from the local area, but from throughout the United States. Beginning in October 1983, the use of full-time Church service personnel was expanded into most operations of the Department.[94] Concurrently, the role of part-time volunteers was expanded to include all the functions performed by those in full-time service. By 1989 these groups were contributing over a million hours of service annually to the central operations of the Department.[95]

At first, Church service personnel and part-time volunteers all worked under the Department's Church Service Organization Presidency. In 1990, however, both the full- and part-time volunteers were called as family history missionaries and were organized in much the same way as those on a Church proselyting mission. During 1993 an average of 800 family history missionaries (350–400 full-time) served at Church headquarters.[96] What was once only an adjunct service had become a major part of the Department's work, with the missionaries and employees serving together as equal partners.

Family History Library/FamilySearch Center

The research collection housed in the Family History Library in Salt Lake City has consistently attracted thousands of people daily from all corners of the globe. The average number of visitors in March and April 1975 was 1,662 per day. The number peaked during 1977, in the wake of the *Roots* phenomenon, at an average attendance of 2,580 visitors per day.[97] By 1992 the count was consistently equaling the 1977 high, with over 2,500 people entering library doors daily.[98] This number reflects both the religiously motivated activity of Church members and the continuing popularity of genealogy as an avocation.

As elsewhere in the library world, properly serving the growing patronage has been a continuing problem. In 1976 library hours, which were from 8 A.M. to 9 P.M., were extended so the library was open from 7:30 A.M. to 10 P.M.[99] That same year, library staff began to teach classes to provide the necessary background for effective use of genealogical sources.[100] In 1977 patrons were asked to refile their own films, leaving the staff with more time to do other important things.[101] In addition to walk-in users, the library received thousands of requests for information by mail each month. Reference consultants answered these requests along with fulfilling their other duties. In July 1980, a correspondence section was organized from existing staff, who responded to the mail full-time, providing answers as complete as staff time would permit. In 1993 this unit answered 2,000 research requests each month as well as an additional 3,000 photocopy requests.[102]

At the 1980 World Conference on Records, President Spencer W. Kimball announced that a new library would be built to house the Department's collection. Groundbreaking occurred in May 1983. The building was dedicated two and one-half years later, in October

1985. The $8.5 million facility encompasses 136,000 square feet and at that time held 250 more patron seats than the old facility. Facilities to provide book and microfilm copies were also expanded. In the words of the library director, David Mayfield, the new library is "undoubtedly the largest, most modern and best-equipped genealogical library in the world."[103]

In 1993 a new facility dedicated to promoting family history work was finished. This new facility was the FamilySearch Center in the newly renovated Joseph Smith Memorial Building (formerly the Hotel Utah). At the heart of the center are 133 individual FamilySearch workstations, each equipped with a computer. Additionally, the facility houses 15,000 archive binders containing compiled genealogies received by the Department prior to automation.[104] In the year since the opening, an average of two out of three patrons have found data on their families in the center's automated files. The center hosts 1,500 to 2,000 visitors per day.[105]

Conclusion

With an eye to helping more members become actively involved in providing ordinances for their ancestors, the Family History Department has decentralized and simplified many of its programs in response to the needs of a growing Church. Another benefit realized by the many who have been involved in this work was noted by Elder Richard G. Scott in 1987:

> There is substantial refining, spiritual activity associated with identifying your ancestors. It does something to you. It makes of you a more Christ-like person. . . . We must not simply speak of all the dead who must be redeemed, but we must speak of the work of helping ourselves become the kind of people we need to become to be worthy to receive the Savior.[106]

The efforts of individuals to advance the cause of family history have been enhanced by the Department for a hundred years. It intends to continue this role in the future. The envisioned partnership between the Department and its patrons may be underpinned by a religious motive, but the information it holds can be shared by all and enjoyed for a variety of purposes. Thus, the Department offers its facilities and holdings to the world and hopes mutual benefits will occur from the exchange of ideas and information.

NOTES

[1]Spencer W. Kimball, "A Report of My Stewardship," *Ensign* 11 (May 1981): 5.

[2]George Fudge, oral history interview by Bruce Blumell, 1977, James Moyle Oral History Program (hereafter cited as JMOHP), Archives Division, Historical Department, The Church of Jesus Christ of Latter-day Saints, Salt Lake City (hereafter cited as LDS Church Archives), 68; Theodore M. Burton, oral history interview by Bruce Blumell, 1977, JMOHP, 38.

[3]Thomas Daniels, oral history interview by James B. Allen, 1977, JMOHP, 2–3; *Church News,* 27 December 1975; Boyd K. Packer, transcript of talk given in a meeting with Genealogical Department employees, 18 November 1975, Family History Department of the Church (hereafter cited as FHD), 3–4 (hereafter cited as Packer, meeting with Genealogical Dept.).

[4]Henry Christiansen files, 1975, FHD.

[5]Henry Christiansen, oral history interview by Bruce Blumell, 1977, JMOHP, 72.

[6]Packer, meeting with Genealogical Dept., 12.

[7]Daniels, interview, 3–7.

[8]Fudge, interview, 64–65; *Church News,* 27 December 1975.

[9]Arlene Eakle, personal interview by Jessie Embry, 17 January 1977; Daniels, interview, 14–15; Frank Smith, interview by Bruce Blumell, 1976, typescript, JMOHP, 45.

[10]Some information not specifically documented in this and later sections is based on the personal knowledge of Kahlile Mehr, who had discussions with various Genealogical Society administrators over time, who was personally involved in some of the events and programs discussed, and who has studied the various internal reports of the Department that are compiled for official use only.

[11]Management Meeting Minutes, 19 March 1974, FHD.

[12]Packer, meeting with Genealogical Dept., 4–5.

[13]Packer, meeting with Genealogical Dept., 7.

[14]Managing Director's Minutes, 23 December 1976.

[15]Fudge, interview, 53–54.

[16]Lynne Hollstein, "New Program Speeds Temple Work," *Church News,* 22 April 1978, 3.

[17]Historical Report, a monthly report compiled for use in the Department, March 1978, FHD.

[18]"Our Genealogical Responsibility," attached to Managing Director's Minutes, 24 April 1978, FHD, typescript, 2–4.

[19]J. Thomas Fyans, "Ours Is a Shared Ancestry," *Ensign* 8 (November 1978): 28.

[20]Ezra Taft Benson, "Worthy of All Acceptation," *Ensign* 8 (November 1978): 30.

[21]Council of the Twelve to the Presidents of the First Quorum of the Seventy, 15 November 1979, copy in the possession of Kahlile Mehr.

[22]Extract from minutes of the meeting of the Council of the Twelve with the Presidency of the First Quorum of the Seventy, 26 March 1980, copy in the possession of Kahlile Mehr.

[23]Spencer W. Kimball, "No Unhallowed Hand Can Stop the Work," *Ensign* 10 (May 1980): 5.

[24]A. Theodore Tuttle, "Eternal Links That Bind," *Ensign* 10 (May 1980): 40.

[25]Benson, "Worthy of All Acceptation," 30.

[26]Council of the Twelve to All Stake, Mission, and District Presidents, Bishops and Branch Presidents in the United States and Canada, 21 June 1979, LDS Church Archives. This letter was intended for reading in all sacrament meetings.

[27]Ezra Taft Benson, 9 July 1981, cited by David Ottesen, "Priesthood Family History Program," 23, document in possession of Kahlile Mehr.

[28]Management Meeting Minutes, 26 July 1982.

[29]*Memorandum,* July 1987, FHD.

[30]Theodore Burton to George Durrant, 11 January 1977, attached to Managing Director's Minutes, 13 January 1977, FHD.

[31]*Memorandum,* August 1987, FHD.

[32]The other committees were Melchizedek Priesthood, Missionary, and Correlation.

[33]*Memorandum,* July 1985, FHD.

[34]Managing Director's Minutes, 18 February 1986.

[35]Planning Meeting Minutes, 6 March 1990, FHD.

[36]Planning Meeting Minutes, 24 May 1991.

[37]Leadership Council Minutes, 23 March 1992, FHD.

[38]Coordination Meeting Minutes, 14 September 1992, FHD.

[39]Globalization Team Minutes, 3 May 1993, 5, FHD.

[40]Globalization Team Minutes, 3 May 1993, 4.

[41]See chapter 5 for a discussion of branch libraries. The name was changed in 1987 in connection with renaming the Genealogical Department to the Family History Department.

[42]"Family History Center Microfilm Circulation, 1978–1994," internal FHD document, typescript in possession of Kahlile Mehr.

[43]Bradley Stewart, personal interview by Jessie Embry, 22 February 1977; Fudge, interview, 50–51.

[44]*Family History Centers Memorandum,* May 1994, FHD.

[45]Management Meeting Minutes, 24 April 1978.

[46]Management Meeting Minutes, 13 November 1978.

[47]Historical Report, September 1979, FHD.

[48]A newsletter known as the *Genealogical Observer* was published from 1964 to 1972.

[49]Management Meeting Minutes, 27 June 1983.

[50]"Total Number of Family History Centers" and "Family History Centers: 1964–1994," internal FHD documents in the possession of Kahlile Mehr.

[51]"Audit of Multi-Regional Branch Genealogical Libraries," 12 April 1985, attached to Managing Director's Minutes, 7 May 1985, FHD, typescript; also Glade Nelson, previously the director of library extension services, telephone interview by Kahlile Mehr, August 1994.

[52]Multiregional centers were redesignated as multistake centers in 1991.

[53]Genealogy Department to Joseph Wirthlin, Europe Area President, n.d., in Managing Director's Minutes, 9 April 1985, FHD.

[54]Leadership Council Minutes, 17 December 1991.

[55]Typescript excerpt in the possession of Kahlile Mehr.

[56]Management Meeting Minutes, 13 December 1976.

[57]"Microfilm Ordering Centers Background Detail," internal FHD document in the possession of Kahlile Mehr. "Genealogical Society—Quarterly Historical Report, Library Division, Quarter Ending 23 June 1973," internal FHD document in the possession of Kahlile Mehr.

[58]"Genealogical Department 1983—Semi-annual Report (Prepared 18 August 1983)," internal FHD document in the possession of Kahlile Mehr; *Memorandum,* July 1985.

[59]David Mayfield, telephone interview by Kahlile Mehr, 20 July 1993.

[60]"Family History Service Centers: Serving the Member of the Church in International Areas," September 1990, internal FHD document, typescript, in the possession of Kahlile Mehr.

[61]Historical Report, March 1977, FHD.

[62]Historical Report, September 1978.

[63]Historical Report, June 1979.

[64]*Memorandum,* May 1985, FHD.

[65]"Audit of Multi-Regional Branch Genealogical Libraries," 12 April 1985, attached to Managing Directors Minutes, 7 May 1985, FHD, typescript.

[66]*Memorandum,* October 1989, FHD.

[67]"Family History Center Microfilm Circulation, 1978–1994," internal FHD document, typescript in possession of Kahlile Mehr.

[68]Management Meeting Minutes, 22 November 1982.

[69]Management Meeting Minutes, 25 October 1982.

[70]*Memorandum,* January 1988, FHD.

[71]*Memorandum,* May 1989.

[72]"Suggestions for Priesthood Leaders," attachment to First Presidency to General Authorities, Regional Representatives, Stake Mission and District Presidents, Bishops, and Branch Presidencies in Countries Where FamilySearch Is Authorized, 8 November 1993.

[73]Management Meeting Minutes, 9 January 1978.

[74]"Names Provided by Church Members," internal FHD document in the possession of Kahlile Mehr; "Temple and Family History Executive Council: Family History Quarterly Report, 15 May 1991," FHD; also, "Patron Endowment Entries Received," graph for 1980–88, internal FHD document in the possession of Kahlile Mehr.

[75]Hartman Rector Jr. address given at employee meeting, 3 November 1993, FHD, notes in the possession of Kahlile Mehr.

[76]Managing Director's Minutes, 2 November 1981.

[77]*Memorandum,* December 1988, FHD.

[78]"Thousands Research Daily in Library," *Church News,* 17 September 1977.

[79]Of the registered participants, 38 percent were from outside Utah, and 4 percent were from outside the United States.

[80]Thomas E. Daniels, "A Brief History of the 1980 World Conference on Records," typescript in the possession of James B. Allen, 28.

[81]Historical Report, May 1976, FHD.

[82]Dennis Neuenschwander to Ted Powell, 2 December 1980, Management Meeting Minutes, 5 January 1981, FHD.

[83]Charles Hillinger, "Cave Hides Genealogical Gold Mine," *Los Angeles Times,* 29 September 1976.

[84]Robert William Fogel, "From the Marxist to the Mormons," *Literary Times Supplement,* 13 June 1975, 669.

[85]Ted F. Powell, "Saving the Past for the Future—Tales of International Search and Cooperation," *American Archivist* 39 (July 1976): 314.

[86]Powell, "Saving the Past," 317-18.

[87]Coordination Meeting Minutes, 6 December 1993.

[88]*Memorandum,* December 1993, FHD.

[89]Ted F. Powell to Wm. Grant Bangerter, 26 April 1977, in Management Meeting Minutes, 25 March 1977, FHD.

[90]"Statement of Understanding: Missionaries with Other Missionary Assignments," Management Meeting Minutes, 12 April 1980, FHD, typescript.

[91]Don Jessee, telephone interview by Kahlile Mehr, January 1994.

[92]Management Meeting Minutes, 6 February 1978.

[93]Historical Report, January 1982, FHD.

[94]Zelda Merritt, comp., "Experiences and Impressions of Genealogical Missionaries, 1981-1986," typescript, preface, FHD.

[95]*Memorandum,* March 1990, FHD.

[96]Leadership Council Minutes, 10 April 1993.

[97]Historical Report, April 1976, April 1977, FHD.

[98]*Memorandum,* January 1993, FHD.

[99]Historical Report, February 1976.

[100]Historical Report, June 1976.

[101]Historical Report, October 1977.

[102]Jimmy Parker, telephone interview by Kahlile Mehr, July 1994.

[103]R. Scott Lloyd, "Genealogical Library Moves into New Home," *Church News,* 20 October 1985.

[104]The archive binders contained the family group sheets submitted for temple work and the group sheets turned in as part of the Church-sponsored three- and four-generation programs. Of course, such records, compiled by researchers with varying levels of skill, were not perfect. However, they at least provided a good starting place for those interested in genealogical research.

[105]Paul Brooks, telephone interview by Kahlile Mehr, July 1994.

[106]*Genealogical Church Service Mission Journal: 10 Oct. 1986-10 Apr. 1987,* Mission Journals, v. 3, 157, LDS Church Archives.

Chapter 8

Automating the Records

In April 1964, Elder Howard W. Hunter, then president of the Genealogical Society, attended a week-long computer seminar sponsored by IBM in San Jose, California. After the first day, he wrote in his journal: "I was amazed in having been able to write a computer program in one day without previous experience." On the fifth day he was less ebullient: "The material is so concentrated and given so rapidly, it keeps one under a constant strain to keep up." The session concluded with a "look into the future and what we might expect in new data processing equipment."[1] Elder Hunter had glimpsed the potential of computer technology to manage and process names for temple ordinance work; it was under his direction that automation was implemented.

The Family History Department began the massive project of automating its data and gathering further records from the genealogical community in automated format in the early 1970s. Automation resulted in several amazing new programs designed to facilitate the two overriding purposes of the Department: processing names for temple ordinances and assisting researchers. It also opened the door for many more Church members to be involved in and responsible for genealogical work even though they lacked the skills necessary to do research in the primary sources. The ultimate promise of automation was to reduce research to keystrokes at a computer terminal, thus eliminating the complexities and frustrations of dealing with original records and cumbersome volumes. Computer programs beckoned to an increasingly computer-literate world. As a result, a larger spectrum of people than ever before began to participate in family history activity.[2]

GIANT

In 1969 the Department unveiled a comprehensive computer system designed to automate the submission of names for temple ordinance work. Introduced to the public as the Names Tabulation Program, it was known within the Department as GIANT. It combined the names extracted from genealogical sources under the Records Tabulation Program (R-TAB) with the names from manual method of patron name submission. All names went into one computer system, programmed to detect duplicates and confirm unique entries. It served as the primary names-processing system for the next twenty years.

The use of GIANT implied a fundamental change of concept—family groups no longer needed to be identified before temple ordinances could be performed. Subsequent to the 1894 revelation of President Woodruff concerning the sealing of families, the identification of family groups became an integral part of family history research. Under the new system, Church members were no longer required to compile group sheets to clear names for temple work. Instead, they filled out magenta-colored Individual Entry and Marriage Entry forms with fields designed to simplify data entry.

Extracted names from the Names Tabulation Program could not be placed into families without research. Consequently, only individual ordinances such as baptisms and endowments were performed for these names. Sealings, either of spouses to each other or of children to parents, were not performed. The Department had hoped that Church members would use the alphabetized parish register printout provided by R-TAB to identify family members, then place them in family group sheets to submit to the temples for sealing ordinances. However, few members took those steps.

President N. Eldon Tanner asked George Fudge if a way could be found to solve the problem of how to do sealings for individually extracted names. Complicating the issue, however, was the policy that temple ordinances be performed in order: baptisms, endowments, then sealings. As Fudge sat in his office pondering the problem, the question came to him one day, "When do these ordinances become effective?" The answer, he reasoned, was that their ultimate validity depended upon the worthiness of the individuals for whom the ordinances were performed and upon whether they were performed by the proper authority in the proper place and officially recorded. Furthermore, as he reviewed the scriptures, Fudge found nothing implying that the order in which proxy ordinances were performed had any impact on their validity.

This discovery could have a tremendous, almost revolutionary, effect on the traditional pattern. Children could be sealed to their parents even if they were not yet tied together in family groups and even if the names of the parents were not yet known. If a child were sealed to parents (that is, if the word *parents,* rather than specific names, was used in the temple ceremony), there would be no doubt that the child would, in fact, be sealed to his or her correct parents. Fudge proposed, therefore, that proxy sealing of spouses be performed from marriage records, whether or not the spouses had been endowed, and that proxy sealing of children to parents be performed from birth or christening records, whether or not the parents had been endowed or sealed. Elder Howard W. Hunter took this new concept to the First Presidency, who approved it, and it was quickly put into effect.[3]

GIANT made "individual" ordinance work a comprehensive principle for all name submissions, but it also caused serious concerns. Professional researchers saw it as a threat to their livelihood. Some family organizations complained they wished to do sealings for their family only when all of the children were represented by proxies at the same time.[4] One Department board member privately expressed his reservations, saying that the new approach was misguided and wrong. Even some General Authorities did not readily accept the change. After Harold B. Lee became President of the Church, he questioned the policy and, for a short time, abrogated the sealings of parents for whom baptism and endowments had not yet been performed. However, his successor, President Spencer W. Kimball, reconsidered the issue and, with the support the Council of the Twelve, confirmed the principle of performing sealing ordinances without first identifying family groups.[5]

Although the most important result of this change was that all ordinances could be provided for individually extracted names, the new policy considerably reduced the genealogical research load. The Department continued to emphasize family responsibility in compiling family groups even though the names were submitted for temple work individually, but so far as its own work was concerned the Department deferred the matter of identifying family groups for extracted names.

The heart of GIANT was a master file containing genealogical and temple ordinance data for individuals. It served as the basis for a multiplicity of functions: (1) data entry, (2) standardized place names uniquely identified by geographical coordinates, (3) standardized surnames, (4) a duplication check that compared names against the mass file, (5) printed ordinance lists sent out to the temple, (6) clearance notices mailed to those who submitted the names, (7) mass file update, (8) a microfiche output known initially as the Computer File Index (CFI) but later as the International Genealogical Index (IGI), (9) a batch number index that identified the source of the name submission, (10) and a listing of all extraction sources, known as the Parish and Vital Records List (PVRL).

GIANT had one major shortcoming. It required that all persons in the system be identified by a basic set of data—name and event date and place—from a *single* source. This feature of the system restricted the submission of many names from the United States, a country that does not have single-source records for most of its population. An alternative was needed to handle the submission of names when a piece of required data was missing or when multiple sources were merged into a composite. In response to this problem, the Department developed the Family Entry System as a supplement to GIANT.

Implemented in January 1979, Family Entry cleared names based on family relations rather than on dates and places of birth and marriage (the data GIANT required). The data used in this process could be derived from various sources, and precise dates or places were not required. The system assisted the submission of names, not only from U.S. records, but also from oral genealogies.

After two decades, the GIANT technology, once on the cutting edge of computer processing, was stretched to its limits.

Computer center of the GIANT system, 1968. Shown are Ivan Pack, programmer (left), and Delbert Roach, library director (right).

By the late 1980s, a replacement was obviously needed. For a time, development efforts focused on creating a bigger and more complex central system. In the end, another change in policy resulted in a smaller, decentralized system known as TempleReady.

TempleReady

A major task of the Genealogical Society since the creation of the Temple Index Bureau card index (TIB) in 1927 was to reduce duplicate ordinances by checking name submissions against a central ordinance file. This function and the related processes of assuring complete and accurate data were called "names clearance." The creation in 1970 of an automated ordinance file in the GIANT system made names clearance a two-step process. First, a computer check of name submissions was made against GIANT. Next, a manual check was made against the TIB. In the manual check, employees identified individuals whose temple endowment had been performed by shuffling down narrow isles and thumbing through a forty-year compilation of cards filed in 700 filing cabinets.

Two important developments profoundly altered the process of names clearance in the late 1980s. One was technological. Powerful and inexpensive microcomputers made it possible for virtually anyone to do data processing virtually anywhere, and compact-disc technology made the distribution of large databases feasible. Martell Gee, head of systems development in the Department, recognized the possibility of creating a compact-disc version of the file of completed proxy temple work (the International Genealogical Index, or IGI). He won approval for a test project, and in a relatively short period, his staff produced a prototype that proved the concept was feasible.[6]

The second development to alter the procedure of names clearance was a change in policy. The long-range goals, adopted in 1976 (see table in chapter 7), envisioned the day when this responsibility would be returned to the members, with whom it had resided before 1927. At a special meeting in December 1988, Department management decided to pursue the concept of placing computers in meetinghouses to permit members to clear names for themselves.[7] The proposal was approved by the First Presidency in May 1989. In the words of the Department's executive director, Elder J. Richard Clarke, this historic decision would "revolutionize family history work."[8] He hoped to make family history work easy for anyone who would try and to propel the Church into a new era of family history activity.

The name eventually given to this plan was TempleReady. The program permitted members to match names they desired to submit for temple work against the record of temple ordinances in the automated IGI. An individual would either type in a name on the computer or transfer data from a diskette created by the Personal Ancestral File program. TempleReady would prompt the user to enter the appropriate compact disc of the IGI, compare the names, and display possible matches. The individual could accept or reject the match, or even skip this function and have the computer automatically decide if the name matched anything already in the file of completed work. The end product was a submission diskette that could be taken directly to the temple. This simplification reinvigorated researchers, who could take the results of their research directly to the temple. It also transferred the burden of supplying temple names from the Church back to the individual, reducing reliance on the name extraction program.

TempleReady employed name-checking routines that excelled those in the GIANT system by increasing the number of matches for variant spellings. The new algorithms weighed each match and computed a probability that two entries represented the same person. Tests showed that 80 percent of the names cleared by GIANT would be eliminated as duplicates by TempleReady.[9]

TempleReady was tested as the "Names Clearance System"[10] in the Salt Lake Mt. Olympus Stake, beginning in July 1990. During the next eight months, the number of stake members clearing names jumped from 31 to 283 per month, and the number of names cleared rose from 426 to 6,700. An average of eight or nine names was cleared each hour during the pilot. The test phase was expanded to sixteen stakes in May 1991. In September, John Jarman observed to his fellow directors, "The program has been so easy to use, and the clearance of names occurs so quickly, that members of the Church have one of two reactions—utter disbelief or overwhelming joy once they realize that the work is now ready to go to the temple."[11]

Word of the program spread. In November 1991, the Department received approval to expand the test to over two hundred stakes in the U.S. and Canada. Shipment to these stakes began on 31 December 1991.[12] In November 1993, the Department released the program (as part of the FamilySearch package) to all English-speaking stakes in the Church. A new era had dawned in the history of temple work.

In addition to the pilot in the stakes, in 1991 the Department distributed TempleReady to all temples except those in Japan, Taiwan, and Korea (which continued to use non-Roman-script manual systems). Even though the pilot had not been translated into languages other than English, the program was so easy to use that workers had little need to refer to the written instructions.[13]

Temple Recording

Before long, automation reached inside the temples themselves, and for good reason. In the 1970s, the ordinance lists created by GIANT inundated the temples with nearly fourteen tons of paper every year.[14] The printed forms needed to be checked manually for print quality, sent to the temples, updated with proxy names and ordinance dates, and returned to the Department for ordinance data entry into GIANT. It was a paper-flow quagmire. This problem, together with the rising cost of paper due to a shortage in the United States, led to the development of the automated Temple Recording System (TRS).

Discussion of such a system began in 1974 but was not pursued seriously until the adoption of the 1976 long-range goal to use modern technology in recording completed temple work. In October 1977, a formal project was initiated.[15] The technical challenge was so enormous that developing the system took three and one-half years. This system used multiple identical minicomputers working together to provide the desired capacity and redundancy. A spare computer could take over if any of the others went down. Each computer handled a different set of ordinances, and names were passed from one computer to the next as the ordinances were completed. The number of computers varied to match the volume of work performed in a particular temple.

The system also produced automated statistics and controlled information on lost temple recommends. Because each patron's temple recommend was placed in a plastic holder with a magnetized strip on which personal identification data was encoded, the system even alerted the receptionist at the door if it was the recommend holder's birthday.[16]

In February 1981, TRS was introduced in the Salt Lake Temple. The system soon produced the desired benefits. Much of the work of recording temple ordinances performed became paperless, and the clerical staff was reduced from twenty-two to nine.[17] As efficiency increased, the automated data could be rearranged to meet any informational need, or it could be transferred into other systems. Temple workers found the system easy to use, an important consideration as many had little computer experience. TRS was implemented at the Jordan River Temple when it opened in December 1981. The Provo, Ogden, and Swiss Temples were refitted to use it in 1982, and, by 1986, it was put into use in eighteen more temples.[18]

As important as it was, however, the Temple Recording System was never implemented in all the temples, partly because technology quickly passed it by and partly because of still another change in policy. In September 1989, the First Presidency paved the way for a less expensive system. They decided to eliminate the recording of the names of proxies, witnesses, and officiators. Only information on the person for whom the work was done and ordinance dates would be collected and stored by the system. This decision was in response to the "pressing need for less complex temple procedures and reduced personnel requirements."[19] It also reflected the general effort throughout the 1980s to simplify policies and practices as the Church experienced rapid worldwide growth.

The Temple Department had been established in 1979 to administer all affairs related to temples. Created when TRS was under development, it played a major role in fielding that system. It now began work on a new automated program consistent with the simplified recording requirements. The new system, named the Ordinance Recording System (ORS), was designed for simple installation and operation by temple personnel with minimal support from Church headquarters. It also integrated into the temple-recording process those patron submissions created through TempleReady. The system was piloted in the Logan Temple in 1990 and implemented in most other temples the following year.[20]

This system consisted of few procedures and minimal computer support. Names of ancestors were received at the temple on computer diskette, supplied by the Department or directly by Church members. The temple printed out slips as needed for ordinance work each day. The person serving as proxy received a slip and returned it after the ordinance work was completed. These slips were then collected and used to update the database. Global update, which allowed more than one record to be updated at a time, permitted quick recording. The whole procedure was supported by no more than two or three personal computers, two printers, and a few clerks. Once the temple record was complete, it was sent on disk to the Family History Department. There it was entered into the Completed Ordinance File (COF). Begun in the summer of 1991, this file had grown to twenty-one million names by 1994.[21]

Stake Record Extraction

Meanwhile, the objectives of simplifying family history work, decentralizing headquarters functions, and involving the Church members were embodied in the stake record extraction program. This program consisted of the Department sending genealogical sources on film to stakes and Church members extracting all names from those sources onto cards and returning the cards to Department headquarters for names clearance processing. This program sidestepped the research process and the complexities of putting names together into families. The process of transcribing could be performed wherever there was access to a film reader.

Prior to stake record extraction, extensive extraction was performed at Department headquarters. In 1977 most of the two hundred employees in the Temple Services Division extracted names from New England, British, Spanish, German, and Swedish records. Sometimes this work was extremely difficult and slow, for the records were difficult to read. Managing Director George Fudge proposed the concept of decentralized extraction to Elder Boyd K. Packer, whose immediate response was, "That's inspired."[22]

The idea for extraction at the stake level originated in 1976, when Elder L. Tom Perry challenged members of the St. George Utah Stake to submit as many names for temple work as ordinances they performed. Seeing no way to meet this goal under the current system, stake leaders wrote to the Department asking for their own extraction program.[23] The Department approved their request in January 1977.[24]

Two rooms were reserved in the St. George Tabernacle, and ten microfilm readers installed. Leaders in the St. George and St. George East stakes called twenty-seven local Church members as missionaries to carry out the program. The Department sent microfilms of German and English genealogical sources. It also sent instructors to teach procedures as well as the paleographic skills needed to analyze and transcribe names written in archaic scripts. Extraction began in May. After three months, the two stakes had extracted 80,000 names, well exceeding the challenge delivered the year before. The excitement and dedication of the local people is illustrated by the comment of Alvin Gentry, a stake genealogical leader. "We have fun here," he reported. "We really enjoy it. In fact, we have trouble getting the workers to take their breaks and to work only four hours a day. Many of them want to stay on working longer."[25]

With the success of the St. George program, Department officials were satisfied that stake extraction would work. In November 1977, therefore, they sought and immediately received the approval of the First Presidency to expand the program Churchwide. Six additional stakes applied for the program that same month—Las Vegas South, Grantsville (Utah), Orem North (Utah), Salt Lake Ensign, Salt Lake Wilford, and Santaquin (Utah).[26]

The formidable task of training began. Extensive resources both in the stakes and at Department headquarters were required to prepare and distribute training materials. In the process, the Department not only instructed the stakes, but also learned by their experience. It found, for example, that decentralization also required simplification. The large binders used at Church headquarters were reduced to a few sheets of instructions for use in the stakes. The decentralized program was such a success, however, that it eventually eliminated the need to employ staff to continue extraction at the Department headquarters.[27]

Important measures were taken to insure the integrity of the extracted data. Duplicate extractions were made and compared in order to reduce transcription errors, and in 1979 the cards were routed through an audit unit at Church headquarters. The quality of the extraction was high, with 97 percent of the batches passing the audit during 1979. Another attempt was the request that stakes become accredited. To become accredited, stake trainers were required to pass a test of their ability to extract records in the language assigned to the project. In 1979 trainers were accredited in 60 percent of the approved projects.[28]

At first the receipt of names from stake extraction was slow. By the end of 1978, only thirty-four stakes were actually extracting records, and only 75,000 names from the program had been cleared by the Department for temple work.[29] This number was not a huge return on the investment in time and effort. To some degree, the limited success resulted from the fact that many name cards remained in the stakes pending the extraction of all names in an extraction batch. But it also reflected the inevitable time required to start a new program, train the staff, and produce results. The number of stakes turning in extraction cards increased substantially to 109 in 1979, with 404 stakes having received batches. The program matured during the next decade. By 1985, it had produced enough names to supply current temple needs and to serve as a year's supply in advance. In that year, 841 extraction sites totaled an estimated 12,000 people working four to eight hours per week and producing about 10 million names a year.[30] By 1991 the stake extraction program had produced 115 million names.[31]

At first the stakes filled out a card for each name extracted and mailed the cards directly to the Department for data entry. As minicomputers became more available locally, however, a regional Volunteer Data Entry Program (VDE) was launched. The first site was set up in the Orem Utah West Stake on 18 October 1982. Stake extraction centers throughout the Provo Temple District sent their cards to the new site instead of to Salt Lake City.[32] By the end of the year, five more VDE centers had been established. Early in 1983, these centers were averaging data entry of 60,000 names per week.[33]

Outside of the United States, the Department introduced the extraction program at temple service centers (later family history service centers). They provided names for work at newly built temples in South America, Asia, and later in Europe. In 1977 extraction began in Mexico City, and in the following year, it was introduced in São Paulo and Tokyo. Anticipating the construction of the East German temple at Freiberg, local members produced 35,000 names before the temple groundbreaking in April 1983.[34] Likewise, members in Chile extracted 115,000 names prior to the dedication of the Chilean temple in 1983.[35] The Department gradually expanded the program beyond the temple service centers into international stakes in general.

Family Record Extraction

Another form of extraction took shape in the late 1980s. Known as the Family Record Extraction Program (FREP), it was designed to index a variety of family history sources. The first use of FREP was automating all temple ordinance data prior to 1970, as envisioned by the 1976 long-range goals. To reach this goal, the Department involved thousands of Church members.

Creating such an automated master temple file was discussed in 1976 by Department management, who considered converting the manual TIB file either through optical character recognition or computer keyboarding. At the time, however, the costs to proceed were judged to be too high.[36] When the discussion resumed in 1981, Department management dropped the idea of TIB conversion in favor of extracting data directly from the original temple records.[37]

In late 1984, it was proposed that films of pre-1970 temple records would be printed on a continuous roll of paper through a process known as copyflow, cut into batches, and sent to the homes of Church members for manual transcription. The data would then be entered locally on personal computers and returned to Department headquarters on computer diskette.[38] Thus began FREP.

Elder Richard G. Scott was a driving force behind FREP. He had been appointed an assistant executive director of the Department in 1981 and had become its executive director in late 1984. Recognizing that the average member of the Church had difficulty getting involved in family history activity, he had proposed taking the program to the members in their homes. The basic vision of FREP implements his proposal by combining the contributions of the computer with the contributions of numerous people sitting in the comfort of their own homes and using no more than pen and paper. This simple vision has the potential of involving virtually anyone in this Herculean indexing task.

Before such a proposal could be implemented, the Department had to write new software, establish procedures, prepare instructional materials, install new equipment, obtain approval from various administrative levels, and field test the entire concept. The new software, which became known as Universal Data Entry (UDE), employed user-defined templates. This feature permitted anything to be indexed after a template had been fashioned to fit the nature of the information in the source being indexed. Department staff designed different forms for the different temple record formats. Family history missionaries at Church headquarters were assigned to prepare the extraction batches for transmission to the stakes. The video, *A Unique Opportunity to Serve,* was created to introduce the program and explain its purpose to Church members who would be asked to volunteer their time. New copyflow printers to produce the paper copy for extraction were installed at the Granite Mountain Records Vault.

The pilot program for FREP was conducted from October 1986 through April 1987 in twelve stakes in Utah, Maine, Illinois, California, Montana, Georgia, Washington, Texas, Maryland, and Kansas.[39] Then, with all preliminary tasks completed, the Department was ready to deploy the system. But the initial starting date of 1 July 1987 was delayed six months because of announcements in the computer industry that hardware better suited for the program would soon be available.

In early 1988, Elder Scott expected all 1,000 stakes in the United States and Canada eventually to be enrolled. After only eighteen months, more than half of that goal had been achieved, with 650 stakes cooperating in the program.[40] In its second year of production, FREP was evaluated. The Church Correlation Department surveyed 110 stake coordinators, investigated thirty-four stakes in depth, and conducted interviews in seventy-six other stakes. As might be expected, not all stakes were equally effective in implementing the program. Thirty-seven percent of the stakes were fully organized, and 40 percent were partially organized. Sixteen percent had just entered the program. In the average stake, seventy-five people were involved, and the average extractor donated five hours per week to the project. Of those involved, 75 to 90 percent said they looked forward to the work. Less pleasing was the fact the priesthood leadership was not very involved in the process.[41] Overall, however, the program was achieving the purpose of involving a significant segment of the membership of the Church in family history activity.

Initially, the goal was to finish indexing the temple records in five years. After three years, only one-fourth of the batches had been returned, but the rate of return was rising steadily. While an average of 500 batches came back to the Department each month of 1989, the rate doubled to 1,000 per month in 1990 and then to 1,500 in 1991. To speed up the process, the Department introduced in 1989 software that permitted direct entry from copyflow prints to computer diskette, eliminating the hand transcription step. This change took advantage of the increasing presence of personal computers in homes. By 1995 the project was virtually complete, with only a few hundred of the 100,000 batches generated by the program still outstanding. In total, 50,000 members had participated.[42]

A major restructuring of the extraction programs occurred in February 1994, when the Church merged Family Record Extraction and Stake Record Extraction. The new program, administered primarily at the ward level, was designed to have the records of a country extracted by those living in that country. Local units were given wider responsibility to choose what they wished to extract. At the same time, new family history sources were added to the extraction list.

As originally conceived, FREP could be used to extract data from any family history source. When the temple records were exhausted, the Department began to distribute other valuable family history sources. The traditional list of extracted records—christening, birth, and marriage records—has been augmented by new sources such as U.S. civil death records, Ellis Island (New York) passenger lists, and Canadian census schedules for 1871 and 1881. As Elder Scott had envisioned, meaningful family history work could be performed in the homes of all members who were willing to help share the task of identifying those who had lived in generations gone by.

CFI/IGI

Automation also provided the means to effectively distribute ordinance data. The database of names in GIANT, known as the Mass File, was made available on microfiche in 1975. The set of microfiche, called the Computer File Index (CFI), provided researchers a manual check of the database in order to prevent resubmission of names for which temple work had already been performed. A batch number in each entry also provided a trace back to the source from which the name came.

The CFI consisted of extracted names gathered under the Records Tabulation Program (R-TAB) and names submitted by Church members since 1970. The entries were filed alphabetically under the country in which the ancestor was born or married. The 1975 CFI consisted of approximately 30 million names on 2,689 microfiche. It was sent to one hundred branch libraries for $208 per set, the amount needed to recover the cost of producing the fiche.[43]

The fourth edition, renamed the International Genealogical Index (IGI), was published in 1981. The new name reflected the research value of the file. Because it contained large numbers of names from original records, the index served as an index to original records as much as it did to temple ordinances. It grew substantially between each edition, expanding from 34 million names in 1975, to 81 million in 1981, 108 million in 1984, 147 million in 1988, and 187 million in 1992. This was an average increase of 9 million names each year.[44]

As the index became a more comprehensive research tool, demand for the file by genealogists not affiliated with the Church expanded. In 1984 the index was offered for sale to the general public. It was of particular value in British research. The 1988 index contained names extracted from British records over the previous twenty-five years, amounting to 58 million of the 147 million names in the file.[45]

The 1988 IGI became an even more powerful research tool with the introduction of the compact disc version. This not only permitted automated searching, but also expanded search possibilities. A member could retrieve names of children by entering the names of the parents. A person could then reconstitute tentative family groups from the individual name entries. The primary purpose of the IGI, however, from the Department's perspective, continued to be as an index to ordinances. Combined with TempleReady, the compact-disc version could be used for names clearance by the individual member, as previously discussed.

The 1992 edition of the IGI on microfiche was a totally new product, including 187 million names, not only from the Mass File in GIANT (162.5 million), but also from other ordinance files: pre-1970 temple records created by the Family Record Extraction Program (17.5 million), records from the Family Entry System

(4.5 million), and Completed Ordinance File records created by the Ordinance Recording System (2.5 million). At the same time, extracted names in the Mass File for which ordinance work had not been performed were withheld pending the creation of the Extraction Resource File (22 million names).[46] Eventually, this file will be made available as a source of names from which members can select those they wish to submit for ordinance work.

Creating a compact-disc version of IGI became problematic. Amassing the names from the various files created in different databases and by different systems was a technical nightmare. Also, the available computer power was insufficient to handle such a leviathan task. The 1992 compact-disc version was delayed until November 1993, but because of the delay, additional names became available. The new disc version contained fourteen million more names than the microfiche version published the year before.[47] The delay also resulted in another benefit: data compression technology had developed to the degree that it could be used to provide a quantum increase in the storage capacity of a disc. While fifty million names were added to the IGI between 1988 and 1993, the number of discs was reduced from fifty-eight to thirty-three.[48]

In only two decades, the Department and countless Church volunteers have created what is probably the largest name database in existence. Yet this achievement is only the beginning in the Department's quest to identify, as nearly as possible, all the people who have ever lived.

Cooperative Indexing

In the 1980s, the Department embarked on creating automated indexes to major research sources. The precedent was set by the 1982 decision to index the 1880 U.S. federal census. This project was particularly needed by U.S. researchers because a national civil registration system was nonexistent in the U.S. prior to the 1880 census. U.S. research was further complicated because of a highly mobile population and because record-keeping practices had created a random array of record types throughout the nation. By 1990 more than half of the fifty-million census entries were transcribed.[49]

In 1985 the Department's executive director, Elder Richard G. Scott, proposed expanding the program to involve not only Church members, but also any other people willing to help with indexing. The first major project in the Cooperative Indexing program was the 1881 British census. Discussions concerning this project began in 1985 with the British Genealogical Record Users Committee and the Federation of Family History Societies in England. The resulting agreement provided that the Federation be in charge of transcription and the Department provide paper copies of the census, data entry software, hardware, and outputs at cost. Beginning in February 1988, the first of over eight thousand volunteers from family history societies throughout the British Isles began transcribing the thirty million names in the 1881 census. Data entry began in 1989. In 1991 the first outputs for individual counties—Cambridge, Denbigh, and Flint—were published. In 1992 sixty-two data entry sites at Church facilities in England continued to work on the program. They were supported by a staff of thirty full-time missionaries and ten volunteers at Church headquarters.[50]

In 1994, Anthony J. Camp, director of the Society of Genealogists, referred to this project as "the largest joint [genealogical] project ever undertaken in England, . . . an almost foolhardy idea. . . . But the results are revolutionizing genealogical research in England, Scotland, and Wales; and giving beginners in the subject, a flying start when they most need it." As of December 1994, 99 percent of the census entries had been transcribed and 82 percent of the data entered on computer discs. Index fiche had been produced for 42 of the 91 counties in the British Isles. Referring to the assistance of the Church and the Family History Department, Camp said, "Their contribution has been absolutely magnificent and generations of genealogists yet to come will be in their debt."[51]

In 1991 the U.S. Federation of Genealogical Societies[52] approached the Department in behalf of the National Park Service with the proposal that the Department provide data entry software, for creating a database from records in the National Archives concerning Civil War participants. The Park Service envisioned such a database as a significant resource in answering queries by visitors to battlefield sites. The Federation of Genealogical Societies assumed the responsibility to coordinate the extraction. Many other cooperative projects are being discussed as possible future ventures.

Ancestral File

Along with automating ordinance files and research sources, the Department developed an unprecedented computer research file to help people avoid duplication of research efforts. Known as Ancestral File, it provides the results of countless research hours in the form of pedigree charts, family group records, descendant charts, and assorted other reports. As a source of completed research, it helps researchers take advantage of the work done by other genealogists. As an automated file, it can be made available anywhere a computer might be installed. Open to submissions from all researchers, it serves as a focal point of cooperation between the Department and genealogical researchers throughout the world.

Ancestral File was an automated extension of the original concept of the Four- Generation Program, which began in the early 1960s. Submissions to the Department were kept in heavy black binders at the main library and on film in the branch libraries. As countless researchers discovered, sheets submitted by different people for the same family contained numerous discrepancies. Before automating the file, Department leaders felt that as many discrepancies as possible should be eliminated from the sheets. Thus, when the call for four-generation sheets was renewed in 1978, accuracy became the watchword of the program.[53] The Department asked families to coordinate their efforts and submit a single set of sheets as well as a pedigree chart. These new submissions became the major data source for the initial release of the automated file.

The target date for submission of four generations to Ancestral File was 1 July 1981. In a frenzy of activity, Church members submitted more sheets in the last two weeks of June than in the previous two years of the program.[54] The target date had been perceived as a deadline. The Department worked for several years to clear up this misunderstanding and encourage continued submissions to the file. In the meantime, the Department had a mountain of paper containing genealogical information and a task of unknown dimensions to provide access to the data. The sheets were microfilmed and indexed on microfiche by name of submitter and by surname of the first person on the pedigree.

In 1982 the Department sought to increase the usefulness of the file by soliciting submissions beyond four generations. A letter was sent to several hundred family organizations requesting the extended research. The Department also drew upon the compiled records in its Medieval Records Section. Created in 1972, this group of specialists and volunteers had compiled approximately 25,000 family group records, representing 100,000 individuals of selected royal, noble, and pre-1500 families.[55] These two sources of data began to expand the file, fulfilling the intent of having the file serve as a collecting point for all genealogies back as far as sources would permit.

Programming to automate Ancestral File began in 1984. It was a major step into the unknown, especially in light of the variable relationships between people and the possible ways of searching and retrieving such information. Through a rigorous process of defining user needs and expectations before programming began, the Department resolved issues regarding retrieval requirements, inputs, outputs, and privacy. In 1987 the Church purchased a mainframe computer exclusively for Department use, the CYBER 180 model 992. This would serve as the main computer tool in making Ancestral File a reality.

Ancestral File data entry software became available in October 1984.[56] Because of wide variations in the way information was recorded on the submitted sheets, data entry was divided into two steps: sheets were coded, and then relationships were marked with a standard code, the order of dates and places were regularized, and surnames were marked. While some coding and data entry were done at Department headquarters, most of it was performed at special sites in Logan, Ogden, and Provo. With the data entry nearing completion, a prototype of the file was released in 1987 for testing in the Family History Library.

Considerable work went into making Ancestral File both effective and user friendly. Response time, in particular, was considered crucial to user satisfaction. It dropped from minutes to seconds as the search routine was improved. The file, comprised of four million names, was installed in the Family History Library in April 1988.[57]

A major obstacle that had to be overcome in the creation of the file was the existence of countless duplicate submissions. Because many Church members have common ancestries, different descendants had submitted information on the same family lines. The computer was assigned the task of merging these duplicate submissions while not merging persons with similar identities. Even though the name of each person who submitted entries was retained, merging eliminated the possibility of determining who submitted what piece of data. The initial merge pared the submitted 8.2 million records down to 4.5 million.[58] Routines designed to detect duplications eliminated 90 percent of them, although, unfortunately, existing technology was insufficient to detect all duplicates resulting from variant spellings and birth dates.[59]

In 1988 the Department decided to invite submissions from the entire genealogical community. The benefit would be clearly evident to anyone using the system. Ancestral File was seen as the central system for promoting cooperation among genealogists.

While a production system was in operation as early as 1988, the file was not distributed Churchwide until September 1990 and then as part of FamilySearch. In articles in Church and genealogical community periodicals, press releases, and presentations at professional meetings, the concerted efforts of a decade were released to the public. It was an unprecedented undertaking for the Church, unequaled in scale anywhere. Ancestral File became the starting point for anyone interested in commencing new research.

In 1991 new features were introduced, including descendant charts and a correction system to provide users a means to revise the file. The 1992 edition reduced the number of compact-disc swaps during searching.[60] From 1990 to 1993, the file grew from seven to fifteen million names. The file continues to grow, limited mainly by the capacity of the Department to process contributions and produce new releases.[61]

As with most software development, great strides forward were accompanied by some faltering steps. The Department continues to work on several unresolved problems regarding source citations, correctness of the merge process, errors in the data, identifying submitters, making the edit/correction capability easier to use, and accommodating diacritics or non-Roman characters.[62] Despite these drawbacks, the file accomplishes its basic purpose of expanding the possibilities for all genealogical researchers.

Patrons using the computers in the FamilySearch Center located in the Joseph Smith Memorial Building, 1993.

Personal Ancestral File

By the 1980s, the personal computer was revolutionizing not only how businesses and institutions managed information, but also what went on in households, especially in the United States. The Department responded by developing a personal computer application whereby individuals could record the names and relationships of their ancestors. Personal Ancestral File (PAF) was initiated in 1983 as a part of the Ancestral File project. It was released in April 1984 and sold for $35, a price that covered little more than the costs of the manual and diskettes. Within six months, 4,000 copies had been sold.[63]

The earliest version of Personal Ancestral File had one glaring deficiency—poor response time. Release 2.0, a complete rewrite that was available in April 1986, corrected this problem.

More significantly, the new version introduced a genealogical communications format known as GEnealogical Data COMmunications (GEDCOM), the purpose of which was to establish a standard for sharing data between programs or computers or both. GEDCOM eventually became a standard for data communication of genealogical information in the genealogical community at large. The Department encouraged other developers to write GEDCOM-compatible programs similar to PAF. It launched a registration program, where staff reviewed programs sent in by developers and certified whether they were fully compatible with the GEDCOM standard. By late 1994, thirty programs had been registered.[64]

Meanwhile, in April 1988, release 2.1 was made available for IBM, IBM-compatible, and Macintosh computers. This release allowed transfer of PAF information on computer diskette to Ancestral File. Consequently, submissions would reflect exactly what was typed in at the point of origin and be added to the file without waiting in a queue at a data entry site. This release also allowed temple name submission on computer diskette. Routines were added to the program that enhanced the accuracy of submissions. For example, the system automatically prompted the submitter to correct inconsistencies such as death dates that preceded birth dates.

Other refinements have been added. Prior to the general release of Ancestral File to family history centers in 1990, PAF was upgraded to increase the ease of data transfer between it and the parent system. Release 2.2, issued in November 1989, permitted the match-merging of records from other data bases. It also introduced the ability to convert pieces of a large data transfer from Ancestral File. The program was upgraded again in 1994 (version 2.31) to make it fully "compatible with TempleReady, using the same rules to check and qualify names."[65] By that time, ten years after its original release, over 300,000 copies of PAF had been sold.[66]

Personal Ancestry File had another less profound, but significant, impact. The program printed out family group records in the common letter-size format. From the early twentieth century, the Department had required legal-size family group sheets to be used in submitting information. Because PAF was about to be released, the Department reviewed this matter, opted in favor of letter size, and adopted an evolutionary strategy for introducing the form.[67] In 1987 it was adopted as the standard submission form for temple ordinances and was widely circulated in the publication *Come unto Christ through Temple Ordinances and Covenants.* It also became the primary form for the manual submission of research to Ancestral File.

Automated Catalog

As the Department automated names processing, it began to consider automating its library. The task was equal to, if not greater than, developing GIANT. The library was receiving approximately forty thousand new rolls of microfilm and thousands of new books each year. Keeping the card catalog updated, particularly the microfilm copy provided to the branch libraries, was an acute problem. Automated library cataloging systems were still in their infancy in the early 1970s, however, and they focused primarily on book collections. Acquiring, handling, cataloging, and distributing information contained on microfilmed manuscripts was a unique problem. As the Department studied the challenge from 1970 to 1976, it envisioned a total system with various modules that would identify genealogical sources worldwide, control the microfilming of those sources, process the microfilms, catalog them, and provide public access to the collection.[68] In 1976, the Department decided to proceed with the cataloging program.

A key decision made at the outset was that records would be cataloged in the language of the record or of the country from which they originated.[69] Because national boundaries had changed, it was necessary to provide catalog headings for each country in which a given locality had been included during modern times. Thus, from its inception, the catalog was intended to meet the needs of an international audience.

The Department also decided to provide a content description for each film in the collection. This decision resulted in descriptions much more detailed than those in any other computer catalog of the time. The catalog also pioneered such concepts as real-time cataloging and automated authority control.[70]

In 1987 the computer catalog totally replaced the card catalog. Information was provided in two formats—microfiche and compact

Research carrels in the Family History Library at 35 North West Temple, ca. 1986.

disc. The compact-disc catalog was first made available with Ancestral File at the Family History Library in 1988 as part of the Genealogical Information System, the prototype for FamilySearch.

Headquarters Systems

In addition to providing such a multitude of automated programs for public use, the Department saw the need to automate its operations at headquarters. In the late 1960s, for example, no integrated system controlled the various stages of microfilm production. Prints were not being sent to donors, some films were not getting evaluated, and some rolls were being misplaced. These problems prompted the development of the Microfilm Production Control System.[71] Packets of punch cards were created for batches of one to nine films. Each punch card represented a film processing task. When the task was completed, the card was posted to the control system that was implemented in 1972. This system functioned well but became antiquated during the 1970s, when the computer processing environment moved from batch-mode to real-time processing.[72]

Discussion of a replacement system began in 1982 .[73] The Microfilm Production and Monitoring System was installed in 1986. It tracked films through the various tasks preceding storage of the master film in the vault and the printing of films for circulation. The system played a key roll in handling the Department's large number of filming projects in the late 1980s.

By 1973 the Department had implemented a system to account for circulating films from the time they were ordered until they were returned. This system produced bar-code labels for the circulating films and bills for orders. The program was enhanced in 1990 to improve microfiche ordering and other functions.[74]

In 1990 to 1991 a bibliographic index system was developed to provide surname access to information on genealogies prior to 1500. It was used in-house to compile sources for assembling pedigrees that were then added to Ancestral File.[75]

Family Registry

In the 1980s, the Department introduced the Family Registry as a tool to facilitate further cooperation among researchers. Originally, the concept was to provide a listing of family organizations. Such organizations were seen as key elements in getting families to work together on their ancestry. The Registry would allow people to identify family organizations that they could join or consult. In 1983 this concept was augmented by providing a tool to help researchers working on the same line contact each other.

Registration began in October 1983. A brochure was mailed to priesthood leaders; training materials, posters, brochures, and registration forms were sent to family history centers in the United States and Canada; a mailer was sent to 10,000 family organizations; and the program was officially announced in the *Church News* on 18 December 1983. After a year, nearly 100,000 registrations had been received, and an average of nearly 2,000 were coming in each week.[76] At that point, the Registry was expanded to family history center patrons in the British Isles, Australia, New Zealand, and South Africa.

Unlike the Pedigree Referral Service, the Registry permitted two types of entries—individual or family/surname organization. These entries were arranged alphabetically in a microfiche set. Accompanying the entries was information needed to contact the person or organization submitting the name. The actual submission forms were filmed in a separate set of fiche by sequential submission number.[77] This number served as the link between the two sets of microfiche.

The first edition of the Registry, containing 27,757 entries, was released in May 1984. Along with distributing it to family history centers, the Department sent it to over one hundred public libraries. It was published quarterly through 1989, then annually thereafter. By 1993 there were 348,898 registrations in the file.[78]

FamilySearch

The automation efforts of the Department have been tied together under an umbrella system. Known initially as the Genealogical Information System (GIS), it was renamed FamilySearch in 1989. An embodiment of the 1976 long-range goal of creating a central genealogical file, the project involved folding several computer databases into a single system that is now the beginning point for family history research in the Church. The decision made in February 1983 to provide automated access to large files of genealogical sources was as seminal as had been the 1938 decision to microfilm the world's records. Just as the decision to microfilm defined the nature of the Society's work for the decades that followed, so the decision to develop FamilySearch will define the nature of the Department's work for the coming years.

In 1985, Elder Richard G. Scott, executive director of the Department, enunciated the perspective from which this decision was made:

> We really have two options. . . . The first option could be to merely automate what is currently being done in research. . . . The other option is to fundamentally simplify genealogical research using those tools [computers]. . . . In order to do that, we need to enter into the computer large quantities of data that are now either on paper or on microfilm or microfiche, then use the computer to arrange the data so that it is usable.[79]

The development process continued throughout the 1980s as numerous analysts, programmers, other staff members, and users contributed to the project. A new database manager known as the Associated Information Management system was specifically designed to handle the genealogical data to be included in FamilySearch. The prototype was first made available at the Family History Library in 1986. Originally, the system was designed to be on-line, but concerns about telecommunication costs and security dictated another means of distribution. The answer was found in the emerging compact-disc technology, first demonstrated to Department management in 1985.[80] The Department produced a compact-disc prototype of the Family History Library Catalog in 1986, followed by disc versions of International Genealogical Index and Ancestral File.

In 1989 the compact-disc version of all these databases, now called FamilySearch, was tested at the Family History Library and seven family history centers. With the technology available and the program defined, the Department proposed that computers and disc readers be distributed to all family history centers and Church meetinghouses. The proposal was approved.

The automated catalog, the automated International Genealogical Index, and Ancestral File were developed concurrently, but separately from one another. All of these database projects were unified in the product released as FamilySearch. In time, other elements were added: TempleReady, the Social Security Death Index, and Military Index (U.S. military deaths in Vietnam and Korea). The latter two indexes are databases created by the U.S. government and are in the public domain. The Department created search software to provide easy access to the information.

FamilySearch was announced to the Church in a letter from the First Presidency dated 2 April 1990. With this announcement, the computer came of age as a key genealogical tool for every Church member. While 2,000 machines were purchased or distributed to local Church units from 1985 to 1988 for local administrative purposes, almost 3,000 were added in 1989, and about 3,000 more in 1990. Of these computers, 1,725 were dedicated to family history programs, including Family Record Extraction as well as FamilySearch.[81]

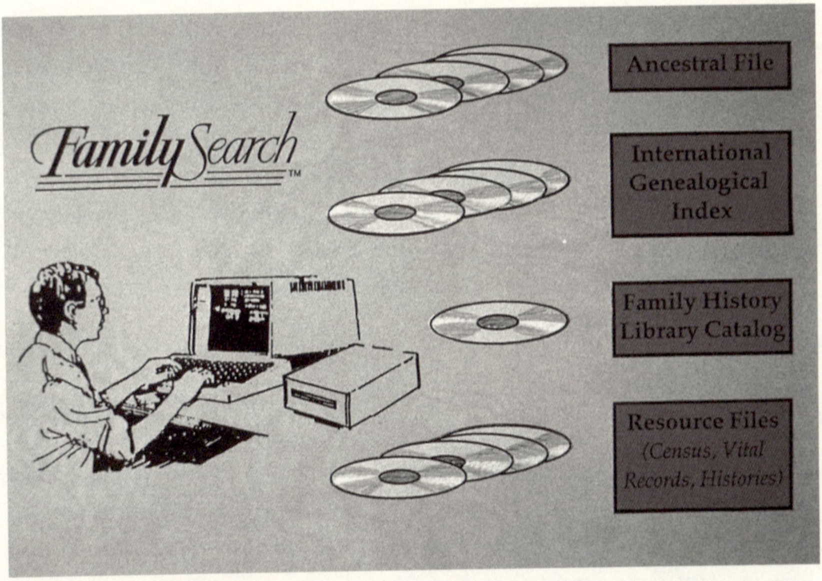

FamilySearch databases, 1990. FamilySearch makes use of the personal computer to distribute information about millions of names and family history sources.

In 1990 the system was distributed to 627 family history centers in the United States and Canada. A year later, the decision was made to expand the distribution to stake centers without family history centers, to public libraries, and even to the homes of some Church members.[82] At first distribution outside of centers was done to selected sites to permit further field testing of the system. In early 1992, the system began to be shipped internationally, with units going to Great Britain, Ireland, Australia, and New Zealand. By late 1994, systems had been distributed to a total 376 Church sites outside the United States.[83]

In 1990 and 1991, respectively, the Library of Congress in Washington, D.C., and the Victoria State Library in Melbourne became test sites for FamilySearch workstations.[84] Judith Reid at the Library of Congress reported that only minimal effort was needed to teach library patrons how to use the program on their own.[85]

In 1992 the system became more broadly available. The Department signed a contract in March 1992 with Dynix Corporation, an outside firm, for release of the system to public libraries, archives, and genealogical and historical societies. By late 1994 FamilySearch was available in over one hundred libraries in the United States, Canada, France, Germany, Ireland, New Zealand, and Great Britain.[86]

On a test basis, FamilySearch was distributed to approximately forty home sites in late 1992.[87] Further testing of the mechanics of distributing and pricing the product to the home market occurred in 1994, reaching over eight hundred homes in the United States and Canada.[88]

Even with the tremendous capacity of compact discs, the databases on these files were so large that using the system required a good deal of "disc swapping" in and out of the disc reader. This inconvenience was eliminated at the Family History Library, the FamilySearch Center, and Brigham Young University by the installation of a local area network (LAN) in late 1991. For family history centers, significant progress was made in 1993 with the implementation of new techniques to further compress the data so that more would fit on each compact disc.

The response to FamilySearch was enthusiastic. The system provided convenient and quick access to large amounts of information. The user could print out the information or transfer it to diskette for personal use. At a demonstration of the system in Stockholm in 1990, an archivist searched his own lines back to the twelfth century. He compared a published pedigree with the file and found no discrepancies, except that the file extended the line back further than the book. Many European archivists who saw the system demonstrated that year "were visibly moved" by its capabilities.[89]

From the beginning, extensive efforts had been made to design the system to accommodate widely diverse users, to be forgiving of errors, and to be self-instructional. Still, some problems required one-of-one help. In December 1991, the Department consolidated its Personal Ancestral File and TempleReady customer support units to handle telephone requests for help in using all products.[90]

Computer Complexities

The advent of the computer in family history work has greatly expanded genealogical activity in the Church. It has provided tools for everyone to make significant contributions to family history work. But even though the computer has become a dominant and beneficial tool, it is not a panacea. Corrupted information in Ancestral File is difficult to detect; TempleReady uses an incomplete database of temple ordinance work, resulting in the occasional clearance of duplicate submissions. There is still a time lag between the completion of new ordinance work and the entry of the data either to the International Genealogical Index or Ancestral File, and Church members can submit names from Ancestral File that are missing ordinance dates.[91] From Ancestral File hundreds, if not thousands, of submissions can be quickly generated, but if members bypass research altogether and simply focus on clearing names from this file, extensive duplication will certainly occur before the files can be updated.

At the same time, some people are computerphobes, always fearing the worst as they try to become familiar with computer technology. Many anecdotal stories tell of problems coping with the new technology, such as those that occur when users do not understand basic computer routines, file management, or the proper treatment of diskettes. In one extreme example, an older person in Salt Lake County tried to record the data by rolling a floppy diskette into a typewriter and typing on it, then wondered why the computer could not read it. Such incidents only serve to illustrate the trepidation and lack of understanding with which many people enter the computer world.

The majority of Church members are still without computers in their homes. The Church is rapidly expanding into countries where computers are rare, where only manual systems will function, and where basic texts must be translated before even the rudiments of the family history program can function. Aware of this, the Department has focused efforts on simple manual systems for such areas.

Despite these problems, the computer holds great promise. Automation is taking family history work out of the library or archive and into the home. The edges of this possibility are only dimly visible at present because the technology to reach them in any comprehensive fashion is not yet widely available. Nevertheless, the potential of what can be achieved through technology was expressed by Church president Howard W. Hunter in his address at the centennial commemoration of the Family History Department on 13 November 1994:

> In recent years we have begun using information technology to hasten the sacred work of providing ordinances for the deceased. The role of technology in this work has been accelerated by the Lord himself, who has had a guiding hand in its developments and will continue to do so. However, we stand only on the threshold of what we can do with these tools. I feel that our most enthusiastic projections can capture only a tiny glimpse of how these tools can help us—and of the eternal consequences of these efforts.[92]

NOTES

[1]Eleanor Knowles, *Howard W. Hunter* (Salt Lake City: Deseret Book, 1994), 189, quoting Howard W. Hunter, personal journal.

[2]Some information not specifically documented in this and later sections is based on the personal knowledge of Kahlile Mehr, who had discussions with various Genealogical Society administrators over time, who was personally involved in some of the events and programs discussed, and who has studied the various internal reports of the Department that are compiled for official use only.

[3]George Fudge, oral history interview by Bruce Blumell, 1976, typescript, James Moyle Oral History Program, Archives Division, Historical Department, The Church of Jesus Christ of Latter-day Saints (hereafter cited as LDS Church Archives), 17; George Fudge, oral history interviews by John Jarman and George Durrant, 31 May–31 July 1984, typescript, copy in the possession of Kahlile Mehr, 27–28, 37–38.

[4]This opportunity was preserved in the new system. Family sealing lists could be requested, allowing people to have families sealed at the same time. See Fudge, 1984 interview, 34.

[5]Fudge, 1984 interview, 29, 31.

[6]Martel Gee, personal interview by Kahlile Mehr, 10 September 1993.

[7]John Jarman, telephone interview by Kahlile Mehr, 19 March 1993.

[8]Jarman, interview.

[9]Leadership Council Minutes, 21 August 1990, Family History Department of the Church (hereafter cited as FHD).

[10]The name was changed to TempleReady in early 1991.

[11]Leadership Council Minutes, 24 September 1991.

[12]Leadership Council Minutes, 6 January 1992.

[13]Leadership Council Minutes, 5 November 1991.

[14]Fudge, 1984 interview, 140.

[15]*Memorandum,* February 1985, FHD.

[16]*Memorandum,* March 1985.

[17]*Memorandum,* March 1985.

[18]"Temple Ordinance Chronology," reference aid, Family History Library, FHD.

[19]*Memorandum,* November 1989.

[20]*Memorandum,* September/October 1990.

[21]Paul Starkey, telephone conversation with Kahlile Mehr, 26 January 1995.

[22]Fudge, 1984 interview, 49.

[23]Lynn Hollstein, "Pilot Program in St. George Provides Names for Temple Work," *Church News,* 4 February 1978.

[24]Managing Director's Minutes, 20 January 1977, FHD.

[25]Hollstein, "Pilot Program."

[26]Historical Report, September 1977, FHD.

[27]Danish, Norwegian, Swedish, Icelandic, and French records were extracted by paid staff until 1982. *Memorandum,* June 1987, FHD.

[28]"Survey Summary of the Record Extraction Program," 1 May–25 June 1979, in Historical Report, June 1979, FHD.

[29]Historical Report, December 1978.

[30]*Memorandum,* August 1985, FHD.

[31]Employee meeting, Family History Library, 6 February 1991, notes in possession of Kahlile Mehr.

[32]Historical Report, October 1982, FHD.

[33]Management Meeting Minutes, 1 August 1983.

[34]Historical Report, April 1983, FHD.

[35]Management Meeting Minutes, 18 July 1983.

[36]Managing Director's Minutes, 5 January 1977, FHD.

[37]Management Meeting Minutes, 30 March 1981.

[38]Management Meeting Minutes, 12 November 1984.

[39]*Memorandum,* January 1988.

[40]Managing Director's Minutes, 16 May 1989.

[41]Managing Director's Minutes, 12 September 1989.

[42]Hartman Rector Jr. (address given at employee meeting, 3 November 1993), notes in the possession of Kahlile Mehr.

[43]Management Meeting Minutes, 6 May 1975, 16 August 1978.

[44]There were also editions in 1976 and 1978.

[45]*News of the Family History Library* 1, no. 1 (July/August 1989), FHD.

[46]"Sources of Names in the International Genealogical Index," internal FHD document compiled by Elizabeth L. Nichols, 17 September 1992.

[47]*News of the Family History Library* 5, no. 4 (Fall 1993), FHD.

[48]Paul Starkey, personal interview by Kahlile Mehr, 27 August 1993, notes in possession of Kahlile Mehr.

[49]"Cooperation with Nonmembers to Compile Lineage-Linked Records of the Families of Man," Director's Council Minutes, 6 June 1989, FHD, typescript.

[50]*Memorandum,* March 1992, FHD.

[51]Anthony J. Camp, lecture, 6 October 1994, Salt Lake City, notes in the possession of Kahlile Mehr; "British-Scottish 1881 Census Project Production Update," 6 December 1994, FHD.

[52]Founded in 1976 as an umbrella organization to coordinate on the national level the work of genealogical societies and family history organizations in the United States.

[53]Family group sheets received after 1 July 1979 were kept separate from those received earlier. Only the later group sheets were included in Ancestral File.

[54]Management Meeting Minutes, 1 July 1981, FHD.

[55]The section began as the Royalty Identification Project in 1968 and became a unit in 1972. It was renamed the Medieval Families Unit in 1988. Robert Gunderson, the original supervisor, continues to serve in this role today.

[56]The software was called Original Data Entry (ODE).

[57]David M. Mayfield to Family History Library Professional Staff. 17 February 1988, copy in possession of Kahlile Mehr.

[58]10.3 million names were submitted, but they included the names of the living. Information on living individuals had not been entered at first. Later, the decision was made to enter data on the living but to display the names only of Church members and to display the term "Living" instead of names for those without an LDS baptism date.

[59]John Jarman to Executive Directors, 25 May 1989, Director's Council Minutes, 23 May 1989, FHD.

[60]*Memorandum,* November/December 1992, FHD.

[61]"Enabling Members Transition Team," 1 September 1993, internal document, FHD, typescript, 2-3.

[62]"Enabling Members," 2-4, 6.

[63]"Genealogical Department Third Quarter Report, 1984," internal FHD document in possession of Kahlile Mehr.

[64]Greg Brown to Kahlile Mehr, memo, November 1994, copy in possession of Kahlile Mehr.

[65]*Memorandum,* December 1993, FHD.

[66]Blair Keddington, telephone conversation with Kahlile Mehr, November 1994.

[67]Management Meeting Minutes, 3 January 1984.

[68]"Feasible Ideal System Target (FIST) for the Genealogical Society Library System," October 1972, FHD, typescript.

[69]English summary notes were added to records cataloged in a foreign language.

[70]Melvin Olsen to Kahlile Mehr, 15 October 1993, letter in the possession of Kahlile Mehr. An authority is a standardized spelling of a person, place, or thing. An authority is used so that all sources referring to that thing are located in the same place in the catalog.

[71]Melvin Olsen, telephone interview by Kahlile Mehr, 5 October 1993.

[72]In batch-mode processing, transactions are put in a queue and processed all at the same time, usually after hours. In real-time, transactions become effective when they are made.

[73]Micrographics Division Managers Council, 9 November 1982, FHD.

[74]Dennis Meldrum, telephone interview by Kahlile Mehr, 11 October 1993.

[75]Robert Gunderson, telephone interview by Kahlile Mehr, 11 October 1993.

[76]Gary Christiansen, telephone interview by Kahlilc Mehr, 21 April 1993. Christiansen was in charge of data entry for Family Registry.

[77]The fiche set of submission forms was not sent out with the index after July 1985.

[78]Gary Christiansen to Michael Petersen, memo, 16 April 1993, FHD.

[79]*Memorandum,* May 1985, FHD.

[80]Managing Directors Meeting Minutes, 12 March 1985, FHD.

[81]Fred Lundberg, "Estimates of Local Unit Computers—Full Systems: Stakes, Meetinghouses, and Family History Centers; United States and Canada," 21 February 1992, internal document, FHD, typescript.

[82]Leadership Council Minutes, 22 March 1991.

[83]"International FamilySearch Shipments," 23 November 1994, internal FHD document in the possession of Kahlile Mehr.

[84]"Family History Quarterly Report," 15 May 1991, FHD, typescript.

[85]*Memorandum,* September 1991, FHD.

[86]Greg Brown to Kahlile Mehr, memo, November 1994, in possession of Kahlile Mehr.

[87]Leadership Council Minutes, 14 December 1992, FHD.

[88]Greg Brown to Kahlile Mehr, memo, November 1994, in possession of Kahlile Mehr.

[89]*Memorandum,* November 1990, FHD.

[90]*Memorandum,* December 1991.

[91]*A Member's Guide to Temple and Family History* Work (Salt Lake City: The Church of Jesus Christ of Latter-day Saints, 1993), 13.

[92]Howard W. Hunter, "We Have a Work to Do" (address given at Family History Department Commemorative Fireside, Salt Lake City, 13 November 1994), FHD, typescript, 4.

Epilogue

A New Century

The Genealogical Society of Utah was one of several genealogical societies that originated in the United States during the last half of the nineteenth century. In 1894 a proclamation by Church president Wilford Woodruff clearly enunciated the obligation of LDS Church members to trace their ancestry and perform temple ordinances in their behalf. Before the year was out, a society was in place to assist in that work. Thus, unlike the other genealogical societies, it was founded for religious purposes.

Two of the Society's most important challenges have always been to reduce the complexities of identifying ancestry and to develop programs that effectively mobilize participation from a broad spectrum of Church members. The solutions have varied as the Church has emerged from relative isolation to broad international involvement. Methodology has undergone several incarnations as the tools of genealogy have evolved from paper to computers. But the purpose has remained constant—to turn the hearts of the children to their ancestors in order to encourage the living to complete the sacred temple ordinances in behalf of the dead.

Two of the Society's most significant contributions have been gathering records and automating them. Prior to the advent of microfilming, most genealogical records lay hidden in countless vaults, archives, sheds, attics, and cellars. The information compiled by unnumbered scribes in many ages was at risk of being lost forever. Microfilming has provided the means to preserve this priceless information, gather it in a central locale, and make it available for research. Genealogical microfilmers are still busy photographing vital records from around the world. The master films are secured in the cavernous, steel-reinforced vaults blasted from the interior of a granite mountain near Salt Lake City.

Traditionally focused on helping members wend their way through the complexities of researching their own ancestry, the Society simplified family history research in recent decades with programs reflecting collective responsibility for all ancestors. These programs took advantage of common skills so that family history name extraction and cooperative indexing involved anyone who could read, write, or type. Undergirded by the advent of the computer, these programs have begun to replace paper records with digitized files.

Since its inception, the Genealogical Society has learned from and worked with institutions outside the Church. It has shared its resources with the genealogical community at large, hosted two world conferences on genealogical records, and participated in many national and international meetings of genealogists and record keepers. Society efforts to promote genealogical research were enhanced by the *Roots* phenomenon of the late 1970s, when many people began to more fully appreciate the value of family history.

With the growth of the Church, the number of temple patrons eventually exceeded the supply of names generated through the research process. After attempting a variety of marginally successful programs, the Society received approval for a fundamental change in procedure. In 1961 the Records Tabulation Program, later called Name Extraction, supplemented the arduous process of perusing countless records for a single name with a simpler process of extracting many names from a single document. The delays inherent in research no longer restrained the vicarious ordinance work in the temples. The plethora of names generated by this new procedure enabled an unprecedented increase in temple construction, spreading the opportunity for temple worship to the membership of the Church in many parts of the world. More recently, through a computer program named TempleReady, the responsibility for clearing names for temple ordinances was transferred directly to the members, propelling the Church into a new era of family history activity.

Nevertheless, the Church does not aim to provide a simple family history research program that replaces all individual research effort. For several decades, collective programs have nourished members who are unskilled in research. While these programs produce the opportunity to do temple work for most ancestors, researchers with pencils in hand must still seek out those individuals missing from their family lines.

The Genealogical Society, now known as the Family History Department of the Church, has helped countless people identify their ancestors as far back as available records permit. At this centennial juncture, the Department looks forward to a second century of identifying and documenting the lineages of mankind for the purpose of completing temple ordinances in their behalf.

Howard W. Hunter, a past president of the Genealogical Society, became President of the Church in June 1994. His long service in family history makes him particularly well suited to give this program renewed emphasis. In November 1994, President Hunter effectively inaugurated the next century of genealogical work in his address at the Centennial Commemorative Fireside:

> I look back in wonder at the tapestry woven by the Lord in the furthering of temple and family history work. When I was president of the Genealogical Society of Utah, we had visions of how it would move forward mightily. Now we are observing something glorious occurring throughout the world. The gospel is moving forward to encompass every nation, kindred, tongue, and people. Temples are located throughout the earth, and the Spirit of Elijah is touching the hearts of many members, who are doing family history and temple ordinance work at an unprecedented pace. . . .
>
> With regard to temple and family history work, I have one overriding message: This work must hasten. . . . The great work of the temples and all that supports it must expand. It is imperative![1]

As the Family History Department celebrates its centennial anniversary, almost fifty temples are in operation, and others are either being built or planned throughout the world. Consistent with President Hunter's message, leaders in the Family History Department are planning even greater efforts to make names available for temple work. They envision more extensive international genealogical activity. They hope for a world in which educational resources on family history will become common in libraries and schools, and community groups will promote and support family history as an activity that strengthens cultural, social, and familial ties. Sources will be preserved from loss or destruction by caring record custodians, who will make protected originals or copies increasingly accessible for researchers. A vast international network of trained volunteers will help the untrained develop their skills in the use of family history resources. Powerful, easy-to-use software programs—all sharing a common format for data exchange—will be widely available from diverse providers. The compiled record of all families, preserved in the Ancestral File or a more refined system, will be valued both in and out of the Church as the repository for the vital records of mankind and as the exchange place for ancestral information.

As a result, Church members around the world will more easily and quickly review large amounts of family history information in their homes. Family history programs will be tailored to the needs of the members in each country. Instructions and computer systems in each language will be clear and simple to understand. As the Saints seek spiritual guidance in genealogical research, families will be strengthened, troubled hearts will be healed, and Church members will be brought closer to the Savior through their service to others. Temples will be spread across the earth, and members will participate regularly in sacred ordinances.[2] When such a vision is achieved, the Spirit of Elijah will be felt in greater measure throughout the earth as the hearts of the children turn to their fathers.

NOTES

[1]Howard W. Hunter, "We Have a Work to Do" (address given at the Family History Department Commemorative Fireside, Salt Lake City, Utah, 13 November 1994), FHD, typescript, 1, 2, 3.

[2]"Family History Long Range Directives, Proposed April 1994," internal document, FHD, 7-8.

Appendix I: Historical Milestones

1836 Elijah. This ancient prophet appeared in the Kirtland Temple in fulfillment of Malachi's prophecy that he would come to "turn the heart of the fathers to the children, and the heart of the children to their fathers." Members of the LDS Church believe that since that time the "Spirit of Elijah" has motivated the increased genealogical activity of Latter-day Saints as well as others.

1840 Baptism for the dead. The first proxy baptisms for the dead were performed at Nauvoo, Illinois, in the Mississippi River.

1842 The endowment. Joseph Smith introduced the endowment ceremony to those who would later introduce it to the general membership of the Church.

1845 Nauvoo Temple. In November the first endowments were given in the Nauvoo Temple to the general membership of the Church.

1877 St. George Temple. In January the first proxy endowments for the dead were performed in the St. George Temple.

1894 Revelation on sealings; organization of the Genealogical Society. President Wilford Woodruff received an important revelation on sealings; this revelation affirmed the importance of eternal family units, the necessity of sealing families under priesthood authority, and the obligation of Church members to trace their lineages for this purpose. The Genealogical Society of Utah was created in November 1894 to coordinate the work of the Church to accomplish this purpose.

1910 *Utah Genealogical and Historical Magazine*. The first issue was published in January. The magazine continued as the official voice of the Society for the next thirty years.

1918 Vision of the redemption of the dead. President Joseph F. Smith received a vision that showed the Savior's visit to the spirit world and expounded the doctrine of redemption of the dead (D&C 138). In 1976 this revelation was added to the canon of LDS scripture.

1927 Temple Records Index Bureau card index. The Society instituted the checking of all name submissions against a card file index of all endowments performed. The index was maintained through 1969, when new endowments began to be recorded in GIANT. It was still used through 1990 to check name submissions for temple work to avoid duplication. Out of every five names submitted, the index identified one as being a person for whom ordinances had been performed.

1938 Microfilming Program. The Society's extensive microfilming project permits the gathering of family history sources to the Family History Library and from there to family history centers. The microfilmed records provide the sources for the name extraction program.

1961 Records Tabulation. The first name extraction program permitted volunteers to extract names from original records and to send them to the temples for ordinance work. This program was replaced by Stake Record Extraction.

1963 Granite Mountain Records Vault. The completion of this facility assured safe, long-term storage of the microfilm camera masters of the genealogical records filmed in all parts of the world.

1964 Branch libraries/family history centers. Through these facilities, located in LDS Church buildings throughout the world, researchers can gain access to global records by ordering microfilms of sources from the collection in Utah.

1966 Four-Generation Program. Through this program, the Church encouraged all families to compile their own records and ensure that temple work had been performed for ancestors at least four generations back. The program was expanded in 1976, when the Church requested that families consolidate and verify the information on their family group records. These revised records provided the initial data for Ancestral File.

1969 World Conference on Records. Hosted by the Society, this conference introduced the genealogical program of the Church to a world audience. The Society found this conference so beneficial they sponsored a second conference in 1980.

1969 GIANT. This system automated names processing and initiated the automated storage of massive name files, primarily the International Genealogical Index. GIANT functioned until 1990, when it was replaced by a program called TempleReady.

1976 New scripture. President Spencer W. Kimball submitted two revelations to be added to the canon of LDS scripture. These revelations concern work for the dead and are included in the Doctrine and Covenants as Section 137 (given to Joseph Smith Jr. in 1836) and Section 138 (given to Joseph F. Smith in 1918).

1978 Stake Record Extraction. This program involved many members in family history work through the decentralized extraction of names. Stake Record Extraction provided a foundation for the expansion of temple work in the 1980s.

1981 Temple Recording System. This was the first system to automate the recording of temple work. It was replaced in 1990 by the Ordinance Recording System, which functioned in connection with TempleReady to simplify recordkeeping procedures for temple work.

1988 Family Record Extraction; Cooperative Indexing. Family Record Extraction first involved Church members in indexing all pre-1970 temple records and later in indexing major genealogical sources. Family Record Extraction and Stake Record Extraction were combined in 1994. Co-operative Indexing involves the genealogical community outside the Church in indexing sources.

1990 FamilySearch. Through compact-disc technology, the FamilySearch system provides researchers access to an ever-increasing storehouse of information through personal computers. It provides automated access to Ancestral File, the International Genealogical Index, the Library Catalog, and several other smaller databases.

1993 TempleReady. This system was distributed to all English-speaking stakes, enabling members to clear their own family names for temple work—a function that had been performed by the Society since 1927, when the Temple Index Bureau was created.

Appendix II: Microfilm Places and Operators, 1938–1994

Year	Initial Project Date	No.	Area	Microfilm Operator
1938	Nov. 11	1	United States	Ernst Koehler
1945	Dec. 15	2	England	James Cunningham
1946	Jun. 1	3	Denmark	Arthur Hasso
1947	Oct. 7	4	Wales	John Leach
	Dec. 29	5	Netherlands	Rinze Schippers
1948	Jun. 12	6	Norway	Hilmar Freidel
	Aug. 27	7	Italy	James Black
	Sep. 21	8	Switzerland/Basel	James Black
	Oct. 19	9	Sweden	Anton Bolgar (Rekolid Filming Company)
	Dec. 15	10	Finland	Rekolid Filming Company
1949	Jul. 1	11	East Germany	Paul Langheinrich
	Sep. 10	12	Ireland	Ralph Blakeburn
1951	Jun. 11	13	Scotland	Ralph Blakeburn
1952	May 1	14	West Germany	West German Archives
	Oct. 1	15	Iceland	Michael McAleer and David Ainge
	Nov. 20	16	Mexico	Delbert Roach
1957	Jun. 28	17	Canada	Lloyd Hughes
1958	Jun. 30	18	Belgium	P. de La Mairieu
1959	Apr. 1	19	France	Gerard de Villeneuve
	Apr. 20	20	Australia	Ronald Pollard
	Jul. 1	21	New Zealand	Elwin Jensen
1960	Apr. 1	22	Bahamas	Dakota Microfilming of Miami
	Nov. 7	23	Luxembourg	J. Poos
1961	Jan. 1	24	Hungary	Ivan Borsa
1965	Apr. 25	25	Argentina	Maria Sule
1966	May 6	26	Austria	M. Volgger

Year	Initial Project Date	No.	Area	Microfilm Operator
1967	Nov. 17	27	Poland	Anna Jelen
1969	Feb. 1	28	Guatemala	Harold Brown
1970	Apr. 7	29	Fiji	Molimau Tupa'i
1972	Jun. 21	30	Korea	Central National Library
	Jun.	31	Panama	Johann Meyer
	Oct. 7	32	Faeroe Islands	Maxine Geer
1973	Mar. 30	33	Chile	Luis Maureira Aipe
	Sep. 15	34	Philippines	Braulio S. Garcia and Nenita Balita
1974	Jan. 26	35	French Polynesia	E. Stewart Shaver
	Feb. 16	36	Cook Islands	J. Moosman
	Feb. 23	37	American Samoa	Molimau Tupa'i
	May	38	Japan	Shigeru Takahashi
1975	May 24	39	Madeira (Portugal)	Julio de Freitas
	Jun.	40	South Africa	South African National Film Board
	Jun. 21	41	Costa Rica	Mercedes Gamboa
	Aug. 2	42	Spain	Kim A. Langdorf
	Sep. 20	43	Taiwan	Huang Han-Chin
	Nov. 22	44	Hong Kong	B. Wong
1976	May 1	45	Peru	Wilfredo Rojas
	May 22	46	Macao	J. W. T.
	Jul. 24	47	Brazil	Wilson Roberto Gomes
	Sep. 11	48	El Salvador	Zeniff Mejia
1977	Feb. 4	49	Western Samoa	M. S. Davies
	Jul. 30	50	Zimbabwe	Halima Siddick
	Dec. 17	51	Bolivia	Carlos Ferrari
1978	Mar.	52	Namibia	E. Munn (South African National Film Board)
	Apr. 15	53	Liechtenstein	Irene Doring
	Apr. 15	54	Barbados	Jay Davis
1979	Feb. 24	55	Indonesia	Bambang Leo Antoatmono
	Mar. 31	56	Honduras	Pablo Zaldana
	May 12	57	Sri Lanka	Padmabandu Mayadunne
	Sep. 1	58	Paraguay	Dante Ortez
	Sep. 15	59	Greece	Jorge Rojas
	Nov. 10	60	Israel	Israel National Archives
1980	May 23	61	Turkey	Steve Baldridge

Year	Initial Project Date	No.	Area	Microfilm Operator
1981	Jan. 24	62	Ecuador	Carlos Perez
	Feb. 20	63	St. Helena	Steve Baldridge
	Apr. 13	64	Dominican Republic	Victor A. Navarro
	Nov. 1	65	India	S. K. Kashyap
1982	Jan. 30	66	Papua New Guinea	John and Olive Peterson
	May 12	67	China	Shuying Li
	Jun. 19	68	Uruguay	Carlos Ferrari
1983	Feb. 26	69	Gambia	Steve Baldridge
	Apr. 30	70	Singapore	Amir Butar Butar
	Jun. 18	71	Jamaica	V. C. Soffe
1985	Mar. 20	72	Yugoslavia/Croatia	Ljerka Jagic
	Oct. 12	73	Belize	Edmundo Abel Penate
1986	Jul. 5	74	Goa	Mario Fernandes
	Dec. 16	75	Mauritius (purchase film)	
1987	Feb. 7	76	Egypt	Steve Baldridge
	Feb. 14	77	Puerto Rico	L. A. Encarnacion
1988	Jul. 23	78	Colombia	Edilberto Moreno
	Sep. 3	79	Grenada	W. W. and E. S. Bullock
	Dec. 14	80	Virgin Islands, U.S. (purchase film)	
1990	Sep. 22	81	St. Kitts and Nevis	N. and E. Sanderson
1991	Mar. 1	82	Gibralter	Gloria Ruiz
	Mar. 9	83	Bermuda	Wolete Sion Selassie
	Apr. 13	84	Anguilla	N. and E. Sanderson
	Apr. 27	85	Turks and Caicos	Roger Faris
	May 25	86	Kiribati	Geoff and Mavis Draper
	Jul. 6	87	Bulgaria	Ivo Vaclov
	Sep. 7	88	Slovakia	Stefan Pechy
	Oct. 10	89	Br. Virgin Islands	Deloy Mendenhall and Lowell Dayton
	Nov. 30	90	Venezuela	Wilfredo Quintero
	Dec. 14	91	Dominica	David and Trevelene Hall
1992	Apr. 4	92	Estonia	Mati Merioja
	Jul. 30	93	Russia	Olga Mikhailova
	Sep. 26	94	Slovenia	Margareta Klasinc
1993	Jan. 22	95	Belarus	Evgenia Ramzaeva
	Mar. 13	96	Antigua and Barbuda	David and Trevelene Hall
	Sep. 28	97	Armenia	Larisa Khachatrian
	Oct. 2	98	Albania	Natasha Beqaj

Year	Initial Project Date	No.	Area	Microfilm Operator
1994	Feb. 5	99	Niue	Kenneth and Donna Pulham
	Apr. 2	100	Ukraine	Anna Kolodjeko and Alla Artuhova
	May 21	101	Lithuania	Maxim Shestakov

Source: James M. Black, "Microfilming Experiences of James M. Black, 1938–1972, in Service with the Genealogical Society," FHD, typescript (film 1313899); Operator reports from microfilming operators, Cataloging Department, Family History Library, FHD.

Appendix III: Microfilm Production, 1938–1994

Year	Rolls	Total Rolls	Exposures	Total Exposures
1938	12	12		
1939	138	150		
1940	377	527		
1941	607	1,134		
1942	614	1,748		
1943	235	1,983		
1944	24	2,007		
1945	69	2,076		
1946	462	2,538		2,333,664
1947	4,501	7,039	4,138,623	6,472,287
1948	10,012	17,051	9,205,930	15,678,217
1949	17,643	34,694	16,222,556	31,900,773
1950	15,384	50,078	12,906,877	44,807,650
1951	13,307	63,385	14,676,914	59,484,564
1952	17,268	80,653	19,045,686	78,530,250
1953	15,590	96,243	19,586,450	98,116,700
1954	13,324	109,567	15,536,300	113,653,000
1955	18,703	128,270	21,332,350	134,985,350
1956	16,128	144,398	17,695,600	152,680,950
1957	17,467	161,865	17,528,550	170,209,500
1958	27,984	189,849	29,530,800	199,740,300
1959	56,989	246,838	45,337,550	245,077,850
1960	22,746	269,584	17,167,100	262,244,950
1961	35,497	305,081	31,275,750	293,520,700
1962	27,203	332,284	18,180,100	311,700,800
1963	29,298	361,582	22,823,300	334,524,100

Year	Rolls	Total Rolls	Exposures	Total Exposures
1964	26,276	387,858	16,638,350	351,162,450
1965	41,498	429,356	29,679,958	380,842,408
1966	46,516	475,872	29,427,042	410,269,450
1967	42,031	517,903	36,230,722	446,500,172
1968	46,721	564,624	40,372,502	486,872,674
1969	50,882	615,506	43,860,284	530,732,958
1970	44,830	660,336	38,643,460	569,376,418
1971	52,755	713,091	45,474,810	614,851,228
1972	43,110	756,201	37,160,820	652,012,048
1973	40,660	796,861	35,048,920	687,060,968
1974	40,148	837,009	34,607,576	721,668,544
1975	39,539	876,548	34,082,618	755,751,162
1976	44,637	921,185	38,477,094	794,228,256
1977	52,063	973,248	44,878,306	839,106,562
1978	52,567	1,025,815	45,312,754	884,419,316
1979	49,730	1,075,545	34,247,260	918,666,576
1980	37,918	1,113,463	34,204,126	952,870,702
1981	31,243	1,144,706	35,621,229	988,491,931
1982	43,981	1,188,687	51,181,008	1,039,672,939
1983	34,131	1,222,818	39,853,135	1,079,526,074
1984	38,587	1,261,405	51,298,543	1,130,824,617
1985	30,468	1,291,873	46,888,003	1,177,712,620
1986	44,016	1,335,889	72,772,304	1,250,484,924
1987	47,105	1,382,994	85,693,350	1,336,178,274
1988	60,367	1,443,361	102,036,896	1,438,215,170
1989	66,041	1,509,402	109,024,213	1,547,239,383
1990	69,800	1,579,202	112,814,446	1,660,053,829
1991	53,716	1,632,918	99,177,068	1,759,230,897
1992	66,007	1,698,925	137,645,895	1,896,876,792
1993	51,901	1,750,826	94,108,126	1,990,984,918
1994	54,921	1,805,747	90,334,109	2,081,319,027

Source: Data from multiple internal FHD documents compiled by Kahlile Mehr.

Bibliography

Daniel B. McKinlay

This bibliography is made up of Latter-day Saint essays, speeches, manuals, articles, and books that relate to the following subjects: genealogy, family history, vicarious ordinances for the dead in temples, and the eternal priesthood organization of the family. Most of the talks and articles were published by Brigham Young University or by various LDS Church organizations. The bibliography does not pretend to be exhaustive, but contains a substantial representation of the topics indicated.

List of Abbreviations

CR — *Official Report of the Semi-Annual Conference of The Church of Jesus Christ of Latter-day Saints.* Salt Lake City: Deseret News, 1897–1964; The Church of Jesus Christ of Latter-day Saints, 1965–present.

EM — *Encyclopedia of Mormonism.* Edited by Daniel H. Ludlow. 5 vols. New York: Macmillan, 1992.

GRSDA — *Genealogical Research Seminar Devotional Addresses.* Compiled by the Priesthood Genealogical Research Seminar. Provo, Utah: Brigham Young University Press, 1967–1971.

IE — *Improvement Era.* 73 vols. Salt Lake City: The Church of Jesus Christ of Latter-day Saints, 1897–1970.

MS — *Millennial Star.* 130 vols. Manchester, England: Parley P. Pratt, 1840–1937 (vols. 1–99); London: British Mission of The Church of Jesus Christ of Latter-day Saints, 1938–1970 (vols. 100–130).

SY — *Speeches of the Year.* Compiled by Brigham Young University. Provo, Utah: Brigham Young University Press, 1953–present.

UGHM — *Utah Genealogical and Historical Magazine.* 31 vols. Salt Lake City: Genealogical Society of Utah, 1910–1940.

Allen, James B., and Jessie L. Embry. "'Provoking the Brethren to Good Works': Susa Young Gates, the Relief Society, and Genealogy." *BYU Studies* 31 (Spring 1991): 115-38.

Anderson, James H. "Elijah's Saving Mission." *UGHM* 27 (April 1936): 67-75. First published in *MS* 96 (13 September 1934): 577-83.

———. "From Abraham to Modern Britain—Racial Traits." *MS* 90 (24 May 1928): 321-26.

———. "The Salt Lake Temple." *The Contributor* 14 (April 1893): 243-303.

———. "Temple Ceremonies." *IE* 32 (October 1929): 969-71.

Anderson, Lewis. Conference address. *CR* (October 1910): 88-90.

Anderson, Nephi. "Genealogy's Place in the Plan of Salvation." *UGHM* 3 (January 1912): 12-22.

———. "The Gospel to the Dead." *MS* 66 (11 August 1904): 504-5.

———. "The 'Larger Hope' for the Dead." *UGHM* 4 (October 1913): 157-63.

Anderson, Richard L. "Peter's Letters: Progression for the Living and the Dead." *Ensign* 21 (October 1991): 6-10.

"Avoid Rejection: Be a Happy Genealogist." *Ensign* 3 (November 1973): 34-35.

Babcock, George Milton. "Gathering Genealogy by Letter Writing." *UGHM* 5 (April 1914): 74-77.

Badger, Virginia M. "The Family Tree Club." *IE* 60 (February 1957): 86-88.

Ballard, Melvin J. "The Inspiration of Temple Work." *UGHM* 23 (October 1932): 145-50.

Bangerter, W. Grant. "What Temples Are For." *Ensign* 12 (May 1982): 71-72.

Banning, Pierson W. "Relation of History to Genealogy." *UGHM* 11 (October 1920): 151-54.

Barlow, Helen. "The Importance of Genealogical Work." *IE* 57 (November 1954): 802.

Barton, Patricia T. "Finding Grandma Toth." *Ensign* 21 (April 1991): 59-60.

Beebe, Clara W. "Temple Work." *Children's Friend* 23 (November 1924): 342.

Beeley, Arthur L. "Salvation for the Dead." *UGHM* 6 (July 1915): 107-11. First published in *MS* 76 (26 November 1914): 753-56.

Belnap, W. Dean. "How to Start a Family Organization and Keep It Going." *Ensign* 2 (August 1972): 81-82.

———. "Involving Youth in Genealogy." *IE* 72 (July 1969): 64.

Bennett, Archibald F. *Adventures in Research: Genealogical Training Class—Teachers Supplement for The Church of Jesus Christ of Latter-day Saints.* Salt Lake City: Deseret Sunday School Union Board, 1943.

———. "The Beginning of the Blessing." *IE* 56 (April 1953): 228–29, 292–94.

———. "A Century of Sacred Service." *IE* 50 (July 1947): 461–63, 491–93.

———. "The Children of Ephraim." *UGHM* 21 (April 1930): 67–85.

———. "Eight Ways to Avoid Duplications." *IE* 47 (July 1944): 455–56.

———. *Family Exaltation.* Salt Lake City: Deseret Book, 1957.

———. "Finding Ancestors by the Co-operative Method." *UGHM* 19 (July 1928): 97–112.

———. "For a Wise Purpose." *MS* 100 (31 March 1938): 194–96, 203.

———. "The Genealogical Society of Utah." *IE* 38 (April 1935): 225–26.

———. "Genealogy: Partner of Temple Work." *IE* 39 (April 1936): 244–46.

———. "The Growth of the Temple Index Bureau: 'A World-wide Clearinghouse.'" *IE* 39 (April 1936): 218–21.

———. *A Guide for Genealogical Research.* Salt Lake City: Genealogical Society of The Church of Jesus Christ of Latter-day Saints, 1951.

———. "The Hearts of the Children." *MS* 95 (15 June 1933): 391, 394–97.

———. "How Can a Quorum Encourage the Gathering and Compiling of Genealogy." *IE* 49 (February 1946): 106–8.

———. "The Keystone of the Gospel." *MS* 109 (October 1947): 290–91, 317–18.

———. "The Lineage of Queen Elizabeth II." *IE* 56 (May 1953): 316–18, 345–50.

———. *Methods of Tracing Pedigrees.* Salt Lake City: Genealogical Society of Utah, 1936.

———. *Proving Your Pedigree.* Salt Lake City: Deseret Sunday School Union Board, 1951.

———. "Put on Thy Strength, O Zion!" *IE* 55 (October 1952): 718–20.

———. *Saviors on Mount Zion.* Salt Lake City: Deseret Sunday School Union Board, 1950.

———. "The Way to Happiness and Exaltation." *MS* 124 (August 1962): 190–92.

———. "Why Men and Women Compile Genealogies." *IE* 44 (December 1941): 750–52.

Bennion, Howard S. *Genealogical Research: A Practical Mission.* Salt Lake City: Deseret Sunday School Union, 1962.

Bennion, Roy B. "Genealogy—Love That Transcends Time." *Ensign* 17 (August 1987): 11–13.

Benson, Ezra Taft. "What I Hope You Will Teach Your Children about the Temple." *Ensign* 15 (August 1985): 6–10.

———. "Worthy of All Acceptation." *Ensign* 8 (November 1978): 30–32.

Betts, Margaret E. "Genealogy Is Exciting." *IE* 61 (September 1958): 658–59.

Bitton, Davis. "Great-Grandfather's Family." *Ensign* 7 (February 1977): 48–51.

Bitton, Davis. *Guide to Mormon Diaries and Autobiographies.* Provo, Utah: Brigham Young University Press, 1977.

———. "That Your Children May Know." *Ensign* 3 (November 1973): 43-48.

Black, Susan Easton. "The Search for Early Members of the Church." *Ensign* 19 (July 1989): 28-31.

Bloxham, Ben. Seminar address. *GRSDA 1966,* 17-25.

Bohn, William J. "Three Other New Testament Temples." *Ensign* 21 (July 1991): 21-25.

"The Book of Remembrance." *IE* 69 (April 1966): 294-95.

"The Book of You." *New Era* 23 (September 1993): 34-35.

Bowring, Benjamin L. "Family Responsibility in Genealogy." *CR* (April 1959): 38-42.

———. "Youth and Temple Work." *MS* 124 (June 1962): 124-25.

Boyer, Selvoy J. "The Purpose of the Temple." *MS* 124 (April 1962): 78-79.

Brace, William Raymond. *The Utah Genealogical Society.* Master's thesis, University of Chicago, 1956.

"Branch Genealogical Libraries." *IE* 69 (September 1966): 790-91.

"Branch Genealogical Libraries Now Being Established." *IE* 68 (March 1965): 220-21, 235.

Brewster, Verlean D. "Home Movies—Starring Our Ancestors!" *Ensign* 23 (August 1993): 66-67.

Brickey, Wayne. "The New Scope of What We Have Called Genealogy." *Ensign* 7 (January 1977): 41-44.

Brimley, Wilford C. "Salvation for the Dead." *MS* 74 (29 August 1912): 545-48.

Brockbank, Bernard P. "Our Brother's Keeper." *GRSDA 1967,* 62-69.

Brough, Monte J. "Everyone's Blessing." *Ensign* 24 (December 1994): 16-20.

Brown, Hugh B. "History of the Temple." *MS* 127 (February 1965): 45-47.

———. "Modern Temples." Parts 1 and 2. *MS* 108 (April 1946): 97-99; (May 1946): 141-43.

———. "Temple Building." In *Continuing the Quest,* 47-55. Salt Lake City: Deseret Book, 1961.

Brown, Victor L., and Lois Brown. "Questions about Temple Marriage." *New Era* 17 (February 1987): 30-31.

Bryan, Max A. "The Priesthood and Genealogy." *MS* 127 (February 1965): 62-63.

———. "Priesthood and Genealogy." *MS* 127 (November-December 1965): 413-14.

Bryson, Leah Y. "Happy History to You." *Ensign* 23 (January 1993): 73.

Buckmiller, LeRoy J. "Going to the Temple." *MS* 129 (January 1967): 68-69.

———. "Going to the Temple." *MS* 129 (August 1967): 22-23.

Burton, Theodore M. "The Era Asks about Genealogy in the Church Today." *IE* 71 (February 1968): 51-57.

———. "Genealogy: A Personal Responsibility." *Ensign* 3 (January 1973): 52-54.

———. "The GIANT System." *IE* 72 (June 1969): 108-9, 111.

———. "The Gospel—and the Dead." *IE* 67 (June 1964): 488-89.

———. "I Have a Question." *Ensign* 5 (March 1975): 32-33.

———. "The Importance of Temples." *IE* 70 (December 1967): 80-82.

———. "The Inspiration of a Family Record." *Ensign* 7 (January 1977): 13-17.

———. "A Modern Sacrifice." *IE* 69 (June 1966): 508-10.

———. "Neither Cryptic nor Hidden." *Ensign* 7 (May 1977): 28-30.

———. "The Power of Elijah." *Ensign* 4 (May 1974): 61-62, 67.

———. "The Priesthood and Family Exaltation." *GRSDA 1967,* 1-12.

———. "Priesthood Correlation Program—Genealogy." *GRSDA 1967,* 13-30.

———. "Priesthood Responsibility." *IE* 70 (June 1967): 50-51.

———. "Prove Thy Lineage." *IE* 71 (December 1968): 81-82.

———. "Salvation for the Dead—a Missionary Activity." *Ensign* 5 (May 1975): 69-71.

———. "Seek and Ye Shall Find." *GRSDA 1969,* 3-15.

———. Seminar address. *GRSDA 1966,* 4-14.

———. "The Spirit and Power of Elijah." *IE* 73 (December 1970): 57-59.

———. "The Temples of God." *IE* 69 (December 1966): 1111-12.

———. "What Is the Granite Mountain Records Vault?" *IE* 69 (August 1966): 698-701, 734-35.

———. "Why Genealogy?" *IE* 72 (July 1969): 4-6.

———. "With Whom Will We Share Exaltation?" *Ensign* 1 (August 1971): 33-35.

———. "The Work of Elijah." *IE* 68 (June 1965): 532-34.

Busche, F. Enzio. "University for Eternal Life." *Ensign* 19 (May 1989): 71-73.

Caldwell, C. Max. *An Analysis of the Role of Temples in the Establishment of Zion*. Provo, Utah: Brigham Young University Press, 1971.

Callis, Charles A. "Justice for the Dead." *MS* 98 (13 August 1936): 514-15.

Cannon, Annie Wells. "Our Pioneer Mothers: A Tribute." *UGHM* 5 (July 1914): 144-47.

Cannon, David H. Conference address. *CR* (April 1913): 103-8.

Cannon, Donald Q., Larry E. Dahl, and John W. Welch. "The Restoration of Major Doctrines through Joseph Smith: Priesthood, the Word of God, and the Temple." *Ensign* 19 (February 1989): 6-13.

"Can You Prove It?" *IE* 42 (August 1939): 492.

Card, Joseph Y. "The Cardston Temple." *IE* 26 (September 1923): 1001-9.

Carpenter, J. Hatten. "The 'Mormon' People and Their Progenitors." *UGHM* 11 (October 1920): 163-69.
———. "Preservation of the Purity of Israel's Race." *UGHM* 21 (October 1930): 163-71.
Cerny, Johni, and Wendy Elliott, eds. *The Library: A Guide to the LDS Family History Library.* Salt Lake City: Ancestry Publishing, 1988.
"The Chain That Binds." *IE* 42 (September 1939): 546.
Christenson, Joseph. "The Growth of Temple Work." *UGHM* 27 (April 1936): 90-93.
Christiansen, ElRay L. "A Foundation Stone of the Gospel." *IE* 65 (December 1962): 956-57.
———. "If You Would Be Eternally Rich." *GRSDA 1968,* 3-11.
———. "The Importance of Temples." *MS* 118 (August 1956): 234-39.
———. "Of the Most Worth unto You." *GRSDA 1967,* 94-103.
———. "The Primary Purpose of the Present Dispensation." *IE* 63 (June 1960): 409-11.
———. "Temples—Avenues to Exaltation." *SY* (August 1970).
———. "Why Temples?" *IE* 71 (June 1968): 104-6.
———. "Work for the Living and the Dead." *IE* 57 (June 1954): 418-19.
Christiansen, Henry E. "Genealogical Sources in Denmark." *UGHM* 31 (October 1940): 200-211.
———. "I Have a Question." *Ensign* 7 (January 1977): 71-72.
The Church of Jesus Christ of Latter-day Saints. *Birthright Blessings: Genealogical Training Class Sunday School Lessons for The Church of Jesus Christ of Latter-day Saints.* Salt Lake City: Deseret Sunday School Union Board, 1942.
———. *A Book of Remembrance: A Lesson Book for First Year Junior Genealogical Classes.* Salt Lake City: Genealogical Society of Utah, 1936.
———. *Church Service on Genealogical Committees: Course for Senior and Junior Classes for 1935.* Salt Lake City: Genealogical Society of Utah, 1935.
———. *Come unto Christ through Temple Ordinances*. Salt Lake City: The Church of Jesus Christ of Latter-day Saints, 1987.
———. *Discovering Your Family Tree.* Salt Lake City: The Church of Jesus Christ of Latter-day Saints, 1989.
———. *Family Exaltation and You.* Salt Lake City: The First Presidency, 1973.
———. *Guide to Research.* 3d ed. Salt Lake City: The Church of Jesus Christ of Latter-day Saints, 1994 (pamphlet 30971).
———. *A Guide to Research, Family History Library.* Salt Lake City: The Church of Jesus Christ of Latter-day Saints, 1988.
———. *Handbook for Genealogy and Temple Work.* Salt Lake City: Genealogical Society of Utah, 1949.

———. *The Latter-day Saint Family.* Salt Lake City: Deseret Sunday School Union Board, 1946.

———. *A Member's Guide to Temple and Family History Work: Ordinances and Covenants.* Salt Lake City: The Church of Jesus Christ of Latter-day Saints, 1993.

———. *Out of the Books: Genealogical Training Class Sunday School Lessons for The Church of Jesus Christ of Latter-day Saints.* Salt Lake City: Deseret Sunday School Union Board, 1940.

———. *Research Outlines.* Salt Lake City: The Church of Jesus Christ of Latter-day Saints, 1986– (various item numbers). This is a series of publications dealing with specific research topics. Research outlines exist for the United States as a whole as well as for individual states, Canada as a whole as well as individual provinces, Latin America, Germany, Norway, Sweden, Denmark, France, England, Wales, Ireland, Philippines, U.S. military records, tracing immigrant origins, and LDS records.

———. *Teaching One Another: Study Course for Senior Genealogical Classes, 1939–40.* Salt Lake City: Genealogical Society of Utah, 1938.

———. *Temple and Family History Leadership Handbook.* Salt Lake City: The Church of Jesus Christ of Latter-day Saints, 1992.

———. *Temples and the Latter-day Saints.* Salt Lake City: The Church of Jesus Christ of Latter-day Saints, 1973.

———. *Temples of The Church of Jesus Christ of Latter-day Saints.* The *Ensign* of The Church of Jesus Christ of Latter-day Saints, 1988.

———. *Ten Basic Steps in Genealogy.* Salt Lake City: Genealogical Society of The Church of Jesus Christ of Latter-day Saints, 1963.

———. *Where Do I Start?* Salt Lake City: The Church of Jesus Christ of Latter-day Saints, 1992, 1993 (pamphlet 32916).

———. *Why Family History?* Salt Lake City: The Church of Jesus Christ of Latter-day Saints, 1982, 1989 (pamphlet 30961).

———. *World Conference on Records and Genealogical Seminar.* 11 vols. Salt Lake City: Genealogical Society of The Church of Jesus Christ of Latter-day Saints, 1969.

———. *World Conference on Records: Preserving Our Heritage.* (12–15 August 1980). 13 vols. Salt Lake City: [Genealogical Society of The Church of Jesus Christ of Latter-day Saints, n.d.].

Clark, Harold Glen. "Four Blessings of the Temple." *Ensign* 13 (October 1983): 68–71.

Clark, J. Reuben, Jr. "President Clark Explains Necessity and Uses of Temple." *MS* 116 (April 1954): 93–96.

Clark, Wilfred. "Salvation for the Dead." *MS* 116 (March 1954): 83–84, 88.

Clarke, J. Richard. "A Conversation with Elder J. Richard Clarke about FamilySearch." *Ensign* 20 (November 1990): 110–12.

Clarke, J. Richard, *cont.* "Our Kindred Family—Expression of Eternal Love." *Ensign* 19 (May 1989): 60-62.

———. "The Temple: What It Means to You." *New Era* 23 (April 1993): 4-7.

Clawson, Rudger. Conference address. *CR* (October 1931): 75-79.

———. Conference address. *CR* (October 1940): 121-24.

———. "The Fathers without Us Not Perfect." *MS* 72 (8 September 1910): 568-73.

———. "The Hawaiian Temple." *MS* 82 (8 January 1920): 27-32.

———. "A Plea for Temple Work." *UGHM* 28 (January 1937): 1-4. First published in *CR* (October 1936): 115-18.

———. "Spiritual Wealth through Temple Work." *UGHM* 5 (January 1914): 25-30. First published in *CR* (October 1900): 8-12.

———. "Temple Building and Work for the Dead." *UGHM* 5 (July 1914): 121-24. First published in *CR* (October 1908): 71-75.

———. "The Temple of the Lord." *UGHM* 9 (October 1918): 154-59.

Clissold, Edward L. "The Church and Temple Work." *CR* (April 1959): 42-44.

Colket, Meredith B., Jr. "Prominent American Genealogical Societies." *IE* 72 (July 1969): 8-9.

Conrad, Agnes C. "Sources for Family History in Hawaii." *Proceedings, First Annual Conference, Mormon History in the Pacific, August 1-2, 1980* (August 1980): 10-19.

Cook, Doris. "John Francis Cook: He Made Genealogy Live." *MS* 120 (March 1958): 79-82.

Cook, John F. "The Hearts of the Children." *MS* 96 (15 February 1934): 107-8.

Cowan, Richard O. *Bibliography on Temples and Temple Work*. Provo, Utah: Brigham Young University Press, 1982.

———. *The Living Church: The Unfolding of the Program and Organization of The Church of Jesus Christ of Latter-day Saints during the Twentieth Century*. Provo, Utah: Brigham Young University Press, 1974.

Cowley, Matthew. "Make It Easy for Them to Believe." In *Matthew Cowley Speaks,* compiled by Deseret Book, 118-23. Salt Lake City: Deseret Book, 1954.

Cowley, Matthias F. "Salvation for the Dead." In *Cowley's Talks on Doctrine,* 120-35. Chicago: Northern States Mission of The Church of Jesus Christ of Latter-day Saints, 1905.

Crowley, Ariel L. "The Epistle of Kallikrates and Baptism for the Dead." *IE* 48 (July 1945): 386, 430.

Cummings, B. F. "Compiling and Assembling a Genealogy." Parts 1 and 2. *UGHM* 6 (April 1915): 69-74; (July 1915): 111-17.

———. "Genealogy and the Spirit of Elijah." *UGHM* 7 (April 1916): 69-72.

———. "Research Work and the Genealogical Society of Utah." *UGHM* 8 (July 1917): 133–38.

Cunningham, James R. "Forging Everlasting Links." *MS* 125 (September 1963): 247, 255.

———. "The Genealogical Work of the Latter-day Saints." *Genealogist's Magazine* 14 (September 1964): 369–73.

———. "Microfilming in Ireland and Wales." *IE* 55 (April 1952): 235–95.

———. "Searching for the Right Name in the Right Place." *MS* 125 (August 1963): 211–12.

Curtis, Theodore E. "Vicarious Work for the Dead." *IE* 20 (December 1916): 106–10.

Damson, Lori Stephenson. "Even in an Ordinary Ward." *New Era* 17 (November 1987): 8–11.

Daniels, Thomas E. "I Have a Question." *Ensign* 4 (March 1974): 23–25.

———. "I Have a Question." *Ensign* 4 (July 1974): 14.

———. "I Have a Question." *Ensign* 21 (October 1991): 62.

Davidson, W. B. "Salvation for the Dead." *MS* 73 (16 November 1911): 721–24.

DeMille, Janice F. *The St. George Temple: First 100 Years.* Hurricane, Utah: Homestead Publishers, 1977.

Denny, Eula. "I Have a Question." *Ensign* 21 (June 1991): 53.

Deputy, Marilyn, and Maren Jeppsen. "25 Terrific Ideas for Family History Fun." *New Era* 16 (March 1986): 34–37.

Derrick, Royden G. "The Heritage of Royal Families." *Ensign* 9 (May 1979): 26–28.

———. *Promoting the Basic Points of Emphasis through Example: Leadership in Genealogical Work.* Salt Lake City: n.p., 1980.

———. *Temples in the Last Days.* Salt Lake City: Bookcraft, 1987.

Dulong, John Patrick. "Genealogical Groups in Changing Organizational Environment: From Lineage to Heritage." Ph.D. diss., Wayne State University Press, 1986.

Durrant, George D. *The Case of the Missing Ancestors: The Fun of Sleuthing Out Your Family History.* Orem, Utah: Keepsake, 1991.

———. "Doing Genealogy: Finding That Glorious, Elusive Condition Called 'Balance.'" *Ensign* 15 (April 1985): 18–23.

———. *Fun and Names: Or, How to Dig Your Family History without Really Prying.* Salt Lake City: Bookcraft, 1980.

———. "Genealogical Society of Utah." *EM* 2:537–38.

———. "Genealogy and Temple Work." *Ensign* 13 (August 1983): 18–20.

Durrant, George D., and Noel Barton. "To Go Forward, Go Back." *Ensign* 8 (February 1978): 26–29.

Dyer, Alvin R. "Three Challenges." *IE* 65 (December 1962): 908–11.

Edmunds, John K. "Temple Teachings through the Ages." *Ensign* 4 (August 1974): 48–55.

Edmunds, John K. *Through Temple Doors.* Salt Lake City: Bookcraft, 1978.

"Effective Family Organizations." *IE* 68 (April 1965): 312-13.

Ehat, Andrew F. *Joseph Smith's Introduction of Temple Ordinances and the 1844 Mormon Succession Question.* Master's thesis, Brigham Young University, 1982.

Ellsworth, German E. Conference address. *CR* (April 1914): 79-83.

Embry, Jessie L. "Missionaries for the Dead: The Story of the Genealogical Missionaries of the Nineteenth Century." *BYU Studies* 17 (Spring 1977): 355-60.

"English Probate Jurisdictions." *IE* 71 (October 1968): 82-83.

Esplin, Ronald K. "God Will Protect Me until My Work Is Done." *Ensign* 19 (August 1989): 16-21.

Evans, Beatrice C. "What's the Use?" *IE* 43 (October 1940): 601, 619.

Evans, Richard L. "Eternal Assurances." *IE* 68 (February 1965): 144-45.

———. "For the Living and the Dead." *MS* 89 (8 December 1927): 776-77.

Evans, Teri. "Baby Stories." *Ensign* 21 (December 1991): 58.

Everton, George B. "Genealogical Help through Relatives." *IE* 68 (July 1965): 614-15.

Everton, Walter M. "Early Training Is Best." *IE* 41 (August 1938): 495.

———. "Write Your Life Story." *IE* 44 (May 1941): 300.

Fairbanks, Martin. "Home Is Where Family History Is." *Ensign* 23 (July 1993): 73.

"Family History Moments." *Church News.* (21 January 1989-present). A column published on the last page of the *Church News* every four or five weeks. From 3 March 1985-21 January 1989, the column was entitled "Genealogy Moments."

Farrow, Echo. "The Desire of Their Hearts." *New Era* 18 (November 1988): 44.

Faust, James E. "The Keys of the Kingdom." *Ensign* 5 (November 1975): 55-57.

Feldman, Margie L. "I Saw My Eternal Family." *Ensign* 23 (April 1993): 61-62.

Finlayson, Mary. "Elijah, Spirit Of." *EM* 2:452.

Fitches, J. W. "The Spirits in Prison." *MS* 73 (5 October 1911): 625-28.

Forbis, Dianne D. "It's Child's Play: How to Help Your Child Begin a Journal." *Ensign* 7 (January 1977): 29.

Fox, Ruth May. "Youth and Temples." *IE* 39 (April 1936): 224-26.

Fudge, George H. "I Have a Question." *Ensign* 7 (January 1977): 74-75.

———. "I Have a Question." *Ensign* 16 (March 1986): 49-50.

Fyans, J. Thomas. "Ours Is a Shared Ancestry." *Ensign* 8 (November 1978): 28-29.

Galbraeth, John J. "Genealogy among the American Indians." *MS* 95 (1 June 1933): 364-66.

Gardner, Bryan B. "The Exciting Influence of Elijah." *MS* 120 (November 1958): 341–45.

Gardner, Cynthia M. "Book of Remembrance." *EM* 1:217.

Gardner, David E. "Hearts Turned to Their Fathers: A New Series of Notes on Genealogy." *MS* 128 (September 1966): 37–38.

Gardner, David E., Derek Harland, and Frank Smith. *A Basic Course in Genealogy, Volume 1: An Introduction to Record Keeping and Research.* Salt Lake City: Bookcraft, 1958.

Gates, Susa Young. "Genealogical and Temple Activity." *IE* 30 (October 1927): 1101–3.

———. "Genealogical Societies and the Work for the Dead." *UGHM* 10 (July 1919): 97–104.

———. "Genealogy in the Relief Society." *UGHM* 7 (January 1916): 41–45.

———. "Going Abroad for Genealogy: United States." *UGHM* 5 (April 1914): 88-91.

———. "Hints for Pedigree Hunters." *UGHM* 6 (January 1915): 17–22.

———. "How to Begin Genealogical Research." *MS* 91 (5 December 1929): 778–79.

———. "Hunting Pedigrees in Scotland." *UGHM* 7 (January 1916): 31–33.

———. "Importance of Record Keeping." *UGHM* 5 (January 1914): 16–19.

———. "Lessons in Genealogy." Parts 1-6. *UGHM* 2 (October 1911): 163–69; 3 (January 1912): 23–29; (April 1912): 76–83; (July 1912): 123–32; (October 1912): 186–94; 4 (April 1913): 93–101.

———. "Pedigree Hunting." *UGHM* 6 (July 1915): 126–30.

———. "Sandwich Island Genealogy." *UGHM* 10 (October 1919): 145–52.

———. "Sources of Information for the British Searcher." *UGHM* 6 (April 1915): 55-60.

———. "The Way of the Pedigree Hunter." *UGHM* 7 (July 1916): 109–12.

Gaunt, LaRene P. "A Day in Heaven." *Ensign* 21 (December 1991): 33–37.

———. "Doing 'Homework' for the Lord." *Ensign* 21 (March 1991): 54–57.

———. "Family History Wellspring." *Ensign* 23 (August 1993): 22–26.

———. "FamilySearch—Stepping-Stone to the Temple." *Ensign* 22 (August 1992): 12–19.

———. "Finding Joy in Temple Service." *Ensign* 24 (October 1994): 6–10.

———. "Leading the Way." *Ensign* 25 (January 1995): 54–59.

———. "The Power of God Was with Us." *Ensign* 23 (March 1993): 28–31.

"Genealogical Record Sources in Denmark." *IE* 71 (September 1968): 84–87.

"Genealogical Research." *IE* 62 (May 1959): 350–52, 364.

Gerlach, Larry R., and Michael L. Nicholls. "The Mormon Genealogical Society and Research Opportunities in Early American History." *William and Mary Quarterly, 3d Series* 32 (October 1975): 625–29.

"Getting Started on Your Family History." *New Era* 19 (September 1989): 40.

Gordon, Margaret E. P. "Research through Correspondence." *IE* 54 (April 1951): 227, 288.

Grant, Heber J. Conference address. *CR* (April 1924): 5–8.

———. "A Family Temple Night." *IE* 47 (July 1944): 425, 471.

———. "An Inspired Message." *UGHM* 22 (July 1931): 106–9.

———. "On Going to the Temple." *IE* 44 (August 1941): 459.

———. "Sacredness of the Temple." *IE* 11 (March 1908): 361–63.

———. "Temple Work." *CR* (April 1928): 8–9.

Greenwood, Val D. "I Have a Question." *Ensign* 7 (January 1977): 73–74.

Groberg, Delbert V. *The Idaho Falls Temple: The First LDS Temple in Idaho.* Salt Lake City: Publishers Press, 1985.

Groom, Percy. "Genealogy and Its Relation to Temple Work." *UGHM* 15 (January 1924): 33–35.

———. "How to Bring Our Message More Effectively before the People." *UGHM* 15 (April 1924): 71–73.

Gunderson, Robert C. "I Have a Question." *Ensign* 14 (February 1984): 31.

Haab, Sherri Ann. "Family History—Holiday Style." *Ensign* 21 (December 1991): 57.

Hafen, Bruce C. "Planting Promises in the Hearts of the Children." *Ensign* 24 (June 1994): 46–52.

Haigh, Roger M., and Frank J. Sanders. "A Report on Some Latin American Materials in the Genealogical Library of The Church of Jesus Christ of Latter-day Saints at Salt Lake City, Utah." *Latin Americana Research Review* 10 (1975): 193–96.

Haight, David B. "Come to the House of the Lord." *Ensign* 22 (May 1992): 15–17.

———. "Linking the Family of Man." *Ensign* 21 (May 1991): 75–77.

———. "Personal Temple Worship." *Ensign* 23 (May 1993): 23–25.

———. "Symbol of Sacrifice—Monument to Life." *Ensign* 23 (October 1993): 8–11.

———. "Temples and Work Therein." *Ensign* 20 (November 1990): 59–61.

Hamer, Ginger. "Family Fun with Genealogy." *Ensign* 14 (September 1984): 64–66.

Hanks, S. Bruce. "Where All May Be Saved." *MS* 101 (30 March 1939): 202–3, 206.

Hanny, Nellie F. D. "Testing Your Own Accuracy." *IE* 47 (August 1944): 504.

Harland, Derek. *A Basic Course in Genealogy.* Vol. 2. Salt Lake City: Bookcraft, 1958.

———. *Genealogy in Action.* Salt Lake City: Priesthood Genealogy Committee, 1964.

Harmon, W. Glenn. "Strengthening the Tie That Binds." *IE* 60 (March 1957): 166–67, 206–7.

Hart, David K. "The Necessity of a Temple." *MS* 118 (August 1956): 243–45.

Hartley, William G. "Writing Your History: Some Helpful Ideas." *Ensign* 7 (January 1977): 26–27.

Hasenberg, Syger T. "Names." *MS* 127 (March 1965): 103–5.

———. "Our Books of Remembrance." *MS* 126 (December 1964): 424, 431.

Haskin, Frederic J. "Coats of Arms and How to Obtain Them." *UGHM* 7 (July 1916): 150–53.

———. "Kings as Ancestors." *UGHM* 4 (January 1913): 25–27.

———. "Modern Profession of Genealogy." *UGHM* 5 (January 1914): 13–16.

———. "The New England Historic Genealogical Society." *IE* 46 (April 1943): 238–39.

Hauch-Fausboll, T. H. "Genealogical Research in Denmark." *UGHM* 6 (October 1915): 173–76.

———. "How Is Genealogy to Be Studied." *UGHM* 22 (January 1931): 3–6.

Hawkins, Echo. "Genealogy—A Life-Time's Thrill." *MS* 113 (August 1951): 178–79, 193.

———. "When a Genealogist Climbs a Tree." *MS* 112 (July 1950): 202–3, 207.

Hawkins, Olive. "The Purpose of Genealogical Research and Temple Work." *IE* 56 (July 1953): 509, 549.

Heckscher, Ella. "Genealogical Sources in Sweden." *UGHM* 29 (July 1938): 97–110.

Heinerman, Joseph. *Spirit World Manifestations.* Salt Lake City: Magazine Printing and Publishing, 1978.

———. *Temple Manifestations.* Manti, Utah: Mountain Valley Publishers, 1974.

Higginson, Mollie. "Where Was Christ?" *MS* 77 (2 December 1915): 756–58.

Hilton, W. Bruce. "The Purpose of Keeping Records and Doing Temple Work." *IE* 57 (November 1954): 803.

Hinkley, Gordon B. "Keeping the Temple Holy." *Ensign* 20 (April 1990): 49–52.

———. "Rejoice in This Great Era of Temple Building." *Ensign* 15 (November 1985): 53–54, 59–60.

Hinkley, Gordon B. "The Salt Lake Temple." *Ensign* 23 (March 1993): 2-6.

———. Seminar address. *GRSDA 1970,* 1-6.

———. "This Peaceful House of God." *Ensign* 23 (May 1993): 72-75.

———. "Why These Temples?" *Ensign* 4 (August 1974): 37-41.

Hinze, Sarah Street. "In the Right Place at the Right Time." *Ensign* 21 (February 1991): 65-66.

Holzapfel, Richard Neitzel. "Every Window, Every Spire 'Speaks of the Things of God.'" *Ensign* 23 (March 1993): 7-21.

Horne, Flora B. "History of the Society of Daughters of the Utah Pioneers." *UGHM* 3 (April 1912): 96-104.

Horner, Catherine L. M. "Our Kind of Humor." *IE* 72 (July 1969): 11-12.

Horsley, Richard B. *Mormonism's One Hundred Largest Posterities.* Provo, Utah: Pioneer Book and Research Center, 1983.

———. *Who's Who in Mormon Families.* Provo, Utah: n.p., 1983.

"How to Become 'Saviors on Mount Zion.'" *IE* 42 (June 1939): 364.

Hoyer, Margaret. "Search for Ancestors in the Light of the German 'Racial' Movement." *UGHM* 25 (April 1934): 68-73.

Huber, Carol. "One-Hour Life History." *Ensign* 24 (June 1994): 54.

Hughes, Lloyd S. "Connecticut's Early Records Microfilmed." *IE* 54 (May 1951): 334, 349-50, 352-53.

Hunt, Albert E. "To Prepare the Way." *IE* 61 (March 1958): 152-53, 182, 184.

Hunter, Howard W. "Elijah the Prophet." *Ensign* 1 (December 1971): 70-72.

———. "The Era Asks about the World Conference on Records." *IE* 72 (January 1969): 22-24.

———. "The Great Symbol of Our Membership." *Ensign* 24 (October 1994): 2-5.

———. "The Oakland Temple: Culmination of History." *IE* 68 (February 1965): 140-42.

———. "Primer in Genealogy." *Ensign* 1 (February 1971): 4-5.

———. "A Temple-Motivated People." *Ensign* 25 (February 1995): 2-5.

———. "Temple Ordinances." *GRSDA 1969,* 19-24.

Hunter, Milton R. "A Record-Keeping People." *IE* 61 (March 1958): 154-55, 193, 195-96.

"Impelling Motives of Genealogists." *IE* 42 (March 1939): 172.

"Introduction of Baptism for the Dead." *IE* 42 (April 1939): 251.

Irving, Gordon. "The Law of Adoption: One Phase of the Development of the Mormon Concept of Salvation, 1830-1900." *BYU Studies* 14 (Spring 1974): 291-314.

Ivins, Anthony W. "Israel in History and Genealogy." *MS* 94 (15 September 1932): 599-607. First published in *UGHM* 23 (January 1932): 1-9.

———. "Temples, Ancient and Modern." *UGHM* 15 (July 1924): 97-103.

Jaussi, Laureen R. *Fundamentals of Genealogical Research.* Salt Lake City: Deseret Book, 1966.

Jensen, Marlin K. "A Conversation on Preparing Ourselves for the Temple." *Ensign* 23 (May 1993): 103.

Jensen, Nephi. "Baptism for the Dead." *UGHM* 15 (July 1924): 120-23.

Jenson, Andrew. Conference address. *CR* (April 1913): 77-81.

———. "Danish Names and Genealogy." *UGHM* 4 (April 1913): 75-81.

———. "Importance of Record Keeping." *UGHM* 9 (July 1918): 97-99.

———. "Scandinavian Latter-day Saint Literature." *UGHM* 13 (October 1922): 181-91.

Jeppsen, Maren. "Mormon Battalion Sources at the Genealogical Library." *Pioneer* 34 (March-April 1987): 22.

Jessee, Dean C. "Wilford Woodruff: A Man of Record." *Ensign* 23 (July 1993): 28-31.

Johnson, Lisa A. "The Eternal Road Trip." *New Era* 23 (June 1993): 28-31.

Jones, Ivie H. "The Living, First." *IE* 57 (April 1954): 243, 263.

———. "Record Seeking in the 'Land of Mañana.'" *IE* 54 (March 1951): 151-52.

Jones, Milton J. *Genealogical Research Work Book.* Salt Lake City: LDS Aids, 1965.

Jones, Shirlyn Andersen. "That Day in Manti." *New Era* 24 (February 1994): 8-10.

Killpack, William L. "Temple Work and Its Importance to Us in This Dispensation." *MS* 118 (August 1956): 240-42.

Kimball, Heber C. "President Heber C. Kimball's Teachings." *UGHM* 13 (January 1922): 1-7.

Kimball, Spencer W. "The Angels May Quote from It." *New Era* 5 (October 1975): 4-5.

———. "President Kimball Speaks Out on Personal Journals." *Ensign* 10 (December 1980): 60-61.

———. "Temples and Eternal Marriage." *Ensign* 4 (August 1974): 2-6. First published in *CR* (October 1964): 259-60.

———. "The Things of Eternity—Stand We in Jeopardy?" *Ensign* 7 (January 1977): 3-7.

———. "The True Way of Life and Salvation." *Ensign* 8 (May 1978): 4-7.

———. "We Feel an Urgency." *Ensign* 10 (August 1980): 2-3.

King, David S. "I Have a Question." *Ensign* 23 (February 1993): 29-30.

Kirkham, E. Kay. *The ABC's of American Genealogical Research.* Salt Lake City: Deseret Book, 1955.

Kirkham, E. Kay. *Professional Techniques and Tactics in American Genealogical Research.* Logan, Utah: Everton, 1973.

———. *Research in American Genealogy: A Practical Approach to Genealogical Research.* Salt Lake City: Deseret Book, 1956.

Kirkham, E. Kay. *Simplified Genealogy for Americans.* Salt Lake City: Deseret Book, 1977.

Kirkham, Francis W. "Spiritual Educational Values in Genealogy." *UGHM* 30 (April 1939): 71–74.

Kirkham, James M. "Family Gatherings." *IE* 43 (November 1940): 667.

———. "Temple Activities in the Missions." *IE* 39 (April 1936): 236–38.

———. "Why Build Temples?" *MS* 99 (11 November 1937): 722–24, 732–33.

Komatsu, Adncy Y. "The Blessing of Building a Temple." *Ensign* 6 (May 1976): 101–2.

———. "The House of the Lord." *Ensign* 13 (November 1983): 27–28.

Kruckenberg, Janet. "A Catalog of Events." *Ensign* 24 (June 1994): 68.

Kunz, Phillip R. "Family Organizations." *EM* 2:497–98.

Lambert, G. C. "Building Temples." *MS* 46 (9 June 1884): 360–61.

Larsen, Dean L. "The Importance of the Temple for Living Members." *Ensign* 23 (April 1993): 10–12.

Law, Craig. *The Logan Temple: Logan Temple Centennial, 1884–1984.* Logan, Utah: Logan Temple Centennial Commemoration Committee, 1984.

Lee, Harold B. "Correlation and Priesthood Genealogy." *GRSDA 1968,* 55–73.

———. "Preparing to Meet the Lord." *IE* 68 (February 1965): 121–25.

———. Seminar address. *GRSDA 1970,* 27–35.

Lee, S. Norman. "Concerning the Redemption of the Dead." *MS* 72 (1 December 1910): 760–64.

LeSueur, J. W. "The Arizona Temple." *IE* 30 (October 1927): 1063–72.

Linder, Bill R. "How to Get a Going Family Organization Going." *IE* 73 (February 1970): 38–39.

Littke, Joseph C. "The Mission and Travels of the Israelitish Peoples." *UGHM* 25 (January 1934): 1–13.

Little, Harriet F. "Where There's a Will There's a Way." *UGHM* 22 (October 1931): 177–80.

Lofthouse, Merrill S. "A Glance Backward: Historical Sketch of the Genealogical Society." *IE* 72 (July 1969): 14–17.

———. *A History of the Genealogical Society of The Church of Jesus Christ of Latter-day Saints to 1970.* Master's thesis, Brigham Young University, 1971.

Lubeck, Kathleen. "Preparing for the Temple Endowment." *New Era* 17 (February 1987): 8–11.

———. "Sweet Is the Work." *New Era* 19 (February 1989): 28–31.

Lund, Anthon H. Conference address. *CR* (October 1900): 24–27.

———. Conference address. *CR* (October 1903): 80–83.

Lundwall, Nels B., comp. *Temples of the Most High.* Salt Lake City: Bookcraft, 1941. Multiple editions.

Lyman, Richard R. "Salvation for Both Living and Dead." *MS* 99 (1 April 1937): 200-201.

Madsen, Truman G. "Elijah and the Turning of the Hearts." In *The Radiant Life*, 105-15. Salt Lake City: Bookcraft, 1994.

———. "House of Glory." In *The Highest in Us,* 93-107. Salt Lake City: Bookcraft, 1978.

"Major Genealogical Record Sources in Germany." *IE* 70 (September 1967): 70-72.

"Major Genealogical Record Sources in Ireland." *IE* 70 (May 1967): 22-24.

"Major Genealogical Record Sources in the Netherlands." *IE* 71 (August 1968): 30-32.

"Major Genealogical Record Sources in Norway." *IE* 71 (April 1968): 54-56.

"Major Genealogical Record Sources in Scotland." *IE* 70 (June 1967): 10-12.

"Major Genealogical Record Sources in Sweden." *IE* 71 (February 1968): 22-24.

"Major Genealogical Record Sources in Switzerland." *IE* 71 (March 1968): 30-32.

"Major Genealogical Record Sources in the United States." *IE* 70 (July 1967): 50-53.

Malan, Asta J. "Genealogy Family Night." *IE* 68 (June 1965): 564-65.

The Manti Temple. Manti, Utah: Manti Temple Centennial Committee, 1988.

Mayfield, David M. "Ancestral File." *EM* 1:39.

———. "I Have a Question." *Ensign* 22 (February 1992): 52.

———. "Personal Ancestral File." *EM* 3:1077.

Mayfield, David M., and A. Gregory Brown. "Family Search." *Genealogical Computing* 10 (July 1990): 1.

McAllister, Duncan M. "How to Begin Temple Work." *MS* 86 (29 May 1924): 339-41. First published in *UGHM* 15 (April 1924): 78-80.

———. "The Purpose of Temples." *IE* 30 (October 1927): 1080-87.

———. "Temple Ceremonies." *IE* 21 (January 1918): 208-13.

———. "Temple Work." *UGHM* 16 (October 1925): 168-72. First published in *MS* 87 (24 September 1925): 617-21.

McAllister, Duncan M., and E. Wesley Smith. "Genealogical Records Relationship." *IE* 23 (September 1920): 962-66.

McConkie, Bruce R. "The Eternal Family Concept." *GRSDA 1967,* 81-93.

———. "A New Commandment: Save Thyself and Thy Kindred." *Ensign* 6 (August 1976): 7-11.

McConkie, Bruce R. "Why the Latter-day Saints Build Temples." *IE* 58 (December 1955): 920.

McKay, David O. "'None Other Name.'" *IE* 66 (November 1963): 924-25.

McKay, David O. "President David O. McKay's Dedication Address." *MS* 115 (September 1953): 198-99, 215.

———. "The Purpose of the Temple." *IE* 58 (November 1955): 793-94.

———. "Responsibilities of Those Who Enter the Temple." *IE* 68 (February 1965): 92-93, 145.

———. "The Salt Lake Temple." *IE* 71 (April 1968): 2-3.

———. "Salvation for the Dead." *MS* 85 (25 October 1923): 680-82.

McKinlay, Daniel B. "Temple Imagery in the Epistles of Peter." In *Temples of the Ancient World: Ritual and Symbolism.* Edited by Donald W. Parry, 492-514. Salt Lake City: Deseret Book and F.A.R.M.S., 1994.

McKinlay, Lynn A. "Patriarchal Order of the Priesthood." *EM* 3:1067.

Mehr, Kahlile. "International Activities and Services of the Genealogical Society of Utah." *Archivum* 37 (1992): 148-57.

———. "The Langheinrich Legacy: Record Gathering in Post-war Germany." *Ensign* 11 (June 1981): 22-25.

———. "The Microfilm Mission of Archibald F. Bennett." *Ensign* 12 (April 1982): 68-72.

———. "Name Extraction Program." *EM* 3: 979-80.

———. *Preserving the Source: Early Microfilming Efforts of the Genealogical Society of Utah, 1938-1950.* Master's thesis, Brigham Young University, 1985.

"Melchizedek Priesthood and Temple Work." *IE* 58 (November 1955): 856-57, 870-71.

Merrill, Joseph F. "Can the Dead Be Saved?" *MS* 98 (20 February 1936): 120-21.

———. "Salvation for the Dead." *MS* 101 (19 October 1939): 658-60, 670.

Merrill, Marriner W. "Temple Work." *IE* 42 (December 1939): 748.

Millet, Robert L. "Beyond the Veil: Two Latter-day Revelations." *Ensign* 15 (October 1985): 8-13.

———. "I Have a Question." *Ensign* 17 (August 1987): 19-21.

Minns, George. "British Records and Their Custodians and Searchers." *UGHM* 16 (October 1925): 153-60.

———. "The History and Manner of British Registration." *UGHM* 2 (April 1911): 75-85.

Monson, Thomas S. "In This Holy House." *IE* 68 (February 1965): 136-37.

———. "The Key of Faith." *GRSDA 1968,* 15-24.

———. "The Temple of the Lord." *Ensign* 23 (May 1993): 4-5.

Morton, William A. "Is Baptism Essential to Salvation?" *IE* 5 (June 1902): 603-8.

Mugleston, Maurine Kinghorn. "Lost in the Fold." *Ensign* 22 (June 1992): 49.

Mulder, William. "The Search Goes On—an Account of Genealogical Activity in the Eastern States Mission." *IE* 43 (August 1940): 495, 498.

Muren, Joseph C. "The Temple Endowment As Taught Anciently." *1971-1972 California Know Your Religion Speeches,* 179-213. BYU California Center.

Naisbitt, Henry W. "Building Temples." Parts 1 and 2. *MS* 39 (27 January 1877): 56-59; (29 January 1877): 72-75.

Nelson, N. L. "Temple Consciousness for the Dead." Parts 1 and 2. *MS* 102 (20 June 1940): 450-52, 460; (27 June 1940): 477-80. First published in *IE* 43 (March 1940): 152-54.

Nelson, Russell M. "The Spirit of Elijah." *Ensign* 24 (November 1994): 84-87.

"The New GIANT System in Genealogy." *IE* 72 (January 1969): 48-49; (February 1969): 52-53.

Nibley, Hugh. "Baptism for the Dead in Ancient Times." Parts 1-5. *IE* 51 (December 1948): 786-88, 836-38; 52 (January 1949): 24-26, 60; (February 1949): 90-91, 109-10, 112; (March 1949): 146-48, 180-83; (April 1949): 212-14. Reprinted in *Mormonism and Early Christianity.* Edited by Todd M. Compton and Stephen D. Ricks. Vol. 4 of *Collected Works of Hugh Nibley,* 100-169. Salt Lake City: Deseret Book and F.A.R.M.S., 1987.

———. "A House of Glory." In *Temples of the Ancient World: Ritual and Symbolism,* edited by Donald W. Parry, 29-47. Salt Lake City: Deseret Book and F.A.R.M.S., 1994.

———. "The Idea of the Temple in History." *MS* 120 (July 1958): 228-37, 247-49. Reprinted as "What Is a Temple?" In *The Temple in Antiquity,* edited by Truman G. Madsen, 39-51. Provo, Utah: Brigham Young University Religious Studies Center, 1983. Also reprinted in *Mormonism and Early Christianity,* edited by Todd M. Compton and Stephen D. Ricks, 355-90. Vol. 4 of *Collected Works of Hugh Nibley*. Salt Lake City: Deseret Book and F.A.R.M.S., 1987.

Nichols, Elizabeth L. "The Family Registry." *Genealogy Digest* 16 (Summer 1985): 26-31.

———. "Questions and Answers on the Name Tabulation Program." *Ensign* 1 (November 1971): 46-51.

Nordgren, Weston N. "Temple Work." *MS* 91 (October 1929): 699-700.

Oaks, Dallin H. "Family History: 'In Wisdom and Order.'" *Ensign* 19 (June 1989): 6-8.

———. "The Secular Purpose of Genealogical Work." *Ensign* 2 (October 1972): 20-24.

Ockey, Ovena Jorgensen. "Survey of Genealogical Conditions in Denmark, Norway, and Sweden." *UGHM* 17 (July 1926): 220-22.

Olsen, Eugene. "Genealogical Stone Walls." *IE* 50 (March 1947): 174.

———. "Government Records Help in Genealogy." *IE* 54 (February 1951): 83.

Olsen, Nolan P. *Logan Temple: The First 100 Years.* Providence, Utah: Keith W. Watkins and Sons, 1978.
Orme, Lafayette. "Baptism for the Dead." *MS* 70 (9 April 1908): 225–29.
Orton, John W. "Genealogical Research in Asia." *IE* 73 (March 1970): 60–63.
Packer, Boyd K. "Covenants." *Ensign* 17 (May 1987): 22–25.
———. "The Family and Eternity." *Ensign* 1 (February 1971): 7–11.
———. "The Holy Temple." *Ensign* 25 (February 1995): 32–36.
———. *The Holy Temple.* Salt Lake City: Bookcraft, 1980.
———. *The Holy Temple.* Salt Lake City: The Church of Jesus Christ of Latter-day Saints, 1982 (pamphlet 30595).
———. "The Redemption of the Dead." *Ensign* 5 (November 1975): 97–99.
———. Seminar address. *GRSDA 1970,* 19–26.
———. "Someone up There Loves You." *Ensign* 7 (January 1977): 8–12.
———. "The Temple, the Priesthood." *Ensign* 23 (May 1993): 18–21.
———. "A Temple to Exalt." *Ensign* 23 (August 1993): 6–15.
Palmer, Douglas D. "The World Conference on Records." *IE* 72 (July 1969): 6–8.
Palmer, Hoyt. "For Those Who Are Waiting: Blessings and Inspiration Reward Genealogists' Searching Process." *Ensign* 4 (August 1974): 70–77.
Parker, Jimmy B. "I Have a Question." *Ensign* 7 (January 1977): 72–73.
Peery, Joseph S. "Why Baptize for the Dead?" *IE* 24 (May 1921): 638–39.
Penrose, Charles W. "Baptism for the Dead." *MS* 100 (3 February 1938): 74–76.
———. "The Genealogical Society of Utah." *UGHM* 7 (January 1916): 8–11.
———. "Salvation for the Dead." *UGHM* 4 (January 1913): 1–18.
———. "Salvation for the Dead." *MS* 100 (27 January 1938): 58–60.
———. "Salvation for the Living and the Dead." *UGHM* 5 (October 1914): 157–72.
———. "Vicarious Work for the Dead." *MS* 71 (11 November 1909): 712–16.
"Pertinent Questions Answered." *IE* 66 (May 1963): 380–81; (June 1963): 456–57; (July 1963): 601; (August 1963): 660–61; (September 1963): 759; (October 1963): 847; (November 1963): 940–41; (December 1963): 1046–47; 67 (February 1964): 104–5; (March 1964): 164–65; (April 1964): 270–71; (May 1964): 366–67.
Perry, L. Tom. "Let Us Go Up to the House of God." *Ensign* 12 (May 1982): 53–54, 59.
Petersen, Mark E. "Early Christian Historians Tell of Baptism for the Dead." *UGHM* 24 (April 1933): 63–64.
———. "For All Live unto Him." *GRSDA 1968,* 27–40.

———. "The Genealogical Society." *IE* 59 (November 1956): 808-9.

———. "The Message of Elijah." *Ensign* 6 (May 1976): 14–16.

———. "The Mission of Elijah." *Ensign* 11 (August 1981): 64–65.

———. "What Started the World on Its Quest for Ancestors?" *UGHM* 27 (January 1936): 1–10.

———. "Why Mormons Build Temples." *Ensign* 2 (January 1972): 42–49, 52-53, 55.

Pomeroy, Frank T. "Why the Latter-day Saints Build Temples." *UGHM* 11 (July 1920): 122–27.

Pope, Hyrum C. "About the Temple in Hawaii." *IE* 23 (December 1919): 149–53.

"Popular Education in Genealogy." *IE* 67 (February 1964): 104–5.

Porter, Arthur C. "Why Are They Baptized for the Dead?" *MS* 100 (31 March 1938): 197–98, 204.

Powell, Ted F. *The Miracle of Microfilm: The Foundation of the Largest Genealogical Record Collection in the World.* N.p., n.d.

———. "Saving the Past for the Future: Tales of International Search and Cooperation." *American Archivist* 39 (1976): 311–18.

Pratt, David H. "Family History, Genealogy." *EM* 2:492–94.

———. "Genealogy: The Great Equalizer." *IE* 72 (October 1969): 76–77.

Pratt, Orson. "Elijah's Latter-day Mission." *UGHM* 30 (April 1939): 65–71; (July 1939): 129–33.

Pratt, Parley P. "Celestial Family Organization." *IE* 64 (August 1961): 580–81, 603–4. First published in *MS* 5 (May 1845): 189–94.

Pratte, Paul Alfred. "Temple of Refuge in the Pacific." *IE* 72 (December 1969): 26–27.

Price, J. Robert. "From the Temples of Our Lord." *MS* 124 (December 1962): 312–14.

"Questions and Answers." *New Era* 24 (January 1994): 16–18.

Rand, Lawrence W. "Books of Remembrance or Books of Encumbrance? A Fresh Approach for Bogged-Down Genealogists." *IE* 73 (September 1970): 30–33.

Read, Lenet Hadley. "Elijah and Elisha." *Ensign* 18 (March 1988): 24–28.

"Records Full of Genealogical Wealth." *IE* 42 (February 1939): 108–9.

Rector, Connie. *The Celestial Connection: Faith-Promoting Stories on Family Research.* Salt Lake City: Bookcraft, 1980.

———. *Links of Forever: Inspirational Stories of Lineage and Love.* Salt Lake City: Bookcraft, 1977.

Rector, Hartman, Jr. "Roots and Branches." *BYU 1981 Fireside and Devotional Speeches*, 10 February 1981.

———. "Turning the Hearts." *Ensign* 11 (May 1981): 73–75.

Rich, Wendell O. "In His Name." *IE* 37 (December 1934): 726–27.

Richards, Franklin D. (1821–1899). "Ephraim and Manasseh in America." *UGHM* 23 (April 1932): 66–71.

Richards, Franklin D. (1821-1899). "The Temple of the Lord." *UGHM* 11 (October 1920): 145-50.

Richards, Franklin D. (1900-1987). "Happiness and Joy in Temple Work." *Ensign* 16 (November 1986): 70-72.

———. "Leadership Preparation for Motivating Family Research and Temple Work." In *GRSDA 1967*, 70-80.

Richards, George F. "All May Be Saved." *IE* 39 (April 1936): 200-203.

———. "Blessings from Temple Service." *UGHM* 27 (October 1936): 145-52.

———. "Genealogy and Temple Work." *UGHM* 13 (July 1922): 97-104.

———. "Genealogy and Temple Work." *UGHM* 15 (January 1924): 1-5.

———. "The Importance of Genealogical and Temple Work." *IE* 45 (May 1942): 288, 324-25.

———. "Importance of Genealogical Research." *MS* 86 (3 April 1924): 209-12. First published in *CR* (October 1923): 65-69.

———. "Latter-day Temples." *IE* 33 (May 1930): 470-73.

———. "This Is My Work and My Glory." *IE* 53 (May 1950): 368, 406, 408.

Richards, LeGrand. "God Moves in a Mysterious Way His Wonders to Perform." *Ensign* 7 (May 1977): 62-63.

———. "The Lord Hath Spoken." *IE* 68 (February 1965): 138-40.

———. "Our Holy Temples." *SY* (April 1972).

———. "Spiritual Implications of Genealogical Work." *GRSDA 1969*, 43-54.

Ricks, Stephen D. "The Appearance of Elijah and Moses in the Kirtland Temple and the Jewish Passover." *BYU Studies* 23 (Fall 1983): 483-86.

Ridlon, G. T. "Importance of Family History." *UGHM* 3 (October 1912): 182-86.

Rigby, Mary Noel. "One Day at the Temple." *Ensign* 23 (February 1993): 43.

Roberts, B. H. Conference address. *CR* (October 1905): 43-48.

Roberts, David R. "Books of Remembrance." *IE* 51 (August 1948): 524.

———. "Books of Remembrance." *IE* 52 (August 1949): 529.

Robertson, Paul David. "Family Ties." *Ensign* 21 (February 1991): 64-65.

Robinson, Joseph E. "Salvation for the Dead." *UGHM* 8 (October 1917): 160-65.

Rollings, Virginia H. "If Anybody Wants to Listen." *New Era* 18 (July 1988): 36-39.

Romney, Marion G. Seminar address. *GRSDA 1970*, 13-18.

———. "Temples—the Gates to Heaven." *Ensign* 1 (March 1971): 12-16.

Romney, Richard M. "Generations of Service." *New Era* 18 (March 1988): 39.

———. "House of Holiness." *New Era* 17 (February 1987): 20-29.

Roskelly, Samuel. "Temple Work." *MS* 67 (5 January 1905): 6.

Royall, Paul F. "Changes on Our Mind." *IE* 72 (July 1969): 9–10.

———. "Every Man in His Place." Brigham Young University Six-Stake Fireside address (January 1965).

———. "Family Togetherness—Parents, Children, and God." Brigham Young University Education Week Devotional (12 June 1963).

———. "Genealogy Is People." *GRSDA 1967,* 41-61.

———. "God's Work Shall Be Accomplished." *GRSDA 1967,* 31–40.

———. Seminar address. *GRSDA 1966,* 26–35.

———. "That Our Children May Know." *Ensign* 1 (October 1971): 6–8.

Sapp, Edwin Greenlaw. "Find Iby." *Ensign* 21 (July 1991): 42–43.

Sargeant, Linda M. "The Book That Changed the Night." *Ensign* 23 (January 1993): 72–73.

Satterfield, Ammon Y. "Divine Guidance in Gathering Genealogy." *IE* 57 (March 1954): 164, 187.

Schooneveldt, J. C., Jr. "Genealogical Records in the Netherlands." *UGHM* 23 (April 1932): 76–80.

Schueler, Donald G. "Our Family Trees Have Roots in Utah's Mountain Vaults." *Smithsonian* 12 (December 1981): 86–95.

Scott, Richard G. "Redemption: The Harvest of Love." *Ensign* 20 (November 1990): 5–7.

Searle, Don L. "A 'Magnificent and Enduring Monument.'" *Ensign* 23 (March 1993): 22–27.

Shortridge, Laura S. "A Journal of Letters." *Ensign* 24 (February 1994): 71–72.

Shoumatoff, Alex. *The Mountain of Names: A History of the Human Family.* New York: n.p., 1985.

———. "A Reporter at Large: The Mountain of Names." *New Yorker* 61 (May 1985): 51–101.

Simmonds, A. J. "A Record among You." *IE* 70 (March 1967): 14–15.

Simmons, Paul. "Beyond the Fourth Generation: Continuing Family Research to Redeem the Dead." *Ensign* 11 (October 1981): 20–23.

Simpson, Robert L. "The House of the Lord." *Ensign* 10 (November 1980): 10–11.

———. "A Most Urgent and Important Work." *GRSDA 1969,* 27–40.

Sjodahl, Janne M. *Temples Ancient and Modern: Including an Account of the Laying of the Capstone on the Salt Lake Temple.* Salt Lake City: Deseret News, 1892.

Slorance, Andrew J. *Genealogy and the Mormons*. N.p., n.d.

Smith, Andrew K. "Extending the Benefits of the Research Clearing House to Those Compiling Their Own Genealogy." *UGHM* 18 (October 1927): 151–53.

———. "The Genealogical Research Bureau." *UGHM* 19 (July 1928): 113–23.

———. "Vicarious Offerings: The Research Clearing House." *UGHM* 18 (January 1927): 9–16.

Smith, David A. Conference address. *CR* (October 1921): 140–43.

Smith, Eldred G. "As Pertaining to Our Salvation." *IE* 57 (December 1954): 886–87.

———. "Do Not Procrastinate!" *Ensign* 4 (November 1974): 25–26.

———. "The Eternity of the Family." *MS* 129 (February 1967): 20–22.

———. "Family Research." *Ensign* 5 (November 1975): 106–8.

———. "Our Responsibility to Our Dead." *IE* 65 (June 1962): 436–39.

———. "Patriarchal Order of the Priesthood." *IE* 55 (June 1952): 425–26.

———. Seminar address. *GRSDA 1970,* 7–12.

———. "The Spirit of Elijah." *MS* 129 (September 1967): 16–17.

———. "Temples Are Essential." *IE* 72 (December 1969): 59–61.

———. "Why Do Latter-day Saints Build Temples?" *Ensign* 3 (January 1973): 55–56.

———. "Work for the Dead." *IE* 62 (June 1959): 462–63.

Smith, Frank Miller. "Monument to Spirituality: Sacrifice, Dreams, and Faith Build the Washington Temple." *Ensign* 4 (August 1974): 7–13.

Smith, George Albert. "The Tenth Temple." *IE* 48 (October 1945): 561, 602.

Smith, Hyrum G. Conference address. *CR* (October 1923): 100–101.

———. "The Day of Ephraim." *UGHM* 20 (July 1929): 123–26.

Smith, James E., and Phillip R. Kunz. "The Kinship of the World." *Ensign* 7 (January 1977): 65–68.

Smith, Joseph, Jr. "Baptism for the Dead." *Times and Seasons* 3 (April 1842): 759–61.

Smith, Joseph F. "Temples and Temple Work." *UGHM* 7 (January 1916): 24–30.

Smith, Joseph Fielding. "The Coming of Elijah." *Ensign* 2 (January 1972): 2–5.

———. Conference address. *CR* (October 1911): 118–22.

———. Conference address. *CR* (April 1912): 67–71.

———. "Differences in Genealogical Lineages." *IE* 63 (March 1960): 144–45.

———. "The Duties of the Priesthood in Temple Work." *IE* 62 (February 1959): 98–99, 111. First published in *UGHM* 30 (January 1939): 1–4.

———. "Elijah's Mission to the World." *IE* 51 (May 1948): 277, 315–16.

———. *Elijah the Prophet and His Mission.* Salt Lake City: Deseret Book, 1957.

———. "Elijah the Prophet and His Mission." *UGHM* 12 (January 1921): 1–20.

———. "The Essential Value of Genealogical Research." *UGHM* 9 (January 1918): 14–21.

———. "For Whom Is Vicarious Work Done?" *IE* 67 (July 1964): 566–67.

———. "Genealogy: A Summary of Important Instructions." *IE* 46 (January 1943): 47.

———. "Hearts of the Children—Turned to the Fathers." *MS* 102 (12 December 1940): 850-52, 864.

———. "Heirs to Exaltation." *UGHM* 26 (April 1935): 49-62.

———. "The Historical Background of the Prophet Joseph Smith." *IE* 44 (December 1941): 716-17, 762-63.

———. "History and History Recorders." *UGHM* 16 (April 1925): 52-59.

———. "Justice for the Dead." *MS* 95 (15 June 1933): 387-91.

———. "The Keys of the Priesthood Restored." *UGHM* 27 (July 1936): 98-102.

———. "The Keys Restored by Elijah." *UGHM* 27 (April 1936): 49-53.

———. "Latter-day Temple Work." *UGHM* 31 (October 1940): 193-200.

———. "The Mission of Ephraim." *UGHM* 21 (January 1930): 1-4.

———. "The Necessity of Working on Our Own Lineage." *IE* 45 (May 1942): 289, 325-26.

———. "Privileges concerning Temples and Other Ordinances." *IE* 30 (June 1927): 736-38.

———. "The Prophet's Vision of Salvation for the Dead." *IE* 58 (February 1955): 79.

———. "Salvation for the Dead." Parts 1 and 2. *IE* 20 (January 1917): 196-99; (February 1917): 360-64.

———. "Salvation for the Dead." *MS* 89 (8 December 1927): 769-75, 782-83. First published in *UGHM* 17 (April 1926): 145-56.

———. "Salvation Universal." *Ensign* 1 (February 1971): 2-3. First published in *IE* 13 (February 1910): 352.

———. "Salvation Universal." Parts 1-5. *IE* 13 (November 1909): 38-45; (December 1909): 144-51; (January 1910): 244-51; (February 1910): 351-55; (March 1910): 453-57.

———. "Saviors on Mount Zion." *IE* 68 (February 1965): 111-12.

———. "Temples and the Sacred Rites Therein." *UGHM* 21 (April 1930): 53-57.

———. "Temple Work." *IE* 62 (June 1959): 430-31.

———. "Thoughts on Temple Work and Salvation." *UGHM* 20 (January 1929): 40-43.

———. "Why Are Baptisms for the Dead Performed below the Surface of the Earth in Our Temples?" *IE* 63 (May 1960): 304-5.

Smith, Laura Lee. "A Friendly Library." *Ensign* 17 (July 1987): 50-54.

Snow, Erastus. "Redemption for the Dead." *MS* 91 (19 September 1929): 593-95.

Sorensen, Donna D. *Genealogical Research: A Practical Mission, Teacher's Supplement.* Salt Lake City: Deseret Sunday School Union Board, 1962.

Sorensen, Parry D. "Malachi's Promise, Elijah's Mission." *MS* 99 (1 April 1937): 198-99, 205.

Sowby, Laurie Williams. "Meeting Our Relatives on Paper." *Ensign* 23 (July 1993): 66-67.

Sperry, Kip. "From Kirtland to Computers: The Growth of Family History Record Keeping." In *The Heavens Are Open: The 1992 Sperry Symposium on the Doctrine and Covenants and Church History,* 290-301. Salt Lake City: Deseret Book, 1993.

Sperry, Sidney B. "The Meaning of Peter's Confession." Parts 1 and 2. *IE* 52 (July 1949): 430-31, 471-72; (August 1949): 496-98, 537.

"The Spirit of Elijah." *UGHM* 4 (July 1913): 105-12.

Stewart, Ora Pate. "Family Reunion." *IE* 47 (August 1944): 504, 522.

Stillwell, Glen F. "How to Have Fun Making History." *IE* 72 (October 1969): 72-73.

Sudweeks, Joseph. *The Principles and Practice of Genealogy.* Salt Lake City: Deseret Sunday School Union Board, 1949.

Summerhays, Richard B. "The Genealogical Society of Utah." *IE* 30 (October 1927): 1104-6.

———. "How Temple Work Helps the Living." *IE* 39 (April 1936): 240-43, 253-54, 260.

Talmage, James E. "As to Genealogy." *MS* 87 (8 October 1925): 648-49.

———. Conference address. *CR* (April 1912): 124-29.

———. "Genealogy and Work for the Dead." *UGHM* 10 (April 1919): 49-61.

———. *The House of the Lord.* Salt Lake City: Deseret News, 1912. Multiple editions.

———. "In the Realm of the Dead." *UGHM* 20 (October 1929): 155-60.

———. "The Living and the Dead." *UGHM* 9 (July 1918): 124-31.

———. "Present Need of Temples." *IE* 16 (November 1912): 3-22.

———. "What's in a Name?" *UGHM* 4 (October 1913): 169-75.

———. "Why Are They Then Baptized for the Dead?" *MS* 79 (19 April 1917): 241-43.

———. "Why Do the Latter-day Saints Build Temples?" Parts 1 and 2. *MS* 76 (2 July 1914): 417-20; (9 July 1914): 433-37. First published in *IE* 17 (June 1914): 712-24.

Tanner, N. Eldon. "The Heavens Are Open." *IE* 67 (June 1964): 459-61.

———. "Saviors on Mount Zion." *IE* 66 (November 1963): 928-29, 984, 986-87.

———. "Seek Out Your Dead." *IE* 68 (February 1965): 125-27.

———. "Why Do We Doubt?" *GRSDA 1969,* 71-81.

Teasdale, George. "Spiritual Manifestations in the Manti Temple." *MS* 50 (13 August 1888): 520-23.

Telford, Ted A. "Chinese Materials on Microfilm at the Genealogical Society of Utah." *Ch'ing-shih Wen-t'i* 4 (June 1980): 106-13.

"Temple Events." *Church News* (10 March 1985-present). A column published on the last page of the *Church News* every four or five weeks. From January 1992–March 1993, the column was entitled "Temple Centennial."

"Temples and Temple Building." *UGHM* 12 (July 1921): 113–22.

Thomas, Janet. "Names and Faces." *New Era* 24 (February 1994): 30–33.

———. "Turning Their Hearts." *New Era* 22 (March 1992): 20–22.

"Thoughts for Your Inspirational Talk: Temple Work." *IE* 60 (September 1957): 616.

Tice, Richard. "Doing Temple Work at Home." *Ensign* 20 (July 1990): 24–27.

———. "Temple Ancestor Day." *Ensign* 19 (July 1989): 12–15.

Tingey, Earl C. "Redemption of the Dead." *Ensign* 21 (May 1991): 26–27.

Todd, Jay M. "In His Holy House." *Ensign* 23 (March 1993): 32.

———. "Reports of the Faithful." *IE* 72 (July 1969): 18, 20, 22–24.

———. "Salvation for the Dead." *Ensign* 25 (February 1995): 46–51.

Tolman, William O. *The History of Temples and Temple Ordinances—Ancient and Modern.* Provo, Utah: Brigham Young University Press, 1964.

Turner, Danette. "Pictures for a Lifetime." *Ensign* 24 (July 1994): 72–73.

Tuttle, A. Theodore. "Eternal Links That Bind." *Ensign* 10 (May 1980): 40–41.

———. "The First and the Last Words." *Ensign* 12 (May 1982): 65–66.

———. "The Key to Our Redemption." *SY* (September 1980): 105–12.

Tvedtnes, John A. "Elijah: Champion of Israel's God." *Ensign* 20 (July 1990): 52–57.

Ursenbach, O. "Preparing for the Millennial Reign." *MS* 124 (September 1962): 232–34.

Vandenberg, John H. "Memory Is a Poor Record." *GRSDA 1968,* 43–51.

Van Orden, Bruce A. "Redeeming the Dead as Taught in the Old Testament." In *A Witness of Jesus Christ: The 1989 Sperry Symposium on the Old Testament,* 261–70. Salt Lake City: Deseret Book 1990.

Wach, Elizabeth O. "Me, a Records Extractor?" *Ensign* 13 (September 1983): 51–53.

Waddoups, William W. "Genealogical and Temple Work in Polynesia." *UGHM* 31 (July 1940): 161–63.

Wallace, Arthur. *Successful Family Organizations.* Los Angeles: Los Angeles Temple Genealogical Library, 1965.

Warner, Elisha. "The Temple Endowment of Light and Truth." *MS* 120 (March 1958): 63–67, 78.

Warner, Terry. "A Temple for Great Britain." *MS* 120 (September 1958): 266–75.

Watt, Ronald G. "Genealogy and History at LDS Church Headquarters." *Genealogical Journal* 11 (Spring 1982): 3–13.

Webb, Jon. "Beyond Pen and Ink: 18 Ways to Record Family History." *Ensign* 7 (January 1977): 18–21.

Wells, Gawain, and Gayle J. Wells. "Hidden Benefits of Keeping a History." *Ensign* 16 (July 1986): 47-51.

West, Joseph A. "Importance of Temple Work and Tithing." *IE* 29 (December 1925): 153-55.

Westergaard, James C. "A Worthwhile Bequest." *IE* 44 (May 1941): 300.

"What Is the Four-Generation Program?" *Ensign* 2 (March 1972): 52-54.

Whitney, Orson F. Conference address. *CR* (October 1920): 30-36.

———. "Two Great Phases of the Lord's Work." *IE* 24 (February 1921): 281-88.

———. "The Welding Link." *IE* 28 (January 1925): 187-96.

"Why Family Organizations?" *IE* 68 (August 1965): 700-701.

Wickman, Lance B. "Stand Ye in Holy Places." *Ensign* 24 (November 1994): 82-83.

Widtsoe, John A. "The Beginnings of Modern Temple Work." *IE* 30 (October 1927): 1073-79.

———. "Elijah, the Tishbite." *UGHM* 27 (April 1936): 53-60.

———. "European Program for Genealogical Study, Research and Exchange." *UGHM* 21 (January 1930): 33-35.

———. "Fundamentals of Temple Doctrine." *UGHM* 13 (July 1922): 129-35.

———. "Gathering Genealogical Records." *IE* 38 (January 1935): 39.

———. "Genealogical Activities in Europe." *UGHM* 22 (July 1931): 97-106.

———. "The House of the Lord." *IE* 72 (July 1969): 13-14. First published in *IE* 48 (October 1945): 584.

———. "The Joys of Temple Work." *IE* 71 (April 1968): 8-9.

———. "Looking toward the Temple." *Ensign* 2 (January 1972): 56-58. First published in *IE* 65 (October 1962): 706-10, 765.

———. "The Meaning and Importance of Records." *UGHM* 11 (July 1920): 97-103.

———. "Obtaining Scandinavian Genealogies." *UGHM* 19 (January 1928): 1-8.

———. "Salvation for the Dead." *MS* 91 (19 September 1929): 600-601.

———. "Serving Our Dead." *MS* 89 (4 August 1927): 481-85. First published in *CR* (April 1927): 29-32.

———. "The Temple Calls." *IE* 46 (April 1943): 224.

———. "Temple Worship." *UGHM* 12 (April 1921): 49-64.

———. "Universal Brotherhood Will Save the World." *IE* 53 (May 1950): 372, 428-30.

———. "The Way of Salvation." *IE* 46 (May 1943): 278-79.

———. "Work for the Dead." *UGHM* 6 (January 1915): 33-35.

———. "The Worth of Souls." *MS* 96 (1 March 1934): 129-34.

Widtsoe, Osborne J. P. "An Introduction to the Study of English Surnames." Parts 1-4. *UGHM* 1 (January 1910): 12-18; (April 1910): 82-88; (July 1910): 114-23; (October 1910): 153-59.

Wilcox, Charles G. Finney. "Genealogy and Its Place in the Affairs of Human Society." *UGHM* 6 (October 1915): 218–27.

Wimmer, Larry T., and Clayne L. Pope. "The Genealogical Society Library of Salt Lake City: A Source of Data for Economic and Social Historians." *Historical Methods Newsletter* 8 (March 1975): 51–58.

Wood, V. Alfred. *The Alberta Temple: Centre and Symbol of Faith.* Calgary: Detselig Enterprises, 1989.

Woodruff, Wilford, and George Q. Cannon. "The Law of Adoption." *UGHM* 13 (October 1922): 145–58.

Wright, Norman Edgar. *Building an American Pedigree: A Study in Genealogy.* Provo, Utah: Brigham Young University Press, 1974.

———. "Genealogical Research in Perspective." *Ensign* 1 (August 1971): 26–28.

———. *Key to Genealogical Research Essentials.* Provo, Utah: BYU Extension Publications, 1966.

———. *Key to Migration Sources: Great Britain and North America.* Provo, Utah: Brigham Young University Press, 1967.

Wright, Norman E., and David H. Pratt. *Genealogical Research Essentials.* Salt Lake City: Bookcraft, 1977.

Wright, Raymond S. "An International Center for the Study of the Family." *Journal of Family History* 2 (1977): 169–71.

Young, S. Dilworth. "Lord, What Is Thy Purpose?" *GRSDA 1969,* 57–68.

Yuen, Tai Kwok, as told to Marguerite Smith. "Seventy-Generation Pedigree." *Ensign* 21 (February 1991): 66–67.

Zobell, Albert L., Jr. "If the Dead Rise Not." *IE* 43 (September 1940): 530–31.

———. "The Temple at Idaho Falls." *IE* 48 (October 1945): 569.

Scripture Index

Subject Index

Page numbers in *italics* indicate illustrations.

L

M